BREAKING THE CONFEDERACY

ALSO BY JACK H. LEPA
AND FROM MCFARLAND

The Civil War in Tennessee, 1862–1863
(2007; paperback 2011)

The Shenandoah Valley Campaign of 1864
(2003; paperback 2010)

BREAKING THE CONFEDERACY

The Georgia and Tennessee Campaigns of 1864

Jack H. Lepa

McFarland & Company, Inc., Publishers
Jefferson, North Carolina, and London

The present work is a reprint of the illustrated case bound edition of Breaking the Confederacy: The Georgia and Tennessee Campaigns of 1864, *first published in 2005 by McFarland.*

Photographs in this book are from
the collections of the Library of Congress.

LIBRARY OF CONGRESS CATALOGUING-IN-PUBLICATION DATA

Lepa, Jack H., 1949–
Breaking the Confederacy : the Georgia and
Tennessee campaigns of 1864 / Jack H. Lepa.
p. cm.
Includes bibliographical references and index.

ISBN 978-0-7864-6098-4
softcover : 50# alkaline paper ∞

1. Atlanta Campaign, 1864. 2. Sherman's March to the Sea.
3. Nashville, Battle of, Nashville, Tenn., 1864. 4. Franklin, Battle of, Franklin, Tenn., 1864. 5. Georgia — History — Civil War, 1861–1865.
6. Tennessee — History — Civil War, 1861–1865. I. Title.
E476.7.L46 2011 973.7'37 — dc22 2005012766

British Library cataloguing data are available

© 2005 Jack H. Lepa. All rights reserved

No part of this book may be reproduced or transmitted in any form or by any means, electronic or mechanical, including photocopying or recording, or by any information storage and retrieval system, without permission in writing from the publisher.

Cover photograph: Union troops in a captured
Confederate fort near Atlanta, 1864 (Corbis)

Manufactured in the United States of America

*McFarland & Company, Inc., Publishers
Box 611, Jefferson, North Carolina 28640
www.mcfarlandpub.com*

Contents

Preface — 1

1. Still It Goes On — 3
2. Planning the Campaign — 12
3. Armies and Commanders — 21
4. Opening Moves — 32
5. The Bloodletting Begins — 44
6. Slow Movement Through Northern Georgia — 55
7. The Summer of Despair — 66
8. New Tactics Outside Atlanta — 76
9. Battle of Atlanta — 87
10. A City Under Siege — 99
11. Atlanta Is Taken — 110
12. The Occupation of Atlanta — 120
13. Chasing Hood and Planning the "March" — 131
14. The Tide Turns — 142
15. The March Through Georgia — 151
16. Savannah — 162
17. Hood Invades Tennessee — 172
18. Slaughter at Franklin — 183
19. Debacle at Nashville — 193
20. The End in Sight — 207

Notes — 213
Bibliography — 225
Index — 233

Preface

After almost three years of bloody warfare the people of the North were looking forward to the 1864 campaigns with optimism. A new general in chief, the hard-hitting Ulysses S. Grant, was now in charge and it was widely expected that he would roll over the Confederate armies and bring victory and peace by the end of the summer. One of the two main components of Grant's plan was William Tecumseh Sherman and his campaign to destroy the Army of Tennessee and ravage the deep South so that the area could no longer provide support for the Confederate war effort. The fighting and devastation that went on through Georgia and Tennessee during the summer and fall of 1864 was a major factor in determining the course of the war and the final Union victory.

This book describes how the twists and turns on the road to final victory wound through Georgia and Tennessee. General Sherman's strategy of flanking and crushing the Confederates with superior numbers was thwarted time and again by timely Confederate withdrawals to another strong position, but each such withdrawal brought the fighting a little closer to Atlanta. When the Confederates left their fortifications to attack the superior Federal forces—which was exactly what Sherman wanted—they suffered bloody defeats.

Sherman's march to Savannah and the disastrous Confederate invasion of Tennessee were the last major campaigns of the war. Although they were separated by hundreds of miles the campaigns in Georgia and Tennessee had a major effect on the war in Virginia. By the end of 1864 supplies for Lee's army were even scarcer than they had been and the people of the South now knew that no place was safe from death and destruction as long as they continued to support the war.

I would like to thank the staff of the library at the University of Nevada, Las Vegas, for their assistance with research and locating many of the materials used for reference. Also, the staff of the Interlibrary Loan Department of the Las Vegas-Clark County Library District provided invaluable help is finding older and difficult-to-find books that would have been impossible for me to obtain otherwise.

Chapter 1

Still It Goes On

The beginning of the year 1864 brought mixed emotions of hope and despondency to the people in both the Union and the Confederacy. In the North there was optimism based on a string of victories the previous year. The Army of the Potomac's glorious but bloody victory at Gettysburg turned back the Confederacy's final serious threat of invasion and is generally considered the turning point of the war. At the same time Union forces were winning the victory at Gettysburg, Ulysses S. Grant was culminating a long siege with the capture of Vicksburg, Mississippi. Three days later Port Hudson fell to Union troops moving up from New Orleans, giving the Union control of the entire length of the Mississippi River and cutting off the Confederate states west of the river from the rest of the Confederacy. In late November a Union force commanded by Grant, attacked and routed the Confederate Army of Tennessee from what were considered nearly impregnable positions at Lookout Mountain and Missionary Ridge outside Chattanooga, Tennessee, giving the Federal forces control of the state. Yet the optimism of the people of the North was tempered by the fact that victory had appeared tantalizingly close before, only to be snatched away by some unexpected reverse.

In the South there was an air of foreboding. On the first day of the year Dolly Sumner Lunt of Georgia made an entry in her diary that might have been repeated by many in the South:

> A new year is ushered in, but peace comes not with it. Scarcely a family but has given some of its members to the bloody war that is still decimating our nation. Oh, that its ravages may soon be stopped! Will another year find us among carnage and bloodshed? Shall we be a nation or shall we be annihilated.[1]

Robert E. Lee's Army of Northern Virginia was still a foe to be reckoned with but his invasion of the North that ended at Gettysburg had cost the South well over 20,000 irreplaceable veteran soldiers. Combined with the loss of Tennessee and the Federal army's gaining control of the Mississippi River, it appeared to many that the end of the Confederacy might be near. John B. Jones, a clerk in the Confederate War Department, spoke for many southerners when he wrote, "we have experienced the great agony of 1863 and have become so familiar with horrors that we shall fight [in 1864] with desperation."[2]

After nearly three bloody years many believed that the war had reached the point where a final decision might be near. While the people wondered and worried about the future, the leaders on both sides were desperately searching for military and political solutions to win the war.

The war had brought hardships to both sides but the South was suffering from shortages of almost everything, including food for the fighting men, thanks in part to the Federal blockade of the southern coastline. While the shortages that winter were widespread, chronic problems with the Confederacy's deteriorating railroad system caused the most severe problems in Northern Virginia, the all-important area between Washington and Richmond. In addition to the physical effects of hunger, depression and doubt began to take hold of some of the troops. On January 15, J. B. Crawford, a soldier in the 16th Mississippi, wrote to his wife: "I am sorry to tel you that wee are in starvation. Wee have nothing to eat but a little bread and not enough at that. I dont see any prospect of peace for the next few years. My dear wife I am willing to give up my part of the Confederacy to get to com home...."[3]

Even General Lee was having serious concerns. On January 22 he wrote to Confederate secretary of war James A. Seddon:

> A regular supply of provisions to the troops in this army is a matter of great importance. Short rations are having a bad effect upon the men, both morally and physically. Desertions to the enemy are becoming more frequent, and the men cannot continue healthy and vigorous if confined to this spare diet for any length of time. Unless there is a change, I fear the army cannot be kept together.[4]

If the situation was desperate east of the Mississippi, conditions were worse in the Trans-Mississippi. When Vicksburg fell in July 1863, the Confederate states west of the Mississippi found that they were cut off from the southern heartland. But the region ranked low on Richmond's list of strategic priorities, so the Trans-Mississippi would have to make do with its own resources—which included an abundant supply of cotton but little of the materials required to sustain war.[5]

The problems facing the Confederacy at the outset of 1864 were formidable: her armies had been battered and driven from vital territory, the fledgling nation was in economic shambles, the ever-mounting toll of dead young soldiers continued unabated, and they were facing an implacable enemy far superior in numbers and resources.

Economic conditions in the South had begun to deteriorate since the start of the conflict. In Alabama, Elizabeth Lyle Saxon wrote:

> The war found us but ill-prepared for the blockade that was soon instituted, and it appears to me, as I recall the facts that existed, that not one person in ten anticipated the results, or else supplies of such character as were needed would have been bought in great quantities before hostilities began. The South, so essentially agricultural, had bought everything from Northern merchants. Cotton had been planted to the exclusion of all other crops, well nigh. Now potatoes, corn and other edibles were planted in larger quantities than ever before.[6]

And from Fayetteville, North Carolina, Mrs. Eliza Stinson wrote:

> Although not subject to the horrors of actual battle, many of our people endured privations never before dreamed of. Those called "the poor" got along as well as ever probably, as they did not scruple to ask for help; but the suffering was among those families who were accustomed to every comfort, and were above asking or even receiving assistance from others, and many families of this class found great difficulty in procuring the bare necessaries of life. I have known cases in which corn bread formed the sole bill of fare at meals in familes accustomed to comfort and even luxury.[7]

Yet, in spite of all these problems there was still hope for the Confederacy. The South still had a formidable army of battle-hardened veterans that were not about to quit fighting. They may have been short of food and clothing but they had plenty of rifles, cannons and courage. As George C. Eggleston wrote,

> [T]he sentiment of the South made it the duty of every man who could bear arms to go straight to the front and stay there. The acceptance of any less actively military position than that of a soldier in the field was held to be little less than a confession of cowardice; and cowardice, in the eyes of the Southerners, is the one sin which may not be pardoned either in this world or the next.... To go where the bullets were whistling was the one course open to gentlemen who held their honor sacred and their reputation dear.[8]

The loss of territory, especially along the Mississippi, meant that Confederate armies could concentrate on defending the southern heartland. Last but perhaps most important, the vast majority of southerners still were willing to go on sacrificing, suffering, and struggling for the Cause. As a whole southerners were a deeply religious people and could not believe that a just God would let them be conquered by the hated Yankees.[9]

After the war a former Confederate soldier wrote about how difficult it was to admit even the possibility of defeat:

> We were convinced, beyond the possibility of a doubt, of the absolute righteousness of our cause, and in spite of history we persuaded ourselves that a people battling for the right could not fail in the end. And so our hearts went on hoping for success long after our heads had learned to expect failure.[10]

No one in the Confederacy was more determined to outlast the North than its president, Jefferson Davis. Davis was a tough-minded man, many would call him stubborn, who fervently believed in the cause that he had been chosen to lead. As a soldier he had learned discipline and self-control but sometimes allowed these traits to be overcome by his zeal for an idea once a decision was made. He vigorously supported his friends and ruthlessly fought against his enemies. Whatever criticisms might fairly be leveled at him no one doubts that he was a fighter. From the beginning he knew that the odds were against the South and, unlike many of his people, he expected a long and costly struggle. But he was still confident that the South could win its independence so long as it did not lose the will to continue the fight. He was determined to continue the war until the Confederacy was either victorious or crushed; there were no other choices.[11]

In February the Confederate Congress passed a series of laws that Davis felt were necessary to enable the South to continue the fight into 1864. These laws affected every segment of southern society. All males between the ages of 17 and 55 were made eligible for some sort of military service and exemptions from service were drastically reduced. Free blacks could be conscripted for noncombatant service. The Confederate currency was devalued and taxes were imposed on virtually all types of property. The South was getting ready for an all-out effort.[12]

Despite the hardships involved, many southerners saw that the new laws were necessary. In a letter dated February 19, Confederate general James Conner wrote:

> I see Congress has also passed the Currency Bill, the Tax Bill, and Military Bill — three very important Acts — and severe as they unquestionably are, I think they will do good. No nation voluntarily subjects itself to such taxation and such sacrifices, unless thoroughly in earnest. I know nothing that will tend so much to convince the North that we are prepared for the worst, and intend to fight it out to the last, as these Acts.[13]

After he got over his depression of January, John B. Jones wrote at the end of February that after a few minor victories in Florida and the far West, confidence in the future was slowly returning:

> But we shall probably end the war this year — and independence will compensate for all. The whole male population, pretty much, will be in the field this year, and our armies will be strong. So far we have the prestige of success, and our men are resolved to keep it, if the dissensions of the leaders do not interfere with the general purpose.[14]

Along with all the obvious military and economic factors that affected the Confederacy's fight for independence there was one more problem that the people of the South had to overcome: their own government. George Eggleston remembered:

> The history of the Confederacy, when it shall be fully and fairly written, will appear the story of a dream to those who shall read it, and there are parts of it at least which already seem a nightmare to those of us who helped make it. Founded upon a constitution which jealously withheld from it nearly all the powers of government, without even the poor privilege of existing beyond the moment when some one of the States composing it should see fit to put it to death, the Richmond government nevertheless grew speedily into a despotism, and for four years wielded absolute power over an obedient and uncomplaining people.[15]

As Eggleston saw it, the government of the Confederacy "tolerated no questioning, brooked no resistance, listened to no remonstrance." Taxes of all kinds were levied on a people that were already living well below previous standards and in many cases near the point of starvation. The conscription policy made virtually every white male a prospective soldier and those who had originally enlisted for a specific term of months or years found those terms arbitrarily extended through the duration of the war. Throughout the South, government officials looking for men avoiding the draft subjected citizens to unannounced visits in their homes. A stifling system of guards and passports was developed to preserve order and prevent desertion from the army. "In short, a government constitutionally weak beyond all precedent was able for four years to exercise in a particularly offensive way all the powers of absolutism, and that, too, over a people who had been living under republican rule for generations."[16]

Many die-hard Confederates could rationalize all the sacrifices the people made because it was for the Cause. But at some point these extraordinary efforts may have become self-defeating. As the resources of the South dwindled most of the men who might have developed more efficient ways to farm or run the factories were instead being used as cannon fodder in the army.

Aside from the universal fear for the safety of loved ones during a war, most of the people in the North suffered from few of the problems faced in the South. Unlike southern civilians whose lives and property were frequently put at risk by Federal raids and battling armies, about the only areas of Union-controlled territory where civilians were threatened was in the border states, especially Kentucky and Tennessee. Many civilians were killed or driven from their homes by violent supporters of both sides. In March, Union chaplain G. S. Bradley wrote from Tennessee:

> During the last two months, over 4,000 refugees have applied for assistance.... The story they tell of suffering at the hands of the rebels, is a sad one. As a general thing, every man, thus driven out, has his man selected to kill when the war is over. Society in those sections will for years be in a most unsafe condition. Those who have suffered are bound to have revenge.

This desire for revenge, especially in the North, was one of the biggest problems President Lincoln knew he would have to overcome if the nation was ever going to heal and become one again.[17]

The two most important concerns of the Federal government were how to win the war and what to do with their defeated countrymen afterward. Based on the events of 1863 the war seemed to be going in the right direction and in December, President Lincoln announced a plan he hoped would smooth the way for the rebellious states to re-enter the Union. Excluding only a few major offenders from its lenient terms, it offered a full pardon with restoration of all rights to property, except in slaves, to all persons implicated in the rebellion who would swear thereafter to uphold the Constitution, the Union, the Emancipation Proclamation, and all laws pertaining to slaves. The president announced further that when, in any state, one-tenth of those who had voted in the election of 1860 had taken this oath of allegiance, they could re-establish a state government, republican in form, and he would recognize it and grant it federal protection.[18]

The president's proposal was meant to be a compromise between the peace party and the radicals. As might be expected, however, this compromise was rejected by both groups. Peace Democrats in the North condemned the president's pardon and reconstruction plan as excessively harsh. The radical Republicans wanted to impose significantly tougher terms on a beaten South to punish them for the death and destruction they had caused. Caught between these two groups the president was not interested in revenge but absolutely demanded the rebellious states return to the Union and abandon slavery.[19]

Abraham Lincoln's stand against slavery was fueled by personal and political motives. In a letter to A. G. Hodges of Frankfort, Kentucky, the president defended the Emancipation Proclamation as necessary to preserve the country:

> I am naturally antislavery. If slavery is not wrong, nothing is wrong. It was in the oath I took that I would to the best of my ability, preserve, protect, and defend the Constitution of the United States. I could not take the office without taking the oath. Nor was it my view that I might take an oath to get power, and break the oath in using the power. I did understand, however, that my oath to preserve the Constitution to the best of my ability imposed upon me the duty of preserving by every indispensable means, that government — that nation, of which that Constitution was the organic law. I felt that measures otherwise unconstitutional might become lawful by becoming indispensable to the preservation of the Constitution through the preservation of the nation. Right or wrong, I assumed this ground, and now avow it.[20]

On the point that the people of the South must accept the new laws related to slavery, President Lincoln wrote:

> Those laws and proclamations were enacted and put forth for the purpose of aiding in the suppression of the rebellion. To give them their fullest effects, there had to be a pledge for their maintenance. In my judgment they have aided and will further aid the cause for which they were intended. To now abandon them would be not only to relinquish a lever of power, but would also be a cruel and an astonishing breach of faith. I may add, at this point, that while I remain in my present position I shall not attempt to retract or modify the Emancipation Proclamation, nor shall I return to slavery any person who is free by the terms of that proclamation, or by any of the acts of Congress.[21]

Many Republican senators, though less vindictive than the radicals, were afraid that Lincoln's readiness to forgive and forget might result in future political problems for Republicans and the nation as a whole. A restored South could very well join in an alliance with Northern Democrats and once again become dominant in the government. If this were to happen there was little to prevent them from weakening or circumventing the anti-slavery laws, and reversing all the gains that had been won at such a terrible cost during the war. This political warfare between Republicans and Democrats and between different factions within the Republican Party caused President Lincoln almost as much anguish as the war itself.[22]

The vast majority of Northern Democrats may have disagreed with many of the president's policies but they were still truly called "the loyal opposition." They wanted to preserve the Union as much as their political opponents, but they also believed that to a great extent the South was provoked into secession by the antislavery program of overzealous Republicans. Most Northern Democrats also supported the war effort. Some of the Union's best generals and hardest-fighting troops were Democrats, but there was a growing dissatisfaction with how the war was being conducted.[23]

Many people from both parties believed the Federal government had overstepped its authority by drafting citizens into the army. Other actions that had raised protests included allowing military authorities to arrest citizens alleged to be disloyal without sufficient proof or trial, and suspending some of the very constitutional rights and legal protections that soldiers were supposedly fighting to protect. Some Democrats also feared that the Republicans were using the war as an excuse to curtail certain civil liberties and to gain enough power to control the national and state governments indefinitely. They also believed that the Emancipation Proclamation was unconstitutional and relatively useless since the only slaves actually set free were those in Confederate territory controlled by the Union army. In addition, the threat to set free millions of former slaves only served to stiffen southern resistance and prolong the war. For these, and many more politically motivated reasons, the Democrats became more interested in just ending the war than in winning it. At the very least they were not especially interested in allowing the Republicans to receive all the credit for winning the war and all the power that would come afterward.[24]

The Republican response to the complaints of the Democrats was to call them southern sympathizers and proslavery traitors, labeling them "copperheads." While there were certainly some Democrats whose hatred of the Lincoln administration overpowered their common sense, these were only a handful and as a whole the Democrats were as patriotic as any other group. The Democrats were a political party composed of practical politicians bitter over the loss of power they had grown accustomed to wielding. They resented the newly enfranchised Republicans who took away their power and were desperate to get it back. They were a party made of up of white men who are frightened by the very idea of free blacks becoming part of their society. And, finally, many Democrats simply found it intolerable that Americans should be slaughtering one another by the thousands for what they believed was no valid reason.[25]

During the last two years both political parties clearly learned that the course of the war would determine the course of politics. This relationship between war and politics would be even more important in the presidential election year of 1864. If the Federal armies moved forward that spring and fought their way to victory, or at least won enough battles to make it appear that victory was near, the Lincoln administration and the Republican Party would surely remain in power. But, if the Union armies suffered defeat or were stalemated by the smaller Confederate forces with no sign of progress toward victory, the administration would almost surely be voted out of office. In addition, the citizens of the North had been sickened by the number of their husbands and sons who had already been killed and crippled; had the casualty lists increased significantly, with no sign of progress toward victory, then there was a good possibility that many people would decide that the war was not winnable and that further sacrifice was pointless. This belief could have caused enough northerners to give up on the war and turn to the seductive promise of the Democrats that the restoration of peace would bring the restoration of the Union. What many may not have realized or wanted to accept was that the South did not want reunion, on any terms. The southern people had not sacrificed as much as they had just to return to the status quo; they were fighting to become an independent nation.[26]

Never before had the connection between military operations and the public's perception of what was happening on the battlefield been so critical as in the spring and summer of 1864. The war was everything: high taxes, poor economic conditions, tightening of civil rights, and all the other things that Americans usually worried about were overshadowed by the war. The only thing that really mattered was whether or not the public could see that progress was being made toward victory. What occurred on the battlefields, and what it cost, would determine who would win the election in November. And who occupied the White House would determine if the war would be fought out to the end, or just ended, and along with this decision lay the future of the nation.[27]

As was obvious by this time everything in the future depended on the armies. Although there were clear differences in size and the amount of equipment available both armies had one problem in common: filling the ranks. The Confederacy came up with a simple, straightforward solution: just put everyone in the army. The Union decided to take a more complicated route. The ranks of the men who volunteered to fight for the Union when the war started had been terribly thinned by battle and sickness. The only way to bring the Federal armies up to full strength was by the use of draftees. Under normal circumstances most draftees could be turned into decent soldiers through discipline and hard work. Unfortunately the Federal conscription policies brought many of the lowest forms of humanity into the army.

Each state in the North was given a quota of men that were to be delivered to the Federal army. It did not matter if these men were volunteers or draftees. Eventually a system of paying cash bounties to encourage men to enlist was developed. In addition, any man who was drafted could pay a fee of $300, a great deal of money in 1864, and be exempt from the draft. Naturally, the average workingman or farmer had little enthusiasm for fighting and dying simply because he was poor.[28]

The real problems, however, came with the bounties. What seemed like a good idea at first, giving men a little bonus cash for risking their lives, was soon corrupted. Because the competition for men was so fierce the amount of the bounties grew until it was not unheard of for a man to receive $800 to $1,000 for enlisting. This kind of money quickly brought out thousands of the kind of men that no army on earth would want. A new kind of soldier came into being—the professional bounty-jumper. These men, many of whom were just plain criminals, found they could earn a great deal of money by enlisting, collecting the bounty, deserting at the first opportunity, and enlisting for another bounty somewhere else. With the limited means of identification and record keeping during the Civil War many men were able to get away with this for as long as their nerve held up, or until they were caught and shot.[29]

Considering how much money was being eaten up by the war, the amount of money lost to these men was less important than how they affected the army. Many units had to be operated as if they were guarding prisoners instead of training soldiers. Most bounty men could not be made to fight and at the first sign of battle they would run away if they could. In most cases a regiment that had to rely on bounty men to fill its ranks was better off with fewer but more reliable men especially when it came to standing in a line of battle. The fact of the matter is that although the

Union armies of 1864 were as large as in previous years, they were simply not as good an instrument of war as in the past. Considering how much depended on the coming campaign, and the quality of the men they would be fighting against, the Federal advantage in numbers might not have been as overwhelming as it appeared.[30]

Chapter 2
Planning the Campaign

The story of the 1864 campaigns west of the Appalachian Mountains really begins on November 25, 1863. On that day the Confederate Army of Tennessee broke and ran from its seemingly impregnable position on Missionary Ridge, outside of Chattanooga, Tennessee. This debacle cost the Confederacy its last foothold in that state and began the slide toward defeat for the South that included the loss of Atlanta, Sherman's campaign to Savannah, and the twin disasters of Franklin and Nashville a year later.

Throughout the war the Federal armies west of the Appalachian Mountains were more successful than their comrades in Virginia. It was in the West that Ulysses Grant built his reputation as a hard-driving winner that led to his promotion as the only lieutenant general in the army and appointment as general in chief. Just as important for the Union cause in the West was the appointment of Maj. Gen. William T. Sherman as Grant's successor as commander of the Military Division of the Mississippi. Sherman received the order of his promotion on March 14, along with a request to meet Grant in Nashville and accompany him as he traveled to Washington. The best of friends, the two men would meet in person to discuss the coming campaign and what they expected to accomplish.[1]

Sherman went along as far as Cincinnati. With their wives visiting in another room, Generals Grant and Sherman, at the time the two most powerful men in the Federal army, spent many hours in the parlor of the Burnet House bent over their maps and discussing how to formulate a campaign that would end the war. When they finally emerged the basic strategy for the rest of the war had been developed and it was brilliant because of its simplicity.[2]

In his official report Grant wrote:

> General Sherman was instructed to move against Johnston's army, to break it up, and to go into the interior of the enemy's country as far as he could, inflicting all the damage he could upon their war resources; if the enemy in his front showed signs of joining Lee, to follow him up to the full extent of his ability, while I would prevent the concentration of Lee upon him if it was in the power of the Army of the Potomac to do so. More specific written instructions were not given, for the reason

that I had talked over with him the plans of the campaign, and was satisfied that he understood them and would execute them to the fullest extent possible.[3]

This plan for the coming campaign was deceptively simple; they would attack everywhere at the same time. The main blows would be aimed at Robert E. Lee's Army of Northern Virginia and the Confederate capital of Richmond and Joseph E. Johnston's Army of Tennessee and the manufacturing and transportation center of Atlanta. Grant would oversee the Army of the Potomac in the east and Sherman would command in the west. Several other, smaller movements would be launched at the same time to prevent Confederate reinforcements from being sent to the two main fronts. Maj. Gen. Franz Sigel was to take a small army up the Shenandoah Valley, meet another column from West Virginia, and destroy railroads and supplies. Maj. Gen. Benjamin Butler commanded an army of 30,000 that was to threaten Richmond from the east while Grant moved down from the north. The beauty of this plan was that it didn't really matter which of the two men succeeded in achieving his goals. If Lee were beaten and Richmond captured the Confederacy would almost surely fall apart, and if Sherman could destroy Johnston and take Atlanta all that would be left of the Confederacy were the states along the east coast, with Sherman in position to march north and eventually link up with Grant to smother Lee.[4]

Since early in the war General Grant

> had been impressed with the idea that active and continuous operations of all the troops that could be brought into the field, regardless of season and weather, were necessary to a speedy termination of the war. The resources of the enemy and his numerical strength were far inferior to ours, but as an offset to this we had a vast territory, with a population hostile to the Government, to garrison, and long lines of river and railroad communications to protect, to enable us to supply the operating armies.[5]

General Grant realized that there had never been a nationally coordinated effort to attack the Confederacy from multiple directions at the same time. In a letter to General Sherman on April 4, Grant outlined the basic idea of the coming campaign: "It is my design, if the enemy keep quiet and allow me to take the initiative in the spring campaign, to work all parts of the army together, and somewhat towards a common centre."[6]

The main Federal armies in the East and West always had previously acted independently of each other, allowing the Confederates to use their shorter interior lines of communication to move troops from inactive areas to a more seriously threatened location. Grant was "firm in the conviction that no peace could be had that would be stable and conducive to the happiness of the people, both North and South, until the military power of the rebellion was entirely broken."[7]

Now that he had the authority to do something about it Grant was determined,

> first, to use the greatest number of troops practicable against the armed force of the enemy, preventing him from using the same force at different seasons against first one and then another of our armies, and the possibility of repose for refitting and producing necessary supplies for carrying on resistance; second, to hammer contin-

uously against the armed force of the enemy and his resources until, by mere attrition, if in no other way, there should be nothing left to him but an equal submission with the loyal section of our common country to the constitution and laws of the land.[8]

The old strategy of attacking and capturing and then holding a specific place, or fighting a brief campaign then allowing both sides to pull back and regroup was not working. Adam Badeau, one of General Grant's aides, wrote that, "During three long weary years the nation had watched in anxiety and gloom the various movements of the different armies, and the result was still increasing gloom and ever additional anxiety."[9]

With Ulysses S. Grant was coming a new type of warfare. This new way of waging war meant not only unrelenting pressure on the Confederate armies in the field but now the farms that fed the armies, the factories that produced the materials to carry on the war, and the railroads that transported those materials were also legitimate targets. In order to end the rebellion the will of the southern people to continue their support of the war had to be ground down and snuffed out. Grant was bringing total war to the South and in William T. Sherman the new general in chief had a willing and able disciple.

One example of the new type of warfare that was coming to the South was Sherman's raid on Meridian, Mississippi, in February. Before General Grant was promoted to general in chief, he preceded Sherman as commander of the Military Division of Mississippi. During the winter Grant was desperately trying to get some sort of offensive movement going in the Deep South. His target of choice was Mobile, Alabama, but the Lincoln administration insisted instead on a campaign to the Red River in Louisiana, which ended in a humiliating disaster for the Union.[10]

In an attempt to salvage something of his plans for Mobile, General Grant had Sherman take about 20,000 men on a raid to Meridian. The objective was to destroy railroad tracks and capture or destroy the vast amount of supplies at Meridian. Grant also hoped, rather unrealistically, that somehow Sherman might be able to continue on and capture Mobile on his own. General Sherman left Vicksburg on February 3 and easily made his way across Mississippi to Meridian by the 14th. Sherman's men destroyed about 55 miles of tracks and over 50 bridges and culverts in eastern Mississippi, both above and below the city of Meridian. A cavalry force that was intended to join Sherman was beaten back by Nathan Bedford Forrest and Sherman soon returned to Vicksburg. Little of military value was accomplished but the nature of the campaign is what is important; it was a raid not to win a battle but to destroy property.[11]

In his report General Sherman gave a taste of how future campaigns would be conducted:

> On the 16th began a systematic and thorough destruction of the railroads centering at Meridian. The immense depots, warehouses, and length of sidetrack demonstrated the importance to the enemy of that place.... For five days 10,000 men worked hard and with a will in that work of destruction, with axes, crowbars, sledges, clawbars, and with fire, and I have no hesitation in pronouncing the work well done. Merid-

ian, with its depots, store-houses, arsenal, hospitals, offices, hotels, and cantonments no longer exists.

This is the kind of warfare the South could expect from now on.[12]

Just over 100 miles south from Washington, D.C., Jefferson Davis sat in his office in Richmond, facing a growing gulf between the dream of Confederate independence and the reality of the situation at the beginning of 1864. The defeats of the previous year left the Confederate chief executive with the difficult task of rebuilding his armies.

Unlike President Lincoln, Davis did not have a general in chief; he commanded the Confederacy's armed forces. Davis was a graduate of the United States Military Academy, served as an officer in the regular army for seven years, and was wounded in the Mexican War. Before the war he had been United States secretary of war, so he certainly understood what it took to put armies in the field. His office was the headquarters for the Confederate armies and he would play a major role in determining the strategy for the coming year.[13]

One of the most important decisions Davis had to make was to find a new commander for the Army of Tennessee. The lack of success west of the mountains was a major reason why the Confederacy had the problems it now faced. Braxton Bragg had been relieved after the debacle at Chattanooga and it was imperative to find someone who not only possessed the knowledge and experience to command a large army but also could rally the dispirited troops so that they would once again be willing to risk life and limb for the Cause. After some serious deliberations Davis chose Joseph E. Johnston as the new commander of the Army of Tennessee.

President Davis had already determined that Johnston's first task would be to prepare his army to attack Sherman's forces in Tennessee and, if successful, carry the war north into Kentucky. Johnston was offered reinforcements in the form of Leonidas Polk's corps from Mississippi, part of the Army of Tennessee on detached assignment, and Longstreet's troops in East Tennessee, if he would move forward. With Sherman's armies still separated, Confederate lieutenant general John Bell Hood understood that, "The President and General Bragg, and also General Lee, were desirous that the offensive be assumed, and an attempt be made to drive the Federals to the Ohio river, before a large Army could be concentrated to move against us."[14]

On March 12 General Bragg wrote to Johnston, trying to convince him to make the advance:

> It is needless, General, for me to impress upon you the great importance, not to say necessity, of reclaiming the provision country of Tennessee and Kentucky; and from my knowledge of the country and people, I believe that other great advantages may accrue especially in obtaining men to fill your ranks.[15]

Johnston insisted that his army was not in any condition to launch a major operation at this time and he "pointed out the necessity of great preparations to take the offensive, such as large additions to the number of troops, an ample supply of field transportation, subsistence stores, and forage, a bridge equipage, and fresh artillery horses."[16]

The powers in Richmond, however, apparently could not or would not believe that the Army of Tennessee was in as poor condition as Johnston reported. On February 18 Johnston received a plan for the new campaign that was being insisted on:

> It prescribed my invasion of Tennessee with an army of 75,000 men, including Longstreet's corps, then near Morristown, Tennessee. When necessary supplies and transportation were collected at Dalton, the additional troops, except Longstreet's, would be sent there; and this army and Longstreet's corps would march to meet at Kingston, on the Tennessee River, and thence into the valley of Duck River.[17]

Johnston replied that he believed that Sherman's forces could defeat this plan in at least two different ways, "either by attacking one of our two bodies of troops on the march, with their united forces, or by advancing against Dalton before our forces there should be equipped for the field; for it was certain that they would be able to take the field before we could be ready."[18]

Of course, General Johnston had his own recommendation on what should be done with any reinforcements sent to the Army of Tennessee: "[T]he additional troops should be sent to Dalton in time to give us the means to beat the Federal army there, and then pursue it into Tennessee, which would be a more favorable mode of invasion than the other."[19]

This plan was unacceptable to Richmond as Bragg wrote on the 21st, "Troops can only be drawn from other points for advance. Upon your decision of that point further action must depend."[20] In other words, Johnston would not receive reinforcements, especially Longstreet's Corps, if they were just going to sit in Dalton and wait for the Federals to attack; they could be more useful elsewhere.

Newly appointed lieutenant general John Bell Hood, who frequently wrote to President Davis outside normal military channels, later wrote that Johnston

> immediately took the ground that he did not very well know the country through which it was proposed to pass to the rear of the enemy; that there were difficulties to be encountered, etc., etc.; he desired Polk's and Longstreet's forces to join him at Dalton, where, this large Army being concentrated, he considered he should be left to decide and act for the best; in other words, be left to move forward, stand his ground or retreat, as might seem most expedient.[21]

Here was a classic military impasse: A far-away government trying to push a commander to act, even though the man who was actually on the scene had a much-clearer view of the situation, and the commander in the field asking the government to continue to supply him with difficult-to-come-by resources but offering no promise to use those resources as his superiors wished.

In a letter to President Davis, Johnston wrote that he

> believed that the Federal forces in Tennessee were not weaker, but if anything stronger, than at Missionary Ridge; that defeat beyond the Tennessee would probably prove ruinous to us, resulting in the loss of his army, the occupation of Georgia by the enemy, the "piercing of the Confederacy in its vitals," and the loss of all the southwestern territory.[22]

Johnston was well aware of what his commander in chief expected him to do but was not about to be pushed into a campaign he felt would be a mistake. "Your Excellency well impresses upon me the importance of recovering the territory we have lost. I feel it deeply, but difficulties appear to me in the way." After once again enumerating all the reasons why he could not launch an attack Johnston added, "I can see no other mode of taking the offensive here, than to beat the enemy when he advances, and then move forward. But, to make victory probable, the army must be strengthened."[23]

General Johnston proposed, "to stand on the defensive until strengthened, 'to watch, prepare, and strike,' as soon as possible." After defeating the Federal advance Johnston intended to move to Cleveland, Tennessee, cut the railroad and isolate East Tennessee. At the same time Johnston wanted a large cavalry force sent into Middle Tennessee, behind the Federal forces. These operations, he thought, would result in forcing the Federal army to evacuate the Tennessee Valley, and make an advance into the heart of the state safely practicable.[24]

In addition to the differences with the authorities in Richmond concerning how to use his army, throughout the term of his command Johnston was plagued by some of his subordinates going behind his back to inform those same authorities of his actions, or lack of them. General Hood was in frequent communication with their mutual superiors. On March 7 Hood wrote to Davis that he was "exceedingly anxious, as I expressed to you before leaving Richmond, to have this Army strengthened, so as to enable us to move to the rear of the enemy and with a certainty of success. An addition of ten or fifteen thousand (10,000 or 15,000) men will allow us to advance."[25]

On April 13 Hood wrote to Bragg that he was

> sorry to inform you that I have done all in my power to induce General Johnston to accept the proposition you made to move forward. He will not consent, as he desires the troops to be sent here, and it be left to him as to what use should be made of them.
> When we are to be in better condition to drive the enemy from our country, I am not able to comprehend. To regain Tennessee would be of more value to us than half a dozen victories in Virginia.[26]

By the end of April the Army of Tennessee once again looked and acted like the proud and confident force it had been. While Johnston still called for reinforcements he must have been pleased with the transformation of his command. The men were better clothed and fed and discipline had improved which meant better control and coordination between units on the battlefield.[27]

In addition to improving the morale and physical condition of his army Johnston had apparently made the decision as to how the army was to be used during the coming campaign. When Bragg commanded the army his philosophy was to attack whenever the army had been strong enough, and the army had suffered high casualties and defeat. Johnston was not going to make the same mistakes; he was sure that rashness was not the answer, so the Army of Tennessee was committed to a defensive policy before the first shot was fired. Most of the terrain between Chattanooga and Atlanta favored a defensive strategy. The western end of the Appalachian Range left a series of ridges running roughly north and south across the most direct route between the two cities. Johnston would let Sherman smash his armies to bits against well-dug-in Confederate fortifications.[28]

While Joe Johnston was rebuilding his army and the messages were flying back and forth between Dalton and Richmond, General Sherman was steadily building up his invasion force. Sherman's problems centered not on manpower but on supplying his armies for several months, over a single railroad line, while operating hundreds of miles from his bases. He later wrote:

> The great question of the campaign was one of supplies. Nashville, our chief depot, was itself partially in a hostile country, and even the routes of supply from Louisville to Nashville by rail, and by way of the Cumberland River, had to be guarded. Chattanooga [our starting-point] was one hundred and thirty-six miles in front of Nashville, and every foot of the way, especially the many bridges, trestles, and culverts, had to be strongly guarded against the acts of a local hostile population and of the enemy's cavalry. Then, of course, as we advanced into Georgia, it was manifest that we should have to repair the railroad, use it, and guard it likewise.[29]

In addition to needing mountains of supplies to feed, clothe, and arm his men Sherman also realized that when the armies headed south "ordinary prudence dictated that we should have an accumulation at the front, in case of interruption to the railway by the act of the enemy, or by common accident."[30]

The key to building up this needed surplus was to increase the flow of supplies from Nashville to Chattanooga. Nashville itself was actually overstocked with provisions and forage, its huge warehouses filled to capacity. The problem was a bottleneck on the railroad. There was an overall lack of freight cars and all too often the locomotives pulled passenger cars filled with soldiers returning from leave, civilians on the way to visit relatives in the army, and preachers and politicians come down to save souls or get votes.[31]

It was calculated that 130 carloads of supplies had to be delivered to Chattanooga daily in order to supply the needs of the army and build the required surplus. When Colonel Anderson, the chief quartermaster, informed Sherman that he did not have nearly enough cars or locomotives to meet these requirements the commanding general took drastic action:

> On the 6th of April, I issued a general order, limiting the use of the railroad-cars to transporting only the essential articles of food, ammunition, and supplies for the army proper, forbidding any further issues to citizens, and cutting off all civil traffic; requiring the commanders of posts within thirty miles of Nashville to haul out their own stores in wagons; requiring all troops destined for the front to march, and all beef-cattle to be driven on their own legs. This was a great help, but of course it naturally raised a howl.[32]

Restricting the use of the railroad to purely military freight helped to improve the efficiency of the railroad system but there were still not enough freight cars available to allow the accumulation of supplies that were needed before the opening of the campaign. Sherman then instructed his chief quartermaster, "to hold on to all trains that arrived at Nashville from Louisville, and to allow none to go back until he had secured enough to fill the requirements of our problem." It didn't happen overnight but sufficient supplies were accumulated and from the time Sherman's host moved south to their entrance into Atlanta they suffered no severe shortages of food or munitions.[33]

Another example of General Sherman's thoroughness was that he had blockhouses built to guard every bridge along the over 300 miles of railroad track from the Ohio River to Chattanooga. Col. William Wright commanded a corps of 5,000 construction workers based in camps along the track. Sherman knew that he could never total protect his railroad lines from Confederate raiders so he tried to minimize the damage and make preparations to repair it as quickly as possible. If any campaign was ever won before the first gun was fired it was this one.[34]

Clearly and properly Sherman's main assignment was to destroy the Army of Tennessee. However, if the Confederates were forced to retreat it would be natural for Johnston to fall back toward his base of supplies and defend Atlanta with all his strength, making the city Sherman's target by default. With four railroads radiating from the Atlanta area it provided the main transportation connection with what was left of the Confederacy east of the Mississippi. During the war years Atlanta had become one of the principal manufacturing centers of the South and its rolling mill was one of the few outside Richmond that could mass produce steel rails for the Confederacy's railroads. Another important consideration for both sides was that the geography of the South made the route through Atlanta the "back door" to the heart of the Confederacy along the East Coast.[35]

In addition to the importance of Atlanta there were many other areas of Georgia that had become important manufacturing centers. Augusta had both light and heavy industrial plants and its canal furnished the waterpower for the increased industrial expansion during the war. Soon it was manufacturing shoes, clothing, wagons, and other equipment for the army. There was also a huge gunpowder mill there, the largest in the world, which produced almost 3 million pounds of gunpowder over the course of the war. Macon also contained a rail center and was the home of the state arsenal. The prisoners in the state penitentiary at Milledgeville had been put to work producing weapons. Put simply, in addition to the Confederate army, the state of Georgia itself contained a wealth of targets for Sherman's invaders.[36]

Georgia had also become a major source of supplies for the Army of Northern Virginia, and these supplies traveled on the railroads that went through Atlanta. If the Federal army could gain control of Atlanta, the rest of Georgia and the states of Alabama and Mississippi would not be able to resist for very long. The loss of these states together with the Confederate states already under Federal control and those in the west that were cut off by the Mississippi River would reduce the territory controlled by the Confederacy to just North and South Carolina and Virginia. The loss of Atlanta and what would probably follow could very well mean the death of the Confederacy.[37]

On April 19 General Grant sent a message to Sherman confirming his instructions for the coming campaign and proposing what action to take if the Confederate armies decide to abandon one of the two main fronts:

> [I]f the two main attacks, yours and the one from here, should promise great success, the enemy may, in a fit of desperation, abandon one part of their line of defense, and throw their whole strength upon the other, believing a single defeat without any victory to sustain them better than a defeat all along their line, and hoping too, at the same time, that the army, meeting with no resistance, will rest perfectly satisfied with their laurels, having penetrated to a given point south, thereby enabling them to throw their force first upon one and then on the other.
>
> With the majority of military commanders they might do this.
>
> But you have had too much experience in traveling light, and subsisting upon the country, to be caught by any such ruse. I hope my experience has not been thrown away. My directions, then, would be, if the enemy in your front show signs of joining Lee, follow him up to the full extent of your ability. I will prevent the concentration of Lee upon your front, if it is in the power of this army to do it.[38]

No matter what strategy the Confederates might come up with General Grant wanted to be sure that he had an answer for it.

As April drew to a close the opening of the campaign was just days away. President Lincoln, who never claimed to be a military man, was grateful that he could trust General Grant with running the military aspects of the war effort and told him so in a letter on April 30:

> Not expecting to see you before the spring campaign opens, I wish to express in this way my entire satisfaction with what you have done up to this time, so far as I understand it. The particulars of your plans I neither know nor seek to know. You are vigilant and self-reliant, and, pleased with this, I wish not to obtrude any restraints or constraints upon you. While I am very anxious that any great disaster or capture of our men in great numbers shall be avoided, I know that these points are less likely to escape your attention than they would mine. If there be anything wanting which is within my power to give, do not fail to let me know it. And now, with a brave army and a just cause, may God sustain you.[39]

Chapter 3

Armies and Commanders

The armies contesting for control of Georgia and Tennessee were made up of mostly veteran troops led by seasoned officers. So far during the war, the Federal armies in the West had usually bested their Confederate foes but, although confident of ultimate victory, few of the Federal officers and men had anything but the utmost respect for the fighting ability of their enemy.

General Sherman's command, the Military Division of the Mississippi, consisted of four military departments: the Ohio, the Cumberland, the Tennessee, and Arkansas. Geographically this embraced all the territory from the Alleghanies to the western border of Arkansas. Three Federal armies were assigned to Sherman's command.[1]

The Army of the Ohio was commanded by Maj. Gen. John M. Schofield, a scholarly looking former professor with blond hair and a flowing beard. A graduate of the Military Academy in the Class of 1853, he could sometimes be too easygoing but Sherman considered him a capable army commander and cool under fire. The Army of the Ohio originally contained the Ninth and Twenty-third Army Corps, and was stationed at Knoxville, Tennessee. They had been facing a Confederate force commanded by Lt. Gen. James Longstreet, who had been recalled to Virginia to join Lee's army before the spring campaign began. The Ninth Corps was also moving to Virginia to reinforce the Army of the Potomac. When Sherman began to concentrate his forces three divisions of the Twenty-third Corps were left behind to guard East Tennessee giving Schofield command of only two divisions, commanded by Brig. Gens. Miles S. Hascall and Jacob D. Cox.[2]

The Army of the Cumberland, based in Chattanooga and the largest of Sherman's armies, was commanded by Maj. Gen. George H. Thomas. It contained the Fourth, Fourteenth, and Twentieth Corps, commanded respectively by Maj. Gens. Oliver O. Howard, John M. Palmer, and Joseph Hooker. The Fourth Corps included three divisions commanded by John Newton, David S. Stanley, and Thomas J. Wood. The Fourteenth Corps contained the divisions of Absalom Baird, Jefferson C. Davis, and Richard W. Johnson. The three divisions of the Twentieth Corps were led by Daniel Butterfield, John W. Geary, and Alpheus S. Williams.[3]

George Thomas was the most experienced and dependable of Sherman's army commanders. He earned the nickname "the Rock of Chickamauga" by saving the army from probable total destruction with his immovable defensive stand during that terrible battle. He was a little taller than average with a heavy, square body and short dark hair and beard with more than a little gray. Thomas was not a fast starter but rather was cautious and conservative, always weighing all the factors before taking action, but when he did strike the blow was overpowering. He was pretty much the opposite of Sherman, but totally dependable on or off the battlefield. His normal expression was serious, even grave, and it was often difficult to judge his mood because he was always calm and under control, displaying little emotion.[4]

The Army of the Tennessee, stationed at Huntsville, Alabama, was commanded by Maj. Gen. James Birdseye McPherson. This army was comprised of the Fifteenth and portions of the Sixteenth and Seventeenth corps, under Maj. Gens. John A. Logan, Grenville M. Dodge, and Frank P. Blair Jr. The Fifteenth Corps contained divisions commanded by Brig. Gens. Peter J. Osterhaus, Morgan L. Smith, John E. Smith, and William Harrow. The Sixteenth Corps had present the divisions of Thomas E.G. Ransom, John M. Corse, and Thomas W. Sweeney. The Seventeenth Corps was made up of divisions under Charles R. Woods, and Miles D. Leggett. Both the Sixteenth and Seventeenth corps were missing divisions, Stephen A. Hurlbut's at Memphis and Henry W. Slocum's at Vicksburg. Another absent division was that of A.J. Smith, who had been assigned to the ill-fated Red River Campaign.[5]

Union Major General William T. Sherman

General McPherson, at 36, was one of the more popular and capable generals in the Union army. So personable that he was able to overcome the natural hatred of the people of Vicksburg when stationed there. He had strict moral principles but could also be lighthearted and gay. Sherman had taken McPherson under his wing and treated him almost like a son.[6]

General Sherman's cavalry force consisted of George Stoneman's division of the Army of the Ohio, Judson Kilpatrick's and Kenner Garrard's divisions of the Army of the Cumberland, and Edward McCook's brigade of the Army of the Tennessee.[7] Sherman had some reservations about his cavalry; they were a little too flashy and reckless for his taste. Most importantly the cavalry did not perform well at Sherman's favorite task, destroying railroads. It seemed they didn't have the patience to tear up tracks and destroy the rails properly so they could not be used again.[8]

Overall, though, General Sherman had every reason to have confidence in his command; the men were tough, hard, and seasoned. Most of the men were from the farms and backwoods of Ohio, Illinois, and Indiana, and other western states. They were used to hard work and living off the land, long marches were no bother and they were ready to fight at the first sound of battle. Perhaps they lacked the discipline and formality of the Army of the Potomac but Sherman didn't really care. He was more concerned with how his men acted in battle than on the parade ground, and marksmanship counted for more than the shine on a man's boots.[9]

The commander of the Federal host, Maj. Gen. William Tecumseh Sherman, was born on February 8, 1820, at Lancaster, Ohio, the sixth child of Charles and Mary Sherman. He was appointed to the Military Academy at West Point in 1836 and graduated in 1840, sixth in his class. During the Mexican War he was employed on an expedition to California, thereby missing out on the opportunity to distinguish himself in battle. He served in the army until 1852 when he left for California to pursue a career in banking until 1857. Not particularly adept in the financial field he accepted the post of superintendent of a small military school in Louisiana that was to eventually become Louisiana State University. Having lived and traveled extensively in the South, Sherman understood how passionate the people were about slavery and states' rights, and actually agreed with most of their public issues, except secession.[10]

When the war broke out Sherman quickly offered his services to the Union and was appointed brigadier general of volunteers in May 1861. After commanding a brigade at the first battle of Bull Run, he was sent West and soon became the commander of the Department of the Cumberland. He did not remain long in this command and was replaced, at his request, and transferred to Maj. Gen. Henry Halleck's command in the West, where he began his long and fruitful connection with the Army of the Tennessee.[11]

Once joined with Grant and Halleck, Sherman climbed steadily through the ranks of high command. As a division commander at the battle of Shiloh, Sherman handled his troops, who had never before been under fire, with skill and courage. During the Vicksburg campaign Sherman showed himself to be a careful and energetic corps commander, improving his reputation with Grant and Halleck although he achieved no great success on the battlefield. When Grant, as commander of the Division of the Mississippi, assumed command at Chattanooga, he gave the Army of the Tennessee to his good friend. And finally, in early 1864, when Grant was promoted to general in chief, he recommended that his most trusted subordinate be given the overall command in the West.[12]

At age 44 Sherman was tall and slim with light reddish-brown hair. His face was lined with wrinkles and his small bright eyes were constantly in motion exhibiting his unbounded energy.

> He is common-place in appearance.... His short, crisp whiskers, which grow unshaven, and which appear to be stunted in growth, are of a dingy red, or what is commonly called "sandy" in color. He has, perhaps, as great a disregard for his personal appearance as he has for what others may say or think of him.[13]

In contrast to his shabby, rather common physical appearance Sherman was untiring in thought and action. He had a nervous, restless energy and looked into every detail, large and small, then quickly made his decision and issued orders. In a conversation the words flowed as if he were always running at top speed and when receiving a report he seldom gave the person time to finish without several interruptions for pointed questions. He seldom waited to hear the whole argument and issued his decision as soon as he had heard enough to understand the idea, and seldom deviated from a decision once made.[14]

General Sherman was not a brilliant battlefield commander but his grasp of strategy and the larger issues of the war were matched by few in or out of the army. He was well aware of the strength of the Confederate positions around Dalton and long before the first Federal soldier marched south he had decided that there would be no futile frontal attacks that might shatter the army just as the campaign got under way. His strengths lay in a dogged determination that refused to let obstacles deter him from the objective. Sherman had this determination because he was totally convinced that he was fighting the just fight. He wrote about himself and Grant that they

> were as brothers.... We both believed in our heart of hearts that the success of the Union cause was not only necessary to the then generation of Americans, but to all future generations. We both professed to be gentlemen and professional soldiers, educated in the science of war by our generous Government for the very occasion which had arisen. Neither of us by nature was a combative man; but with honest hearts and a clear purpose to do what man could we embarked on that campaign which I believe, in its strategy, in its logistics, in its grand and minor tactics, has added new luster to the old science of war.[15]

William T. Sherman was much more complex than is apparent by his public face. In letters to family and friends he revealed other sides that showed he was not the monster the people of the South learned to hate, nor was he the brilliant, all-conquering general that the North loved and admired. Sherman was basically a man doing a job that he would have preferred not to have to do.

Sherman understood what it would take to win this seemingly unending conflict. In a letter to his wife he wrote:

> I would rather occupy my present relation to the military world than any other command and therefore must serve out this campaign which is to be the test. All that has gone before is mere skirmishing. The war now begins, and with heavy well-disciplined masses the issue must be settled in hard fought battles. I think we can whip

them in Alabama and it may be Georgia, but the devils seem to have a determination that cannot but be admired....[16]

Although Sherman despised the fact that his nation had been torn apart he did not hate the South as a whole. Having lived in the South he understood, better than most northerners, their way of life. "We of the North are beyond all question right in our cause but we are not bound to ignore the fact that the people of the South have prejudices which form a part of their nature, and which they cannot throw off without an effort of reason, or by the slower process of natural change."[17]

However, Sherman's concept of reason and natural change ended when it came to secession and war.

> When men take up arms to resist a Rightful Authority we are compelled to use like force, because all reason and argument cease when arms are resorted to.... The people of the South having appealed to War are barred from appealing for protection to our Constitution which they have practically and publicly defied. They have appealed to war and must abide its rules & laws.[18]

A believer in states' rights, up to a point, Sherman always maintained that the Federal government had the ultimate authority, writing that the United States government, "has all rights of sovereignty which they choose to enforce in war, to take their lives, their homes, their lands, their every thing, because they cannot deny that war does exist by their acts, and war is simply power unrestrained by Constitution or compact."[19]

Reflecting on the past and future of the South, Sherman wrote:

> Three years ago, by a little reflection and patience they could have had a hundred years of Peace and Prosperity, but they preferred War. Last year they could have saved their slaves but now it is too late, all the powers of Earth cannot restore to them their slaves any more than their dead Grandfathers. Next year in all probability their lands will be taken, for in War we can take them & rightfully too, and in another year they may beg in vain for their lives, for sooner or later there must be an end to strife.[20]

Fortunately General Sherman's projection of the length of the war was too long by a year.

And in a letter to his brother, United States senator John Sherman, he wrote about the issue of slavery and the bitterness and anger that has been brought on by the war:

> The South have made the interests of Slavery the issue of the war. If they lose the war they lose Slavery. I always assert that we were bound by our Constitutional compact to restore fugitive slaves, but as they broke the Constitution the compact as to them was void, and we were released.
>
> In like manner I admit the right of secession. Men may expatriate themselves. They may go away, but they cannot carry with them the ground which is tied down. Therefore if the people of the South are unwilling to live in the same land with us, let them go, even to Madagascar and if they cannot pay their passage we might help

them, as an act of grace. They allege they cannot abide us, I know that is the feeling of some, but the masses can. I have associated with rebels & have seen our soldiers do it under flags of truce, and during lulls in war, but I do admit that some of them are so embittered that all would be benefited by an eternal separation. They cannot kill us all, but we may them. They must be killed or sent away.[21]

Although Sherman was clearly an advocate of "hard war" he did have another, softer side. This is displayed in a letter to his daughter Maria:

The War is not yet over, and I do not see its end. Many of us must die by it yet, and it may be my fate, but I feel certain our Cause will prevail so that my children will reap the fruits of my labor. Were it not for this I would not feel the same interest in success. People wonder why I don't try to get more fame, but my Dear Minnie will remember that before she was born I lived much in South Carolina and afterwards in Louisiana, and that in every battle I am fighting some of the very families in whose houses I used to spend some happy days. Of course I must fight when the time comes, but whenever a result can be accomplished without battle I prefer it.[22]

By the end of April General Sherman was preparing to unleash on Georgia over 100,000 of some of the best soldiers ever to wear a uniform. Like the soldiers in all armies the men in Sherman's command were only human. Some of them were scared, some were homesick, some of them were confident of victory, and some of them thought the war would never end.

George F. Cram, of the 105th Illinois Regiment, wrote, "Now I begin to see peace dawning. We want a perfect avalanche of men to pour down upon the South and end the war with one glorious sweep. We hope much from the Spring campaign and I do think that it will so stagger the rebellion that a few months more will end it...."[23]

Maj. Flavel Barber wrote in his diary on January 25:

Both sides are strengthening themselves for the terrible struggle in the spring, the struggle which both sides agree will finish the war. Three years of unceasing warfare have pretty well exhausted both parties. Men are difficult to procure to fill up the wasted armies; enthusiasm has entirely subsided North and South, and dogged determination alone remains.

Major Barber was mortally wounded on May 14.[24]

The Campaign of 1864 was to begin the first week of May. All the armies of the United States would be moving forward to crush the Confederacy. William T. Sherman and his host would be ready.

Opposing Sherman and the combined Federal armies was the Army of Tennessee and its new commander, Gen. Joseph Eggleston Johnston. After the defeat at Chattanooga the Army of Tennessee needed a new commander. This army contained some of the toughest and bravest troops in the Confederacy; their ferocity in battle could only be equaled, not surpassed. The real problem was that this army never had leadership worthy of the men. Jefferson Davis spent several weeks agonizing over whom to appoint to command the Confederacy's main military force in the West.

There were five men with the rank of full general in the Confederate army. Since his defeat at Chattanooga, Braxton Bragg was obviously not a candidate nor was the aged Samuel Cooper, thus leaving three men: Robert E. Lee, Joseph E. Johnston, and Pierre G.T. Beauregard.[25]

The best army commander in the Confederacy was, of course, the legendary General Lee. But he could not be spared from the Army of Northern Virginia, soon to be locked in a struggle to the death with the Federal Army of the Potomac. Recommended by Lee, General Beauregard had a colossal ego and was not above self-promotion and criticizing fellow officers. Davis did not like Beauregard and didn't want to deal with him on any level. That left Joseph Johnston, and given the circumstances he was really the only viable choice. Except for Lee and Bragg he had more experience commanding a large army than any other Confederate officer. He had proven his courage on many fields with several wounds to show for his devotion to duty. One trait he had that would be valuable in dealing with the Army of Tennessee was an ability to win the loyalty of subordinates. Finally, and perhaps most importantly, Johnston had a great deal of support from the public, the press, and his many politically powerful friends who believed that his talents were being wasted.[26]

Confederate General Joseph E. Johnston

Despite his many positive traits, however, President Davis disliked Johnston almost as much as Beauregard. Davis believed that Johnston was a personally brave and skillful general but that he was so protective of his reputation that he lacked the nerve to risk it on the outcome of a battle unless success was certain. Since the battlefield is a notoriously unstable place Johnston had become a specialist in the art of retreating. In 1862 he had fallen back to the outskirts of Richmond before being wounded in the battle of Seven Pines. After recovering he was sent west but lost what slim hope there was of saving Vicksburg by being too careful. Davis simply didn't trust Johnston not to slip back into his old habits once in Georgia, but felt there was no other option.[27]

Born into a prominent Virginia family, Joseph E. Johnston graduated near the top of his West Point class in 1829, the same class as Robert E. Lee. Both men's fathers had fought in the Revolutionary War and their sons were close friends. Johnston was a thorough professional, rising steadily in the army serving, and being wounded, in both the Seminole and Mexican wars. Now in his 50s with mostly gray hair and beard, he was a thin, short man with an intelligent face and blue eyes, Johnston was not physically impressive but his mind was as sharp as ever.[28]

Having served with, and commanded, many Union officers before the war, Johnston was well respected by his enemy. General Cox wrote that "Johnston was an officer who, by common consent of the military men of both sides, was reckoned second only to Lee, if second, in the qualities which fit an officer for the responsibility of great commands."[29]

The enmity between Johnston and Davis dated from the beginning of the war when President Davis ranked Johnston fourth among the Confederacy's full generals, instead of first, as Johnston believed he should have been. Over the years the two men had disagreements about almost everything: strategy, personnel, logistics, and army organization. Johnston was often reluctant to take any major risk without specific instructions from Richmond, and then frequently complained about excessive interference. Davis, on the other hand, felt Johnston needed to be constantly prodded to take any action at all. Davis also resented Johnston's close ties with his political opponents. The result was a serious lack of trust and communication between the two men. In essence Davis assigned Johnston to command the Army of Tennessee because, hoping for the best, he realized that there was no better alternative.[30]

General Johnston arrived in Dalton on December 27, 1863, and assumed command the next day. What he found there bore little resemblance to the well-clothed and well-fed army that had been described to President Davis by Lt. Gen. William J. Hardee, who had been in temporary command of the Army of Tennessee since Bragg's removal.

> There was a great deficiency of blankets; and it was painful to see the number of bare feet in every regiment. There was a deficiency, in the infantry, of six thousand small-arms. The artillery-horses were generally still so feeble from long, hard service and scarcity of forage, that it would have been impossible to maneuver our batteries in action, or to march with them at any ordinary rate on ordinary roads.

Johnston found it necessary to send about half of the cavalry and artillery horses to rear areas where they could be better fed to build up their strength for the coming campaign.[31]

More disturbing to Johnston than the shortages of food and clothing was the lack of morale and discipline displayed by many of the troops. After the wasted victory at Chickamauga and the humiliating defeats at Chattanooga depression and despair permeated the ranks. Before any kind of offensive movement could be considered Johnston had to restore the physical and spiritual well-being of his army.[32]

There was one other problem facing General Johnston that winter — lack of men. In a letter to Davis on January 2 he wrote: "According to the return of December 20, the effective total of the army (infantry and artillery) is not quite thirty-six thousand; the number present about forty-three thousand; that present and absent about seventy-seven thousand." If these figures are accurate, the Army of Tennessee was vastly outnumbered by the Federal troops stationed at Chattanooga, before Sherman combined all three of his armies.[33]

Soon after taking command Johnston began a constant stream of requests to President Davis and Confederate secretary of war James A. Seddon for more of everything: men, arms, food, clothing, and shoes. He recommended that slaves could be used to do much of the manual labor that soldiers now were doing, freeing up thousands of men to fight. That suggestion was rejected out of hand but slowly things in Dalton did improve. The system of supply from Atlanta via the Western & Atlantic Railroad was improved, rebuilding the health and morale of the army. The troops were granted furloughs, and drill and exercise were increased to improve their discipline and fighting ability. Johnston also offered an amnesty to the men who had deserted from the army after Missionary Ridge and this brought several thousand men back into the ranks to fight for a commander they trusted and respected.[34]

As the condition of the men in the ranks steadily improved the relations between the general officers remained strained, to say the least. Braxton Bragg, who was frequently difficult for anyone to get along with, had caused a fissure among his subordinate generals. Several had made great efforts to have him removed from command and clashed with his supporters. This rupture was a factor in the army's collapse in late 1863 and Bragg's removal had not healed the bitterness that still lingered when Johnston took command. President Davis appointed General Bragg as his chief military advisor in February and combined with the distrust between Johnston and Davis this led to a continuing division between Johnston supporters and Davis-Bragg loyalists. Some of Johnston's subordinates were sending information to Richmond, outside normal channels, that contradicted Johnston's official statements about the army's condition. This only further weakened the government's confidence in the army commander and weakened even more the level of cooperation between the two groups. Chief among the subordinates who freely communicated with President Davis was John Bell Hood.[35]

Recently promoted, Lieutenant General Hood was only 32 years old but had earned a reputation with the Army of Northern Virginia as a hard-charging leader with unsurpassed bravery on the battlefield. A native of Kentucky, he had moved to Texas and considered that his home. A graduate of the Military Academy in 1853, some of his classmates were McPherson, Schofield, and Philip Sheridan. He quickly rose in rank to become the brigadier general of the famous Texas Brigade, which he gallantly led through the Seven Days battles around Richmond and at Second Bull Run and Antietam. Promoted to major general, in command of one of Longstreet's divisions at Gettysburg, his left arm was so badly wounded as to be useless for the rest of his life.[36]

General Hood was not completely recovered from his Gettysburg wound when he accompanied his division to join Bragg at Chickamauga. On the second day of that battle, leading a brilliant charge with his arm still in a sling, Hood was wounded in the left leg, so severely that it was later amputated. While recovering in Richmond he became acquainted with President Davis who was impressed by Hood's friendly personality and his brilliant war record, and the two became friends. Despite his physical disabilities Hood refused a desk job, so early in 1864 Davis promoted him to lieutenant general and sent him to command a corps in the Army of Tennessee. Davis expected that Hood would not only be an aggressive officer who was constantly pushing Johnston to fight, but also the president's eyes and ears in the high command of the Army of Tennessee.[37]

Hood arrived at Dalton burning with desire to lead his men to great victories, even though he could not stay on a horse unless strapped into the saddle. His aggressive attitude was the exact opposite of his cautious commanding general. On March 7, Hood wrote to Davis:

> I feel that a move from this position, in sufficient force, will relieve our entire country.
>
> I sincerely hope and trust that this opportunity may be given to drive the enemy beyond the limits of the Confederacy. I never before felt that we had it so thoroughly within our power. He, the enemy, is at present weak, and we are strong. I am eager for us to take the initiative, but fear we will not be able to do so unless our Army is increased.[38]

General Johnston could not have been entirely ignorant of Hood's relationship with Davis and his undermining of Johnston's authority. The gradually increasing friction between the army commander and his subordinate would cause the army serious problems as the campaign progressed.

Whatever else concerned him about his new subordinate, Joe Johnston could count on Hood's courage and devotion to the Confederacy. The other corps commanders of the Army of Tennessee were also first-class officers. Lieutenant General Hardee, a native of Georgia, commanded the Second Corps. Accomplished in the theory of war, Hardee was the author of one of the standard military guides of the day, *Hardee's Tactics*. He had fought well at most of the major battles in the West including Shiloh, and Missionary Ridge, but he gave the impression of being a student or dispassionate observer on the battlefield. Hardee also had no problem criticizing his superiors and was instrumental in having Bragg removed and Johnston given the command.[39]

Confederate General John Bell Hood

General Johnston's cavalry commander was the mercurial Joseph "Fighting Joe" Wheeler, another Georgian. Ranked with the great cavalry leaders of the war, Wheeler had a streak of independence that was a common trait of a cavalryman but he sometimes carried it to the point of rashness. The cavalry as a whole lacked discipline and frequently operated more like freelance raiders than an integral part of the army.[40]

This, then, was what Joe Johnston had to work with. An army that was dispirited, hungry, ill-prepared for battle, and vastly outnumbered. He also had to deal with a wide range of personalities among his subordinate commanders and the knowledge that the government in Richmond disliked and distrusted him more than his enemies. By early May, through hard work and commitment to the Cause, the army was improved, fortifications were built and then expanded, and everything that could reasonably be done to prepare the army for the coming campaign was done. It was not a moment too soon for Sherman's massive Federal army was on its way.

Chapter 4

Opening Moves

The small town of Dalton, in northern Georgia, was not chosen as the main base for the Army of Tennessee because of its important strategic position; it was chosen mostly by accident. When Gen. Braxton Bragg was retreating from Missionary Ridge he stopped there for the night and when it was discovered the victorious Federals were not pursuing he decided to stay put.[1]

Dalton sits at the junction of the Western & Atlantic Railroad and the Rome Railroad to East Tennessee, and is protected on the west by a wall of rock known as Rocky Face Ridge which runs for about 25 miles in a north-south direction. About three miles northwest, the Western & Atlantic passed through a gorge in the ridge known as Mill Creek Gap. The towering sides of the gap are called Buzzard's Roost. Union soldier George Pepper described it as "a narrow defile, through which the railroad passes. The name of Buzzard Roost is employed by the natives to signify the idea not only of utter solitude, but of boundless desolation, of untrodden dreariness."[2] About a mile north of the gap the railroad passes through Tunnel Hill then northwest to Chattanooga. Near the southern end of the ridge is Snake Creek Gap, but this was left unguarded by General Johnston, who expected no trouble that far in his rear. There were no natural obstacles to the east of Dalton except for Mill Creek, which flows into the Connasauga River. However, if Sherman were to advance from that direction he would be leaving middle Tennessee open to invasion and the Confederates could easily move between Sherman and his line of supplies in the lower Tennessee Valley. Johnston correctly assumed that Sherman would stick close to the railroad and his defenses were prepared accordingly.[3]

Including the corps of General Polk, then under orders to join him, General Johnston had under his command an overall total of between 65,000 and 70,000 men of all arms. Of course, not all were fighting men. It was a superb army of veterans, with implicit confidence in their commanding general, and capable of great achievements. Like all Confederate armies they didn't have sufficient supplies to create a stockpile for any type of long-term campaign but there was enough for any possible short-term movement its commander could order.[4]

Jefferson Davis later wrote about how much effort and expense was put into

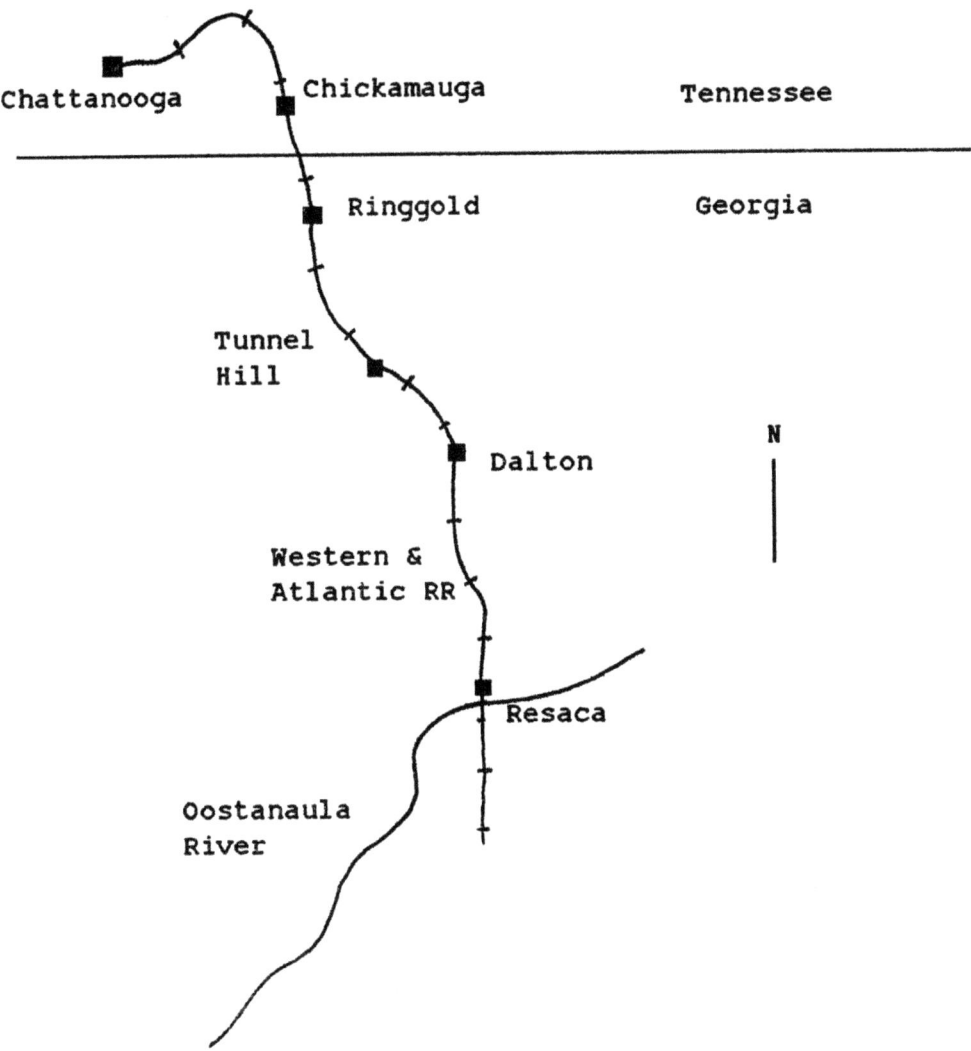

Chattanooga to Resaca

organizing and supplying the Army of Tennessee so that General Johnston could begin the long-sought offensive: "[N]o effort was spared on the part of the Government. Almost all the available military strength of the south and west, in men and supplies, was pressed forward and placed at his disposal."[5]

General Johnston explained why he kept the army at Dalton:

> The disposition of the Confederate army about Dalton was predicated on the belief that General Sherman would attack it there with his whole force. For that reason its entire strength was concentrated there, and the protection of its communications left to Lieutenant-General Polk's troops, then on their way from Alabama. I supposed, from General Sherman's great superiority of numbers, that he intended to decide the contest by a battle, and that he would make that battle as near his own

and as far from our base as possible — that is to say, at Dalton. It is evident that he did not so act, because he thought as I did — that, in the event of his assailing us, the chances would have been very strong in our favor.[6]

Johnston always had to keep in mind the difference in the size of the opposing armies when planning any operation. He also admitted that he had a higher estimation of the quality of the leaders and soldiers of the Federal army than many of his countrymen: "I therefore thought it our policy to stand on the defensive, to spare the blood of our soldiers by fighting under cover habitually, and to attack only when bad position or division of the enemy's forces might give us advantages counterbalancing that of superior numbers."[7]

On the 1st of May the effective strength of the armies that Sherman was preparing to lead south was significantly larger than that of his opponent. The Army of the Cumberland, commanded by Major General Thomas, was the largest with a total of 60,773 infantry, artillery and cavalry. The Army of the Tennessee, Major General McPherson commanding, totaled 24,465. The Army of the Ohio, commanded by Major General Schofield, was the smallest with only 13,559 men. The total for all three armies was 98,797 with over 250 cannon of various sizes. On the morning of May 6 the Army of the Cumberland was camped around Ringgold. General McPherson's troops were at Gordon's Mills on the Chickamauga River and Schofield was at the Georgia border just north of Dalton.[8]

The campaign began on May 6 with Thomas moving toward Tunnel Hill, Schofield on the east moving down toward Dalton from the north, and McPherson marching through the narrow Snake Creek Gap and Sugar Valley on his way to Resaca, 18 miles south of Dalton. The Confederate army was secure behind their fortifications at Dalton, holding the Buzzard Roost Pass, the line of Mill Creek to the north, and the line of railway back toward Atlanta.[9]

Sherman's army ran into the first of many obstacles almost immediately. To strike Dalton in front was impracticable because of Rocky Face Ridge, which soared at least 500 feet high. Buzzard Roost Gap, the pass between Tunnel Hill and Dalton, was narrow, well obstructed by abatis, and flooded by water caused by dams across Mill Creek. The Confederates had also constructed artillery positions all along the length and at the far end commanding the railroad and wagon road that worked its way through the narrow pass.[10]

South of Dalton was the undefended Snake Creek Gap. General Sherman decided that this was "a good practicable way to reach Resaca, a point on the enemy's railroad line of communication, eighteen miles below Dalton." Sherman instructed General McPherson to advance rapidly through Snake Creek Gap and make a "bold attack" on Resaca or any point on the railroad below Dalton. After breaking the railroad McPherson was to fall back and secure Snake Creek Gap. If Johnston retreated to protect his communications, as Sherman expected, McPherson would be in perfect position to attack him in the flank.[11]

As a diversion to draw attention away from McPherson, General Thomas was to demonstrate against Rocky Face from the front while General Schofield pressed down from the north. General Thomas moved from Ringgold on the 7th, occupying

Tunnel Hill, facing the Buzzard Roost Gap. His troops met with little opposition, and easily pushed the enemy's cavalry well through the gap. The next day general Newton's division of the Fourth Corps was able to reach the crest of the north end of Rocky Face Ridge and carried part of the ridge until he reached a point where the crest was too narrow and well protected to enable him to continue. At the same time strong skirmish lines were pushed part of the way up the western slope by Generals Stanley and Wood. These attacks were pressed against multiple lines of works that were nearly artillery proof. Confederate general Stewart reported: "the enemy repeatedly charged them and were as often repulsed with severe loss. It is believed the skirmishers occupying these advanced works could have held them successfully against any force that could have been brought against them."[12]

Union Major General James B. McPherson

On the 9th General Schofield made a strong demonstration from the east pushing the defenders back until reaching their main line of works. While these attacks did not pose any serious threat to the Confederate position the diversion helped to take attention away from McPherson's advance through Snake Creek Gap.[13]

General McPherson reached Snake Creek Gap on the 8th, completely surprising a brigade of Confederate cavalry that was moving up to secure the position. With a detachment of Kilpatrick's cavalry leading the way Dodge's Sixteenth Corps and Logan's Fifteenth Corps moved through the gap and into Sugar Valley.[14]

The Sixteenth Corps was in the lead as McPherson's army moved toward Resaca on the 9th. As General Dodge understood his orders he was to press up close to Resaca while other troops farther north cut the railroad between Resaca and Dalton. Logan's Fifteenth Corps was to follow behind Dodge's men.[15] General Dodge reported that he "advanced steadily, meeting with considerable resistance and skirmishing heavily" until he was within one mile of Resaca where they ran into the Confederate works.[16]

One of Gen. James Cantey's units, the 37th Mississippi, was atop Bald Hill just west of Camp Creek as Dodge's men approached Resaca. The Confederates put up a brave fight but were quickly overwhelmed. McPherson now had a commanding position nearly within musket range of Resaca. One of Dodge's divisions moving to the east reported their skirmishers had actually sighted the railroad. Before the main body could reach the tracks, however, orders were received from McPherson to return to Bald Hill.[17]

The usually aggressive McPherson now surprisingly pulled back to the east end of Snake Creek Gap and dug in. In his report McPherson gave two reasons for his uncharacteristic action: there were several roads coming south from Dalton over which the Confederates could launch a flank attack; and many of his men were out of provisions and he did not want to block the narrow road by sending a wagon train through the gap all the way to Resaca.[18]

General Sherman later wrote: "I got a short note from McPherson that day (written at 2 P.M., when he was within a mile and a half of the railroad, above and near Resaca), and we all felt jubilant." That evening Sherman learned that McPherson had fallen back from Resaca and wrote to his young friend the next morning: "You now have twenty-three thousand men, and General Hooker is in close support, so that you can hold all of Jos. Johnston's army in check should he abandon Dalton. Strengthen your position; fight any thing that comes; and threaten the safety of the railroad all the time."[19] Sherman believed that McPherson should have captured the lightly defended Resaca or put his force on the railroad, daring Johnston to attack.

> Had he done so, I am certain that Johnston would not have ventured to attack him in position, but would have retreated eastward by Spring Place, and we should have captured half his army and all his artillery and wagons at the very beginning of the campaign.
> Such an opportunity does not occur twice in a single life, but at the critical moment McPherson seems to have been a little cautious.[20]

The Confederates realized just as much as Sherman what an opportunity had been missed. General Patrick Cleburne wrote: "[I]f McPherson had hotly pressed his advantage, Sherman supporting him strongly with the bulk of his army, it is impossible to say what the enemy might not have achieved — more than probable a complete victory."[21]

Sherman later admitted that he was "somewhat disappointed at the result" of McPherson's movements. Although the young general did not achieve everything that Sherman was hoping for, the potential advantage of controlling Snake Creek Gap was obvious. On the 10th General Thomas was ordered to send General Hooker's Twentieth Corps to Snake Creek Gap in support of General McPherson, and to quickly follow with General Palmer's Fourteenth Corps. General Howard with the Fourth Corps was instructed to stay at Rocky Face Ridge and continue to threaten Dalton in front, while the rest of the army moved as rapidly as possible through the narrow trail at the bottom of Snake Creek Gap.[22]

Despite all the months the Confederates had to prepare their defenses the route taken by McPherson and later the bulk of Sherman's army was almost unguarded. Neither side had very accurate maps of the area and it is possible that Johnston believed it was too difficult to move a large number of men through Snake Creek Gap. Whatever the reason, the deep valleys and heavy forests west of Rocky Face Ridge hid the Federal movements and General Johnston did not learn of the massive force heading toward Resaca until General Polk informed him. Once he learned of the danger Johnston moved immediately and that night the Confederates evacuated Dalton to concentrate in front of Sherman's advancing troops.[23]

The first important step in the campaign had been successfully taken, and the Confederates had been compelled to evacuate the impregnable lines about Dalton, with only a small loss to Sherman's army.

By the afternoon of May 13th, the arriving Federal units began to take their places near Resaca along the range of rugged, wooded hills that lined the western side of the narrow valley skirting Camp Creek and its tributaries. McPherson's army reoccupied Bald Hill, extending its right flank to the Oostanaula River thus covering the direct road from Snake Creek Gap to Resaca. Thomas' army, except for General Howard's Fourth Corps, was next on McPherson's left. Arriving on the morning of May 14, the Army of the Ohio, commanded by James Schofield, was ordered to extend the line northward along the creek. It was nearly 10 A.M. before all were ready to press toward the Confederate positions east of the intervening creek and valley.[24]

Sherman's men were not the only soldiers heading toward Resaca. Pat Cleburne, who had to make a hurried march from Dalton to support Polk's small force, wrote:

> This movement was rendered necessary by the untoward circumstances of Snake Creek Gap not being adequately occupied to resist the heavy force thrown against it, under the sagacious and enterprising McPherson. How this gap, which opened upon our rear and line of communication, from which it was distant at Resaca only five miles, was neglected I cannot imagine.[25]

During the day of the 13th both armies were consolidating around Resaca. Johnston moved quickly on a relatively good road and had most of his men in the area by the end of the day. The Confederate position was a strong one and now that it was properly manned presented a serious obstacle to Sherman's army. Polk's troops were on the left, facing mostly west, in front of Resaca. Hardee's corps was dug in on the east side of Camp Creek Valley and joined with Hood's men who continued the line from a relatively sharp turn to the east and the Connasauga River.[26]

That same day, General Logan sent the divisions of Generals Osterhaus and Harrow down the road to Resaca and engaged Confederate skirmishers "over broken and irregular ground, with heavy growths of timber and underbrush, with occasional small cleared fields."[27] It took time to fight their way forward but in the afternoon Logan's men captured the Camp Creek hills. This position overlooked the Confederate fortifications, the town itself and the railroad and bridge over the Oostenaula River. Logan placed artillery on the hills and "opened vigorously, causing considerable confusion and interrupting the passage of railroad trains."[28]

The real fighting at Resaca began on the 14th. About noon two divisions of Schofield's army, one commanded by Brig. Gen. Jacob D. Cox and the other by Brig. Gen. Henry M. Judah, attacked the Confederate line north of town. Schofield's troops were supported on the south by Palmer's Fourteenth Corps from Thomas' army.

Hardee's corps manned the Confederate defenses with Cleburne's division in the center, William B. Bate to his right and Cheatham on the left.[29]

The Federal attack was poorly coordinated and achieved nothing but increasing the casualty lists. Brig. Gen. Nathaniel C. McLean, commander of one of Judah's brigades, reported that he advanced through brush and undergrowth and over a ridge before coming into contact with the Confederates, where they ran into a

> storm of death which was hurled upon them from every quarter, and their advance continued until they were broken up by a bog and creek into which they plunged more than waist deep. To climb the opposite bank under such a murderous fire was more than they could do, especially when we found the works so strong that with the force then attacking there was not the slightest chance of success.[30]

To the right of Judah's troops, Brig. Gen. Richard W. Johnson, commander of Palmer's First Division, ran into just as much trouble in his area. Johnson's men advanced and as his division left the cover of the woods where they were formed Cleburne's defenders "opened upon it with terrible effect." The Union troops were unable to reach the enemy lines and fell back behind Camp Creek.[31]

On the northern end of the Federal line Cox's attack was delayed while he waited for Howard's Corps to get into position. It was during this delay that the Federal attacks from the right were beaten back allowing the Confederates to concentrate their fire, especially artillery, on Cox when he did move forward. With the failure of Judah's attack the right of Cox was left unprotected. The attackers carried the first line of Confederate rifle pits but "the enemy immediately opened with both artillery and musketry from their second line, which extended far beyond both flanks of the division." Cox's men were able to hold on to their position until portions of Gen. David S. Stanley's division of the Fourth Corps relieved them after 3:00 P.M.[32]

By midafternoon the attempt to carry the Confederate line near Camp Creek was abandoned. On the northern end of the Federal line elements of General Howard's 4th Corps arrived from Dalton and took position on Cox's left, extending the Federal line to the east opposite Hood's corps.[33]

As Howard's men formed their line it was discovered that there was a gap between the extreme left of the Federal line and the Connasauga River. General Johnston had spent the morning with Hood's Corps and it didn't take long for him to realize he had an opportunity to turn the Federal flank. Two of Hood's divisions commanded by Carter Stevenson and A.P. Stewart were chosen for the task, but it was almost 5 P.M. before the movement got underway.[34]

General Stewart's men were on the extreme right of the Confederate line with their left connecting with Stevenson near the Resaca-Dalton road. The Confederate plan was for Stevenson's regiments to serve as the pivot for the attack with Stewart wheeling around toward the exposed Federal flank. Both Confederate divisions began their advance as planned but Stewart's men had so much more distance to cover that they never did make contact with the enemy.[35]

Stevenson's brigades, however, hit the Federal line almost immediately. From their positions on the hills east of the Dalton road the Federals could see the Confederates forming for the attack and sent reinforcements to the skirmish lines, most of whom were quickly captured as Stevenson's men rushed forward. The attack first hit the left of Stanley's division and confusion in the Federal ranks soon followed. As they fell back the Federal troops passed a hill with Capt. Peter Simonson's 5th Indiana Battery positioned on the top. Federal officers tried to rally the frightened men here to halt the Confederate advance and protect the guns.[36]

The attacking rebels soon directed most of their attention at the battery but as Simonson reported, "A very rapid fire of canister was opened on the advancing foe, which quickly cleared the field; the greater portion of the enemy's troops going into the woods toward our left."[37] The Confederates soon resumed the attack but the timely arrival of Col. J.S. Robinson's brigade of William's division from Hooker's corps quickly blunted the attack and Stevenson's men were beaten back leaving numerous prisoners in Federal hands.[38]

The only real Federal success of the day occurred on the far right in front of Resaca. General McPherson was instructed to launch an attack against Polk to prevent him from sending reinforcements north to aid Hardee and Hood. About 5:30 P.M. the assault was launched across Camp Creek, some of the men crossed on a bridge, some waded across holding their weapons over their heads, others floated over on logs. The assaulting force consisted of Brig. Gen. Charles R. Woods' brigade of the First Division, the Third Missouri Infantry of the Third Brigade, and Brig. Gen. Giles A. Smith's brigade of the Second Division. The ground was marshy with many fallen trees and thickets, making it difficult for the troops to keep in their lines. The rebel infantry poured in a destructive fire and artillery from the enemy forts joined in to meet the advancing men with a storm of lead and iron. In spite of the strong Confederate fire General Logan saw that

> neither thicket, nor slough, nor shot, nor shell, distracted for a moment the attention of the stormers from their objective point. Lines temporarily disarranged were reorganized without slackening the speed, until, without firing a shot, they, at the point of the bayonet, planted their colors on the summits of the conquered hills.[39]

Later in the evening the Confederates tried to reclaim the hills with a series of attacks. The first one was repulsed by the troops who had captured the hills. The size of the Confederate force was large enough that they were endangering the flanks of the defenders and Gen. A.J. Lightburn's brigade of the Second Division was sent across the creek as reinforcements just in time to join the fight and repel the attackers after savage fighting that lasted well after dark, the red flame from the muskets clearly showing the position of the opposing forces.[40]

A minor movement that was to become hugely important later was made late in the afternoon of the 14th when part of Gen. Thomas Sweeny's division of the Sixteenth Corps was able to cross the Oostenaula River at Lay's Ferry several miles south of Resaca. Confederate forces from General Polk's corps were hurried south to intercept the Federals but Sweeny pulled back across the river before they arrived. Finding no enemy the Confederates withdrew, leaving the ferry unguarded.[41]

During the morning of the 15th there was skirmishing along the whole front, but it was in the north that the major fighting occurred. General Hooker's entire corps had now arrived and was in line with Howard's corps. Johnston had brought reinforcements from both Hardee and Polk to strengthen Hood's line. Both sides had decided to make their main effort in the same place.[42]

It took Hooker until noon to move his troops to the left and begin his advance. "He, with a column of brigades, very handsomely drove the enemy before him, seized and held two important heights." Howard, on Hooker's right, was the pivot for the advance but despite some hard fighting the Federal advance stalled.[43]

The main force of Hooker's attack fell on Stevenson's Confederates. He reported: "The assaults of the enemy were in heavy force and made with the utmost impetuosity, but were met with a cool, steady fire, which each time mowed down their ranks and drove them back, leaving the ground thickly covered in places with their dead."[44]

With the Federal attack beaten back General Johnston decided it was now time to launch his own assault. About 4:00 P.M. Hood sent his men forward in a repetition of the attack on the previous day: Stewart, on the far right, swinging around to attack the Federal left with Stevenson holding the pivot position. Stewart's men "moved forward with great spirit and determination and soon engaged the enemy."[45] But his advance ran into trouble almost immediately, as he reported: "We encountered the enemy in heavy force and protected by breast-works of logs. The ground over which a portion of Stovall's brigade passed was covered with a dense undergrowth and brush. Regiments in consequence became separated, and the brigade soon began to fall back."[46] Stevenson advanced his troops in support of Stewart but was unable to make a connection with Stewart's left and was forced to fall back without having much effect on the battle.[47]

While the attack was in progress Johnston received information that immediately changed the entire picture. South of Resaca Union forces under General Sweeny again crossed the Oostenaula at Lay's Ferry, this time with a much larger force than the day before. Walker's Confederates again advanced to remove this threat but Sweeny's entire division was able to entrench and held its ground, in effect cutting Johnston's communications and threatening the rear of the Confederate army.[48]

General Johnston knew that his position at Resaca was compromised and as he reported, "This made it necessary to abandon the thought of fighting north of the river." Hood was ordered to abandon his attack but Stewart had already advanced before being informed of the change in orders. The Confederates suffered heavy casualties before pulling back to their works.[49]

Johnston's position at Resaca was a strong one but Sweeny's comparatively small force in his rear was a potential disaster in the making. Unable to delay any longer, "the army was ordered to cross the Oostenaula that night, destroying the bridges behind it.[50]

On the morning of the 16th Sherman entered Resaca and immediately set his men to repairing bridges and crossing the river. McPherson was ordered to cross the remainder of his army at Lay's Ferry. The Fourth and Fourteenth Corps of Thomas' army crossed at Resaca. Schofield's Twenty-third and Hooker's Twentieth Corps crossed the Connasauga about two miles above the town with Stoneman's cavalry on the extreme left.[51]

The country south of Resaca and between the Oostanaula and Etowah rivers is much more open and less broken than any other portion of northern Georgia. The railroad, after crossing the river at Resaca, runs south and crosses the Etowah River at Allatoona, where a spur of rugged and high hills on the south side of the river is traversed by a deep gorge, the famous Allatoona Pass.[52]

The great numerical superiority of the Federal army forced Johnston to refuse battle in this open ground unless Sherman made some sort of blunder that would give the Confederates a decided advantage. Johnston decided therefore "to fall back slowly until circumstances should put the chances of battle in our favor."[53]

At Adairsville, Johnston looked for a position from which he could give battle, but there too the terrain was unsuitable for defense and the Confederate commander was forced to continue his retreat after a brief stand on the 17th. As he fell back, however, Johnston saw that he might have a possibility of overwhelming and destroying part of Sherman's army. There were two roads leading south from Adairsville — one south to Kingston, the other southeast to Cassville. It seemed likely that Sherman would divide his armies so as to use both roads. This would give Johnston the opportunity to attack one column before the other could come to its aid. Sherman's pursuit of the Confederates brought about exactly the situation Johnston was hoping for. McPherson and the bulk of Thomas' army took the road toward Kingston while Schofield and Hooker's corps of Thomas' army moved along the road to Cassville.[54]

The weather had been very warm and the constant marching and fighting was beginning to take a physical and mental toll on the men of both armies. Union sergeant Hamlin Coe wrote that on the 18th, "We were marched beyond reason today, and hundreds of the boys were tired out and lay by the roadside. I kept up but I am the tiredest man that ever lived. When will this running fight ever cease?"[55]

And from near Cassville on May 18, John Hagan wrote to his wife:

> I beleave when we make a Stand we will give the yankees a thrashing but I fear we will never get the country back. I beleave unless we get heavey reinforcements soon that the yanks will take Atlanta easey. the truth is we have run until I am getting out of heart & we must make a Stand Soon or the armey will be demoralized, but all is in good Spirits now & beleave Gen Johnston will make a stand & whip the yankees badley.[56]

On the morning of May 19, General Johnston ordered Hood to march along a country road a mile or so east of the Adairsville-Cassville Road and form his corps for battle facing west. While Polk attacked the head of the Federal column, Hood was to assail its left flank. However, as Hood was moving into position he received a report that enemy soldiers were approaching from the right.[57]

This could have been a disaster, for with Hood formed facing west, these Federals would have been in position to attack the exposed flank and rear of his corps. As it turned out the report was a mistake but by then it was too late to mount an effective attack so Hood fell back to rejoin Polk. Johnston, believing that the opportunity for a successful battle had passed, ordered Hood and Polk to move to a new line east and south of Cassville, where they were joined by Hardee who had been pushed out of Kingston.[58]

Johnston later wrote: "Expecting to be attacked I drew up the troops in what seemed to me an excellent position — a bold ridge immediately in rear of Cassville, with an open valley before it."[59]

General Johnston issued a general order saying that the retreat had gone as far as was necessary for strategic purposes, that the time had come for trying conclusions with the Federal army and he would give battle where he was.[60]

This was the news that the Confederate soldiers had been waiting for and Pvt. William E. Bevens of the 1st Arkansas was as happy as the rest:

> General Johnston rode along the line and told the men he was going to give battle. The soldiers threw their caps into the air and shouted themselves hoarse with joy at the thought of going into a fight which they felt in their souls would be successful. It was inspiring to see such enthusiasm in battle scarred veterans who knew what fighting meant. It was not theory with them, it was knowledge gained in bloody experience.[61]

Frank Montgomery, a cavalry officer from Mississippi, wrote that Johnston's order "was received with the greatest enthusiasm, cheer after cheer could be heard in every direction."[62]

The Federal artillery began firing soon after they arrived on the scene and continued until dark. As Johnston was inspecting his lines with Brigadier Francis General Shoupe, chief of artillery, Shoupe pointed out to Johnston what he thought was a weak point near General Polk's right, a space of 150 or 200 yards, which Shoupe believed could be vulnerable to artillery fire from a hill about a mile from the right of the Confederate lines.[63]

When Johnston returned to his tent an invitation to a meeting with his corps commanders at General Polk's headquarters was waiting for him. Generals Polk and Hood were present but not General Hardee. Both officers told Johnston that it was doubtful that they could hold their positions because at least part of each was enfiladed by Federal artillery. It was, in fact, the area mentioned by Shoupe that was of the greatest concern to Polk. Both generals urged Johnston to abandon the position and fall back across the Etowah River.[64]

According to General Hood, whose recollection of the council differs markedly from Johnston's, he and Polk told Johnston that the line could not be held against an attack but that it was a good position from which to move against the enemy. Johnston, however, was unwilling to risk an offensive battle.[65]

After a discussion of more than an hour Johnston came to a decision: "Although the position was the best we had occupied, I yielded at last, in the belief that the confidence of the commanders of two of the three corps of the army, of their inability to resist the enemy, would inevitably be communicated to their troops, and produce that inability."[66]

Lieutenant General Hardee, who arrived after Polk and Hood had made their case, said he was confident his corps could hold its ground. But it was too late and the position was abandoned before daybreak. "The army crossed the Etowah on the 20th," Johnston later wrote, "a step which I have regretted ever since."[67]

Many a Federal soldier breathed a heavy sigh of relief when he awoke and found the Confederate lines empty; he knew he would live another day. Rice C. Bull, of the 123rd New York, wrote:

> It was very quiet and we thought it strange that there was no musketry firing but soon we learned the reason. News travels fast in the Army and it was known that the Johnnies had abandoned their works and gone. To say that was pleasant news put it mildly; it seemed too good to be true. The line they held looked so strong with fortifications so well built, it was unbelievable that it would be abandoned without a fight. We had felt that we could only drive them out at great loss to ourselves.[68]

The privates were not the only members of the Federal army to feel relief and be thankful they didn't have to assault those forbidding Confederate works. General Howard remembered:

> The morning of the 21st of May, bright and clear, showed us a country picturesque in its natural features, with farm and woodland as quiet and peaceful as if there had been no war. So Sherman, taking up his headquarters at Kingston, a little hamlet on the railway, gave to his armies three days' rest.[69]

Once again the Confederate soldiers had abandoned their position in the night, and many were not happy about it. John W. Cotton wrote home: "I don't know when we will make at stand at but general Johnston determed to fite them some where he has been trying to get them to fite him now for 2 weaks but they wont do it they keep flanking him and he is oblige to fall back to keep them from cutting him off from his supplies."[70]

Speaking of the first phase of the campaign, Union soldier G.W. Lewis, of the 124th Ohio Infantry, pretty well summed up the feelings of most of his comrades. "The experience of one day did not vary much from that of another. It was march and skirmish every day. The country from Resaca to the Etowah river was the most absolutely desolated of any that we ever left behind us."[71]

Chapter 5

The Bloodletting Begins

After failing in his attempt to cut off and destroy Schofield's army near Cassville, General Johnston pulled his troops back across the Etowah River and occupied a formidable position above Allatoona Pass. Sherman was familiar with the Allatoona area and had no intention of attacking the Confederate position.

> I knew the strength of Allatoona Pass, having ridden through it twenty years ago, and knew it would reduce our strength by forcing us to operate by the head of a single column. I determined not to attempt it but to pass the range by other more devious and difficult natural roads that would admit of more equal terms with the enemy should he attempt to meet us.[1]

General Sherman decided to leave the railroad behind and since he was

> [s]atisfied that the enemy could and would hold us in check at the Allatoona Pass, I resolved, without even attempting it in front, to turn it by a circuit to the right, and, having supplied our wagons for twenty days' absence from our railroad, I left a garrison at Rome and Kingston, and on the 23d put the army in motion for Dallas.

In order to move quickly all nonessential equipment was to be left behind. The men would carry little other than their weapons, ammunition, and a day or two of rations. If the army was delayed by bad weather or fighting the 20 days of rations would have to be stretched to last 30 days.[2]

The goal of the Federal army was to complete a giant sweep to the right. If this movement could be accomplished without too much opposition Sherman's men could circle around through the hills and suddenly appear on the railroad near Marietta, well behind the Confederate lines and dangerously close to Atlanta. If Sherman could accomplish this move he would be able to cut off the Army of Tennessee from its supply depot at Atlanta. Johnston would then have to either fight Sherman's much-larger army to regain control of the railroad or retreat far enough down the line to reestablish contact with Atlanta. A major Federal victory either way, or so Sherman believed.[3]

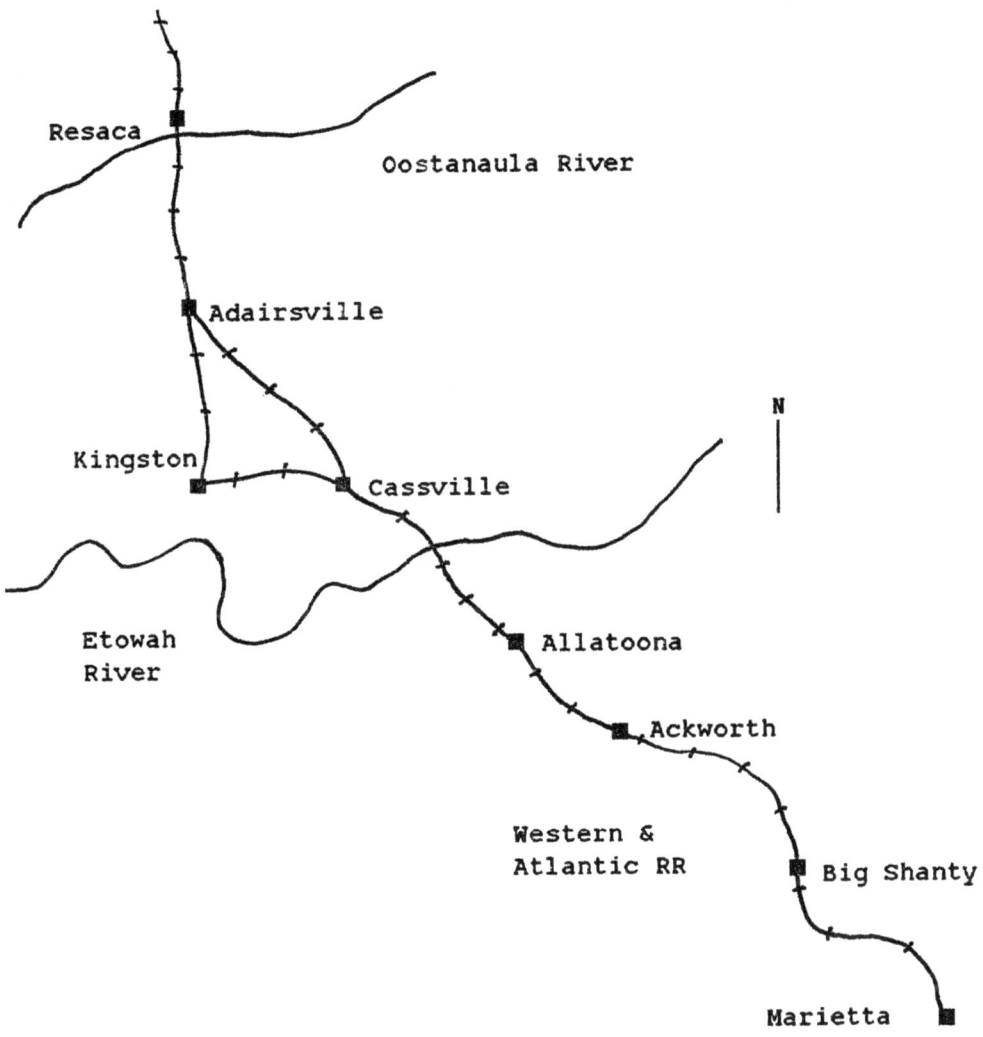

Resaca to Marietta

The country the Federals were moving through was "desolate enough" as General Howard described it with, "old pine forests, half cleared, with tall burnt and blackened stumps; very few openings and very few farms, and those few small and poor; other parts covered with trees having dense underbrush, which the skirmishers had great difficulty in penetrating." The terrain was also filled with ravines and steep hills along with "many lagoons and small streams bordered with treacherous quicksands." All of which slowed the Federal advance to a crawl, allowing Johnston to move his troops to counter Sherman's flanking movement.[4]

Once again, General Johnston's Confederates used the terrain to form a defensive line of great natural strength. General Hardee's corps was stationed on the left, at Dallas, with Polk's corps in the center and Hood's troops on the right, near New Hope. "As I now look back," wrote General Howard years later,

> I wonder that we did not approach those well-chosen Confederate lines with more caution. But we did not know. We thought that the Confederates were not yet thoroughly prepared, and we hoped that by a tremendous onslaught we might gain a great advantage, shorten the battle, and so shorten the war.[5]

On May 25 General Hooker's Twentieth Corps, the leading unit of the Army of the Cumberland, approached the strategic road junction at New Hope Church. As the Federals moved forward they pushed back a force of Confederate cavalry and were able to capture a bridge over Pumpkin Vine Creek. About two miles from the bridge the leading Federal division, commanded by General Geary, ran into the Confederate lines and the advance abruptly halted.[6]

This part of the Confederate defensive line was manned by Stewart's division of Hood's Corps, backed up by plenty of artillery. Believing that he faced a superior force Hooker halted his leading troops and waited for the rest of his corps to come up. General Sherman, who was accompanying Thomas and Hooker, thought that they had found the left flank of the enemy and pressed Hooker to attack as soon as possible. Despite sending back orders for his other two divisions to hurry forward it was not until about 4:00 P.M. that Hooker was able to concentrate his entire corps.[7]

By the time the Federals were ready to advance the rain that had been falling for much of the day had turned into a thunderstorm. Hooker's troops were formed in columns of brigades, with one brigade behind another, giving the attackers the ability to quickly exploit the hoped-for breakthrough. Unfortunately, this also caused the Federal line to be virtually the same width across the front as was Stewart's defenders, who were able to mass their fire against the front of the Federal line.[8]

Union soldier Rice C. Bull, of the 123rd New York Volunteer Infantry, would remember this day for the rest of his life:

Union Major General Joseph Hooker

> As we neared the front there were all the evidences of battle, wounded men being brought back, ammunition wagons and ambulances hurrying to the front, cowardly skulkers who would not stay on the firing line except a bayonet was at their back getting to the rear, men, horses and even mules wild with excitement. There is nothing that tests men's nerves more than marching up to a line of battle that is already engaged; they know they are soon to take their place on the firing line. While making the advance they can see, hear, and think, but can do nothing to take their minds off the dreadful work they know is before them. Until their own battle line is formed and they are facing the front and firing their nerves are almost at the breaking point; then the strain relaxes and the fear and nervousness passes away. As we neared the firing line the noise was deafening, the air was filled with the fumes of burning powder; the lazy whining of bullets almost spent, the shot and shell from the enemy batteries tearing through the trees caused every head to duck as they passed over us.[9]

As the Union columns reached the Confederate lines they were met with a hail of bullets and artillery fire that decimated their ranks. Brig. Gen. Randall L. Gibson, commanding one of Stewart's brigades, reported: "We had hardly taken post when the enemy advanced in great force, driving in my skirmishers and assailing with vigor our main lines. The battle lasted two hours, hotly and stubbornly contested, and resulted in the complete repulse of the enemy at all points."[10]

General Howard observed that "Again and again Hooker's brave men went forward through the forest only to run upon log barricades, which were so thoroughly manned by the enemy, and so protected by well-posted artillery, that to take them under a galling fire was impossible." To make the scene even more ghastly the storm now reached its height of intensity and the field was pounded with rain while thunder and lightning added even more terrifying sounds to that of the raging battle.[11]

Col. John Coburn, of the Thirty-third Indiana Infantry, reported:

> During this advance the enemy poured in upon us a tremendous fire of artillery, raking the ground on which we stood. Shells, grape-shot, canister, railroad spikes, and every deadly missile rained around us. The fight continued until long after dark; a cold and heavy rain closed in, and the men went to work in the darkness to hunt up logs and sticks with which to make rude breast-works.[12]

After about two hours of bloody repulses the Federal troops stopped where they were and dug in. General Geary reported that his command

> was halted close under the enemy's batteries and intrenchments.... The night was intensely dark, and a very severe thunder-storm, with cold pelting rain, added to the gloom. It was, therefore, impossible to form a regular line with the troops, and all the dispositions of them we could make was by the fitful flashes of lightning. Breast-works were thrown up as fast as possible during the night....[13]

The Union troops were close enough to the Confederate line that they kept up a steady fire from behind the crude works that the men were able to build in the dark. Hooker lost about 1,500 men that afternoon while the Confederate losses were likely below 600. Capt. Lovick P. Thomas of the Forty-second Georgia Infantry attributed the low Confederate losses in his unit to "the fact of the great surprise of the enemy in meeting this force there and the stubborn resistance of our men, causing, when our first volley was given, great confusion among them, and was followed on their part by very wild shooting."[14]

After the battle, Confederate soldier Thomas Stokes wrote home about what he had seen as he surveyed the battlefield:

> The next morning I had the privilege of walking over the whole ground, and such a scene! Here lay the wounded, the dying and the dead, hundreds upon hundreds, in every conceivable position; some with contorted features, showing the agony of death, others as if quietly sleeping. I noticed some soft beardless faces which ill comported with the savage warfare in which they had been engaged. Hundreds of letters from mothers, sisters, and friends were found upon them.... Though they had been my enemies, my heart bled at the sickening scene.[15]

Two days later, on the 27th, General Howard led Wood's division from his Fourth Corps and Johnson's division of Palmer's Fourteenth Corps to the far left of the Federal lines in an attempt to find the right end of the Confederate line. Connected on his right with General Cox's division of Schofield's Army of the Ohio, General Howard had Wood on the right and Johnson on the left when he found what he thought was the flank of the Confederate army. "The ground was carefully reconnoitered by General Wood and myself. We still found a line of works to our right, but they did not seem to cover General Wood's front, and they were new, the enemy still working hard upon them."[16]

There was some skirmishing as the Federals probed the Confederate lines to find a weak point and it was not until after 5:00 P.M. that Howard was satisfied that he could turn the enemy position. He was mistaken. General Wood's division, with Hazen's brigade in the lead, ran into trouble almost immediately. The reason that Howard could not tell for sure where the Confederate line ended was because the terrain was densely wooded, and filled with hills and ravines. General William B. Hazen later wrote that as his troops were moving forward they had to work their way "through a dense wood, and our advance in the attack was through a wood so thick that we could keep our direction only by the compass."[17]

Even worse than the terrain the Federal troops had to cross was the fact that Pat Cleburne's division was waiting for them. General Cleburne had arrived on the end of the Confederate line on the afternoon of the 26th. The main line went north and south so Cleburne continued that line but also placed Govan's brigade to the east along a ridge line. "The position was in the main covered with trees and undergrowth, which served as a screen along our lines, concealed us, and were left standing as far as practicable for that purpose." When Cleburne learned that the Federal attack was forming he quickly transferred Granbury's brigade to the far right, next to Daniel Goven's Brigade. It was here that the majority of the fighting occurred.[18]

Hazen later wrote:

> No attack could have been made in better form, nor persisted in with more determination; but as a column attack it was a failure. The several brigades, instead of striking in such rapid succession that each might benefit by the advantage gained by

those before it, were put in at intervals of forty minutes. This resulted in separate attacks by detachments, with ample warning to the enemy to get ready and repair damage.[19]

General Hazen's comments illuminated only a portion of the problems that plagued the Federal assault that day. A brigade from Schofield's army, commanded by General McLean, had been sent to the right as a diversion to draw attention away from the point of attack. Unfortunately they did not open fire or show themselves to the enemy, therefore they attracted little attention. General Johnson was to provide support for Wood's troops but his advance brigade halted briefly to cross Pickett's Mill Creek to drive away enemy skirmishers that were firing on the Federals.[20]

Confederate Major General Patrick Cleburne

The nonexistent diversion on the right and the delay by Johnson allowed Cleburne's troops to concentrate their fire on Wood's advancing men and as Cleburne reported, Granbury's men "awaited them with calm determination, and as they appeared upon the slope slaughtered them with deliberate aim. The piles of his dead on this front, pronounced by the officers in this army who have seen most service to be greater than they had ever seen before...."[21]

General Hazen commented that

> my command had worn itself out in a close fight of just forty-five minutes, losing over five hundred men, and I had sent back all my staff and several other officers to hurry up the other lines, we began to fall back man by man, company by company, and regiment by regiment, from sheer necessity.[22]

With the attack obviously a failure, Howard pulled his survivors back and entrenched near the Confederate lines. The Union forces lost about 1,500 men while the Confederate loss was only about 500. Although the battle was a decided Confederate victory, Howard claimed that "a position was secured near Pickett's Mills of the greatest importance to the subsequent movements of the army."[23]

Despite two attacks, and two repulses, Sherman still wanted to get around the flank of Johnston's army and General McPherson had begun to shift his army to the left so that the rest of the army could continue the move to envelop the Confederate right. On the far right of the Union armies John Logan's corps moved into the vicinity of the town of Dallas on the 26th. General Logan set up his line with "Harrow's division on the right.... Morgan L. Smith in the center, crossing the Marietta road, and Osterhaus on the left, connecting with General Dodge's command."[24]

Early on the morning of the 27th Gen. Peter J. Osterhaus, commanding the First Division of the 15th Corps, reported that on the left of the corps line, "the rebels attacked on the left flank of Second Brigade, throwing an enfilading fire into its lines, and compelling them to fall back." Osterhaus brought up the Third Brigade and after a tough fight, "we soon gained all the ground lost at the outset of the rebel attack, and more too."[25]

Brig. Gen. Charles C. Walcutt, commander of the Second Brigade, Fourth Division, reported that in front of his lines on the right of the 15th Corps, "At 1 P.M. the enemy commenced a terrific shelling. He seemed to have control of the road, but fortunately did me no harm whatever. As soon as the shelling ceased, the enemy, who had formed his lines during the shelling, made a vigorous assault on my line." Because of the surprise and quickness of the attack, Walcutt had to send the Sixth Iowa forward, "which they did most gallantly, meeting the enemy with bayonets fixed. The fight soon became general along my front. The men reserved their fire handsomely until the enemy's line reached the base of the hill, when they opened, scattering and driving the enemy with great loss."[26]

For most of the remainder of the day a constant skirmish fire made it interesting for the soldiers of both armies as the Federal troops built a solid line of intrenchments with good artillery support and connected on the left with the Sixteenth Corps.[27]

During most of the morning and early afternoon of the 28th firing between the skirmish lines continued and gradually increased as the day wore on. About 3:30 in the afternoon General Hardee launched his corps in a desperate attack on Logan's position. The first part of the Federal line to feel the fury of the Confederate attack was on the right under the command of General Harrow. This was considered the weakest part of the Federal position because of a ridge that rose to the right and was not heavily fortified. Logan reported:

> It had been considered impracticable to carry our line far enough forward across this ridge to overcome this objectionable point, without weakening it too much elsewhere.... The enemy at this point approached within 150 yards, without having been seen or exposed to our fire. His assault was made in column of regiments, and with the utmost dash and confidence. Three guns of the First Iowa Battery, which had been run out on the skirmish line, were temporarily surrounded by the enemy.

Logan did not consider these guns as lost because any Confederates who got close to them were shot down.[28]

The Confederates closed on the Union lines through a deadly fire from muskets and artillery. General Logan reported:

> As line upon line of the enemy debouched upon the open plateau, within eighty yards of our works, they were met by a front and flank fire from brave men, who stood unflinchingly to their guns.... Line after line was sent back broken to their works, and in half an hour the assault was over, their dead and wounded only occupying the ground on which they advanced.[29]

Shortly after Hardee's men attacked Harrow's portion of the line the troops of Smith and Osterhaus were hit with the same violent attacks. But, as General Logan's report indicated, "The nature of the ground on these fronts being less favorable for the enemy than that on Harrow's front, they were repulsed very handsomely, and with great loss."[30] Before General Osterhaus' line was attacked he had been ordered by General Logan to take his Second Brigade to the extreme right to support that portion of the Federal line. Upon his return to the rest of his division, Osterhaus saw the enemy emerge from a ravine in front of his division and "come up to within fifty yards of my line, but only to be mowed down by the hundred and to fall back broken and shattered."[31]

The Confederate attack never had much chance of succeeding. Lt. Lot Young of the "Orphan Brigade," Kentuckians who fought for the Confederacy, later wrote, "The actual time under fire did not in my judgment exceed thirty minutes." Due to a mix-up in orders Young's troops were not supported on the left which

> enabled the enemy to deliver an oblique fire upon us from his infantry on the left, as well as from his two lines directly in front.... To push forward meant certain and complete annihilation; to remain where we were some seventy-five or eighty yards in their front, meant the same, only a little slower death. The order to "fall back" having been given, we were only too glad to attempt our escape from the death trap into which we had been ordered.[32]

Overall the main Confederate assault lasted only a little over an hour but many of the attackers, unable to move for fear of sharpshooter fire, had to hold their positions on the field until dark. Logan reported his total loss at fewer than 400 total. He also reported that his men buried over 300 Confederates in front of his lines, and that the total Confederate casualties could be as many as 2,000.[33]

Col. Francis T. Sherman, of the 88th Illinois, wrote a letter to his father from near Dallas, in which he gave a perceptive analysis of Johnston's strategy:

> The rebels fight very obstinately and tenaciously, fortifying their position strongly. Notwithstanding we are slowly but surely pressing them, and they are losing as many men as we. The issue is not as yet certain that we shall be able to destroy their army and close the rebellion in the west. So far they have held their positions just long enough for us to get ready to give them the finishing touch, when they pull up and under cover of night retire to some new point. This tactic is the best one they can adopt and works our troops with harassing marches and continual exposure which, if followed up, in time will break us all down.[34]

The fight at Dallas was the last large battle along the current line. Sherman now decided it was time to forego any more attacks on the strong Confederate positions and return to the previously successful tactic of the flanking movement.

> The ground was very difficult, being densely wooded and composed of ridges and spurs of flinty ground, very barren as to forage and difficult for roads. It took us nearly a week to feel well up to the enemy, who continued, of course, to strengthen his position so that by the 31st of May it became necessary for me to order the direct assault or to turn the enemy's works. The railroad and main Georgia road being to our left, I resolved to pass the enemy's right flank and place the whole army in front of Allatoona Pass.[35]

The first move was for General McPherson to pull his Army of the Tennessee out of the Dallas area and replace Hooker at New Hope Church. Most of the troop movements had to take place behind the front lines because the armies were so close to each other there was a constant skirmishing fire. Once a new right flank was established Thomas and Schofield were to move eastward as far as possible. General McPherson arrived on June 1 and the movement of the rest of the army began almost immediately, but now the weather became a factor.[36]

So far the campaign had been blessed with excellent weather. It had been good marching weather, warm and dry with only a few days of rain, but all that changed on the 25th during the fighting at New Hope Church. Rice Bull wrote:

> There had been little rain and no extreme heat; while it was dry and dusty it had been easy traveling. On May 25th the weather changed and I find recorded in my diary that for twenty-one days it stormed every day. It did not rain continuously but during some part of every day it hit us, usually in thunder storms of the most violent sort. It was such a time of great activity that these storms either caught us on the march or in breastworks where we had no protection. After one of these rains the men would be as wet as if they had fallen in a stream. As it was warm weather a wetting did not make us cold but the ground was so saturated with water it was almost impossible to find a place in which one could rest. We would cut limbs from the bushes and lay them under our tents to keep as much as we could out of the mud, but this did not make comfortable beds. Although the excessive rains retarded our movements we were active. Our trains were well up in front but could only be moved with great difficulty; the wagons would sink in the mud up to their axles and they could not be moved by the mules alone. The men had to take a hand, pry up the wheels and corduroy the roads to solid ground.[37]

The rains turned what few roads there were into muddy trails. It was impossible to keep to any schedule and it was not until the afternoon of June 3rd that Schofield's army made it to the right of the Confederate lines. As it turned out, however, the delay did not have a great effect on events. As soon as the movement to the east began Sherman had sent cavalry detachments under Generals Stoneman and Garrard to secure both ends of Allatoona Pass. Both officers quickly accomplished their assignments and even before the infantry could get there the Federal army was in control of Allatoona Pass.[38]

Despite the Federal efforts at secrecy there was no fooling General Johnston who understood almost immediately what Sherman was trying to accomplish. General Howard noted: "He therefore withdrew Polk, who was located at his center, and marched him parallel to those of us who took up the movement, always keeping time and pace with our march to the left. Then began and continued for a considerable time a race of breastworks and intrenchments."[39]

In addition to the drastic change in the weather, during the fighting in the woods around New Hope and Dallas several other significant changes occurred that would have an enormous effect on how the rest of the campaign was conducted. The first, and most obvious, concerned the day-to-day fighting. Starting in late May, and continuing through the remainder of the campaign until the Federals entered Atlanta, the armies were in almost constant contact. Previously about the only time the men constructed any type of breastworks was when a battle was imminent, and usually these were hastily piled rocks, tree branches, and railroad ties, anything that would afford at least a little protection. On most days, however, the troops were on the move and building fortifications was not a major consideration.[40]

This situation changed once the armies reached Dallas. Sherman was constantly trying to move south, along the railroad, while at the same time looking for an opening to destroy the Confederate army. General Johnston, on the other hand, was perfectly happy to move with Sherman and block his movements, hoping to frustrate the Union commander into a blunder. As skirmish fire and sharp-shooting became routine and exchanges of artillery fire occurred frequently the men on both sides were forced to build more elaborate protection for themselves.[41]

One Union solder remembered that

> [i]t had become almost a habit with us as soon as we halted close to the enemy to build breastworks; every man would dig in as though his life depended on his work. In many cases it did. It was surprising how quickly we could construct a trench that would protect us from musketry.[42]

Most units were able to create a modest but functional trench system in a few hours. A shallow trench could be quickly dug using bayonets, tin plates, boards, and even bare hands, with the dirt piled up on the side facing the enemy. For even greater protection they would place a log or tree trunk on top of the dirt and scoop out small openings beneath the log. The headlog protected the heads of the men as they fired on the enemy through the small openings. The headlog would also have some type of support to keep it from falling back into the trench if it were struck by a cannonball. With little more than their rifles and eyes exposed, troops taking cover behind this simple but effective protection had a much greater chance of surviving a battle.[43]

When time permitted there were additional modifications that could be done to make earthworks nearly impregnable. The underbrush in front of the works would be cut away to give a clear field of fire. Small trees could be cut down with their tops facing the enemy and still attached at the base. This would keep the attackers from pulling the trees aside and slow the advance, keeping them under fire longer. Sometimes telegraph wire would be strung between the trees and stumps creating an even more difficult obstacle for attackers soldiers to overcome. These techniques gave the defenders an even greater advantage than they already had and made any competent commander hesitate to order a mass attack when facing a well-fortified position.[44]

The second factor that affected the campaign was Joseph Johnston's relationship with his corps commanders. Originally Johnston welcomed General Hood as a vigorous and reliable subordinate. However, at Resaca and again at Cassville, Hood had given bad, or at least misleading, advice to Johnston. In addition, it did not take long for Johnston to realize that his subordinate was writing letters to friends back in Richmond in which he criticized many of Johnston's decisions. There is little doubt that much of this criticism would have reached the ears of Jefferson Davis. Over the next several weeks the differences between the two men grew and eventually they became personal and professional enemies for life. At the same time Johnston gradually became more impressed with General Hardee's abilities and as they grew closer they began to look at Hood, Davis and Bragg as their common enemies. These divisions within the command structure could not help but diminish the efficiency of the Army of Tennessee.[45]

A third, and potentially most important, development became clear after the battles at the end of May. From the start of his term as commander of the Army of Tennessee, Johnston had been telling Davis and Bragg that he really wanted to advance into Tennessee, but only when the time was right. He expected "to beat the enemy when he advances and then to move forward."[46]

The problem with this strategy was that General Sherman simply refused to cooperate by allowing himself to be beaten in battle. By the end of May it was obvious that Sherman was not going to smash his army against the strong Confederate fortifications. Unless the Federals suffered massive casualties and were forced to retreat there would be no opportunity for Johnston to begin the long-promised offensive.

Another part of General Johnston's strategy that failed was his theory that as Sherman advanced into Georgia the single railroad that served as the Federal supply line could be broken often enough and severely enough to cause the Federal army to run short of supplies, adding to the possibility they would eventually have to fall back. What Johnston, or even Sherman for that matter, could not know was how quickly Colonel Wright's repair crews could have broken track back in service. At Resaca, for instance, the engineers were able to rebuild the railroad bridge over the Oostanaula in only three days.[47]

The sum of all these factors was that Joe Johnston was unable to find or create a good opportunity to destroy, or at least cripple, Sherman's army. The Federal commander simply did not make too many mistakes, and the few times the Confederates did have a chance to seriously damage Sherman's army, such as at Cassville, Johnston or his subordinates seemed to find a reason not to take advantage of the situation. It was easier to play it safe, block a Federal movement, and then continue to retreat when flanked out of position. But the Army of Tennessee would soon be running out of room.

Chapter 6

Slow Movement Through Northern Georgia

The weather for most of June was simply terrible. Rice Bull remembered that "[t]he first twenty days of the month it rained nearly every day; not light showers but fierce rains that covered the land with water and made roads next to impassable. Our trains and artillery were almost lost in the mud. The men were wet most of the time and many were ill."[1] Union sergeant Hamlin A. Coe also had less than fond memories of the summer weather in northern Georgia. "The boys stand around wet to the skin and in mud half knee deep. They look as though they had lost their last friend. These are sorry old times."[2]

After Allatoona Pass was secured and General Schofield made his push across the railroad near Ackworth the Federal left was well past Johnston's right. Now it was time for another of Sherman's flanking movements. Unfortunately the rainy weather slowed down the Union forces and once again Johnston was able to pull his army out of danger during the night. Any movement in that country was difficult but a night march in the rain was especially trying. Edward McMorries of the 1st Alabama remembered

> the army began its retreat to Lost Mountain, a distance of six miles, a march the most memorable in the long service of the regiment. A chilly rain was falling in intermittent showers, the night was so intensely dark that the hand could not be seen an inch before the eyes, while the angry peals of thunder leaping from cliff to cliff along the mountain crests blended into one prolonged, continuous roar. All nature seemed up in arms against us. Men as they struggled along the road, each for himself, and with no respect for military order, sank to their knees in mud from which with difficulty they extricated themselves.[3]

On the 8th of June, Maj. Gen. Frank P. Blair met Sherman's army at Ackworth with two divisions of the Seventeenth Corps that had been on furlough. These fresh troops replaced almost all the losses in combat and the detachments left behind to garrison captured towns and guard the railroad. The Federal army was back to full

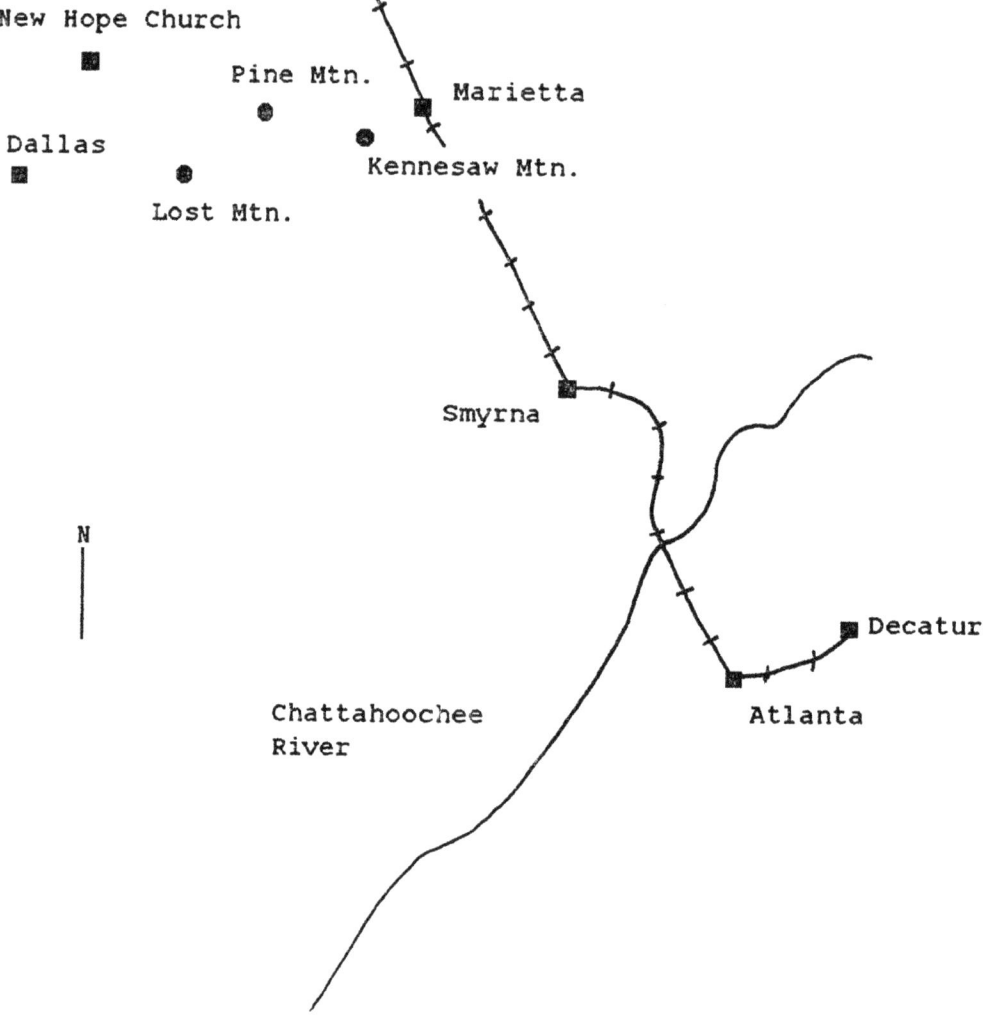

Marietta to Atlanta

strength and the next day they moved forward along the railroad to Big Shanty. Just past Big Shanty the tracks bend east then south again to Marietta. To the west of Marietta lies the forbidding Kennesaw Mountain range, with Johnston's army perched on the high ground.[4]

As the Federal army moved through the countryside the soldiers foraged liberally. General Blair later wrote:

> As we pass through the country, we leave it as though all the locusts of Egypt had been upon it. There is not a single blade of grass left upon the earth. Wheat fields are eaten to the ground, and the rising corn is beginning to yield its quota to the sustenance of our animals. The provisions of the people is also taken without compunction, and they are left in utter want.[5]

The Army of Tennessee had also been reinforced and despite the constant retreating most of the soldiers were spoiling for a fight and confident of the outcome. Alex Spence, a soldier in the 1st Arkansas Regiment, wrote to his parents on June 7:

> Notwithstanding, we have been retreating, I never saw our Army in better spirits. All are confident we will whip the Yankees. If they ever advance near here, they will certainly be the worst whipped set of men the sun ever shone on. Tis said one of Genl Johnston's principal motives for falling back was so as to be able to gain a complete victory when we do fight the Federals.[6]

The new Confederate defensive position was over 10 miles long in the shape of a long arc. Confederate engineers had made excellent use of the mountains that tower over the landscape by laying out a formidable system of fortifications that blocked the way south. On the left Johnston anchored his line on Lost Mountain with Pine Mountain in the center and the right resting on Brush Mountain, just north of Marietta. West of town and about two miles south of the right side of the Confederate line is the rugged Kennesaw Mountain, actually a high ridge about two miles long with two distinct peaks. The highest, "Big" Kennesaw, dominates the northeastern end with "Little" Kennesaw in the center.[7]

Henry Wright, of the 6th Iowa, described what he saw as the Union troops moved down the railroad:

> [T]he first view was had of Kenesaw Mountain, a bold and striking twin mountain, lying in the immediate front, with a range of rugged hills extending to the northeast beyond Noonday creek and terminating at Brush Mountain. Pine Hill lying to the right and west, and still beyond it in the distance the dim outline of Lost Mountain could be seen.
> The vast and beautiful landscape was enchanting to behold, presenting a rural scene of quiet and beauty, soon to be rudely disturbed by a clash of arms.[8]

General Sherman also appreciated the beauty of the countryside, up to a point. "The scene was enchanting; too beautiful to be disturbed by the harsh clamor of war; but the Chattahoochee lay beyond, and I had to reach it."[9] Sherman spread his army out along the front of the Confederate lines. McPherson went to the east, toward Marietta, with the right of his army on the railroad. General Thomas occupied the center position opposite Kennesaw and Pine Mountain and Schofield was on the right facing Lost Mountain. The long Confederate lines meant that Johnston's army was stretched thin and Sherman began to look for any opening that might allow him to break through.[10]

During the next week Sherman's troops marched and skirmished every day in an effort to flank or break the Confederate lines, and once again the weather played a part in determining troop movements. George Cram wrote to his mother, "The weather has been most unpromising. For ten or twelve days it has rained more or less and at one time it rained fifty hours without stopping. This has placed the roads in such a condition that the team cannot get full rations to us and artillery cannot be moved."[11]

The rain brought misery to the men in the field. John Hill Ferguson, of the 10th Illinois, wrote home saying that he and his comrades

[h]uddled up together and only got up to eat when our darky would bring us some coffee. With that and some hard tack, a meal was soon compleated, and again we huddled up in our tents, covering with a blanket, our tents leaking and dripping on us all the time, the ground around us knee deep in mud.[12]

In many places the lines were so close that soldiers could yell back and forth and pickets from both armies occasionally came in contact with one another. While the generals planned new battles the men doing the fighting were more than ready for a truce. Hamlin Coe wrote in his diary: "This morning some of our boys had quite a time exchanging papers with the Rebs, and they seemed to have a good time between themselves. Among other agreements was one to discontinue firing upon pickets."[13] Gen. Alpheus Williams recorded: "For the last few days our pickets have completely fraternized. They have been exchanging papers, coffee, tobacco, and the like. Isn't it strange that men in mortal strife one hour are on affectionate terms the next, and apparently fast friends."[14]

Not only did the closeness of the lines promote friendly contact between the men, it also made it easier to kill each other, and except for a relatively few isolated points the firing seldom ceased for very long. L.W. Day, of the 101st Ohio wrote:

> By this time we had become so accustomed to skirmish firing that unless we were in the line actually participating, we scarcely noticed it. Now and then, when it became unusually severe, the boys would straighten up, make some characteristic remark and then forget all about it. Not so with those in the skirmish line. There the quick eye and ready shot were exceedingly necessary to good health and a whole skin. No soldier on either side was so foolish as to stand bolt upright, when a tree, a log, a stump, a stone or a hole in the ground, or anything else, would afford a shelter.[15]

Starting on the 11th, General Sherman began movements intended to break the Confederate line between Kennesaw and Pine mountains. Pine Mountain was out at the top edge of the arc from Lost Mountain to Kennesaw and Sherman positioned his troops to isolate it from the rest of the Confederate lines. It took a few days but gradually Hooker worked into position on the right, Howard's corps came up on the left, and Palmer moved between the mountain and the railroad.[16]

On June 14, during a brief lull in the rain, Johnston, Hardee and Polk went up Pine Mountain to survey the advancing Federal lines in their front. Federal artillery fire had been falling on the Confederate position all morning and after a brief look the generals had turned to leave when Polk was struck by a shell and killed instantly. Having seen for himself that the Federal forces were closing in on the position, Johnston abandoned the Pine Mountain works during the night of June 14, moving closer to Marietta to defenses that had been prepared in advance.[17]

Over the next few days Sherman "continued to press at all points, skirmishing in dense forests of timber and across most difficult ravines." By moving first against one end of Johnston's line, and then against the other, Sherman gradually increased the pressure. Inevitably, Johnston was forced to contract his thinly manned lines once again.[18]

Union soldier Rice Bull described the process of how Johnston was forced to abandon his works:

> We would advance to a point beyond their extreme left and make a left wheel on their line; after pushing as far as we could we would rapidly fortify with a large artillery force placed in the line with us. Well on the enemy's flank our batteries would have a cross fire on them and within twenty-four hours, generally, they would find their line untenable and fall back to a new position, we in close pursuit.[19]

On the evening of the 18th General Howard was informed that the enemy in his front appeared to be withdrawing from the Lost Mountain positions:

> I directed General Newton to move up his entire division in support. General Baird's division, of the Fourteenth Corps, came up very promptly on the left. General Wood having gained the ridge east of Mud Creek, intrenched the position, making a continuous work. As soon as it was dark Newton's division intrenched strongly within less than 100 yards of the enemy's works. The advantage gained by these movements was great.[20]

The Confederate army now occupied a line based on Kennesaw Ridge. General Hood's corps was stationed on the far right to protect Marietta. In the center, perched on the Kennesaw Mountains was Maj. Gen. William W. Loring, temporarily commanding Polk's corps. Hardee's corps protected the left of the line extending south behind Noyes' Creek entrenched in rolling, hilly terrain.[21]

With the possible exception of the Rocky Face Ridge position, this line around Kennesaw was the strongest position the Confederates occupied during the campaign. Confederate batteries lined the crest of the mountains and from the heights they could see the Federal camps and observe every troop movement. There were frequent artillery duels that filled the air with thunder and smoke but did little actual harm. The Confederates were too well protected in their fortifications and most of the Federal army was up so close to the mountain that the majority of Confederate shells flew harmlessly overhead.[22]

While the soldiers were accustomed to the terrible noise of artillery the civilians in Marietta were now learning firsthand the terrors of war. Mrs. Irby Morgan wrote:

> The enemy were advancing, and soon old Kennesaw resounded with the roar of artillery. We would go out at night and listen to the reverberation of that old mountain, knowing that every shot was the death knell of some dear one. O the tension was fearful! How my heart would go out to our dear boys and the loved ones at home! But all we could do was to bow our heads in prayer and beg God to help us all and sustain us by his grace. Nearer and nearer the sounds would come, the excitement increasing. The scene beggared description — the town was almost in a frenzy of excitement ... that boom, boom, boom got to be every minute, resounding from hilltop to hilltop. We could see the smoke from the firing. O it was a grand but awful sight![23]

The fighting along the front lines was mostly artillery fire and sharpshooting until June 22. Generals Hooker and Schofield were advancing on the Federal right, north of Powder Springs near the Kolb house. General Johnston learned of the flanking movement and brought Hood over from the right to block the way. Rather than digging in and forcing the Federals to attack, Hood, believing he faced only a small advance party, decided to launch his own assault.[24]

The Confederate attack fell mostly on General Williams' division of Hooker's corps and General Hascall's division of Schofield's army. The Federal advance troops were pushed back but as General Stevenson of Hood's corps reported, "The fire under which this was done was exceedingly heavy, and the artillery of the enemy, which was massed in large force and admirably posted, was served with a rapidity and fatal precision which could not be surpassed."[25]

Unfortunately for Hood's men the troops they forced back were just one regiment, the Fourteenth Kentucky, sent out to delay the attackers until Hooker and Schofield could prepare the rest of their force. The Confederates soon ran into two well-dug-in Federal divisions and were cut down in droves. Part of the Confederate force advanced over open ground but further south they faced rougher terrain that held up the advance. On the northern end of the battlefield General Hooker's artillery had a clear field of fire and decimated the right side of the Confederate line. By early evening the fighting had ended with Hood losing about 1,000 men and the Federal losses about 300. After the battle Hood dug in across Schofield's path, as Johnston had originally wanted him to do.[26]

Hooker was never one of Sherman's favorites and this was the battle that produced the final split between them. While the fighting was going on Hooker had sent word to Sherman that he was being attacked by three Confederate corps and inferred that Schofield was somehow to blame. This would have been virtually Johnston's entire army and Sherman was justifiably skeptical. The next day Sherman rode down to Kolb's Farm and basically told Hooker what he thought of his exaggerated report.[27]

In a letter to General Halleck on the 23rd, Sherman tried to summarize the campaign to this point:

> We continue to press forward on the principle of an advance against fortified positions. The whole country is one vast fort, and Johnston must have at least fifty miles of connected trenches, with abatis and finished batteries.... Our lines are now in close contact, and the fighting is incessant, with a good deal of artillery-fire. As fast as we gain one position the enemy has another all ready, but I think he will soon have to let go Kenesaw, which is the key to the whole country.[28]

General Sherman now faced a difficult decision. His armies were stretched out in a long north-south line. The roads were still in terrible condition and it would be at least several days before they could be used by heavy wagons and artillery, if the rain did not return. Sherman had two basic options: continue flanking movements or try to break the Confederate lines with a frontal assault. The only thing he could not do was just sit where he was. Federal inaction could allow Johnston to send part of his command to break the precious railroad connection to Sherman's supply depots.[29]

So far in the campaign General Sherman had carefully avoided making a costly attack on a fortified position, but now he was considering doing just that. In his memoirs Sherman wrote:

> During the 24th and 25th of June General Schofield extended his right as far as prudent, so as to compel the enemy to thin out his lines correspondingly, with the intention to make two strong assaults at points where success would give us the greatest advantage. I had consulted Generals Thomas, McPherson, and Schofield, and we all agreed that we could not with prudence stretch out any more, and therefore there was no alternative but to attack "fortified lines," a thing carefully avoided up to that time. I reasoned, if we could make a breach anywhere near the rebel canter, and thrust in a strong head of column, that with the one moiety of our army we could hold in check the corresponding wing of the enemy, and with the other sweep in flank and overwhelm the other half.[30]

Sherman also gave another reason for deciding to make a frontal assault.

> I perceived that the enemy and our own officers had settled down into a conviction that I would not assault fortified lines. All looked to me to outflank.
> An army to be efficient must not settle down to a single mode of offense, but must be prepared to execute any plan which promises success. I wanted, therefore, for the moral effect to make a successful assault against the enemy behind his breast-works, and resolved to attempt it at that point where success would give the largest fruits of victory. Therefore, on the 24th of June, I ordered that an assault should be made at two points south of Kenesaw on the 27th.[31]

The operation against Kennesaw was carefully planned. Attacks on both ends of the Confederate lines were made to create diversions and draw attention away from the main assault in the center. Schofield advanced on the south, against Hood's troops, and while his men gained little ground they posed enough of a threat to hold the Confederates in their front and prevent the transfer of troops from that area to bolster the center.[32]

On the left, General McPherson's army also advanced and Brig. Gen. Morgan L. Smith's division of Logan's corps got into a serious engagement with Loring's Confederates on the west side of Kennesaw Mountain, suffering heavy casualties. In his report Logan described what his men faced that morning:

> They moved forward gallantly, engaging the enemy almost immediately after leaving our line of works. The advance was continued steadily in the face of a destructive fire from three batteries of about twelve pieces, throwing canister and shell, and from musketry fire from sharpshooters of the enemy ... and rifle-pits also. After a most stubborn and destructive resistance they succeeded in taking and holding two lines of the enemy's rifle-pits and advanced toward the succeeding works of the enemy, which were found to be impossible to be carried by assault.[33]

Henry Wright, of the 6th Iowa, later wrote about what he witnessed during the attack:

> The ascent of the mountain slope, leading up to the crest, was found to be steep and rugged, covered with brush and felled trees, ledges of rock, and an abatis ingeniously and firmly constructed, rendering the advance in the line of battle entirely impracticable. The fire maintained by the enemy, with small arms and artillery, was terrific and deadly, officers and men falling thick and fast all along the lines in the assaulting column.[34]

After repeated efforts to reach the main Confederate line the pointless slaughter was ended and the surviving troops were pulled back about 100 yards, setting up temporary works. The final verdict on the assault in Logan's front was that the "[c]ommanding officers state most positively that the position could not be gained in two hours without any opposing force."[35]

The main attack was made by General Thomas in the center. Two separate Federal assaults took place, one against Loring's left and the other against Cheatham's front. Brig. Gen. John Newton was to lead Howard's corps in the attack on the left against Cleburne's tough fighters. The other column from Thomas' army was commanded by Brig. Gen. Jefferson C. Davis and was headed straight up the mountain against Frank Cheatham's Tennessee troops.[36]

General Davis decided to make his assault at a spot where the Confederate works "presented a salient angle, and, in the absence of abatis, fallen timber, and other obstructions which generally confront their works, this point seemed the most assailable." Two brigades were to spearhead the assault with the rest of his troops in reserve. The terrain ahead of the Federal troops was strewn with large rocks and a considerable amount of trees and underbrush.[37]

The terrain in front of General Newton's men was similar to that faced by their comrades to the south. Newton used three brigades in his assault with two in front and one in close support. Following a heavy artillery barrage the Federal troops started forward about 9:00 A.M. Brig. Gen. Charles G. Harker led one of the front brigades with Brig. Gen. George D. Wagner on the left. Because of the closeness of the lines as soon as they began to move out the Federals were hit by Confederate fire. General Wagner reported: "As soon as the head of my column began crossing our works the enemy opened a terrific and deadly fire of artillery and musketry from their main line of works, but, nothing daunted, the column moved forward, charging the works of the enemy, unmindful of the terrific havoc in their ranks."[38]

On Wagner's right General Harker's troops were met with the same destructive fire. General Howard observed, "The enemy's fire was terrific, the missiles passing and crossing and filling the valley. Our men did not stop, unless struck, till they had gained the edge of the felled trees; a few penetrated to fall close to the enemy's parapet; but most sought shelter behind logs and rocks." General Harker was leading his troops, cheering them on and rallying them to make a second effort to continue up the mountainside. It was during this second charge that Harker was mortally wounded after which his men fell back to find whatever cover they could from the storm of lead coming at them from the Confederate works.[39]

General Wagner's men repeatedly attempted to move forward but, "after repeated efforts of both officers and men to get to the enemy's works, the same being defended by heavy lines of abatis, as well as by artillery and infantry, the command fell back for shelter to a ravine close to the enemy's works."[40] General Kimball now joined Wagner to move forward and they ran into the same terrible fire that had beaten back the first attacks. In addition to the fire from the front Cleburne had taken advantage of the absence of Harker's brigade to throw a force down the hill and fire into the flank of Wagner's men as they fell back. Soon after this General Newton sent word for the survivors to fall back to the main works but many were too close to the

Confederate lines to move. Theodore F. Upson later wrote, "We were in a bad fix. We could not go ahead and could not get back. We took cover as best we could and kept up a desultory fire. There we staid til night came and it seemed long in coming."[41]

On a day that saw many examples of extraordinary courage and violence, there was also extraordinary compassion. After the second assault the leaves and undergrowth in front of Cleburne's line caught fire exposing the Federal wounded to a terrible death. Lieutenant Colonel Martin of the First Arkansas called out above the noise of battle to offer a brief truce so that the Federal soldiers could remove their wounded comrades from the burning area. Of course, after the truce was over, the fighting picked up as savagely as before.[42]

The attack of General Davis' brigades to the south fared no better than Newton's. Davis reported that when the signal to begin the attack was given the lead brigades, commanded by Col. John G. Mitchell on the right, and Col. Daniel McCook on the left, "bounded over our own works, in the face of the enemy's fire, and rushed gallantly for the enemy, meeting and disregarding with great coolness the heavy fire, both of artillery and infantry, to which they were subjected, until the enemy's works were reached."[43]

Colonel Mitchell reported that his column struggled through the heavy enemy fire until they reached "the last thin belt of trees separating us from the main works. As the column reached this point ... it was subjected to an enfilading fire of artillery and musketry. Still the column moved on, the summit of the hill was gained, the works were reached, but we could not pass them." Like the other Union troops that morning Mitchell's men had to fall back until they found cover and dug in.[44]

To the left McCook's brigade suffered the same fate as Mitchell's. During the attack McCook was mortally wounded, the next in command quickly fell, and the third commander of the brigade, Col. Caleb Dilworth, "with great personal gallantry held his command to the fierce contest now being fought so near the works that a number of both officers and men were killed and wounded at the trenches." By now it was obvious that this portion of the attack had also failed and still under fire the men "threw up works a few yards from and nearly parallel to those of the enemy." And there they stayed.[45]

Long after the battle General Howard wrote: "Our losses in this assault were heavy indeed, and our gain was nothing. We realized now, as never before, the futility of direct assaults upon intrenched lines which were already well prepared and well manned." The casualties support Howard's conclusion with Johnston losing about 800 men while Sherman's total casualties were about 2,500. One of the casualties was especially disturbing for Sherman. Dan McCook, who died of his wounds, had been Sherman's law partner and friend.[46]

While the slaughter on Kennesaw Mountain was appalling to the participants, it raised no criticism from Sherman's superiors or the public. The carnage in Virginia was so horrific that none of the news from Georgia seemed very bad in comparison. Sherman had learned his lesson, however, and he would order no more frontal attacks against entrenched positions for the rest of the war.[47]

Although the battle on Kennesaw Mountain was clearly a Confederate victory the inevitable was only temporarily postponed. General Schofield's diversion to the south did not fool Johnston into moving troops from the center to meet this threat. Faced with little opposition Schofield kept moving and flanked the Confederate position. On July 1–2 Sherman moved McPherson around behind Thomas to join Schofield in a push toward the Chattahoochee River. Once again Johnston was threatened with being cut off from his supply line back to Atlanta. The Confederate commander could not extend his already-thin lines to block this new threat and was unwilling to run the risk of detaching a portion of his army to meet the flanking column. There was only one thing Johnston could do and on the morning of July 3 as Sherman surveyed the scene of the terrible fighting, "with the first dawn of day I saw our skirmishers appear on the mountain top."[48]

Joe Johnston moved his army back about six miles to Smyrna Camp Ground, where a complete set of fortifications had already been prepared. General Thomas followed the retreating Confederates through Marietta to the new line of works. There was some serious skirmishing along the line with Thomas on the left across the railroad, and McPherson and Schofield on the right. On the 4th of July, McPherson pushed across Nickajack Creek on the western end of the Federal line and Thomas launched a strong skirmish line attack against the Confederate works, capturing an entire line of rifle pits. As Sherman reported: "This had the desired effect, and the next morning the enemy was gone and the army moved to the Chattahoochee, General Thomas' left flank resting on the river near Pace's Ferry, General McPherson's right at the mouth of the Nickajack, and General Schofield in reserve."[49]

Sherman's troops were right behind the Confederates and were expecting Johnston to cross the Chattahoochee, destroying any bridges in the area, and set up a defensive position on the south side of the river. Howard wrote that Sherman "could not at first believe that Johnston would make another stand north of the river." But make a stand he did, in formidable fortifications prepared in advance that covered the railroad and other bridges. The downstream crossings, on Johnston's left, that were not destroyed were covered by small detachments of infantry with artillery.[50]

The Federal army spent about a week in this position and it was a very uncomfortable place. Henry Wright wrote about the conditions faced by the troops among the swamps and bottom land near the Chattahoochee. "The presence of myriads of insects, venomous worms and reptiles, caused great annoyance.... The locality was a genuine fever breeder and many strong men who had withstood all the hardships up to that point were compelled to give up on account of raging fever...." Fortunately the Federal troops would not have to spend too much time in this position.[51]

General Johnston had focused his attention on his left, expecting another flanking movement so that Sherman could swing around toward Atlanta. Sherman had sent General Stoneman's cavalry downstream to find a crossing but they came up empty. To the north Garrard's cavalry and part of Schofield's infantry searched for a way across the river. At the mouth of Soap Creek Schofield found a lightly defended ford and on the morning of the 8th made an elaborate amphibious attack: "The astonished rebels fired a single shot from their single gun, delivered a few random discharges of musketry, and fled.... The crossing was secured without the loss of a man." Federal troops quickly spread out along the riverbank looking for other crossings.[52]

The Federal army now had a secure bridgehead on the Atlanta side of the Chattahoochee River and the massive Confederate works on the north side were suddenly useless. Once again Johnston had no choice but to fall back, this time to the fortifications around Atlanta itself. Sherman reported that by July 9 "we had secured three good and safe points of passage over the Chattahoochee above the enemy, with good roads leading to Atlanta. This was one, if not the chief, object of the campaign, viz, the advancement of our lines from the Tennessee to the Chattahoochee."[53]

By mid–July most of Sherman's troops were across the river and the armies were positioned to cut Atlanta off from the rest of the Confederacy. Thomas' Army of the Cumberland was on the right, north of Atlanta. Schofield was to the east and slightly behind Thomas and McPherson came down on the east of the city between Stone Mountain and Decatur. Johnston, who surprisingly had not opposed the Federal crossing of the Chattahoochee, formed his army inside the arc of the Federal lines. General Alexander Stewart had been appointed permanent commander of Polk's corps, replacing Loring who was given only interim command. Stewart was on the left along Peachtree Creek, with Hardee in the center and Hood on the right. Wheeler's cavalry was assigned to protect Decatur and the Georgia Railroad.[54]

One of Sherman's goals was to cut Atlanta off from the rest of the Confederacy by destroying the railroads that radiated out of the city. This would make Atlanta useless to the Confederates even if Sherman could not actually capture the city. A two-part cavalry raid was planned to cut Confederate rail connections to the west. Maj. General Stoneman was to lead the cavalry division of the Army of the Ohio to destroy the tracks close to Atlanta. Maj. Gen. Lovell H. Rousseau brought a force down from Tennessee to cut the railroad in eastern Alabama. Rousseau's raid was very successful, destroying nearly 30 miles of track and much railroad equipment. Stoneman ran into relatively light resistance and turned back with little accomplished.[55]

To the Federal soldiers who had survived the terrible fighting and the atrocious weather crossing the Chattahoochee seemed to bring about a sudden change in their fortunes. "The weather had become good, and there was great animation and manifest joy on our side. It was gratifying to escape from such fastness and dismal forests as those which had hampered us for over a month, and we now firmly believed that the end of the campaign was sure."[56]

Back on June 26, the day before the attack on Kennesaw Mountain, Sherman had written a letter home:

> I am now 105 miles from Chattanooga, and all our provisions have come over that single road, which is almost daily broken somewhere, but thus far our supplies have been ample. We have devoured the land and our animals eat up the wheat and corn field close. All the people retire before us and desolation is behind. To realize what war is one should follow our tracks....[57]

Now Sherman had brought the war to Atlanta's front door.

Chapter 7

The Summer of Despair

All over the North people were wondering what happened to the victory they had been expecting. This was the summer that the Rebel armies would be destroyed and peace would finally return. Ulysses S. Grant had been given everything he had asked for in men and materiel. The Army of the Potomac in the East and Sherman's combined armies in the West had been expected to roll over their much-smaller opponents and the war would be over by fall. But, instead of a string of victory announcements, all the citizens of the North saw were horrendous casualty lists with very little to show for the losses. By the middle of the summer of 1864 the end of the war seemed farther away than ever.

The campaign that was to bring an end to the war started before dawn on the 4th of May as the men of the Sixth Army Corps of the Army of the Potomac marched out of their camps, crossed the Rapidan River, and headed south. One of them later wrote, "It was a lovely day, and all nature seemed rejoicing at the advent of spring." This would be the last time any of them would have a lovely day for many months.[1]

Grant's route took the Army of the Potomac straight into an area known as the Wilderness, a dark and dreary patch of heavy woods and underbrush with few roads. Although the difficult terrain would help to negate his superior manpower General Grant had his reasons for choosing this difficult route. In addition to keeping his army between Lee and Washington, Grant hoped that by moving quickly he could get through the Wilderness before Lee could bring up his entire army. But the main reason Grant took the Wilderness route was that Lee's army, not the city of Richmond, was the target and Lee was right in front of him.[2]

Horace Porter, one of General Grant's aides, described the terrible fighting in the Wilderness:

> For two days nearly 200,000 veteran troops had struggled in a death-grapple, confronted at each step with almost every obstacle by which nature could bar their path, and groping their way through a tangled forest the impenetrable gloom of which could be likened only to the shadow of death. The undergrowth stayed their progress, the upper growth shut out the light of heaven. Officers could rarely see their troops for any considerable distance, for smoke clouded the vision, and a heavy sky obscured

the sun.... It was a battle fought with the ear, and not with the eye. All circumstances seemed to combine to make the scene one of unutterable horror.... Forest fires raged; ammunition-trains exploded; the dead were roasted in the conflagration; the wounded, roused by its hot breath, dragged themselves along, with their torn and mangled limbs, in the mad energy of despair, to escape the ravages of the flames; and every bush seemed hung with shreds of blood-stained clothing. It was as though Christian men had turned to fiends, and hell itself had usurped the place of earth.[3]

Much more realistic than the northern public, General Grant never really expected to win any easy victories over Lee's army. The Wilderness was just the first of what he expected to be many hard fights. Adam Badeau, another of Grant's aides, wrote that the general

> often explained to those in his confidence that he did not expect by a single effort to overthrow the fabric; it was too firmly established; its leaders were too able and too desperate; its soldiers too experienced and gallant for this; but persistent and repeated attacks in every quarter, he doubted not, would finally complete the ruin of the so-called Confederacy. The practical result of the contest in the Wilderness was therefore far from a disappointment to the chief, or to those who knew his plans.[4]

After the Wilderness came Spotsylvania. An initial Federal success bogged down into slaughter for both sides. At the Bloody Angle men fought all day across the top of the Confederate works, stabbing with bayonets and holding their muskets over the top to shoot down on the enemy on the other side. The dead piled up on top of each other until in some places the survivors were standing on the bodies of their fallen comrades in order to continue the killing.[5]

After a couple of weeks of marching and skirmishing the two armies met again at Cold Harbor on June 3. Another Federal frontal attack against the dug-in Confederates resulted in one of the most tragic days of the war. Elisha Hunt Rhodes summed up when he wrote: "We have had a terrible battle today, and the killed and wounded number in thousands.... Nothing seems to have been gained by the attack today."[6]

Despite horrendous casualties at Cold Harbor, Grant soon continued the move south and was finally able to pull away from the Confederate army by making a swift march around Lee's right flank. For the first time the Army of the Potomac was unopposed as they marched and Grant had them heading for Petersburg, a rail center and gateway to Richmond that the Confederates could not afford to lose. The capture of Petersburg would also give the Federal army Richmond and cut Lee's army off from its supply lines; victory would soon follow.[7]

As the Federal soldiers marched toward Petersburg they could sense that they finally had the advantage over their old opponents. The scorching summer sun caused many men to drop by the roadside but hard marching brought the advance corps to the lightly manned fortifications south of Petersburg with Lee's veterans nowhere in sight. Then, with a tremendous victory within their grasp, the Union army was just a bit too slow. The combination of exhausted troops and cautious generals brought about a slow and careful advance at a time when the door to Petersburg and Richmond was unlocked and could have easily been forced open. The Union troops did capture some of the outer works, at a heavy cost, but the delays allowed Lee's troops time to rush down from Cold Harbor and man the impregnable inner lines of fortifications. Soon both armies settled down into a trench warfare stalemate that produced only casualties.[8]

The opportunity for a Federal victory that summer was gone and bitter disappointment followed. As Adam Badeau wrote:

> The army of the Potomac had neither captured Richmond nor conquered Lee. The contest was still at its height, and apparently undecided. The country was disappointed, weary, anxious; it could discern no light behind the cloud, no way through the darkness; it only saw that its troops were still outside the rebel capital, and still confronted by the rebel army; and as it counted up its losses, it bitterly asked: "How long?"[9]

While the Army of the Potomac was battering itself against the Army of Northern Virginia the other components of Grant's strategy for winning the war were off to an even worse start.

Maj. Gen. Benjamin Butler's expedition was simply an outright failure. A more aggressive leader probably would have won a smashing victory, because when Butler's army landed at Bermuda Hundred on May 5 he faced only a token force of defenders. A swift advance was needed before the Confederates could bring up more troops, instead Butler cautiously edged forward with short tentative advances, halting to dig in whenever a Confederate force put up a fight. Butler wasted more than a week and by the middle of May the Confederates had built a line of fortifications across the narrow neck of the Bermuda Hundred peninsula that ended any chance of moving to Richmond from this direction.[10]

The other part of General Grant's plans in Virginia had also achieved nothing. Described as "a perfect paradise on earth," by a Union soldier from New York, the Shenandoah Valley had been a perfect hell on earth for Federal troops since the beginning of the war and the summer of 1864 brought more of the same.[11]

Sheltered between the western side of the Blue Ridge Mountains and the eastern edge of the Alleghenies, control of the Shenandoah Valley was necessary for a successful campaign in Virginia. The mountains could conceal the movements of Confederate troops heading north and the passes through the mountains allowed troops from either side to attack the flank of the main armies in eastern Virginia.

The first Federal thrust into the valley was led by political appointee Maj. Gen. Franz Sigel who, after wasting valuable time, led his small army to defeat at New Market on May 15. Once again the Union lost an opportunity to gain control of the valley and disrupt the flow of supplies to Lee's army or threaten his flank. Confederate Gen. John D. Imboden, who participated in the campaign, wrote, "there was no secondary battle of the war of more importance than that of New Market."[12]

A few weeks later Maj. Gen. David Hunter led a slightly larger army to victory at Piedmont on June 5. He followed this up with the capture of Lexington and Staunton while heading for the ultimate goal, the railroads and supply depots of Lynchburg. After being reinforced Hunter's army of about 18,000 approached Lynchburg but was forced back by the timely arrival of Confederate troops led by Lt. Gen. Jubal A. Early. Early's corps was dispatched by Lee in a desperate attempt to save his lifeline, which ran through Lynchburg.[13]

General Early actually had a two-part assignment from Lee. After preventing the capture of Lynchburg he was to lead a daring invasion northward through the Shenandoah Valley. The objective was to threaten, or if all the pieces fell into place, capture Washington, D.C. As Lee's two previous invasions had proven, any threat to the capital would produce panic in the north and might pressure Federal authorities into making a mistake. Grant might be forced to send troops north to save the capital and weaken his grip on Petersburg, opening the way for a breakout by the besieged Confederates, or believing that Lee was substantially weaker because of the detached corps Grant might be induced to try another assault on the still-strong Confederate lines, resulting in high casualty lists and more despair in the North. Either result would prolong the war and increase the number of people in the North who wanted an end to the fighting and also increase the chance that Lincoln would not be reelected. And if Early were able to actually capture Washington, even for a day or two, the results could be fantastic. Besides the huge amounts of food and weapons that might be carried away the occupation of the Federal capital would prove to the world that the Confederacy was still very much alive and give an enormous boost to the morale of its beleaguered people.[14]

Henry Kyd Douglas, one of Early's staff officers, wrote, "The audacity of Early's enterprise was its safety; no one who might have taken steps to oppose or cut him off would believe his force so small."[15] Early came amazingly close to actually pulling it off. After two weeks of forced marching and a victory over a small Federal force at the Monocacy River, Early arrived just outside the capital on July 11 but his troops were too exhausted to make any kind of serious attack on the thinly manned works. The next day, in an almost theatrical coincidence, the veteran troops of the Sixth Corps, just arrived from Petersburg, began manning the works while Early was surveying the lines to decide where to attack. Properly manned the fortifications of Washington were too strong to even make an attempt to attack them so Early turned around and went back to the Shenandoah Valley.[16]

Jubal Early's raid brought temporary high hopes to the South and panic and despair to the North. That he accomplished nothing more than taking his army for a long walk was more a matter of bad luck than lack of effort. A.L. Long, Early's chief of artillery, later wrote: "This campaign is remarkable for having accomplished more in proportion to the force employed, and for having given less public satisfaction, than any other campaign of the war."[17]

Horace Greeley, the well-known publisher, summed up the events of the summer and the feelings of the citizens of the North:

> Gen. Grant's determined attack at Cold Harbor was found to have been not merely unsuccessful — that had been frankly and promptly admitted — but an exceeding expensive and damaging failure — damaging not merely in the magnitude of our loss, but in its effect on the morale and efficiency of our chief army. It had extinguished the last hope of crushing Lee north of the James, and of interposing that army between him and the Confederate capital. The failure to seize Petersburg when

it would easily have fallen, and the repeated and costly failures to carry its defenses by assault, or even to flank them on the south — Sheridan's failure to unite with Hunter in Lee's rear — Hunter's failure to carry Lynchburg — Sherman's bloody repulse at Kenesaw, and the slowness of his advance on Atlanta — Early's unresisted swoop down the Valley into Maryland ... and his unpunished demonstration against the defenses of Washington itself — the raids of his troopers up to the suburbs of Baltimore, and even into Pennsylvania; burning Chambersburg — and finally the bloody, wretched fiasco of the Mine explosion before Petersburg — these, and other reverses, relieved by a few and unimpressive triumphs — rendered the midsummer of 1864 one of the gloomiest seasons of our great struggle for the upholders of the National cause.[18]

All the bad news coming from the armies in the field had a predictable effect on the people at home. New York resident George Templeton Strong wrote in his diary for July 23:

Today's atmosphere unwholesome. People seem discouraged, weary, and faint-hearted. But I will not let myself doubt the final issue. What further humiliation and disaster, public and private, we must suffer before we reach the end, God only knows; but this shabbiest and basest of rebellions cannot be destined to triumph....[19]

And, as Adam Badeau wrote: "Until the fall of Atlanta, indeed the gloom at the North was overshadowing. The most hopeful had become weary, the most determined were depressed and disappointed."[20]

In addition to facing an enemy on the battlefields the Federal government also faced enemies at home. There was dissatisfaction and subversion of the war effort from the very beginning but these problems increased in intensity as the election approached. Presidential secretaries Nicolay and Hay explained much of the workings and membership of these groups: "Opposition to the Government by constitutional means was not enough to gratify the vehement and resentful feeling of those Democrats in the North whose zeal for slavery seemed completely to have destroyed in their hearts every impulse of patriotism." Throughout the country secret societies were formed for the purpose of "embarrassing in every way the action of the Government, of communicating information to the rebels in arms, and in many cases of inflicting serious damage to the lives and property of the Unionists."[21]

The largest of the societies was the Knights of the Golden Circle, but as the purpose of these groups was uncovered the names were changed frequently. "These secret organizations possessed a singular charm to uneducated men ... and this attraction, combined with the fact that they could not in plain daylight inflict any injury upon the Government, drove many thousands of the lower class of Democrats into these furtive lodges."[22]

The vast majority of these groups did no real harm except in encouraging troops to desert and hindering the government officials who were involved in enforcing conscription laws. The Lincoln administration did little to disband these groups because the president "never could be made to believe that there was as much crime as folly in their acts and purposes."[23]

The soldiers in the field were not unaware of what was happening back home.

They knew opportunities had been missed and mistakes made, but they also knew that things were not as bad as they looked to the civilians back home. What really upset the fighting men were the many people who worked against the war effort from the safety of their homes. Some had political reasons to oppose the war and some sincerely just wanted the killing to end. To the soldiers who were doing the fighting, however, the reason was unimportant. They reserved their most bitter hatred, not for the enemy they were fighting, but for the enemy at their backs.

Union soldier James T. Miller wrote:

> Dear father you may think me harsh in my denunciations of traitors and treason in the north but I have used the mildest language I could that would even partially express my utter abhorence and detestation of these false black hearted scoundrels in the north who are enducing our men to desert encouraging the enemy ... there can be no doubt but what a very large share of the miseries and distress of this war are justly chargeable to the coperheads of the north and we soldiers hate them a great deal worse than we do the rebles in arms and the English language does not furnish terms mean and harsh enough to express the feelings of the army in regard to the traitors at home.[24]

In addition to the fighting this was also a summer for politics back home as the various parties held their national conventions to nominate presidential candidates. As the summer wore on and the casualty lists grew longer the number of those in the North who favored peace increased. So too did the number of Republicans who felt that President Lincoln's administration was a failure and that he could not be reelected in November.[25]

The first convention to meet was made up mostly of the radical Republicans at Cleveland on May 31. This small group of disaffected Republicans believed that President Lincoln was too conservative in his actions toward ending slavery and too soft to sufficiently punish the South after the war. Their nominee was former explorer and Union general John C. Fremont. Another factor that concerned the Radicals was purely one of political power. If the seceded states were allowed to simply resume their prewar status, as the president proposed, their politicians would most likely reunite with the Democrats and regain control of the government, as had been done before the war.[26]

On June 7, the Republican convention met in Baltimore and Lincoln easily won the nomination. Although there was a sizable minority that would have preferred another candidate the practical politicians that actually ran the party knew that the people were solidly behind the president, and they had to accept the inevitable.[27]

The Republican platform that Lincoln and vice-presidential candidate Andrew Johnson of Tennessee had to run on naturally supported the war and Lincoln's handling of it. The first three resolutions in the platform summarized the most important aspects of the president's policies. The first declared that every citizen had a duty to maintain the integrity of the Union and to join in putting down the rebellion by force of arms. The second committed the government of the United States to reject any compromise with the rebels. The third approved the actions so far taken against slavery, namely the Emancipation Proclamation, but also proposed an amendment to the Constitution permanently prohibiting slavery in the United States.[28]

President Lincoln made no changes in his policies to gain support during the summer. He knew what had to be done and there was no question that he would continue to do what he felt was right, election or no. In a speech at a Sanitary Commission Fair in Philadelphia on June 16 he told the crowd: "It is a pertinent question, often asked in the mind privately, and from one to the other, when is the war to end? We accepted this war for an object, a worthy object, and the war will end when that object is attained. Under God, I hope it never will end until that time."[29]

The Democratic Convention was originally scheduled for July 4 in Chicago. Hoping to take advantage of any negative news and the public's growing resentment of high taxes and the policy of conscription, they postponed it until August 29. The delay would also give the Democrats more time to adapt their campaign to better counter whatever new policies might come out of the Republican convention.[30]

The Democrats were not totally opposed to a war to reunite the Union, just the way it was being fought; but they were opposed to any form of forced emancipation. With the growing dissatisfaction in the North it was very possible that the Democratic Party could win back the White House in the fall. A Democratic victory in November could mean the end to the movement to abolish slavery, and possibly a negotiated settlement to the war that might or might not restore the Union.[31]

The leading contender for the Democratic nomination was George B. McClellan, the former commander of the Army of the Potomac. McClellan was an advocate of a conservative or limited war effort that would do no more than restore the country as it was before the war. He favored preservation of the Union but opposed the effort to force the abolishment of slavery.[32]

A more radical faction of the Democratic Party was a group that believed the war was nothing but a bloody failure and demanded peace at any price. Their leader was the very vocal Clement L. Vallandigham of Ohio.

The Democratic platform announced

> [t]hat this Convention does explicitly declare, as the sense of the American people, that, after four years of failure to restore the Union by the experiment of war, during which, under the pretense of a military necessity of a war power higher than the Constitution, the Constitution itself has been disregarded in every part, and public liberty and private right alike trodden down, and the material prosperity of the country essentially impaired, justice, humanity, liberty, and the public welfare demand that immediate efforts be made for a cessation of hostilities....[33]

A peace negotiated on these terms could give the Confederacy everything it had been fighting for. Victory for the South might be obtained by default and its political and military leaders were well aware of the possibility. If the southern armies could continue to inflict heavy casualties on the Union armies without giving up any significant victories for a few more months the voters of the North might give the Confederacy the independence that it could not win on the battlefield.

Well aware that political turmoil in the North could benefit the southern cause the Confederate government had dispatched agents to the safe haven of Canada where they went to work to aid individuals and groups that supported the peace movement. It was also possible, the southerners believed, to influence public opinion in the North by subsidizing anti–Lincoln newspapers that would help spread the message that the current administration could not achieve a military victory or restore the Union.[34]

Jefferson Davis later wrote:

> Political developments at the North, however, favored the adoption of some action that might influence popular sentiment in the hostile section. The aspect of the peace party was quite encouraging, and it seemed that the real issue to be decided in the Presidential election in that year was the continuance or cessation of the war.[35]

This sentiment brought about one of the more unusual events of the war.

During the summer rumors were circulated that a peaceful settlement was not only possible but was actually desired by the Confederacy. The real problem, it was said, was that the administration was not interested in opening negotiations. Influential publisher Horace Greeley became involved in what he believed was an opportunity to open a dialogue between the two warring governments. He willingly offered to assist several prominent Confederate agents who were living in Canada at the time, and who had persuaded Greeley that they were authorized by the Confederate government to negotiate for peace. They asked Greeley to help convince President Lincoln to offer them a safe conduct to Washington where they would present the southern position and open negotiations for a peace treaty.[36]

President Lincoln was justifiably concerned about any negotiations that recognized the Confederate government as a legitimate entity, but he also knew that he could not just ignore this opportunity. Trying to walk a tightrope, on July 18 he gave Greeley a note containing his terms:

> To whom it may concern: Any proposition which embraces the restoration of peace, the integrity of the whole Union, and the abandonment of slavery, and which comes by and with an authority that can control the armies now at war against the United States, will be received and considered by the executive government of the United States, and will be met by liberal terms on other substantial and collateral points, and the bearer or bearers thereof shall have safe conduct both ways.[37]

Since one of the main goals of the Confederacy was to be recognized as a legitimate nation this type of offer was not what the Confederates were looking for. Considering how badly things were going for the Lincoln administration that summer it is unlikely that this was a real attempt at a negotiated peace but was probably only a plot to further embarrass Lincoln during the campaign and the whole scheme went nowhere.

One of the many problems that President Lincoln faced during the summer was an attempt by the Radicals to force their own terms of reconciliation on states rejoining the Union. To many of the Radical Republicans the president's policy to allow former Confederate states to come back into the Union was too lenient. They were appalled and angered by the rivers of blood and mountains of treasure that had already been expended on this war. The Radicals were in no mood for a fast and friendly reconciliation; they to wanted to punish the traitorous states, and they wanted revenge on the men who had plunged their peaceful nation into this bloodbath.[38]

Two of the leaders of the Radicals were Senator Benjamin Wade of Ohio and Congressman Henry Winter Davis of Maryland. Earlier in the year they sponsored a bill that offered a plan for the restoration of seceded states that differed significantly from the president's "10-percent plan." The Wade-Davis Bill authorized the president, with Senate consent, to appoint a provisional governor in each of the states in rebellion as soon as the military resistance to the United States was ended in that state.[39]

The provisional governor would then enroll any white male citizen of voting age who would take the oath of allegiance to support the Constitution of the United States and obey all its laws. When a majority of those enrolled had taken the oath they would then be allowed to elect delegates to a convention to reestablish a state government. Only those who swore an oath that they had never held an office in the Confederate government, or had taken up arms against the United States, could serve as delegates.[40]

The delegates that framed the new state constitution were free to include any reasonable laws and amendments as they saw fit but the state constitution must include the following: that no Confederate officer who had held the rank of colonel or higher could serve in the state legislature or be elected or appointed governor of the state; that slavery and any form of involuntary servitude was forever abolished; and that any debt owed by the state or Confederate government was considered null and void.[41]

Once the new constitution was completed the authorized voters of the state had to approve it. Then, the new state constitution had to be approved by Congress; only then could the president issue a proclamation recognizing that the state was once more part of the Union and was authorized to elect senators and congressmen. In effect Congress, and not the president, was to have the power to determine when and how the former Confederate states would be welcomed back into the United States. The Radicals also wanted to make sure than none of the leaders of the Confederacy would be able to profit from their treason.[42]

The Wade-Davis Bill was debated for months and finally approved by both houses of Congress just before the Fourth of July adjournment. President Lincoln was in his office in the Capitol signing last-minute bills as they were brought in. When the Wade-Davis Bill was presented for signing he put it aside and continued with his other work. The president told his aides that he refused to be rushed into signing the bill without studying it. What he really did was simply to ignore the bill and let it die, in effect a pocket veto.[43]

During the summer, political problems with the Democrats and members of his own party grew sharper and more divisive. The prominent politician Thurlow Weed wrote to Secretary of State Seward on August 22:

> "When, ten days since, I told Mr. Lincoln that his re-election was an impossibility, I also told him that the information would soon come to him through other chan-

nels. It has doubtless ere this reached him. At any rate nobody here doubts it, nor do I see anybody from other States who authorizes the slightest hope of success.... The people are wild for peace. They are told that the President will only listen to terms of peace on condition that slavery be abandoned.... That something should be done and promptly done to give the Administration a chance for its life is certain.[44]

Add to this the apparent lack of concrete progress on the battlefields and the horrendous casualties that were being reported and it is little wonder that President Lincoln finally began to display his frustration and disappointment. On August 23 he wrote a note to the members of his cabinet:

This morning, as for some days past, it seems exceedingly probable that this administration will not be reëlected. Then it will be my duty to so coöperate with the President-elect as to save the Union between the election and the inauguration; as he will have secured his election on such ground that he cannot possibly save it afterward.[45]

President Lincoln's depression was shared by many of his fellow citizens in the North as they wondered if this terrible war would ever end. In the South the same feelings of dismay and helplessness were spreading as the casualty lists became longer and longer and there was a growing realization that all the loss and sacrifice may have been for nothing. In July, Mary Chesnut wrote in her diary: "I think if I consider the long array of those bright youths and loyal men who have gone to their death almost before my very eyes, my heart might break, too. Is anything worth it—this fearful sacrifice, this awful penalty we pay for war?"[46]

The fearful sacrifice was even more evident in Washington, D.C., this summer. The city was home to huge hospitals that cared for the flood of wounded men who were being brought back from Virginia. As Secretary of the Navy Gideon Welles described:

The wounded soldiers sent to Washington to be nursed were living witnesses of the country's agony. Miles of hospital barracks were erected in Washington, and filled with thousands upon thousands of brave men, maimed and dying. This almost innumerable host, from among the noblest heroes and most patriotic spirits of the land, who had periled their lives and poured forth their blood for their country, was, during that sad summer, an affecting spectacle that grieved the hearts of all, and none more than the president, who was blamed and held responsible for the killed and wounded by a large portion of his countrymen.[47]

The terrible cost and waste of war had come home to both sides and it had to be played out to the bitter end.

Chapter 8
New Tactics Outside Atlanta

Back at the end of May, the Confederate chief of ordnance, Gen. Josiah Gorgas, wrote in his diary, "Johnston verifies all our predictions of him. He is falling back just as fast as his legs can carry him…." In May it would have been reasonable to give Johnston's strategy the benefit of the doubt. Now, in mid–July, with the contending armies just a few miles outside of Atlanta, there was growing concern in the South as to whether Atlanta could be held.[1]

Jefferson Davis, who hadn't really wanted Johnston to command the Army of Tennessee but had settled on him as the best choice available, voiced his own concerns: "The possible fall of the 'Gate City,' with its important railroad communication, vast stores, rolling-mill and foundries, was now contemplated for the first time at its full value, and produced intense anxiety far and wide."[2]

The president was not the only person who realized how important Atlanta was to the Confederacy; plenty of ordinary citizens knew full well how serious the situation had become. Thomas DeLeon wrote that many people "were perfectly aware that, should Atlanta fall and the enemy penetrate to our rear lines of communication, the cause was lost. We might make a fierce resistance for the moment; but without supplies, all organized plan must cease.[3]

On July 10, President Davis sent General Bragg to Georgia to get a firsthand report of the situation. Arriving on the 13th Bragg spent three days meeting with General Johnston and other high-ranking officers, chief among them Hood. Bragg had told Johnston that his was an unofficial visit but there could not have been much doubt that whatever Bragg learned would soon reach Davis. A series of telegrams did indeed inform President Davis of what Bragg saw and heard in Atlanta. On his arrival Bragg wired, "Our army all south of the Chattahoochee, and indications seem to favor an entire evacuation of this place." The next wire brought the news that the "army is sadly depleted, and now reports 10,000 less than the return of 10th June. I find but little encouraging." Yet another telegram informed Davis that, "Nearly all available stores and machinery are removed, and the people have mostly evacuated the town."[4]

General Bragg also had trouble learning what, if anything, Johnston was planning to do to relieve the situation. On the 15th Bragg reported to President Davis:

> I have made General Johnston two visits, and have been received courteously and kindly. He has not sought my advice, and it was not volunteered. I cannot learn that he has any more plan for the future than he has had in the past. It is expected that he will await the enemy on a line some three miles from here, and the impression prevails that he is now more inclined to fight. The enemy is very cautious, and intrenches immediately on taking a new position. The morale of our army is still reported good.[5]

This lack of openness with Bragg could have been caused by Johnston's distrust of anyone connected with Davis.

When Bragg returned to Richmond he carried with him a letter from General Hood in which Hood stated that the army had several opportunities to strike a decisive blow against the Federal army but for some reason failed to take advantage of a situation when it was presented. Hood also recommended that Sherman should be attacked as soon as possible:

> During the campaign from Dalton to the Chattahoochee it is natural to suppose that we have had several chances to strike the enemy a decisive blow. We have failed to take advantage of such opportunities, and find our army south of the Chattahoochee, very much decreased in strength. Our present position is a very difficult one, and we should not, under any circumstances, allow the enemy to gain possession of Atlanta, and deem it excessively important, should we find the enemy intends establishing the Chattahoochee as their line, relying upon interrupting our communications and again virtually dividing our country, that we should attack him, even if we should have to recross the river to do so. I have, general, so often urged that we should force the enemy to give us battle as to almost be regarded reckless by the officers high in rank in this army, since their views have been so directly opposite. I regard it as a great misfortune to our country that we failed to give battle to the enemy many miles north of our present position.[6]

A frustrated Jefferson Davis telegraphed Johnston on the 16th in an attempt to learn what was being done to protect Atlanta. "I wish to hear from you as to present situation, and your plan of operations so specifically as will enable me to anticipate events." Later that same day Johnston wired back,

> As the enemy has double our number, we must be on the defensive. My plan of operations must, therefore, depend upon that of the enemy. It is mainly to watch for an opportunity to fight to advantage. We are trying to put Atlanta in condition to be held for a day or two by the Georgia militia, that army movements may be freer and wider.[7]

General Johnston's reply did nothing to give Davis any confidence that Atlanta would be held, in fact, it sounded as if Johnston was considering moving his army away from the city and leaving the defense of Atlanta to the less-than-capable Georgia State Militia. The possibility that Johnston would pull the army out of Atlanta greatly disturbed Davis because, as he later wrote,

> If the Army of Tennessee was found to be unable to hold positions of great strength like those at Dalton, Resaca, Etowah, Kenesaw, and on the Chattahoochee, I could

not reasonably hope that it would be more successful in the plains below Atlanta, where it would find neither natural nor artificial advantages of position.[8]

General Johnston's refusal to commit to defending Atlanta sealed his fate and President Davis finally came to a decision. On the evening of the 17th the following telegram was sent by Adjutant General Samuel Cooper to Joseph Johnston:

> Lieut. Gen. J.B. Hood has been commissioned to the temporary rank of general under the late law of Congress. I am directed by the Secretary of War to inform you that as you have failed to arrest the advance of the enemy to the vicinity of Atlanta, far in the interior of Georgia, and express no confidence that you can defeat or repel him, you are hereby relieved from the command of the Army and Department of Tennessee, which you will immediately turn over to General Hood.[9]

That same evening Hood received his orders to assume command of the army. He later wrote: "This totally unexpected order so astounded me, and overwhelmed me with sense of the responsibility thereto attached, that I remained in deep thought throughout the night." The next morning he met General Stewart on the way to Johnston's headquarters where he told Johnston, "he should pocket that dispatch, leave me in command of my corps, and fight the battle for Atlanta." Johnston replied that he would not dispute the order unless it were countermanded.[10]

Confederate General Braxton Bragg

On the 18th Hood sent a telegram, also signed by Stewart and Hardee, to Adjutant General Cooper, requesting that Johnston be left in command at least for a while. "There is now heavy skirmishing and indications of a general advance. I deem it dangerous to change the commanders of the army at this particular time, and to be to the interest of the service that no change should be made until the fate of Atlanta is decided."[11]

Despite the request

from his generals to postpone changing commanders, the fact was that President Davis did not want Joseph Johnston in command while the fate of Atlanta was decided. Davis simply did not trust Johnston to stand and fight. Davis quickly sent a reply to Hood's telegram, sending a copy to both Hardee and Stewart:

> A change of commanders, under existing circumstances, was regarded as so objectionable that I only accepted it as the alternative of continuing in a policy which had proved so disastrous. Reluctance to make the change induced me to send a telegram of inquiry to the commanding general on the 16th instant. His reply but confirmed previous apprehensions. There can be but one question which you and I can entertain — that is, what will best promote the public good; and to each of you I confidently look for the sacrifice of every personal consideration in conflict with that object. The order has been executed, and I cannot suspend it without making the case worse than it was before the order was issued.[12]

President Davis later explained his reasons for the change of commanders:

> I resisted the steadily increasing pressure which was brought to bear to induce me to revoke his assignment and only issued the order relieving him from command when I became satisfied that his declared purpose to occupy the works at Atlanta with militia levies and withdraw his army into the open country for freer operations, would inevitably result in the loss of that important point, and where the retreat would cease could not be foretold.[13]

So the change was made and one of the most beloved commanders in the Confederacy was gone, but not forgotten. In his orders turning over command to Hood, Johnston wrote to his men,

> I cannot leave this noble army without expressing my admiration of the high military qualities it has displayed. A long and arduous campaign has made conspicuous every soldierly virtue, endurance of toil, obedience to orders, brilliant courage. The enemy has never attacked but to be repulsed and severely punished. You, soldiers, have never argued but from your courage, and never counted your foes. No longer your leader, I will still watch your career, and will rejoice in your victories. To one and all I offer assurances of my friendship, and bid an affectionate farewell.[14]

When the soldiers received the news of Johnston's removal they were first stunned, then angry, and finally resigned to what ever might come. Edward McMorries, of the 1st Alabama, wrote:

> The news thunderstruck the army. Gloomy forebodings took the place of buoyant hope.... Further, it was believed to be the result of intrigue at Richmond, and of the clamor of non-combatants at home. But for the patriotism of the army there would have been a vehement protest. As it was, there was sullen submission. The army entertained the highest opinion of Gen. Hood as a Major-general. They knew he was loyal, patriotic and brave, but doubted his ability to command the army. Johnston, by daily object lessons of partial engagements in which he was always victorious during his masterful retreat from Dalton to Atlanta, had inspired his men with a

faith and enthusiasm seldom attained by any general.... Johnston they could follow with certainty of victory; Hood, only with apprehension of defeat and disaster.[15]

John Hagen wrote to his wife that,

> This army receved sad news yesterday the grate Genl J.E. Johnston who has led this army to so many glorious victories & he who was loved by all who ever sirved under him sent to us his farwell address ... if the war department only knew what confidence the army has in their grate Leader he would have been retained in prefferance to any one elce. Gen Hood now commands us & I hope he will be successful but the releaving of Gen Joe is dampening to his troops.[16]

And W.J. McMurray, of the 20th Tennessee remembered that he

> witnessed as sad sights as I saw here. Great stalwart, sun-burnt soldiers by the thousands would be seen falling out of line, squatting down by a tree or in a fence corner, weeping like children. This act of the War Department threw a damper over this army from which it never recovered, for "Old Joe," as we called him, was our idol. If we were ragged, barefooted, and half fed, the boys would say: "Old Joe is doing the best he can," and you heard no complaint.[17]

By no means was it just the privates who were unhappy. Capt. Samuel Foster of the Texas Brigade related,

> Gen. Johnston has so endeared himself to his soldiers, that no man can take his place. We have never made a fight under him that we did not get the best of it. He never deceived us once. It is true we have had hard fighting and hard marching, but we always had something to eat.... He was always looking after our comfort and safety. For the first time, we hear men openly talk about going home, by tens [10] and by fifties [50] ... and talk open rebellion against all Military authority. All over camp,(not only among Texas troops) can be seen this demoralization — and at all hours in the afternoon can be heard Hurrah for Joe Johnston and God D — n Jeff Davis.[18]

Frank A. Montgomery, lieutenant colonel of the First Mississippi cavalry wrote: "We marched all day and all night, and I will never forget the gloom of that march. I felt that our cause was at its crisis, that our only hope had been in Johnston ... one of the few really great commanders we had"[19]

Even civilians could see how the change in commanders affected the soldiers of the Army of Tennessee. Fannie Beers, a volunteer nurse, wrote:

> I new nothing of the relative merits of the two commanders and had no means of judging but by the effect upon the soldiers by whom I was then surrounded. The whole post seemed as if stricken by some terrible calamity. Convalescents walked about with lagging steps and gloomy faces. In every ward lay men who wept bitterly or groaned aloud or, covering their faces, refused to speak or eat. From that hour the buoyant, hopeful spirit seemed to die out. I do not think anything was ever the same again. For, when the awful sacrifice of human life which followed the inauguration of the new policy, the decimated army still were forced to retreat, the shadow of doom began to creep slowly upon the land.[20]

8. New Tactics Outside Atlanta

Seldom has a new military commander taken over under more difficult conditions than those faced by John Bell Hood on Monday morning, July 18. His strategic options were limited and he had to hold Atlanta in the face of a confident and much-stronger enemy. There were no more natural obstacles between Sherman and Atlanta. On the 18th McPherson cut the Georgia Railroad near Decatur, leaving only the Macon & Western Railroad as Atlanta's link to the rest of the Confederacy. Under these conditions there was only one action Hood could take, and this was the main reason he was chosen to be the new commander: he would attack.[21]

While the change in command was taking place in Atlanta, Sherman's army was moving outside the city, improving their positions. "On the 17th we began the general movement against Atlanta." By the end of the next day General Thomas had crossed the Chattahoochee and formed his line facing Peachtree Creek, Schofield occupied the center, and McPherson had moved past Stone Mountain and reached Decatur, cutting the railroad and meeting Schofield's troops who had also spread out to reach Decatur.[22]

When General Sherman learned of the change in Confederate commanders he quickly deduced that the style of fighting was about to change. General Schofield had been a classmate of Hood's at the Military Academy and when Sherman asked him what sort of a man Hood was Schofield replied, "Yes, I know him well, and I will tell you the sort of man he is. He'll hit you like h—l, now, before you know it."[23]

Sherman wrote that he learned that Hood

> was bold even to rashness, and courageous in the extreme; I inferred that the change of commanders meant "fight." Notice of this important change was at once sent to all parts of the army, and every division commander was cautioned to be always prepared for battle in any shape. This was just what we wanted, viz., to fight in open ground, on any thing like equal terms, instead of being forced to run up against prepared intrenchments; but, at the same time, the enemy having Atlanta behind him, could choose the time and place of attack, and could at pleasure mass a superior force on our weakest points. Therefore, we had to be constantly ready for sallies.[24]

The Federal commander was about to get his wish.

As Sherman's army advanced toward Atlanta, Hood learned that a gap of about two miles had opened between General Thomas, north of Atlanta at Peachtree Creek and Schofield and McPherson who were more to the northeast. In addition to the gap between the armies, the part of Thomas' army that was on the Atlanta side of Peachtree Creek would be extremely vulnerable until the entire army was across. Hood planned a surprise attack by Gens. A.P. Stewart and Hardee to crush the Federals that had already moved across the creek, while General Cheatham, on the Confederate right, would hold Schofield and McPherson at bay. Hood's first attack as commander of the Army of Tennessee became known as the Battle of Peachtree Creek.[25]

The Confederate attack was scheduled for early afternoon on the 20th of July. The original plan called for each division, beginning with Hardee's right, to move forward in echelon at intervals of about 200 yards. The objective was to sweep the portion of Thomas' army that had crossed Peachtree Creek backward and then down the creek to the left. It looked like a good plan with Hood being able to concentrate two corps on a much smaller Union force.[26]

Just as the Confederates were making their preparations to launch the attack, General Cheatham saw that McPherson's troops were moving faster and farther to the right than had been anticipated. Fearing that the Federals might be making a flank attack of their own Cheatham received Hood's permission to move farther east to block McPherson. He also received General Cleburne's division from Hardee as reinforcement. This took care of one problem but as Cheatham shifted his troops more to the east to block McPherson, a gap opened up between his corps and Hardee's. This forced Hardee to move to the right and Stewart had to follow to keep the Confederate line together. All this shifting of troops took at least three hours, during which time Thomas was able to get the rest of his army across Peachtree Creek.[27]

The terrain just south of Peachtree Creek was rough with woods and ravines scattered through the area and as soon as Thomas' troops crossed to the south side they hastily threw up crude breastworks. On the Federal left Howard's corps was split with Wood and Stanley's divisions separated from Newton by over a mile. Finally, after wasting valuable time in moving to the right, the Confederate attack began about 4:00 P.M.[28]

The assault went badly for the Confederates right from the beginning. Hardee's corps was lined up against the left of the Federal line defended by Howard's 4th Corps. General Bate's division, on Hardee's right, went too far to the east and "finding no enemy in his immediate front, was directed to find, and, if practicable, to turn, their flank, but his advance through an almost impenetrable thicket was necessarily slow."[29]

It appears as if Bate had wandered into the gap between Newton and Wood. Newton, in his report, states that it was Bate's troops that assailed his left and rear. For a while there was a serious threat that the Confederates might be able to gain the rear of Newton through the gap and cut him off from the bridges over the creek. However, the Federal regiments on that flank were aided by some well-placed artillery. As General Howard observed,

> Newton has some eight or ten big guns in reserve, two good batteries, and what is more they are just where they are needed. These, using canister, are leveled upon the enemy's flanking division, and as the swift Confederates advance toward the creek they are cut down like grain before the mowers. The enemy approach within one hundred yards of these guns, but no column of men can live to traverse the remaining distance.[30]

Hardee's center division, commanded by General Walker along with General Maney on his left, struck the Federal line along Newton's front and right and the fighting there was fierce and deadly. Howard wrote that the Confederates came on "in masses rather than lines. They are close upon our men before they are seen."[31] General Newton reported that, "The fire had scarcely subsided on my left and rear when it broke out on my front and right flank where Kimball held. The enemy came completely around his right front."[32]

The slight breastworks that had been thrown up by the Union troops served them well as they fired on the enemy. Colonel Kimball, on the front and right, reported that he saw the Confederates "in two lines of battle, charging with great confidence with a rapidity and an absence of confusion I have never seen equaled," but that after a severe fight, "[h]e was repulsed with terrible loss." During the battle Newton's men were firing in three directions almost simultaneously.[33]

The first attack lasted about 30 minutes, but the Army of Tennessee never gave up that quickly. On the Confederate right another attempt was made to gain the Federal rear through the gap in Howard's divisions. As before, concentrated artillery fire broke up the attack before it could cause any damage. General Newton reported that after the first attack, "the enemy made frequent attacks on my line, though none so severe as the first, and a constant fire had to be kept up along my lines until dark. Owing to the partial protection of the rail barricades, and the fine natural position, my loss was very slight."[34]

Confederate Lieutenant General William Hardee

To the right of Newton's division, the 20th Corps occupied the center area of the Federal lines. General Ward's division, which had just come up earlier that afternoon, and General Geary's division bore the brunt of the attack from Stewart's Confederates. Ward's division was just then moving up to their place beside Newton when Loring's division of Stewart's corps fell upon them. Trying to give the division time to set up in line of battle the Federal skirmishers held their ground until the main Confederate line forced them back under heavy fire.[35]

There had been no time for Ward's men to dig in so he surprised the Confederates by advancing to meet them. As the Federals moved forward they absorbed their skirmishers and then met the Confederates head on. Ward reported:

> The first line of the rebels was shattered in a few minutes, my advance was hardly checked a minute, the enemy had evidently believed themselves in a gap between

general Geary and the Fourth Army Corps. Meeting my line of battle seemed to completely addle their brains. Their first line broke, mixing up with the second line; they were now in the wildest confusion, firing in all directions, some endeavoring to get away, some undecided what to do, others rushing into our lines.[36]

Keeping up his fire all the time Ward advanced his division up to a hill where he made a solid connection with Newton on his left and Geary's division on the right. Ward had no artillery support and with most of the fighting out in the open the casualties for both sides were high. The first attack was over in about half an hour but the firing continued well into the evening. General Ward reported:

The enemy was rallying his men in the woods, keeping up a constant fire on our lines, and made several attempts to charge. We returned the fire vigorously, repulsed the charges before they got far out of the woods. This was kept up briskly until 6 P.M., when the fire began to abate, but a brisk skirmishing fire was kept up until dark.[37]

The main force of General Stewart's attack seems to have fallen on Geary and Williams' division in the center and right of Hooker's corps. The left portion of Geary's line was in open country but his right, and William's division were in wooded country with ravines running all through the area. The difficult terrain forced gaps in the lines between Geary and Williams, and between brigades in Williams' division. General Geary's troops were in the process of fortifying their position, which was in advance of the divisions on either side, when the Confederates struck.[38]

The Confederates fell on Geary's men in a ferocious attack, causing heavy casualties among the Federal skirmishers. The left and center of the line was able to hold position but as Geary's skirmishers were forced back, "Scarcely had they rejoined the main body when the enemy, in immense force, rapidly and fiercely burst upon the right flank of Candy's and Jones' brigades and passed their flanks to their rear, at the same time charging on Candy's front, right, and rear." That side of Geary's division was forced back almost to the bridgehead near Peachtree Creek before they could be stabilized and formed at nearly a right angle to the rest of the division, facing west. The fighting here was as fierce as any that day and it was here that Stewart's troops made their deepest penetrations and the Federals suffered their worst casualties. The firing was so heavy that Howard wrote later, "the trees and thickets afterward seemed to have been bruised and broken by some terrific tornado." Like on the rest of the field the Confederates here were finally pushed back from the Union lines but continued to keep up their fire until after dark.[39]

When the Confederates pushed back the right of Geary's troops that also put them on the left flank of Williams' division, in between the Federal divisions. Like the other Federal divisions Williams' line was first struck on the left and then across its front. One advantage Williams had was that, hearing the sounds of battle heading his way, he was able to place several batteries of artillery on high ground that commanded his left and front. General Williams reported, "Hardly had these dispositions been made before the enemy advanced upon us in great force, driving in our skirmishers with his line of battle, and, under cover of the thickets and undergrowth, coming close upon our lines before being seen."[40]

The terrain played a large part in the battle on this end of the field as Confederate columns were able to move through ravines on both sides of Williams' division, temporarily forcing back troops on both flanks. The Confederates fought just as fiercely here as they did along the rest of the line. Rice Bull of the 123rd New York later wrote:

> During the afternoon the enemy made five charges on our line, coming at times within one hundred feet; yet I did not see a single Johnnie. The clouds of smoke from the muskets of both sides and from Winegar's Battery poured down on us to hide everything but the flash of the enemy's guns that gave us their position.[41]

The fighting on this end of the lines continued until dark with multiple Confederate attacks that only increased their casualties. Bull commented that the firing continued until seven o'clock and that the gunbarrels of their muskets "would get so hot we could scarcely hold them." Parts of the far left of the Confederate line struck the left of Palmer's 14th Corps but they were easily brushed back.[42]

After the battle Hood put most of the blame for the defeat on General Hardee. The delay in launching the attack allowed Thomas to bring his entire army across Peachtree Creek and throw up at least some protection for his troops. The delay was brought about because Hood had ordered Hardee to move "one half division front to the right" and keep in contact with Cheatham's corps facing Schofield and McPherson to the east. Unfortunately Cheatham was not where Hood thought he was and there was about a two-mile gap between Hardee's right and Cheatham's left.[43]

As General Stewart reported, in order to stay connected with the troops on the right he had to move his corps

> fully a mile and a half or two miles to the right, and my right division [Loring's] did not move forward, following the one on its right in the prescribed order, until near 4 o'clock. And, when the assault finally did get under way, Loring's division was struck by an enfilade fire from the right, because the left division of the other corps had not moved up to the attack.[44]

General Loring's report puts the blame for failure on the lack of coordination among the various commands. He reported that

> when engaged in a desperate, though successful, struggle against overwhelming odds in our front, it was with pain that we discovered that the co-operating forces had not yet engaged the enemy, thus enabling him to pour into our ranks an enfilading fire from both directions, which gradually thinned my brave officers and men and enabled the enemy in our front to rally.[45]

General Thomas' army suffered fewer than 2,000 casualties and Stewart and Hardee nearly 5,000. For months Sherman and his commanders had been unable to get the Confederates out in the open. Now, Hood had come out and attacked Sherman and the results were a resounding Federal victory.[46]

This was Hood's first battle as commander of the Army of Tennessee. The idea of catching Thomas in the act of crossing Peachtree Creek was a very good one, but the shifting of entire corps and staggered attack formation was probably poor planning. It might have been better to just launch the attack straightaway. Whatever the cause for the failure one thing was certain: one defeat would not discourage John Bell Hood.

There was another important event that occurred on July 20, 1864. This was the day that the first of many federal artillery shells fell on the city of Atlanta. This first shell exploded at the intersection of East Ellis and Ivy streets. Legend has it that a young couple and their child happened to be walking by at that moment and the child was killed.[47]

Chapter 9

Battle of Atlanta

There would be no respite for either army after the bloody battle along Peachtree Creek. Always looking for an opening that might be exploited, General Hood found one thanks to his cavalry, as he explained:

> The failure on the 20th, rendered urgent the most active measures, in order to save Atlanta even for a short period. Through the vigilance of General Wheeler, I received information, during the night of the 29th, of the exposed position of McPherson's left flank; it was standing out in air, near the Georgia Railroad between Decatur and Atlanta, and a large number of the enemy's wagons had been parked in and around Decatur. The roads were in good condition, and ran in the direction to enable a large body of our Army to march, under cover of darkness, around this exposed flank, and attack in rear.[1]

General Hood's surprising information was entirely correct. As General McPherson moved westward from Decatur toward Atlanta his army moved along the railroad with Logan's Fifteenth Corps and Blair's Seventeenth Corps on the left and Dodge's Sixteenth Corps on the right in a mostly north-south line. As Sherman's armies closed on Atlanta they began to run out of room as the circle of troops contracted. On the north side of the railroad the Sixteenth Corps was squeezed out of position when the Fifteenth Corps connected with General Schofield's Army of the Ohio. As McPherson's army advanced the cavalry division that was guarding the left flank of the army was pulled out to go on a raid to destroy railroad track to the east. This left the end of McPherson's line unprotected and vulnerable to an attack on the flank or rear.[2]

Early on the 21st General Cleburne, who had missed the assault at Peachtree Creek when he was sent to reinforce Cheatham, finally reached the far right of the Confederate line and extended the defenses south of the Georgia Railroad, right in front of McPherson. For most of the day there was vicious fighting along the eastern front as the Federals continued to push toward Atlanta.[3]

A portion of Cleburne's line rested on a hill that had a commanding view of the area and both sides decided that they needed that piece of real estate. Just after sunrise Brig. Gen. Mortimer D. Leggett advanced his Third Division against this hill initiating a series of attacks and counterattacks that lasted for hours. Gen. Frank P. Blair, commander of the Seventeenth Corps, reported: "The enemy made a stubborn resistance, having been strongly re-enforced during the night ... but the Third Division moved upon them at a double-quick and took possession of their works."[4]

The Confederates quickly reformed and made several attempts to drive the Federals off the hill, but General Leggett fought them off in a series of bloody little fights that cost the Confederates dearly. While Leggett's men were repulsing the enemy General Blair reported

> As soon as the Third Division took possession of the hill on their front, I ordered the Fourth Division to advance, to engage the enemy, and prevent them from turning their whole force upon General Leggett. The enemy occupied a line of works in front of the fourth Division, in the edge of a wood, about 600 yards from our intrenchments, the intervening ground being an open field.... The division moved gallantly forward in two lines and were met by a heavy fire of musketry. They continued to advance until nearing the top, when the enemy opened with artillery loaded with grape and canister at such short range, and with such deadly effect, as to stop our advance.[5]

By 9 A.M. General Leggett had placed a battery of artillery on the hill and began sending shells into Atlanta, only about a mile and a half away. General Blair commented, "The position thus secured by General Leggett was one of the greatest importance, and commanded all the ground occupied subsequently by the Army of the Tennessee."[6]

General Hood carefully explained his plan to the corps commanders—Hardee, Stewart, and Cheatham—together with the cavalry commander, Major General Wheeler, and the commander of the Georgia state troops, Maj. Gen. G.W. Smith:

> Stewart, Cheatham, and G.W. Smith, were ordered to occupy soon after dark the positions assigned to them in the new line round the city, and to entrench as thoroughly as possible. General Shoupe, chief of artillery, was ordered to mass artillery on our right. General Hardee was directed to put his corps in motion soon after dusk; to move south on the McDonough road across Entrenchment creek at Cobb's Mills, and to completely turn the left of McPherson's Army and attack at daylight, or as soon thereafter as possible.[7]

In addition to the infantry attack by Hardee's corps, General Wheeler was to move on Hardee's right and join in the assault. General Cheatham's corps, occupying the fortifications on the east side of Atlanta, was to join in the attack as soon as Hardee broke the Federal line from the left with the objective of driving the Federals from right to left and back to Peachtree Creek. Finally, General Smith's state troops would also join the attack once it was in progress. General Stewart was to stay in his fortified position on the left and make sure that General Thomas did not send reinforcements to Schofield and McPherson, and to engage Thomas once the battle became general.[8]

After dark on the 21st the Confederates began their movements to attack McPherson and shift their defensive positions around Atlanta. General Hardee's corps, which was still north of Atlanta, got under way on schedule. General Cheatham's corps, already on the east side of the city, had been fighting all day and the exhausted troops did not begin to move into their new positions until almost midnight. Cleburne's division of Hardee's corps was especially tired after marching to the east on the 20th and then fighting against McPherson's troops most of that day. The weather was typical for Georgia in July, hot and humid, and despite frequent halts for rest, hundreds of Hardee's men fell behind or dropped exhausted along the road. Long before dawn it was obvious that the Confederates would not be able to reach the end of McPherson's line in time to launch the attack on schedule at dawn.[9]

After the exhausting night march it was not until near noon that Hardee was able to form his line of bat-

Confederate Lieutenant General Benjamin F. Cheatham

tle on the flank and rear of McPherson's army. The left of the Confederate line was aiming for the left flank and rear of the Federal Seventeenth Corps, and Hardee's right would sweep around and hit the rear of the Fifteenth Corps to the north. The advance in line was over a rough and broken country, intersected on the right by swamps and heavy woods on the left so dense that it was impossible to preserve the formation and proper angle of attack.[10]

Gen. Giles A. Smith's division of the Seventeenth Corps occupied the extreme left of General McPherson's line. And they were now blessed with an enormous stroke of luck. On the 21st Brig. Gen. John W. Fuller's division of the Sixteenth Corps was moved behind the Seventeenth Corps and on the morning of the 22nd General Dodge's other division, commanded by Brig. Gen. T.W. Sweeney was ordered to take a position on the left of the Seventeenth Corps. Just before noon General Sweeney's men halted behind Fuller's troops to await final orders as to their new position. Maj. W.H. Chamberlin called the movement of Sweeney's division, "the most fortunate for the Union army that could have been ordered, even if the intention of the enemy had been known to us." While the men were resting sporadic firing began coming from the southeast, to the left of and behind the Union line.[11]

General Dodge ordered Fuller to form his troops facing the sound of the firing and as he was riding toward Sweeney's position "Hardee's lines came tearing wildly through the woods with the yells of demons."[12] General Dodge wrote, "Where I stood just at the rear of the Sixteenth Army Corps, I could see the entire line of that corps, and could look up and see the enemy's entire front as they emerged from the woods, and I quickly saw that both of my flanks were overlapped by the enemy."[13]

General Dodge got both of his divisions in line facing southeast as the Confederates pressed their attack. His line, with Sweeney on the left and Fuller on the right, was almost perpendicular to the main line of the Seventeenth Corps which faced west. As General Dodge reported,

> [s]carcely was the line formed when the enemy in three columns emerged from the timber on our left, front, and right. I saw that I could not prolong my line to connect with the Seventeenth Army Corps, a long belt of timber lying between my right and its line of battle that faced west."

This gap between the Sixteenth and Seventeenth Corps would be a source of serious problems all day long.[14]

The right side of the Confederate line, Bate and Walker's divisions, were as surprised to find Dodge's troops in front of them as Dodge was to see the Confederates coming out of the woods. This part of Hardee's line had been assigned to come up behind the Seventeenth Corps while the left of their line struck the Federals in the flank.[15]

As the Confederates advanced they were able to put a column of men past the right of Fuller's troops and behind the Seventeenth Corps. General Dodge sent aides to General Smith to warn him that enemy troops were getting behind him and requesting that the Seventeenth Corps extend to join with his corps, but by this time Smith's men were too hotly engaged to move.[16]

Lt. Col. W.E. Strong, McPherson's chief-of-staff, saw

> [t]he enemy, massed in columns three or four lines deep, moved out of the dense timber several hundred yards from Dodge's position, and, after gaining fairly the open fields, halted and opened fire rapidly on the Sixteenth Corps. They, however, seemed surprised to find our infantry in line of battle prepared for attack, and, after facing for a few minutes the destructive fire from the troops of Generals Fuller and Sweeny, fell back in disorder to the cover of the woods. Here, however, their lines were quickly re-formed, and they again advanced, evidently determined to carry the position.[17]

As General Fuller reported, the Twenty-seventh Ohio and Thirty-ninth Ohio regiments "charged as soon as the enemy's line had again emerged from the woods" and this surprise attack "so thoroughly routed that portion of the enemy's line which was in front of these regiments, and sent them back in such confusion, that his supports retire also, and no enemy afterward showed himself on that part of the field."[18]

The Confederates kept coming on other parts of the field and soon their columns approached the center of Fuller's line, threatening to cut off the Twenty-seventh and Thirty-ninth Ohio regiments. The noise on the battlefield was too loud to transmit orders so as General Fuller reported,

> the colors were moved out from the confused mass toward the approaching enemy, and my sword indicated where the line should be reformed. The men of the Twenty-seventh [Ohio], noting this movement of their colors, and instantly comprehending what was required, with a great shout came up on either side.... The Thirty-ninth [Ohio] instantly formed on their left, bayonets were brought down to a charge, our men advanced, and the rebels, now distant less than a hundred yards, came to a right-about, and ran back into the woods.[19]

Despite this setback along other parts of the field Bate and Walker's Confederates fearlessly attacked. Major Chamberlin wrote,

> Their assaults were repulsed, only to be fearlessly renewed, until the sight of dead and wounded lying in their way, as they charged again and again to break our lines, must have appalled the stoutest hearts. So persistent were their onslaughts that numbers were made prisoners by rushing directly into our lines.[20]

In another part of the field an advancing column of Confederates was brought to a halt and took cover behind a rail fence. General Fuller saw

> a general officer [supposed to be General Walker] rode out from the woods, and swinging his hat made a great effort to urge forward his troops. The next moment his horse went back riderless, and so sharp was the fire of our men that the enemy disappeared almost immediately.... The slaughter here may be judged from the report of Colonel Sheldon, who found as many as 13 dead rebels in a single fence corner.[21]

As the Confederates forced their way between the Sixteenth and Seventeenth Corps they exposed their flank to General Dodge who moved forward the Twelfth Illinois and Eighty-first Ohio. As General Logan wrote these two regiments, "delivered so destructive a fire on the enemy's flank that his column gave way. A charge was made, and the enemy fell back to the woods. General Dodge then withdrew his line a short distance to the rear."[22]

There was still heavy fighting behind and to the right of Dodge's line, where the Confederates had gotten between Dodge and Smith's division. The Seventeenth Corps had swung back a part of their line in an attempt to halt the flow of enemy troops to their rear. General Dodge attempted to close the gap from his side by swinging his right backward, "using the left as a pivot, until my command occupied a line facing a little west of south, and a short distance to the rear of my first line. Temporary intrenchments were immediately thrown up."[23]

General Dodge also tried to get some help for General Sweeney's troops who were out on the end of the line on the far left. General Logan sent Colonel Martin's brigade from the Fifteenth Corps and just as they were forming on the left the Confederates launched yet another attack on that end of the line. Fortunately the enemy did not press the assault as hard as they had earlier and they were soon repulsed.[24]

While Dodge's troops were fighting off the determined Confederates, Gen. Giles A. Smith's division, on the southern end of the main line, was almost surrounded by attackers. With only the briefest warning the divisions of Cleburne and Maney had worked their way through the woods and underbrush and smashed into the end of the Federal left. General Smith had a short line of works running back from his main line to protect the rear of his position and these men were soon pushed backward and doubled on to the main line. With the Confederates flooding around both sides of his line, Smith was soon facing hordes of enemy troops in front, left and rear. The veteran Federal troops in the main line were forced to turn about and fight on the reverse side of their works, and as General Smith reported, "My whole line was now hotly engaged, and although fighting from the opposite side of their works from the one intended ... it afforded them very good protection, while their well directed and rapid volleys were doing great execution in the enemy's ranks." The Confederates were temporarily stopped on this front and pulled back to re-group.[25]

Just as the attack on the rear of the Third Division was fought off another column of Confederates had swept around the end of the line and came up on what had originally been the front of the Federal lines, but was now the rear. Just as quickly as they faced to the rear, Smith's men had to jump up and turn to their original front to face this new threat. General Smith then repositioned some of his troops:

> two regiments of Colonel Hall's brigade were formed perpendicular to the work on which the left rested, the right extending toward Atlanta. Colonel Potts' brigade was formed about seventy-five yards to the rear of Colonel Hall's perpendicular line and parallel to his, both being directed to hold that position against any odds.[26]

The Confederate attack across the original front of the Federal works struck Col. William Hall's short line on the front and right simultaneously, forcing his troops back into the main line where they continued the fight. As soon as Hall's men were out of the way Col. Benjamin F. Potts' longer line opened fire on the advancing enemy. As the Confederates came on General Smith reported

> the main opposition they met was the brigade of Colonel Potts, consisting at that time of not more than 1,000 men, in the open field without cover. They, however, maintained their ground, and after a determined but unsuccessful effort of the enemy to break their lines, he gave way in confusion, and retreated into the woods beyond.[27]

It was now nearly 4:00 P.M., and although the fighting had been raging for over three hours, it was not nearly over. Within minutes of the repulse of the Confederate attack on the west side of Smith's lines they came on again, this time out of the wooded area between the Sixteenth and Seventeenth Corps. Once again General Smith's troops had to jump over their works and fight from the opposite side in what would turn out to be a most desperate fight. The Confederates were able to use the cover from the woods to approach to within 20 yards of the Federal works before they were discovered. Much of the fight was at close quarters, as General Smith wrote:

Regimental commanders, with their colors, and such men as would follow them, would not unfrequently occupy one side of the works and our men the other. Many individual acts of heroism here occurred. The flags of two opposing regiments would meet on the opposite sides of the same works, and would be flaunted by their respective bearers in each other's faces. Men were bayoneted across the works and officers with their swords fought hand-to-hand with men with bayonets. Colonel Belknap, of the Fifteenth Iowa Volunteers, took prisoner Colonel Lampley, of the Forty-fifth Alabama, by pulling him over the works by his coat collar, being several times fired at by men at his side. The enemy's loss in this attack must have been very severe. It lasted for nearly three-quarters of an hour, when they reluctantly retired.[28]

Before the fighting began that morning General McPherson was meeting with General Sherman. When the firing began the young army commander dashed off toward his troops. As McPherson approached the battlefield the noise from artillery and musket fire grew so loud that it was obvious that a major encounter was taking place. McPherson sent off his aides to bring reinforcements from the Fifteenth Corps over to the exposed left flank. He was riding through a wooded area that was thought to be too far away from the lines to be dangerous when suddenly Confederate skirmishers called out for him to surrender. Turning his horse to escape he was shot and killed on the spot. General Logan took over command of the Army of the Tennessee for the duration of the battle.[29]

Despite the efforts of both Generals Dodge and Smith to close the gap between their two corps it was still wide enough to allow large numbers of Confederates to move through the woods and move past the Federal positions to the north, trying to gain the rear of General Leggett's division on the bald hill. About the same time as General Smith's troops were fighting front and back a large force of Confederates made an assault on Leggett's part of the Federal line. As General Logan said, "The most important position in the then field of operations was the Bald Hill, occupied by the Third division, of the Seventeenth Corps. It commanded the whole field occupied by the lines, and covered all ground on which were the trains of the Army of the Tennessee."[30]

One of General McPherson's last orders brought Col. Hugo Wangelin's brigade, the First Division of the Fifteenth Corps, up to the gap between the Sixteenth and Seventeenth Corps and engaged the head of an enemy column that was evidently moving to strike the rear of Leggett's division which was a little to the north. Although Wangelin's brigade was small, he threw it into line of battle and, moving under a heavy fire, steadily pushed the enemy in his front backward until he reached a slight elevation of ground, where he halted his brigade and built a breastwork of rails.[31]

The Second Brigade of the Fourth Division, Fifteenth Corps, was on the right of General Leggett's division. The commander of this brigade, Brig. Gen. Charles C. Walcutt, could tell from the direction of the firing that the Confederates were coming his way in force. General Walcutt quickly ordered his men to change their position and face to the rear. The brigade had scarcely reversed their position when a column of the enemy came rushing forward. Walcutt's brigade poured a heavy musket fire into the advancing Confederates, giving them a bloody reception and forcing them to fall back. They reformed and, moving to the right, attacked the division of General Leggett. This allowed General Walcutt to open an effective fire on the Confederate flank, which was made even more effective by a section of 24-pounder howitzers, belonging to the Seventeenth Corps.[32]

Union soldier George W. Pepper described the combat as the Confederate attacks came from different directions:

> Generals Leggett and Smith both put their men over their works, and met the enemy's mad charge with a terrible volley of musketry. The enemy pushed, however, up to within a few feet of our works, but was finally repulsed with a slaughter almost unparalleled. They fell back, reformed their lines and soon came up again in the same direction, and the conflict for some time was a hand to hand combat, the bayonet and the clubbed muskets were freely used, and the enemy again repulsed, leaving the ground literally carpeted with the dead and wounded. After a quiet of a few minutes, the enemy, a part of Hood's old Corps, was discovered moving upon us from the front. Generals Smith and Leggett placed their men to the rear of their works, and met the charge with the same determined spirit that had characterized them in meeting the former onslaught. The enemy came with deafening yells, and were met with murderous volleys, and again successfully driven back. Again they rallied and forced their way up to our works, and again were repulsed with great slaughter.[33]

Back at the Howard House, General Sherman was receiving reports on the fighting and knew how serious the situation was, but he was confident that the Army of the Tennessee would prevail. He tried to get Generals Thomas and Schofield to take advantage of "the absence from their front of so considerable a body as was evidently engaged on our left, and, if possible, to make a lodgment in Atlanta itself; but they reported that the lines to their front, at all accessible points, were strong, by nature and by art, and were fully manned."[34]

Now in command of the Army of the Tennessee, General Logan reported:

> I therefore gave General Blair, commanding the Seventeenth Corps, the most positive and emphatic orders to hold the hill at whatever cost. It was apparent, also, that our most imminent danger was from the great interval between the Seventeenth and Sixteenth Corps. In order to close it, and at the same time adjust our lines in such manner that the Bald Hill might be held, I ordered General Blair, as soon as it could be done with safety, to bring his Fourth Division back to such a line that its right should connect with Leggett's left, and the left of the division with Colonel Wangelin's brigade. I also ordered General Dodge to swing his right, or refused line, up, so as to connect with the left of Wangelin's brigade.[35]

It was now late in the afternoon and the battle had been raging for over two hours. So far the Confederates had been unable to dislodge the left side of the Federal line, but they did capture a short portion of the main line on the left, and were established in the woods between the Sixteenth and Seventeenth Corps. So far the Confederates had concentrated on the left of the Federal line and there had been no attacks on the Fifteenth Corps holding the right of the Army of the Tennessee, but that was about to change.[36]

Around 4:00 o'clock Cheatham's troops joined the battle as they stormed out of their main line of works around Atlanta. Attacking in columns they moved rapidly against the Second Division of the Fifteenth Corps, commanded by Brig. Gen. Joseph Lightburn. Both sides fought hard and the first Confederate attack was repulsed with heavy losses. Again Cheatham's men came on, and again they were beaten back but as General Logan reported, "The withdrawal of Colonel Martin's brigade from the Second Division, to re-enforce the Sixteenth Corps, made an interval between the right of the Second and the left of the First Division, which was held by a thin line of skirmishers." The only other reserve force that had been in the area was Colonel Wangelin's brigade from the First Division, which had earlier in the day been withdrawn to the gap between the Sixteenth and Seventeenth Corps. Now, when the Confederates were launching attacks from a totally different source, the Fifteenth Corps had no reserve troops to help defend their own lines.[37]

The gap between the First and Second Divisions provided a golden opportunity that every attacking force hopes to find, a thin line of defenders with little or no support to back them up. It was to this point that a column of Cheatham's men were able to move through a deep railroad cut and attack the rear of the line, forcing the Federals back and capturing several pieces of artillery. Gens. Lightburn and Morgan L. Smith worked quickly to reorganize their troops in a ravine behind the line. This breakthrough gave the Confederates a position on the left and rear of the First Division, commanded by Gen. Charles R. Woods, which was located on the right of the Second Division. To protect his position Woods was forced to pull back the left side of his line to face the threat from his side.[38]

General Woods' division was on the far right of the Army of the Tennessee and connected with General Schofield's army to the north. General Sherman, who was overseeing the battle from near the Howard House, ordered Schofield to bring forward all his available artillery, 20 guns in total, and position them to the left of the Howard House where they could fire at the Confederates over the heads of Woods' troops.[39]

General Logan reported that a brief but fierce fight occurred as

> General Woods then moved his First Brigade forward, attacking the enemy in flank and rear, and his Second Brigade in flank and front. At the same time the Second Division, followed at a short distance by Colonel Marsy's brigade, advanced upon the enemy's front. The movement was successful. Woods' division striking the enemy's flank, it began to break, and soon afterward the Second Division charging his front, the line of works, De Gress' battery, and 2 guns of Battery A were recaptured. General Woods swung his left around, and the whole line of the First and Second Divisions was reoccupied with no opposition, except a fierce assault upon the Fourth Iowa, which was repulsed.[40]

About 6:00 o'clock Hood launched another attack from the direction of Atlanta. Gen. Giles Smith had just changed the position of his division to the east side of his works when his left and rear were struck by a heavy fire of musketry and artillery, and his men were forced to abandon another portion of his works. Falling back a short distance General Smith stated that he then

> formed Colonel Potts' brigade in rear of our work, and perpendicular to it, with a portion of Colonel Hall's troops on his right, the remainder occupying the works

vacated by General Leggett's command. This perpendicular line was so nearly enfiladed by the fire from the advancing troops from Atlanta that I was compelled to swing my right still farther back, connecting with a portion of the Third Division, formed across a corn-field, facing south.[41]

The fighting moved along the Federal lines and General Logan reported that

> General Leggett moved out his Second Brigade in a line parallel to that which General Smith then held. Colonel Wangelin's brigade, of the First Division of the Fifteenth Corps, moved forward, and a new line was formed with the Second Brigade of the Third Division, Seventeenth Corps, on the right, the Fourth Division of the Seventeenth Corps the center, and the Third Brigade of the First Division of the Fifteenth Corps on the left. It extended to the crest of Bald Hill, which two regiments of the Seventeenth Corps, the Eleventh Iowa and Sixteenth Wisconsin, held behind an angle of the works, the enemy holding the same works a little below, four of their colors planted within a stone's throw of the colors of the Eleventh Iowa. Upon this line the enemy made an attack in very heavy force. The battle was very severe.[42]

George Pepper remembered that

> [t]here was no pause in the battle. The roar of the strife was ever heard. The artillery bellowed and thundered, and the dreadful echoes went sweeping down the valley, and the paths were filled with the dying and the dead. The sound was deafening — the tumult indescribable. The rebels fought with a fierceness seldom, if ever equaled.[43]

This was to be the final push by the Confederates to break the Federal lines and they put forth every effort that mortal men could, and were met with equal resolve by the Federal troops. General Blair noted that the Confederates,

> advancing up to our breast-works on the crest of the hill, placed their flags side by side with ours, and fought hand-to-hand until it grew so dark that nothing could be seen but the flash of the guns, from the opposite side of the same works. The enemy seemed determined to retake the hill, which was the key-point to the whole of my line, and controlled, to a great extent, the position held by the other corps. General Leggett was equally resolute to hold this important point, and his troops responded nobly to his spirit. The ground over which this assault was made was literally strewn with the enemy's dead, but as the enemy held the ground up to our lines until nearly daylight the next morning, he was able to remove all of his wounded and the dead bodies of many officers.[44]

While the main battle of Atlanta was going on there was a smaller but no less deadly fight about seven miles away near Decatur. Brig. Gen. John W. Sprague's Second Brigade, Fourth Division, of the Sixteenth Corps, was in charge of protecting a massive supply train from Wheeler's cavalry that had moved around the far right of Hardee's advancing force. His fight was a gallant and sometimes seemingly almost hopeless one — giving ground inch by inch, until; finally, he obtained a position that he could not be driven from, and one that protected the entire trains of the army.[45]

General Sprague described his fight with Wheeler's troopers as they seemingly came from all sides:

> There was little difficulty in checking the advance of the enemy in front at any time during the action, but [as] the masses passing to my rear on the right and left would endanger the trains in town and on the road from Roswell, I fell back to the hill at the south line of the town. The line was soon formed with six guns on position, and the fight continued until the town was very nearly enveloped by the superior numbers of the enemy, when I again fell back into the court-house square, fighting from three sides of it.... The trains of the Fifteenth Corps, which were in town when the fight commenced, had all withdrawn and were safe.[46]

Although General Sprague felt he could hold his position the trains coming up from Roswell would be exposed to attack unless he was able to move out to protect them, "so I withdrew from the town on the Roswell road, and made a short stand just north of the place to beat off the enemy who were approaching from the west." The trains passed by the rear of Sprague's line and made it to safety.[47]

General Sherman wrote of the Army of the Tennessee, "nobly did they do their work that day, and terrible was the slaughter done to our enemy, though at sad cost to ourselves." Since Civil War battles were generally very bloody affairs most generals grew to accept that high casualties was a part of winning battles so the "sad cost" that Sherman referred to was most likely the death of General McPherson. The casualties among the fighting men on both sides were high but the Confederates suffered terribly. Sherman reported total casualties of 3,521, while reporting that his men buried or delivered to the Confederates over 3,700 dead. Most estimates give total Confederate casualties of about 8,000 or more.[48]

By any measurement the Battle of Atlanta was a Confederate calamity. General Hood blamed the defeat on General Hardee for not attacking in the correct location. But it could be reasonably argued that Hardee did everything anyone could have done with an exhausted army after a long night march in scorching heat. The real reason the Federals were saved that day was the fantastic luck that had General Dodge's divisions resting at the exact spot and at the exact time that they would be needed most. If Dodge had not been where he was it is doubtful that Gen. Giles Smith's division could have fought off the combined Confederate attacks from flank and rear that would have struck his men almost simultaneously.

In an attempt to put the best face on an obvious defeat General Hood later wrote:

> It became apparent almost immediately after the battle of the 22d that Sherman would make an attack upon our left, in order to destroy the Macon Railroad; and from that moment, I may say, began the siege of Atlanta. The battles of the 20th and 22d checked the enemy's reckless manner of moving and illustrated effectually to Sherman the danger of stretching out his line in such a manner as to form extensive gaps between his Corps, or Armies.[49]

In an effort to blame the defeat on Gen. Joseph Johnston, Hood also wrote, "My failure on the 20th, and 22nd, to bring about a general pitched battle arose from the unfortunate policy pursued from Dalton to Atlanta, and which had wrought such demoralization amid rank and file as to render the men unreliable in battle."[50] Contrary to Hood's excuses, if any soldier in Sherman's army, from the commander on down, were asked if they would like to have the Army of Tennessee fighting for them the answer would surely have been an emphatic yes.

Chapter 10

A City Under Siege

Through the early part of the summer everyday life in Atlanta went on pretty much as before. There was no panic and from the peace and quiet of the city it would seem as if the enemy was over a thousand miles away. The residents knew, of course, that the Yankee army was slowly coming toward them, but confidence in Joe Johnston and his army was high and no one expected to see blue-clad troops in Atlanta, except as prisoners. Mary Gay described what she saw around the city's transportation center: "There was unusual commotion and activity about the depot in Atlanta, and a superficial observer would have been impressed with the businesslike appearance of the little city at that important locality. Men, women, and children moved about as if they meant business."[1]

By the middle of July, however, the citizens of Atlanta finally had to face the fact that the enemy was no longer a distant threat to their city. The enemy had arrived. Parts of Sherman's army were only a few miles from the outskirts of the city, and the defenders were backed up even closer. Government offices and equipment were being moved to Milledgeville and Macon. Gen. Howell Cobb, commanding the Department of Georgia and Florida, moved his headquarters to Macon. Some residents, frightened by the nearness of the gunfire, packed what belongings they could carry and fled south. While many residents were leaving Atlanta others, refugees from the conquered territory, were flooding into the city.[2]

One group of current Atlanta residents that were unable to pick up and leave were the hundreds of wounded Confederate soldiers and the doctors and nurses that cared for them. One of the volunteer nurses, Fannie Beers, wrote about how difficult it was for her to get used to the suffering of her patients:

> At first every death among my patients seemed to me like a personal bereavement. Trying to read or to sing by the bedsides of the dying, uncontrollable tears and sobs would choke my voice. As I looked my last upon dead faces, I would turn away shuddering and sobbing, for a time unfit for duty.

The devotion and courage shown by these civilian volunteers who tended to their wounded countrymen was an inspiration to all.[3]

Many of the people that stayed in their homes tried to prepare for what was expected to be a long siege. Food and other supplies were collected and bomb shelters began appearing in many yards. These were sometimes called "bombproofs" or, sarcastically, "gopher holes," and were basically holes in the ground from six to eight feet deep, with the size dependent on how large a family would be occupying it. Heavy wood planks were laid over the top and then covered with several feet of earth. While there was little that could be done to protect against a direct hit, these shelters did offer safety from near misses and flying shrapnel.[4]

As the Federal army approached Atlanta many of the local citizens were to learn what it meant to be "occupied." The experience of Mary Gay when the invaders arrived at her home was fairly typical:

> Garrard's Cavalry selected our lot, consisting of several acres, for headquarters, and soon what appeared to us to be an immense army train of wagons commenced rolling into it. In less than two hours our barn was demolished and converted into tents....
> Men in groups were playing cards on tables of every size and shape; and whisky and profanity held high carnival. Thus surrounded we could but be apprehensive of danger; and, to assure ourselves of as much safety as possible, we barricaded the doors and windows, and arranged to sit up all night, that is, my mother and myself.[5]

Although the battles on the 20th and 22nd were clear-cut Federal victories, this did not solve Sherman's main problem: how to get into Atlanta. The fortifications that protected the city were as strong as any in the country. Massive earthworks were fronted with ditches and other obstructions. There were forts in strategic locations and artillery commanded all the approaches. To make any type of large, open-field attack against these impregnable fortifications would make the Kennesaw Mountain disaster look like a picnic.[6]

Unwilling to attack Hood in his works, Sherman knew there was another way to bring Atlanta to its knees. With his army now situated mostly on the north and northeast of the city, Sherman decided to shift his troops around to the west. The targets of this movement were the Confederate railroads. The importance of the railroads in this campaign had always been apparent to Sherman; he was never far from the tracks as he moved through northern Georgia, and at Atlanta it was even more obvious that the railroads were the key to victory.[7]

The two railroad lines that were targeted for destruction brought the majority of food and supplies into the city. Heading southwest out of Atlanta the track was shared by both railroads for a few miles until it reached East Point. There, one track split off to the south, ran through Jonesboro, then down to Macon in the center of the state. The other line was the Atlanta & West Point, which went west through Alabama and Mississippi. If Sherman could cut these two rail lines Hood would have to abandon Atlanta or starve.[8]

Sherman decided to move the Army of the Tennessee, now commanded by Maj. Gen. Oliver O. Howard, from the left, around the north side of the city, behind Schofield and Thomas, and place them on the right end of the line, west of Atlanta. While Howard's troops were moving, the rest of Sherman's forces were to remain stationary, providing cover for Howard's men while they were in motion. In addi-

Confederate works outside Atlanta

tion, there was to be a massive, two-part cavalry raid that would provide a distraction and attempt to cut the rail lines south of the city.⁹

The Federal movement began on the night of July 26. General Hood was well aware of what Sherman was trying to do and dispatched his old corps, now commanded by Lt. Gen. Stephen D. Lee, from its position east of the city to intercept Howard. Lee's instructions were to get ahead of Howard "and to take the position most advantageous to prevent or delay the extension of the enemy's right flank." Moving behind Lee was General Stewart's corps, which was to make a surprise attack on Howard's right flank while Lee occupied the center.¹⁰

General Howard's men began arriving at their assigned place in the line on the evening of the 27th with General Dodge forming his troops into line that night, facing the city. General Blair brought his corps up early on the 28th with General Logan arriving on the far right of the line later that morning. The right flank of the Federal line ended near a crossroads and an old meeting house called Ezra Church.¹¹

Stephen Lee's Confederates arrived at the crossroads just after the Federal skirmishers began to move out. He "soon found that the enemy had gained the road, and was gradually driving back our cavalry. Brown's division was at once formed on the left of and obliquely to the road, and Clayton's division on the right." Lee was the youngest lieutenant general in the Confederate army and new to the command of a corps. A more experienced man might have waited until all his troops were concentrated so as to make an overpowering attack. Instead, Lee decided to strike the right end of the Federal line before it could set up a good defensive position. Disregarding his instructions to wait for Stewart, Lee sent his men forward in a series of uncoordinated attacks.[12]

The Confederate assault began about 11:30 A.M., with all but a few troops concentrated on Logan's portion of the line. Logan's troops were still in the act of moving forward to their assigned position and Logan was near the front supervising their placement when,

> just as my command had gained the ridge upon which was situated Ezra Chapel, the enemy suddenly and with the greatest fury assaulted the right and center of my line. The troops had not had a moment to construct even the rudest defenses. The position we occupied, however, at the moment of attack was one of the most favorable that could have been chosen by us, it being the crest of a continuous ridge, in front of the greatest portion of which a good and extensive fire line was opened.[13]

General Logan also reported that the Confederates, "moved forward rapidly and in good order, evidently intending to and confidently believing they would break our lines at the first onset...." But Logan's troops were seasoned veterans of many fights and despite the lack of defensive works they stood their ground and Lee's men ran into a storm of bullets as they made the assault.[14]

General Sherman later wrote that Lee's advance "was magnificent, but founded on an error that cost him sadly, for our men coolly and deliberately cut down his men."[15] Brig. Gen. John C. Brown, commanding one of Lee's divisions, wrote, "my troops were driven with great slaughter."[16] General Lee reported that "as soon as Brown was formed he moved forward ... where he encountered temporary breastworks, from which he was driven back with considerable loss. Clayton's division moved forward as soon as formed, and about ten minutes after Brown's advance, and met with similar results."[17] By sending his divisions in one at a time Lee doomed the attack from the start.

Union soldier George W. Pepper remembered:

> The rebels had massed in a dense piece of wood, and dashed in great force upon Logan. On, on came the rebels, in splendid style ... but the gallant Fifteenth remain rooted in its position.... Showers of balls saluted the rebels as they energetically pushed forward to the attack. The enemy seemed to grow, like Hydra's heads, for, even as they were repulsed, they returned reinforced, to sweep our braves from their position. They yielded not an inch of ground.[18]

Six times the Confederates charged General Logan's men, and six times they were repulsed. During the brief respites between attacks the Federal troops worked at improving their meager defenses, some even running out onto the battlefield to retrieve pieces of wood. At one point the Confederates came close to gaining Logan's rear when they began overlapping the far right end of the Federal line. Fortunately several regiments of reinforcements were rushed over from General Blair's corps, and the danger quickly evaporated.[19]

While General Lee's men were being cut down, Stewart's corps came up and joined in the attack. General Walthall reported that he was ordered to attack about 2:00 o'clock and found the enemy "in strong position and large force on a hill a short distance in front, and failed to dislodge him after a vigorous and persistent effort, in which I lost 152 officers and nearly 1,000 men, Considerably over one-third my force."[20]

One of Walthall's brigade commanders, Brig. Gen. William A. Quarles, reported that his men "gained ground upon them but slowly and at heavy cost." After closing to within 50 paces of Logan's troops Quarles realized that "a farther advance with my line of battle, attenuated by casualties to a mere line of skirmishers, would have been fatal to the few left, and even if successful in driving him from his works, would have been barren of results."[21]

After watching his division being shot to pieces, General Walthall later reported:

> If it had been possible for the daring of officers and the desperate fighting of the men to have overcome such odds in numbers and strength of position as we encountered that day all along my whole line, the enemy must have been beaten, but double the force could not have accomplished what my division was ordered to undertake.[22]

The experience of Logan's men was displayed that afternoon as they coolly stood their ground and shot down the attacking Confederates by the hundreds. General Howard wrote that the battle "was as severe a musketry engagement as it was my fortune to see during the war. Our men, being in position, had the advantage. The slight cover of rails and logs was a great protection. They fired low, and ceased firing when the enemy was driven back, thus keeping cool and self-possessed."[23]

Brig. Gen. William Harrow, commanding the Fourth Division of Logan's corps, reported that his

> line was not entirely formed before the enemy attacked in large force and with great desperation. After a brief struggle their first line gave way; a second was moved forward, but after a severe struggle met a like fate. The woods in our front afforded the enemy an opportunity of reforming his broken lines unperceived. The assault upon my lines was repeated six times between 12 A.M. and 5 P.M., and in every instance were met and repulsed with great slaughter.[24]

Another of Logan's division commanders, Brig. Gen. Charles R. Woods, faced assaults that were "several times repulsed, but after each repulse the enemy charged in greater numbers and with greater determination, but finding, however, that they could not break the lines...." Darkness finally ended the slaughter.[25]

The fighting at Ezra Church was the most lopsided Federal victory of the campaign. Howard's casualties were probably about 600 while estimates of the Confederate casualties vary from about 3,500 to a little below 5,000 men. It was more of a massacre than a battle. In some places the Confederate dead lay in rows two or three deep.[26]

So much damage was done to the Army of Tennessee at Ezra Church that General Hardee, displaying some of his disaffection toward Hood, later wrote:

> This fight of the 28th is mentioned by General Hood in terms to leave an impression of its success, but it was well known throughout the army that so great was the loss in men, organization, and morale in that engagement that no action of the campaign probably did so much to demoralize and dishearten the troops engaged in it.[27]

Writing to his wife the day after the battle Sherman compared the tactics of Hood and Joe Johnston: "Hood is a new man and a fighter and must be watched closer, as he is reckless of the lives of his men."[28]

While Sherman's infantry was cutting down Confederates by the hundreds at Ezra Church his cavalry had already begun their raid. Two separate units of horsemen left their camps to sweep around both sides of Atlanta, destroying railroads as they went. Brig. Gen. Edward McCook, leading about 3,500 troopers, was to cross the Chattahoochee southwest of the city then sweep east to Lovejoy's Station, about 25 miles below Atlanta. At the same time, Major General Stoneman, with about 5,500 men, would leave the Decatur area and ride around Atlanta from the east, meeting McCook at Lovejoy's Station. After destroying the Macon & Western Railroad in the area the combined force was to move south to the valuable rail and manufacturing center of Macon, destroying as much of the railroad and other war-related property as possible. In addition to cutting the railroads that fed Atlanta, Stoneman had convinced Sherman to let them try to reach the hellish prison camp at Andersonville, about 50 miles southwest of Macon, and liberate the thousands of Union soldiers held there.[29]

The cavalry expeditions started out on July 27 and at first all went well. McCook arrived at Lovejoy's Station on schedule and destroyed several miles of track and a large quantity of military supplies, but Stoneman was nowhere to be found. As it turned out Stoneman disregarded his orders almost as soon as he left camp and headed directly for Macon. On the way south he sent out several detachments to attack the railroad from Macon to Savannah, burning the bridge across the Oconee River and destroying a large number of railroad engines and cars at Griswold Station. Stoneman finally reached the Ocmulgee River, outside Macon, but running into well-manned fortifications he was unable to get across the river and was forced to turn back.[30]

Both cavalry columns encountered trouble as they made their way back to the Union lines. After McCook learned that a large force of enemy cavalry was blocking the route to where he was to rendezvous with Stoneman, he decided to return to the Federal lines. General McCook reported that "no serious opposition was met until we commenced our return." It was on the return trip that McCook's troopers came close to disaster. Time after time they had to fight their way through Confederate detachments. Before reaching the safety of the Federal lines McCook lost nearly 600 men and much of his equipment.[31]

Stoneman's part of the raid turned into a disastrous loss of men and equipment. After pulling back from the vicinity of Macon, Stoneman ran into a large Confederate force near Clinton, about 10 miles north of Macon. Sending two brigades ahead to make their way back to safety, Stoneman remained with about 700 troopers to cover their escape. General Stoneman along with about 500 of his men were captured while most of the men from the other two brigades eventually trickled back to the Federal lines, many on foot and unarmed.[32]

The failed raid had pretty well wrecked two divisions of Sherman's cavalry with little to show for the sacrifice. However, this wasted effort did convince him that "cavalry could not, or would not, make a sufficient lodgment on the railroad below Atlanta, and that nothing would suffice but for us to reach it with the main army." This final acceptance of the limitations of his cavalry led Sherman to the decision that would set the stage for the decisive Federal movements around Atlanta.[33]

The first week of August brought more hot weather and the skirmishing was unending. General Sherman continued moving south by bringing Schofield's army around behind the rest of the army on the 1st and extending the Federal lines to East Point. Hood made no more attacks but extended his works right along with the Federal lines, always keeping between Sherman and the railroad. Sherman placed General Palmer's 14th Corps under Schofield's command and on August 4th ordered him to attack the Macon railroad near East Point. Palmer refused to serve under Schofield due to a dispute over seniority and Schofield was unable to launch his attack.[34]

There were several changes in commands about this time. Palmer's refusal to accept orders from Schofield was unacceptable and he resigned to be replaced as commander of the 14th Corps by Maj. Gen. Jefferson C. Davis. General Hooker, who was very unhappy that he was not given command of the Army of the Tennessee after McPherson was killed, resigned command of the 20th Corps, which was given to General Slocum. Sherman never did care much for Hooker; in a letter to his wife Sherman wrote that in looking for a successor to McPherson, "I preferred Howard, who is a man of mind and intellect. He is very honest, sincere & moral even to piety but brave having lost an arm already. But he was a junior Major General to Hooker who took offense and has gone away. I don't regret it — he is envious, imperious, and braggart." Maj. Gen. David S. Stanley succeeded Howard as commander of the Fourth Corps.[35]

Sherman had communicated his concern about what he considered the slow progress of his army to General Grant who wrote back on August 7: "Your progress, instead of appearing slow, has received the universal commendation of all loyal citizens, as well as of the President, War Department, and all persons whose commendation you care for." Back in Washington, Sherman's slow but steady progress toward Atlanta and his relatively low number of casualties must have looked like a victory march when compared to the slaughter and stalemate in Virginia.[36]

Sherman's reply to General Grant illustrates his eagerness to prosecute the war as fully as possible:

> Get the War Department to send us recruits daily as they are made, for we can teach them more war in our camps in one day than they can get at a rendezvous in a month. Also tell Mr. Lincoln that he must not make the least concession in the matter of the September draft. It is right, and popular with the army, and the army is worth considering. I am glad you have given General Sheridan the command of the

forces to defend Washington. He will worry Early to death. Let us give those southern fellows all the fighting they want, and when they are tired we can tell them we are just warming to the work. Any signs of let up on our part is sure to be falsely construed, and for this reason I always remind them that the siege of Troy lasted six years, and Atlanta is a more valuable town than Troy. We must manifest the character of dogged courage and perseverance of our race.[37]

In another telegram on August 7, this one to Henry Halleck, Sherman outlined his plans for the fate of Atlanta:

We keep hammering away all the time, and there is no peace inside or outside of Atlanta. I have sent to Chattanooga for two 30-pounder Parrotts, with which we can pick out almost any house in the town. I am too impatient for a siege, but I do not know but here is as good a place to fight it out as farther inland. One thing is certain, whether we get inside of Atlanta or not, it will be a used-up community by the time we are done with it.[38]

While the telegrams went back and forth the fighting and the dying continued. General Dodge reported:

During August 6, 7, and 8, the entire line advanced to the last range of hills fronting Atlanta, and in plain view of the city. This line was heavily intrenched, strong forts constructed, and batteries casemated, and a steady fire kept up upon the enemy's works and the city. During this advance the enemy contested stubbornly every inch of ground, and, by his excellent artillery practice and continuous musketry fire at close range, inflicted a heavy loss to my command in killed and wounded.[39]

The firing across the lines was constant and the soldiers on both sides had to just sit there and take it. General Thomas reported that although Hood was forced to thin out his forces as he kept pace with the Federal lines moving south,

he formed his troops on very advantageous ridges, strengthened by works of a most impregnable character, rendering an assault on our part unjustifiable from the useless sacrifice of life it would entail. While the enemy was busily engaged fortifying, our troops were not idle. Our position was also soon rendered impregnable to assault, and a constant shelling of the enemy's fortifications and the city of Atlanta was kept up day and night. For the next couple of weeks both armies continued to slowly move down the route of the railroad south of Atlanta, exchanging artillery and musket fire daily.[40]

One of the worst jobs that a soldier had to face when the opposing lines were as close as they now were was serving on picket duty. Rice Bull wrote that a man chosen for picket duty went out to his posts after dark and

watched and listened for any movement of the enemy. This duty was not sought; it was nerve-wracking, dangerous, and the safety of the Army depended on his vigilance. If one wants to know how long a night can be and how black the darkness may become, let him stand some night on the picket line in the face of the enemy. The men sit or stand peering toward the picket line of the enemy, listening as only men listen when their lives depend on their vigilance.[41]

General Sherman could not allow the stalemate on the west side of Atlanta to continue for too long. By mid–August it was obvious that with Grant's forces deadlocked at Petersburg the only place a significant Federal success could occur was in Georgia. Throughout the war, Federal commanders had to take into consideration the political ramifications of their military decisions, and Sherman was well aware of what would happen if President Lincoln was not reelected. With the election only a few months away, it was imperative to show the voters that real progress was being made toward victory.[42]

Fighting Confederates was not the only challenge Sherman was facing in August. During the summer the three-year enlistment term of thousands of veteran troops would be ending, and while many of them would reenlist to see the fight through to the end, many others, who had certainly done their duty, would simply go home. In August alone, nearly 10,000 men would be leaving the army and even if new recruits and draftees filled the ranks, they would have none of the fighting abilities of the men they were replacing. In addition to losing some of his best men Sherman had learned that there were early signs of problems in keeping the army supplied. Delivery of supplies had been hampered by low water in the Tennessee and Cumberland rivers and as the distance between the army and supply depots in Tennessee increased the flow of supplies was slowed.[43]

Another reason for the slowing movement of supplies was Gen. Joseph Wheeler. On August 10, Hood had sent Wheeler and about 4,500 cavalrymen back to northern Georgia to disrupt Sherman's supply lines. He did an admirable job of tearing up track and destroying supply trains, but the effect on the Federal army was less than hoped for. What Wheeler's cavalry expedition really accomplished was to take the eyes of the Confederate army away from the most important part of the campaign. Wheeler ended up going all the way to East Tennessee before he was able to escape into Alabama, away from the main part of the campaign until October.[44]

Since General Sherman would not consider assaulting the massive Confederate fortifications, there appeared to be only one other way to force Hood's army out of Atlanta: bombard the city with artillery fire until they were forced to leave. There had been occasional shelling since the Federal guns came within range at the end of July but nothing like what was about to occur. Starting on August 10 and continuing for over two weeks, Federal guns systematically shelled the city.[45]

In a series of messages Sherman's desire to pound Atlanta into submission was clearly illustrated. On August 7, Thomas was instructed to "Telegraph to Chattanooga and have two 30-pounder Parrotts sent down on the cars, with 1,000 shells and ammunition. Put them into your best position, and knock down the buildings of the town." On the 9th Sherman wrote to General Halleck, "So Hood intends to stand his ground. I threw into Atlanta about 3,000 solid shot and shell to-day...." On August 10 he told Thomas:

> Keep up a steady, persistent fire on Atlanta with the 4½ inch guns and 20-pounder Parrotts, and order them to pay no attention to the side firing by which the enemy may attempt to divert their attention. I think those guns will make Atlanta of less value to them as a large machine-shop and depot of supplies. The inhabitants have, of course, got out.

Whether Sherman really believed the inhabitants of Atlanta had left is debatable, but he apparently didn't care all that much for that same day he ordered Thomas to "[k]eep the big guns going, and damage Atlanta all that is possible."[46]

Inside the city the shrieking shells at first brought terror to the citizens. The damage and death was random, which made it even more frightening, and there was no safe place. Some buildings were struck repeatedly until they were no more than piles of rubble, while others went untouched. Although many of the city's residents had already fled the civilian population had been swelled by war refugees and may have been as high as 10,000. For most of these people there was nowhere else to go and they had to endure the bombardment and pray they would survive.[47]

Once the first wave of fear had passed many of the citizens began to go about their usual daily routine, taking cover when the shelling occasionally intensified. Wallace Reed wrote:

> Many times during the day a busy housewife would unceremoniously drop her sewing, and gathering her little ones together, would make a wild and precipitate plunge for the back yard, where the family would quickly disappear into the bowels of the earth, there to remain until there was a lull in the storm of lead and iron.[48]

The shelling continued sporadically until the 16th when it increased dramatically. The Confederates had placed a large gun near the intersection of Peachtree and Kimball in the business district. The fire from this gun brought a concentrated fire down upon the neighborhood resulting in major damage. The constant shelling created an inferno of noise and the air was filled with the odor of burned powder. The smoke and dust from fires and destroyed buildings was so thick that at times the sun was barely visible.[49]

Fannie Beers described what it was like to be caught in a bombardment:

> The shells still shrieked and exploded; the more treacherous and dangerous solid shot continually demolished objects within our sight. For a few hours I was so utterly demoralized that my only thought was how to escape. But at last I grew calmer; my courage returned, and, urged by the necessity of finding shelter, I ventured out. Not a place could I find. The houses were closed and deserted, in many cases partly demolished by shot or shell, or, having taken fire, charred, smoking, and burnt to the ground.
>
> All day frightened women and children cowered and trembled and hungered and thirsted in their underground places of refuge while the earth above them shook with constant explosions.[50]

General Hood also recalled the courage of the remaining civilian population during the bombardment:

> [I]t was painful, yet strange, to mark how expert grew the old men, women and children, in building their little underground forts, in which to fly for safety during the storm of shot and shell. Often 'mid the darkness of night were they constrained to seek refuge in these dungeons beneath the earth; albeit, I cannot recall one word from their lips, expressive of dissatisfaction or willingness to surrender.[51]

By the end of August it became clear that bombardment was not going to be the answer. No matter how much damage was done Atlanta was too large an area to be effectively destroyed, and with the railroad still open to the south Hood's army could be supplied indefinitely. The railroad was the key, as it had been all along, and Sherman now determined it was time to make the final push that would force Hood to evacuate Atlanta.

Chapter 11

Atlanta Is Taken

On August 10, General Sherman sent a dispatch to General Grant that briefly outlined how he was going to proceed with the campaign:

> Since July 28th, Hood has not attempted to meet us outside his parapets. In order to possess and destroy effectually his communications, I may have to leave a corps at the railroad bridge, well entrenched, and cut loose with the balance to make a circle of desolation around Atlanta. I do not propose to assault his works, which are too strong, nor to proceed by regular approaches. I have lost a good many regiments, and will lose more, by the expiration of service; and this is the only reason why I want reënforcements. We have killed, crippled, and captured more of the enemy than we have lost by his acts.[1]

Realizing that any attack on the Confederate lines would probably be a bloody failure, General Sherman decided to proceed by reverting to his old tactics of moving around the enemy flanks. As long as the railroad to the south was open Hood could sit behind his fortifications indefinitely. It was also apparent that even if the Federal artillery turned the entire city of Atlanta into a pile of rubble that still might not be enough to force the Confederate army out. The only reasonable thing to do was to cut the communications with the south and force Hood to come out and fight or flee.[2]

By August 13, Sherman decided to move the Twentieth Corps to the railroad bridge over the Chattahoochee River to protect his line of communications to that point. With a secure base in his rear, Sherman was then going to take the rest of the army down the west side of the city to permanently cut the railroad below East Point. The movement was set to begin on the 18th.[3]

While the Federal artillery pounded Atlanta and Sherman was planning his next move, General Hood was also looking for a way to end the siege, by forcing Sherman to retreat. The failed attacks that Hood had launched since taking command made it clear that the Federal army was too large to destroy in open battle. So Hood decided that he would try the same tactics Sherman was going to use, cut off the enemy's supplies by destroying the railroad that transported those supplies. Gen. Joseph Wheeler's raid to destroy the Western & Atlantic Railroad in northern Georgia and then cut the railroads between Nashville and Chattanooga was supposed to accomplish just that.[4]

General Wheeler did cause some serious damage but not enough to significantly affect the Federal supply situation. As Sherman himself wrote, "I could not have asked for anything better, for I had provided well against such a contingency, and this detachment left me superior to the enemy in cavalry. I suspended the execution of my orders for the time being...." Sherman decided to give his own cavalry one more chance at destroying the railroad south of the city and postponed the infantry movement.[5]

On August 18, Brig. Gen. Judson Kilpatrick led his cavalry division in a raid to cut the Macon & Western Railroad at Jonesboro, about 15 miles south of Atlanta. Kilpatrick did reach Jonesboro and damage the tracks, but not enough to effectively cut the road for any length of time. Confederate troops closed in on the Federal cavalry and Kilpatrick's only avenue of escape was to the east, riding all the way around Atlanta before arriving back to the Federal lines on the 22nd.[6]

General Sherman, who never had much confidence in his cavalry to begin with, now decided to launch the delayed infantry movement. On the 24th Sherman wired to General Halleck in Washington: "Heavy fires in Atlanta all day, caused by our artillery. I will be all ready, and will commence the movement around Atlanta by the south tomorrow night, and for some time you will hear little of us."[7]

The movement around to the right began on the night of the 25th but Sherman's men had to use great caution when leaving their fortifications. Secrecy was of the utmost importance for if the Confederates learned what was going on and launched an attack while the Federal troops were in the act of pulling back it could result in a catastrophe. The lines of the opposing armies were so close in many areas that Henry Orendorff wrote, "we could & did throw small stones & clods from our skirmish pitts into enemy's & got a similar answer...."[8]

General Williams, who was temporarily in command of the Twentieth Corps, moved first, pulling back to the Chattahoochee and fortifying a position covering the railroad bridge and several nearby ferry crossings. Their sole mission was to stay put and guard the railroad, providing a place to fall back to in case disaster should befall the rest of the Federal army. That same night General Stanley's Fourth Corps pulled out of its works and moved down to a position near Utoy Creek, where they established a defensive position facing north to protect the rear of Sherman's troops as they marched south.[9]

L.W. Day, one of Stanley's soldiers from Ohio later remembered:

> As we plodded along, now on the road, now in the woods, and now across the fields, we could hear the sullen boom of cannon off on our left, and now and then the faint echo of bursting shell. The weather was intensely warm — this being the hottest day we had ever experienced. Very great care was taken, but notwithstanding this, many a boy in blue went down, beneath the merciless rays of a Southern sun....[10]

The next night the rest of the army began to move with General Schofield holding firm near East Point. General Thomas pulled out of his trenches, and pivoting on Schofield, moved behind and to the south with Howard doing the same on the outside of Thomas. It was imperative that the Confederates not discover what was going on. General Howard wrote about how his troops evacuated their works: "In perfect silence, twenty-five thousand men were wakened. Each column started quietly, following its guide, who had familiarized himself with the road that he was to take. Even the ordinary rattle of the wheels of batteries and wagons had been obviated by various contrivances." There was some light artillery fire as the rear of the column pulled out but both Howard and Thomas were able to get away without any serious interference.[11]

During the 27th the Federal infantry, with a cavalry screen in front, continued marching south. About the only opposition they faced was from Confederate cavalry detachments who harassed but could do nothing to halt the massive force as it swung around toward Atlanta's lifeline. "At every favorable ground, for example at the crossing of creeks large enough to bridge," Howard later wrote, the enemy horsemen "would cross over, burn or otherwise destroy the bridge, make a rail obstruction across the road and fire upon Kilpatrick's advance." By the end of the day both Thomas and Howard were near Utoy Creek and facing south with Howard on the far right or farthest away from the railroad.[12]

When Confederate soldiers discovered the abandoned Union lines on the morning of the 27th most believed the enemy had fled. The citizens of Atlanta came out to view the empty trenches and in the city there was rejoicing that they had been spared further bloodshed. Apparently even Hood was briefly fooled by the disappearance of Sherman's troops. He had been receiving glowing reports of how much damage General Wheeler's cavalry was doing in northern Georgia and Tennessee and also some unsubstantiated rumors about food shortages in the Federal camps. When the artillery firing ended and the trenches were discovered abandoned Hood was led to believe that Sherman had turned around and headed back north, leaving Slocum's corps as a rear guard. By the time Hood learned what Sherman was really up to, it was too late to do anything about it.[13]

On August 28, the Union movements continued with Thomas pivoting on Schofield's position and Howard's men racing around Thomas' right side until they reached the Atlanta and West Point Railroad between East Point and Fairburn. Now, Sherman finally had his troops in the position he had been longing for since early August, with thousands of infantry stretched out along several miles of railroad track southwest of Atlanta.[14]

The destruction began immediately and Theodore Upson tells the best way to tear up the track

> is to string the troops out along the track, two men to a tie. The men stick thier guns with their bayonets on into the ground close behind than so as to have them handy in case of an attact, and then at a "Yo heave!" evry man grabs a tie and lifts. Up comes the whole track and slowly tips over. Then with sledge hamers, hand spikes, or any thing else handy, the ties are knocked loose from the rails, the fish plates unbolted, the pine ties made into piles, set on fire, and the rails laid on top. When they get red hot in the center about 20 men get hold of the ends and wind them edgewise around a telegraph pole or small tree. That fixes them. The deep cuts we fill with brush and tree tops and put shells in them that will Explode if the Johnnys try to clean them out.[15]

The Federal troops worked hard tearing up track throughout the night of the 28th and well into the next morning. General Sherman had ordered "one day's work to be expended in destroying that road, and it was done with a will. Twelve and one-half miles were destroyed." To make sure the work was done to his satisfaction Sherman "personally inspected this work."[16]

On the 29th Thomas and Howard continued their march, moving toward the last remaining railroad out of Atlanta, the Macon and Western. Once again Schofield held the position on the far left while the rest of the army moved around on his right. The going was slower due to harassment from Confederate cavalry detachments and lack of good roads in the area. Hood had finally realized what was happening below Atlanta and had dispatched troops to guard Rough and Ready, about three miles southeast of East Point, and Jonesboro.[17]

On the 30th General Howard was ordered to march toward Renfroe's Plantation, about 10 miles southeast of Fairburn and only two miles west of the Flint River, with his ultimate goal being Jonesboro. Thomas would move in the same direction a few miles to the north while Schofield carefully moved east to confront the Confederates at Rough and Ready, all the time still in position north of Thomas to protect the left flank. Howard moved out early in the morning and when he arrived at Renfroe's he decided to continue on to the Flint River.[18]

That afternoon General Logan's corps came upon a bridge that had only been partially destroyed and was defended by Confederate barricades thrown up on the other side of the river. Howard reported:

> The cavalry rushed for the river-bank, and fired so fast that the rebels could with difficulty reply. Under cover of this fire a charge was made across the bridge, and the first and second lines of barricades seized. The enemy made still another stand a few rods to their rear, and opened a sharp fire on our advance, when, as if by a spontaneous impulse, General Logan's skirmishers, now over the river, made a dash upon the enemy.... With considerable skirmishing the advance of the Fifteenth Corps reached the highest ground between Flint River and the railroad.

Howard now had an excellent position from which to advance on the railroad the next day, only about half a mile from the Macon and Western tracks.[19]

Once General Howard had crossed the river Sherman saw that he had a golden opportunity to reach Jonesboro before Hood could bring enough troops and build fortifications strong enough to stop the Federals from destroying the last railroad into Atlanta. Sherman ordered "all the army to turn on Jonesborough, General Howard to keep the enemy busy while General Thomas should move down from the north, with General Schofield on his left. I expected the whole army would close down on Jonesborough by noon of the 1st of September."[20]

Back in Atlanta, General Hood did not seem to realize the extent of the danger to his communication line to the south. Hood clearly understood that Sherman was after the railroad but he did not know the size of the enemy force or its precise location. That evening Hardee sent Hood a message informing him that Federal units had crossed the Flint River and would reach the railroad the next day. With the danger now obvious Hood quickly ordered Hardee to move south with his own corps, commanded by General Cleburne, and Lee's corps, to protect the railroad near Jonesboro.[21]

General Hardee later complained about Hood's tardy reaction to Sherman's movements:

> The opportunity to strike the flank of the enemy exposed during the five days occupied in the movement from Atlanta to Jonesborough was neglected and lost. It was not until the 30th of August in the evening of which day the enemy actually reached the vicinity of Jonesborough, that General Hood was convinced, by information sent him by myself from Rough and Ready, that the enemy were moving upon that place. He then determined to attack what he believed to be only two corps of the enemy at Jonesborough. The enemy had reached Jonesborough before the order was given to move against him.[22]

The Confederate troops were stationed around East Point and Hood's orders to Hardee were to attack the Federal position near the Flint River early on the morning of the 31st. Unfortunately for the Confederates that did not happen due to problems that Hardee reported:

> I left Atlanta by rail and reached Jonesboro before daybreak, expecting to find Lee and Cleburne there. To my disappointment I found that Cleburne, who was in advance, had encountered the enemy in force upon the road which he had been instructed to take, and had been compelled to open another road. This occasioned great delay. Cleburne got into position about nine A.M. and Lee not until eleven A.M. Three brigades of Lee, which had been left on picket, did not get up until 1:30 P.M.

In fact it would be late afternoon before the Confederate attack could be launched. The delay would be costly.[23]

While Confederate troops were racing to Jonesboro, the rest of General Howard's army had come up to support Logan's corps. They had all night and much of the 31st to build fortifications and bring up artillery. The railroad was in range of Howard's guns so that even without actually destroying the track the route was effectively shut down. Howard's position on the ridge was well entrenched with Logan, Hazen and Harrow forming the front lines, and Osterhaus' division in reserve. Osterhaus had placed a battery of guns in advance of the main line and within 800 yards of the railroad. The entire line was well supported by other batteries placed under cover in nearby woods.[24]

While Hardee was waiting for Cleburne and Lee to arrive and get their troops in position he sent a message to Hood advising him of the delay and asking Hood to come down to Jonesboro and assume command. Receiving no answer to his telegram, Hardee launched his assault about 3:00 P.M. and problems developed almost immediately. Hardee had instructed Cleburne

> to turn the enemy's right flank, and Lee to begin the attack when he should hear Cleburne's guns. General Lee, mistaking the guns of Cleburne's skirmishers for the main attack, began the movement before Cleburne became seriously engaged. He encountered formidable breastworks, which he was unable to carry, and after considerable loss was driven back in confusion.[25]

The attack might have lacked perfect coordination but the veteran Confederate soldiers charged Howard's line with all the ferocity they usually displayed. General Logan reported that they "made a sudden and desperate assault on all parts of my line, approaching at points on the left of General Hazen's line (which was the left of my position) within thirty paces." Despite their courageous efforts the Confederate troops had come up against well-entrenched veterans who lacked nothing in courage and ability; the outcome of the battle was a foregone conclusion.[26]

As happened at Ezra Church, General Logan was a force to be reckoned with. Thomas Osborn wrote home:

> This fight at Jonesboro was a bitter little battle and our army showed especial gallantry and great confidence in itself as well as in its officers. I never saw any officer, except perhaps General Hooker, exhibit as great and reckless daring and gallantry on the battlefield as General Logan did at Jonesboro, and his entire corps partook of the spirit which moved him.[27]

The Confederates continued to press forward on the ridge but, as Logan reported, "The most terrible and destructive fire I ever witnessed was directed at the enemy, and in less than one hour he was compelled to retire discomfited and in confusion." Despite the heavy casualties suffered by the Confederates the battle was just beginning, as General Logan reported:

> The enemy made two more assaults, but evidently with far less spirit and determination than the first. The withering and destructive fire which they had received in the first onset had dampened their zeal; and destroyed their confidence in being able to defeat us, and they were, consequently, easily repulsed, though not without severe punishment being inflicted on them.[28]

The left of Cleburne's line had veered off to confront Federal cavalry who were firing on them from the opposite bank of the river and played little part in the battle. The results of the battle are obvious from the casualty figures. Howard reported less than 200 while estimates of Confederate casualties range from 2,000 to 3,000; Logan said his commanders reported about 500 enemy dead in front of his lines.[29]

General Hardee could clearly see that continuing the attack would result in nothing but more Confederate casualties. There was also the very real possibility of a Federal counterattack. "In view of the demoralized condition of Lee's troops, as reported by the same officer, I withdrew a division from Cleburne to support Lee. It now became necessary for me to act on the defensive." One unfortunate aspect of the battle was that it was a wasted effort; the railroad line was already broken north of there by the time the battle ended.[30]

With Howard's troops engaged near Jonesboro, General Sherman had already ordered Schofield and Thomas to advance to the railroad as quickly as possible. On the morning of the 31st General Schofield moved toward Rough and Ready, as did General Stanley's Fourth Corps from Thomas' army. They drove back a small force of Confederate cavalry and approached within a mile of the railroad. Schofield reported that, "The cars were running continually from the direction of Atlanta, stopping in our front and returning, and the resistance in front was rapidly increasing. It was evident that the enemy was re-enforcing the threatened point as rapidly as possible." There was no time to lose so Schofield pushed his troops forward and by 3:00 P.M. they had driven back the Confederates and reached the railroad about a mile and a half below Rough and Ready. General Stanley's corps arrived just afterward and the troops went to work tearing up the Macon and Western tracks. With the railroad firmly in Federal hands General Hardee, and the majority of the Confederate army that was fighting at Jonesboro, was now cut off from Atlanta.[31]

On the morning of September 1 the Confederates faced a perilous situation. As General Hardee explained:

> General Hood was at Atlanta with Stewart's corps and the Georgia militia; my corps was at Jonesborough, thirty miles distant, and Lee's corps on the road from Jonesborough to Atlanta, fifteen miles from each place, and in supporting distance of neither. The Federal commander, on the other hand, had concentrated his whole army upon my corps at Jonesborough, except the one corps left in front of Atlanta, and was now in position to crush in detail the scattered corps of his unwary antagonist. My position at Jonesborough had been taken up on the failure of the attack on the day previous. It was not strong naturally, and there had been little time to strengthen it by art; but it was absolutely necessary to hold the position through the day to secure the evacuation of Atlanta, which had now become a necessity.[32]

During the afternoon General Davis, commanding Thomas' Fourteenth Corps, learned that part of the Confederate lines in his front were not completed. Two divisions were sent forward about 4:00 P.M. and after struggling through heavy brush reached the enemy lines. Davis reported that the Confederates "made a most determined resistance. The fight was short and bloody. The entire line of works was carried, except the extreme left. Elsewhere, at all points, the assault was decisive and complete along the entire line."[33]

Both sides suffered heavy casualties with Davis losing a little over 1,000 men. However, as General Thomas reported, "Two field batteries of four guns each were captured ... together with about 1,000 prisoners. The enemy's loss in killed and wounded was very severe."[34]

More important than the numbers of prisoners or artillery pieces captured was the fact that virtually an entire Confederate brigade had surrendered. The fight had gone out of his men and Hardee knew there was only one thing left to do: save as many of them as possible. Immediately after the fight Sherman had ordered two divisions of General Blair's Seventeenth Corps to swing around Jonesboro to the south to cut off Hardee's escape route, but the Confederates were able to get away under cover of darkness.[35]

In Atlanta, General Hood did not learn of the failed attack at Jonesboro until the morning of the 1st. With the railroad cut and most of the Federal army below Atlanta Hood realized that he had no choice but to evacuate the city. General Stewart's corps had remained in Atlanta and it was decided they would move out on the McDonough Road, several miles east of the Macon & Western tracks, and meet Hardee's troops at Lovejoy's Station, about seven miles south of Jonesboro. Once reunited Hood's army would be in position to protect Macon and the prison camp at Andersonville.[36]

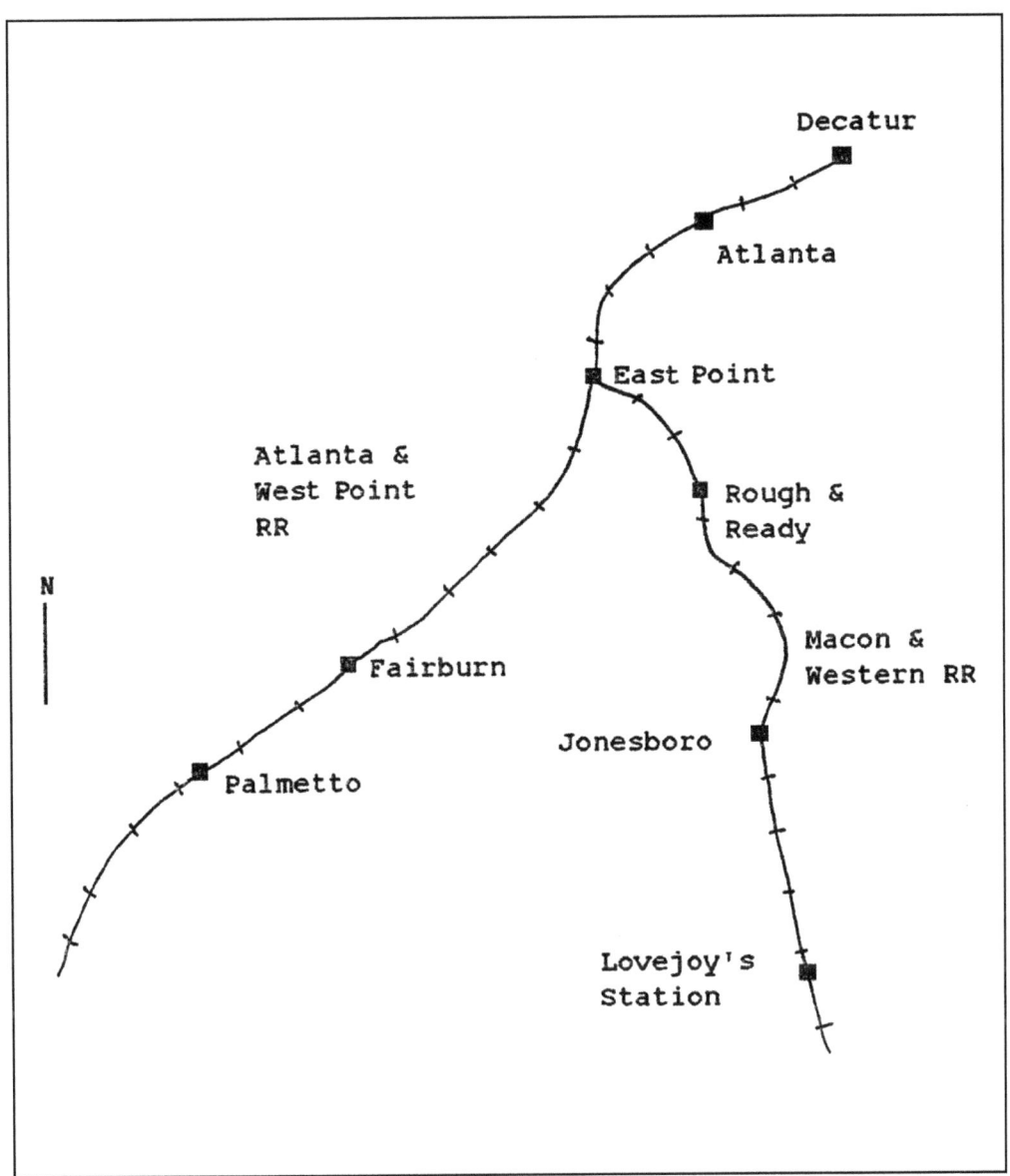

Atlanta to Lovejoy's

While most of the Federal army was pursuing Hardee south of Jonesboro on September 2, Henry Slocum walked into Atlanta. The dull, booming noises that Sherman heard nearly 20 miles away sounded like thunder to the soldiers of the Twentieth Corps, but they knew that the explosions were not the sounds of battle, but rather the sounds of victory.

The next day General Slocum's troops marched into Atlanta, Georgia, with their flags waving and bands playing. Slocum immediately sent what was probably one of the most welcome telegrams ever received by Secretary of War Stanton, "General Sherman has taken Atlanta. The Twentieth Corps occupies the city...."[40]

In his report to General Thomas, which was forwarded to Sherman, Slocum described the capture of the city:

> I sent out a reconnoitering party early on the morning of the 2nd [as I had done on each previous day]. They arrived near Atlanta about 10 A.M., and were met by the mayor, and the city was surrendered to them. I at once moved forward all of my command that could safely be spared from the bridge-heads and occupied the city, and now feel that our position is safe, both at this point as well as at the bridges. We occupy the entire line of rebel works at this place.[41]

While Sherman's troops were facing the new enemy fortifications near Lovejoy's Station rumors began to circulate that Hood had abandoned Atlanta. Nothing was known for sure until Sherman

> received a note in Slocum's own handwriting, stating that he had heard during the night the very sounds that I have referred to; that he had moved rapidly up from the bridge about daylight, and had entered Atlanta unopposed. His letter was dated inside the city, so there was no doubt of the fact. General Thomas's bivouac was but a short distance from mine, and, before giving notice to the army in general orders, I sent one of my staff-officers to show him the note. In a few minutes the officer returned, soon followed by Thomas himself, who again examined the note, so as to be perfectly certain that it was genuine. The news seemed to him too good to be true. He snapped his fingers, whistled, and almost danced, and, as the news spread to the army, the shouts that arose from our men, the wild hallooing and glorious laughter, were to us a full recompense for the labor and toils and hardships through which we had passed in the previous three months.[42]

After learning that he had Atlanta, Sherman decided to hold his position. The closest worthwhile target was Macon, about 65 miles south. Hood's army was again at full strength and now was not the time for a bloody assault on a formidable defensive position. Even if the Confederates could be dislodged the only way to transport sufficient supplies for a Federal army below Atlanta was over the railroads that Sherman's men had recently destroyed. After a long and difficult campaign Sherman's men needed a rest. Slowly the Federal army moved back and by the 8th reached their camps around Atlanta.[43]

Among many of the Confederate soldiers near Lovejoy's Station the reason for the loss of Atlanta was fairly clear. Alex Spence, of the 1st Arkansas Regiment, wrote to his parents:

> Well, contrary to my expectations, we were not able to hold Atlanta. Old Sherman flanked us out of the place. We are now some 30 miles below there on the Macon Rail Road. Genl Hood has been completely "out generaled" by Sherman. Genl Johnston would have done much better with this Army than Hood has.[44]

In a telegram to General Halleck on the 3rd, Sherman described the events of the last week culminating with the occupation of Atlanta. That evening Halleck handed President Lincoln a copy of the message. When the president saw the words "Atlanta is ours and fairly won," he knew that not only had a city been won but also an election and, with Abraham Lincoln firmly in the White House, eventually the war.[45]

Chapter 12

The Occupation of Atlanta

When Slocum's troops entered Atlanta on September 2 they found a city in complete disarray. Much of the business district in the center of town was filled with the lowest class of people, most of whom had nowhere else to go. Dirty, hungry-looking men and women were ransacking the stores, picking up anything they might be able to use or sell from the odds and ends left behind by the store owners. There were plenty of Confederate stragglers and deserters roaming the streets, willing to do whatever it took to survive. Finally, there were the former slaves, ecstatic with their newfound freedom but not really knowing what to do now.[1]

Atlanta was a worn-out and tattered shell of a city, abandoned by its protectors. There was no organized police protection for property or persons. Most of the members of the municipal government had fled or were in hiding. For a brief time the city would be without laws or the means to enforce them, except the mob-like rule of the majority. And, if this situation wasn't bad enough, the only solution to the problems facing the city would have to come from the feared and hated invaders.[2]

During the day of the 2nd and long into the night, Federal troops and wagons flooded into Atlanta. The obvious first step was to make sure they had control of the city. This was quickly accomplished with military precision as the Army of the Cumberland occupied the city and guarded the communication lines with Chattanooga. The Army of the Tennessee was stationed in and around East Point and Schofield's Army of the Ohio occupied Decatur. The men were exhausted from the hard campaign and looked forward to the rest and overdue pay that was promised.[3]

An amazing transformation occurred in Atlanta once the Federal troops arrived and established control over the city. Businesses reopened and the empty stores were quickly stocked with dry goods, food and clothing. Newspapers and magazines from the North suddenly appeared and overall commerce improved dramatically. During the siege it had been nearly impossible to bring supplies into the city and Hood's hungry soldiers took what little food was available. On the heels of the occupying troops Federal quartermasters had brought huge quantities of stores into the city and a depot was opened to help provide basic supplies to the citizens. The soldiers were under strict discipline to behave and although crowds of soldiers and civilians mixed on the streets there very few instances of disorder or women being subjected to indignities.[4]

Evidence of the destruction that occurred during the siege was everywhere and sometimes the result had been tragic. General Geary wrote to his wife, Mary:

> The city is a very pretty place, built much in northern taste and stile, and contained about 15,000 inhabitants. There is scarcely a house that does [not] exhibit in some degree the effects of the battle which so fearfully raged around it. Many of the best are utterly ruined, and many of the ornamental trees are cut down by our shells.[5]

George Washington Baker wrote to his mother:

> I found that our shell[s] had torn the city to pieces considerable as on one side of the City most every house had a shell through it and some were completely riddled. A great good many inoffensive ones were killed as Hood never gave orders for the noncombatants to remove and they curse Hood beyond all account.
>
> In one house there was a girl ironing when a shell burst in the room and 14 Bullets struck her tearing her all to pieces and in one Family of 7 they showed where 5 had been buried killed by one shell so you can judge how pleasant it is to have to run under ground every time you hear a Cannon fired and that fireing continual night and day.[6]

Outside Atlanta the reaction to its fall was as one might have expected. In the North people went wild with joy. Finally they could see that the war was being won and perhaps the end was near. Much of the talk about compromise with the Confederacy or simply letting the South go its own way was ended. The capture of Atlanta also virtually assured the reelection of Abraham Lincoln, and the continuation of the war until victory was won.[7]

Official recognition of Sherman's achievement came quickly. From President Lincoln on September 3:

> The national thanks are tendered by the President to Major-General William T. Sherman, and the gallant officers and soldiers of his command before Atlanta, for the distinguished ability, courage, and perseverance displayed in the campaign in Georgia, which, under divine favor, has resulted in the capture of Atlanta. The marches, battles, sieges, and other military operations that have signalized the campaign must render it famous in the annals of war, and have entitled those who have participated therein to the applause and thanks of the nation.[8]

Praise also came from Sherman's good friend, U.S. Grant:

> [I]t is hardly necessary for me to say that I feel you have accomplished the most gigantic undertaking given to any general in this war, and with a skill and ability that will be acknowledged in history as unsurpassed, if not unequaled. It gives me as much pleasure to record this in your favor as it would in favor of any living man, myself included.[9]

Even General Sherman, who seldom displayed his affection for his men and even less frequently offered his troops praise for doing their job, paid them a compliment on September 8 in Special Field Orders No. 68 when he wrote:

Ruins of Atlanta Railroad Depot

This completed the grand task which had been assigned us by our Government, and your general repeats his personal and official thanks to all the officers and men composing this army for the indomitable courage and perseverance which alone could give success. We have beaten our enemy on every ground he has chosen, and have wrested from him his own Gate City, where were located his foundries, arsenals, and work-shops, deemed secure on account of their distance from the base and the seemingly impregnable obstacles intervening. Nothing is impossible to an army like this, determined to vindicate a Government which has rights wherever our flag has once floated, and is resolved to maintain them at any and all costs.[10]

To the people of the South the loss of Atlanta was clearly seen as the disaster that it was. Thomas DeLeon wrote:

> There was a terrible shock to the people of the South in the fall of Atlanta. They knew its importance so fully that its loss was the more keenly felt. There came sudden revulsion from the hope that had begun once again to throb in the public pulse. The loud murmurs that had arisen after other defeats were wanting now; but a sullen and increasing gloom seemed to settle over the majority of the people. It was as though they were stunned by the violence of the shock and felt already its paralyzing influence.... Even the army itself — while still doggedly determined to strike its hardest to the bitter end — began to feel that it was fighting against hope.[11]

In the Army of Tennessee there was disappointment and a search for excuses to explain away the loss of what was probably the second most important city in the Confederacy.

While his army lay at Jonesboro licking its wounds, John Bell Hood had time to consider how his dreams of a great victory had literally gone up in smoke the night he abandoned Atlanta. He had lost more than a city. In addition to the buildings and railroad equipment consumed by the fires of Atlanta were his army's reserves of powder and ammunition, small arms, and badly needed food.[12]

In addition to reflecting on his material losses Hood was busy requesting aid and spreading the blame for losing Atlanta. On the 8th Hood requested that, "all the reserves of Georgia, under General Cobb, be ordered to this Army ... and that Lieutenant General Taylor be ordered to relieve General Hardee, bringing with him all the troops he can." Unfortunately the dissension among the high command of the Army of Tennessee resurfaced at this time. On September 13, Hood wrote to President Davis:

> In the battle of July 20th, we failed on account of General Hardee. Our success on the 22nd July was not what it should have been, owing to this officer. Our failure on the 31st of August, I am convinced, was greatly owing to him. Please confer with Lieutenant Generals Stewart and S.D. Lee, as to operations around Atlanta. It is of the utmost importance that Hardee should be relieved at once. He commands the best troops of this Army. I must have another commander. Taylor or Cheatham will answer. Hardee handed in his resignation a few days since, but withdrew it. Can General Cobb give me all the reserve regiments he has?[13]

Within a few days of occupying the city General Sherman had to make some difficult decisions about he was going to do with his prize. With the capture of the city the Federal army essentially reversed roles with the Confederates. Atlanta had become a weight around Sherman's neck. Now he was the army commander with a stationary army to feed, dependent on a single railroad line, hundreds of miles from his main supply depots.[14]

The answer to the situation was clear to General Sherman: remove the civilians.

> I was resolved to make Atlanta a pure military garrison or depot, with no civil population to influence military measures. I had seen Memphis, Vicksburg, Natchez, and New Orleans, all captured from the enemy, and each at once was garrisoned by a full division of troops, if not more; so that success was actually crippling our armies in the field by detachments to guard and protect the interests of a hostile population.[15]

While Sherman was not the cold-blooded devil as many people in the South believed him to be he did believe in "hard war." In a letter to General Halleck on September 4th he explained what he had planned for Atlanta:

> I propose to remove all the inhabitants of Atlanta, sending those committed to our cause to the rear, and the rebel families to the front. I will allow no trade, manufactories, nor any citizens there at all, so that we will have the entire use of the railroad back, as also such corn and forage as may be reached by our troops. If the people raise a howl against my barbarity and cruelty I will answer that war is war, and not popularity-seeking. If they want peace, they and their relatives must stop the war.[16]

The decision to basically turn Atlanta into a ghost town was not made to punish the people, or just to show that Sherman had the power to do it, but rather because it seemed like a logical step to take. Sherman could not feed both his army and the city's residents from his one undependable supply line. He also could not just march away, leaving the city intact for the Confederates to move back in and resume business as usual.

> I knew, of course, that such a measure would be strongly criticized, but made up my mind to do it with the absolute certainty of its justness, and that time would sanction its wisdom. I knew that the people of the South would read in this measure two important conclusions: one, that we were in earnest; and the other, if they were sincere in their common and popular clamor "to die in the last ditch," that the opportunity would soon come.[17]

So, the evacuation of the civilian population of Atlanta had become a necessity. The Federal army in Atlanta was far from its base of supplies and its lines of communication were open to frequent interruption by Confederate raiders. Sherman simply did not have the luxury of feeding the families of soldiers who were fighting against him.[18]

Beginning on September 7 a series of lengthy letters passed between Sherman and Hood concerning the evacuation of the civilians from Atlanta. Although the proper military courtesies of the era were maintained, the exchange got progressively more malicious as each man tried to justify his own or condemn the other man's position.

In Sherman's first letter he informed Hood of the action about to be taken and offered as much assistance as could be reasonably given:

> I have deemed it to the interest of the United States that the citizens now residing in Atlanta should remove, those who prefer it to go south, and the rest north. For the latter I can provide food and transportation to points of their election in Ten-

nessee, Kentucky, or farther north. For the former I can provide transportation by cars as far as Rough and Ready, and also wagons; but, that their removal may be made with as little discomfort as possible, it will be necessary for you to help the families from Rough and Ready to the cars at Lovejoy's. If you consent, I will undertake to remove all the families in Atlanta who prefer to go south to Rough and Ready, with all their movable effects.... Atlanta is no place for families or non-combatants, and I have no desire to send them north if you will assist in conveying them south. If this proposition meets your views, I will consent to a truce in the neighborhood of Rough and Ready.... Each of us might send a guard of, say, one hundred men, to maintain order, and limit the truce to, say two days after a certain time appointed.[19]

Hood's response on the 9th was to strenuously protest this action although he realized that he had little choice but to cooperate and accept Sherman's conditions. He added:

And now, sir, permit me to say that the unprecedented measure you propose transcends, in studied and ingenious cruelty, all acts ever before brought to my attention in the dark history of war.
In the name of God and humanity, I protest, believing that you will find that you are expelling from their homes and firesides the wives and children of a brave people.[20]

On September 10, Sherman sent his reply to Hood saying in part:

I say that it is kindness to these families of Atlanta to remove them now, at once, from scenes that women and children should not be exposed to....
In the name of common-sense, I ask you not to appeal to a just God in such a sacrilegious manner. You who, in the midst of peace and prosperity, have plunged a nation into war — dark and cruel war.... If we must be enemies, let us be men, and fight it out as we propose to do, and not deal in such hypocritical appeals to God and humanity. God will judge us in due time, and he will pronounce whether it be more humane to fight with a town full of women and the families of a brave people at our back or to remove them in time to places of safety among their own friends and people.[21]

Hood's lengthy letter of the 12th tries to refute Sherman's letters point by point and is filled with justifications for the war and some personal insults not normally seen in formal military communications of the time:

Had you seen proper to let the matter rest there, I would gladly have allowed your letter to close this correspondence, and, without your expressing it in words, would have been willing to believe that, while "the interests of the United States," in your opinion, compelled you to an act of barbarous cruelty, you regretted the necessity....
I see nothing in your communication which induces me to modify the language of condemnation with which I characterized your order. It but strengthens me in the opinion that it stands "pre-eminent in the dark history of war for studied and ingenious cruelty." Your original order was stripped of all pretenses; you announced the edict for the sole reason that it was "to the interest of the United States."[22]

By the end of his letter Hood seems to have worked himself into a sort of histrionic diatribe:

> You came into our country with your Army, avowedly for the purpose of subjugating free white men, women, and children, and not only intend to rule over them, but you make negroes your allies, and desire to place over us an inferior race, which we have raised from barbarism to its present position, which is the highest ever attained by that race, in any country, in all time. I must, therefore, decline to accept your statements in reference to your kindness toward the people of Atlanta....
>
> You say, "Let us fight it out like men." To this my reply is—for myself, and I believe for all the true men, ay, and women and children, in my country—we will fight you to the death! Better die a thousand deaths than submit to live under you and your Government and your Negro allies![23]

Sherman had the last word in a relatively brief note on the 14th agreeing with Hood that "this discussion by two soldiers is out of place, and profitless." In the closing some of the personal rancor that had been building is obvious:

> I was not bound by the laws of war to give notice of the shelling of Atlanta, a "fortified town, with magazines, arsenals, foundries, and public stores"; you were bound to take notice. See the books.
>
> This is the conclusion of our correspondence, which I did not begin and terminate with satisfaction.[24]

General Sherman also received letters protesting the evacuation from local officials. On September 11, Mayor James M. Calhoun and Councilmen E.E. Rawson and S.C. Wells wrote:

> At first view, it struck us that the measure would involve extraordinary hardship and loss, but since we have seen the practical execution of it so far as it has progressed, and the individual condition of the people, and heard their statements as to the inconvenience, loss, and suffering attending it, we are satisfied that the amount of it will involve in the aggregate consequences appalling and heart-rending.
>
> As you advanced, the people north of this fell back; and before your arrival here, a large portion of the people had retired south, so that the country south of this is already crowded, and without houses enough to accommodate the people, and we are informed that many are now staying in churches and other out-buildings.
>
> This being so, how is it possible for the people still here [mostly women and children] to find any shelter? And how can they live through the winter in the woods—no shelter or subsistence, in the midst of strangers who know them not, and without the power to assist them much, if they were willing to do so?[25]

Sherman's lengthy reply dealt not only with the evacuation but the larger issues of war and peace:

> I have read it carefully, and give full credit to your statements of the distress that will be occasioned, and yet shall not revoke my orders, because they were not designed to meet the humanities of the case, but to prepare for the future struggles in which millions of good people outside of Atlanta have a deep interest. We must have peace, not only at Atlanta, but in all America.... The use of Atlanta for warlike purposes is inconsistent with its character as a home for families. There will be no manufactures, commerce, or agriculture here, for the maintenance of families, and sooner or later want will compel the inhabitants to go.... I cannot discuss this subject with you

fairly, because I cannot impart to you what we propose to do, but I assert that our military plans make it necessary for the inhabitants to go away, and I can only renew my offer of services to make their exodus in any direction as easy and comfortable as possible.

You cannot qualify war in harsher terms than I will. War is cruelty, and you cannot refine it; and those who brought war into our country deserve all the curses and maledictions a people can pour out....

You might as well appeal against the thunder-storm as against these terrible hardships of war. They are inevitable, and the only way the people of Atlanta can hope once more to live in peace and quiet at home, is to stop the war....

We don't want your negroes, or your horses, or your houses, or your lands, or any thing you have, but we do want and will have a just obedience to the laws of the United States.

Now that war comes home to you, you feel very different. You deprecate its horrors but did not feel them when you sent car-loads of soldiers and ammunition, and moulded shells and shot, to carry war into Kentucky and Tennessee, to desolate the homes of hundreds and thousands of good people who only asked to live in peace at their old homes, and under the Government of their inheritance.

But, my dear sirs, when peace does come, you may call on me for any thing. Then will I share with you the last cracker, and watch with you to shield your homes and families against danger from every quarter.[26]

Although Sherman knew from earlier correspondence that the authorities in Washington would approve of his removal of the civilians in Atlanta he received official notice of this from General Halleck on September 28th:

The course which you have pursued in removing rebel families from Atlanta, and in the exchange of prisoners, is fully approved by the War Department. Not only are you justified by the laws and usages of war in removing these people, but I think it was your duty to your own army to do so.

Moreover, I am fully of opinion that the nature of your position, the character of the war, the conduct of the enemy [and especially of non-combatants and women of the territory which we have heretofore conquered and occupied], will justify you in gathering up all the forage and provisions which your army may require, both for a siege of Atlanta and for your supply in your march farther into the enemy's country. Let the disloyal families of the country, thus stripped, go to their husbands, fathers, and natural protectors, in the rebel ranks.... The safety of our armies, and a proper regard for the lives of our soldiers, require that we apply to our inexorable foes the severe rules of war. We certainly are not required to treat the so-called non-combatant rebels better than they themselves treat each other.... We have fed this class of people long enough. Let them go with their husbands and fathers and natural protectors. I would destroy every mill and factory within reach which I did not want for my own use.

I have endeavored to impress these views upon our commanders for the last two years. You are almost the only one who has properly applied them. I do not approve of General Hunter's course in burning private houses or uselessly destroying private property. That is barbarous. But I approve of taking or destroying whatever may serve as supplies to us or to the enemy's army.[27]

One of the residents of Atlanta, Mary Gay, wrote about the despondency and hatred that was generated by the order to evacuate the city:

> [B]y this order, and by others even more oppressive and diabolical, the Nero of the nineteenth century, alias William Tecumseh Sherman, was put upon record as the born leader of the most ruthless, Godless band of men ever organized in the name of patriotism — a band which, but for a few noble spirits who, by the power of mind over matter, exerted a restraining influence, would not have left a Southerner to tell the tale of fiendishness on its route to the sea.[28]

The evacuation took place during the middle of September with both sides declaring a 10-day truce. The number of people who actually had to leave their homes was not that large, only a few thousand. But this was a different time, a time when women and children and the helpless were to be protected and sheltered from the horrors of war. The sight of these pathetic-looking refugees who had been forced from their homes with whatever meager belongings they were allowed to take with them must have been difficult for even the toughest soldier. Rice Bull, a soldier in the 123rd New York, wrote:

> We had one very difficult and unpleasant job in evacuating those civilians who had remained in the city. They were mostly old men and women who were almost helpless to care for themselves. It was heartrending to witness their distress as these old people left their homes with so little to go with, as they said, among strangers.[29]

A guard detachment of 100 men from each army met at Rough and Ready, six miles south of East Point along the Macon Railroad. The transfer went smoothly enough from the Federal point of view; transportation was provided for families that needed it and there were few disputes or problems. Of course, there was nothing the people could do but comply with the orders to leave their homes and the lack of protest only masked the hatred that existed under the surface.[30]

Mary Gay wrote about the exodus from Atlanta at Jonesboro: "I opened wide my eyes and took in the situation in all its horrible details. The entire Southern population of Atlanta, with but an occasional exception, and that of many miles in its vicinity, were dumped out upon the cold ground without shelter and without any of the comforts of home...."[31]

In a conversation with a woman who had been forced from her home Union Major George Nichols learned about that hatred firsthand: "Look here, sir; there are not two nations on the face of this earth whose language, customs, and histories are different ... but what are nearer to each other than the North and South. There are no two peoples in the world who hate each other more."

Nichols replied that: "I understand public feeling at the North pretty well, and such a feeling does not exist there generally."

"Well, sir, we hate you; we will never live with you again."[32]

While the displaced civilians of Atlanta were looking for a new place to live, the Union soldiers occupying their former home were the most comfortable they had been in months. Details were assigned to clean up the camps and soon they had the look of well-kept lawns and parks. The sanitary condition of the camps was frequently inspected and the health and comfort of the troops was never better. Food and clothing was issued in abundance and the men, clean, shaven, and wearing new clothes, looked and felt better than they had for a long time, perhaps since they joined the army.³³

The condition of the Federal troops and their camps was in direct contrast to what remained of the city of Atlanta. George F. Cram described the conditions in the city in a letter to his mother:

> A few citizens still remain who walk the streets with a mournful absent look or stand like statues gazing at the "Boys in blue" as they pass. The houses are closed; blinds drawn tightly down and everything has a sad deserted appearance. Most of them were carried off south. The handsome streets are dug up in crazy places for fortifications; fine shade trees are hacked to pieces, magnificent stores are smoldering ruins; desolation prevails. Atlanta, the beautiful, the "Gate City" is dead.³⁴

Another Union soldier, George Baker, wrote home that he thought

> Atlanta is a very pretty place surrounded with woods and a great many beautiful places in it and a great many northern people in it I should judge who hail the cessation of Shot and Shell with great joy. Perhaps some make it but the main body of the inhabitants are well pleased with our entry into their City and we were pleased to accommodate them in that respect as we shall be in any other nice places they have this way.³⁵

Summer was almost over and Sherman now had to decide what to do next. Keeping his army in camps around Atlanta was the least acceptable option. Despite the capture of Atlanta, Sherman had not actually accomplished the objective of his orders at the opening of the spring campaign, the destruction of the Army of Tennessee. He could pursue Hood and try to bring him to battle, if Hood could be caught. Sherman could take his army back north, but that would give up all that had been won at such a terrible cost. Another option was to move south or east, ignoring Hood's army and striking out through Georgia, carrying the war to places that had so far been untouched by the violence and destruction. General Sherman decided "to await the initiative of the enemy, supposing that he would be forced to resort to some desperate campaign by the clamor raised at the South on account of the great loss to them of the city of Atlanta." Sherman did not have to wait very long before General Hood decided to get back into the war.³⁶

While the Federal army was ensconced in the camps around Atlanta and General Sherman was contemplating what he should do next, down at Lovejoy's Station General Hood was also contemplating the same problem:

> I hereupon decided to operate at the earliest moment possible in the rear of Sherman, as I became more and more convinced of our inability to successfully resist an advance of the Federal Army. I had thought immediately after my arrival at Lovejoy Station that our troops were not disheartened, and telegraphed to Richmond to that effect; but I discovered my error before long....³⁷

With little prospects of receiving reinforcements and unable to stand up to the Federal army in open battle, Hood had only two real options. He could try to take the fight to Sherman's rear and harass the Federals out of Atlanta by breaking the supply lines, or he could just sit and wait, letting Sherman take the initiative and forcing Hood to react as best he could. General Hood explained how he came to his decision:

> The outcome of this stand-still policy, which would have enabled Sherman to advance with all due preparations and have forced us to retreat in his front day after day, would have been the final dispersion of the Army; a greater portion would have returned to their homes, leaving behind a noble band of patriots too proud to desert, yet too weak and disheartened to be of material service. I would have been able to offer just about sufficient resistance to harass and embitter the enemy; to instigate him to perpetrate greater outrages, and commit ten-fold the havoc he actually made in traversing Georgia; and, in lieu of contenting himself with simply cutting the communications of the Army of Northern Virginia with its largest fields for supplies, Sherman would have tarried long enough upon his march to effect irreparable damage.

There was little doubt as to what Hood would do next.[38]

Chapter 13

Chasing Hood and Planning the "March"

During the evacuation of civilians from Atlanta most of Sherman's army was concentrated in the camps around the city. General Hood stayed in the vicinity of Jonesboro occupying himself with sending out requests for supplies and reinforcements. On September 18, the Army of Tennessee moved toward the West Point Railroad and by the 20th Hood had formed his army with the right on the railroad and his left on the Chattahoochee with army headquarters at Palmetto.[1]

Hood had previously issued an invitation to Jefferson Davis to visit the troops and on the 25th the Confederate president arrived at Palmetto. He was there to "ascertain in person the condition of the Army; to confer, as requested, with the corps commanders in regard to the operations around Atlanta, and to obtain the particulars of the proposed campaign in the rear of Sherman."[2]

As Davis wrote later this plan consisted of

> the occupation of a strong position on the enemy's line of communication by the railroad between Atlanta and Chattanooga, the capture of his depots of supplies and the small garrisons left to guard them. If this ... should cause Sherman to move to attack us ... if the tone of the troops justified it, a battle should be joined.

If Sherman did not attack at that point then Hood would move west toward Gadsden, Alabama, where "the largest practicable number of militia and home-guards of both States would be assembled as an auxiliary force, and there a final stand should be made for a decisive battle."[3]

If the Confederate forces were victorious Davis and Hood believed that "the enemy could not retreat through the wasted country behind him, and must surrender or disperse." Another possible scenario was that Sherman would not pursue Hood and instead set out on a march to the seacoast. If the Federal commander decided on this course then,

> the militia, the loyal troops, and others who could be employed, should obstruct the

roads and fords in his front by felling trees, and, by burning bridges and other available means, delay his progress until his provisions should be consumed and absolute want should deplete if not disintegrate his army.

Davis also states that General Beauregard was informed of this plan and approved it.[4]

After approving Hood's basic plan of action Davis left the army on the 27th. The next day another of Hood's wishes was granted when General Hardee was relieved of his command with the Army of Tennessee and assigned to the command of the Department of South Carolina and Florida. During the day of the 29th Hood's army left the camps and began crossing the Chattahoochee to open the next phase of the campaign.[5]

In Atlanta, General Sherman had been waiting to see what Hood would do next. General Thomas had returned to the headquarters of his department in Nashville and General Schofield to his at Knoxville. Now that Hood was on the move, Sherman, leaving Slocum's corps to occupy Atlanta, followed the Confederates. As Sherman wrote, "I had little fear of the enemy's cavalry damaging our roads seriously, for they rarely make a break which could not be repaired in a few days; but it was absolutely necessary to keep General Hood's infantry off our main route of communication and supply."[6]

Hood's troops quickly moved north and on October 4 General Stewart captured Big Shanty and the same day General Loring took Ackworth. Almost 500 Union soldiers were taken prisoner between the two garrisons. In addition the Confederates destroyed over 10 miles of railroad track. The next day Hood approached Allatoona, now a huge Federal supply depot. The warehouses were protected by two small forts manned by a garrison of about 900 men commanded by Lt. Col. John Tourtellotte. The position was nearly impregnable unless attacked by a force large enough to simply overwhelm the defenders. Sherman had purposely avoided it when he moved south toward Atlanta.[7]

Both Hood and Sherman were marching toward Allatoona but Hood got there first. Maj. Gen. S.G. French was ordered to capture the garrison and most importantly over a million rations they were protecting. Sherman's main force was still south of Kennesaw and could do nothing to help the Federal garrison, but Gen. John M. Corse, who had been sent to Rome with an infantry division, could. Using a combination of telegraph lines and signal flags Sherman was able to get a message to Corse on the 4th to send help to Allatoona. That same afternoon Corse and eleven hundred men, with a large supply of ammunition, set out for Allatoona by rail.[8]

General Corse arrived at Allatoona about one o'clock on the morning of October 5. By dawn all the Federal troops had been pulled into the fortifications and French's artillery had begun a bombardment. About 8:30 A.M. French ceased fire and under a flag of truce demanded the surrender of the garrison: "I have placed the forces under my command in such positions that you are surrounded, and to avoid a needless effusion of blood I call on you to surrender your forces at once, and unconditionally. Five minutes will be allowed you to decide." Corse replied saying that "we are prepared for the 'needless effusion of blood' whenever it is agreeable to you."[9]

The fight resumed immediately and it turned into one of the deadliest little battles of the war. French's men came at the Federals from three sides. So many bullets were coming at the Federal soldiers that they barely were able to stand up to fire and frequently just pointed their muskets over the works and pulled the trigger. Officers who tried to stand to set an example were quickly shot down. By midafternoon French gave up trying to take the works and with Sherman's troops closing from the south he withdrew to rejoin the main army. The deadly fight cost the garrison about 700 casualties and at least that many Confederates.[10]

General French rejoined the main army and two days after the fight at Allatoona, the Federal cavalry lost contact with Hood's fast-moving troops. Delayed by bad weather Sherman did not reach Allatoona until the 9th and by then Hood was long gone. There were reports that the Confederates were heading for Rome, so Sherman hurried there only to find that Hood had merely made a demonstration to attract Sherman's attention and then hurried off, where no one could tell.[11]

General Hood's army reappeared at Resaca on October 12, and this time Hood demanded "the immediate and unconditional surrender of the post and garrison under your command, and, should this be acceded to, all white officers and soldiers will be parolled in a few days. If the place is carried by assault, no prisoners will be taken." Apparently the commander of the Federal garrison, Col. Clark R. Weaver, was neither impressed nor unnerved by Hood's threat to basically murder his troops. He replied: "I am somewhat surprised at the concluding paragraph, to the effect, if the place is carried by assault, no prisoners will be taken. In my opinion I can hold this post. If you want it, come and take it."[12]

With Federal reinforcements on the way Hood did not have the time to besiege Resaca, and could not afford to suffer the heavy losses that probably would have occurred in an outright attack. So he went looking for an easier target, which he found the next day at Dalton. Another demand for surrender was sent to a Federal commander but this time, instead of a challenge, Hood came away with the town of Dalton, and about 1,000 Union prisoners. Taking a page out of Sherman's book of war, Hood's troops destroyed about 20 miles of the Western and Atlantic track, from Dalton all the way to Tunnel Hill.[13]

So far Hood's operations in northern Georgia were turning out better than he had originally planned. This success induced Hood to "change my original plan to draw Sherman to the Alabama line and then give battle." He decided to advance toward the Tennessee River. By threatening the railroad and bridges over the river, Hood felt that "Sherman would be compelled still further to detach and divide his forces, whilst at the same time he continued his march northward. I intended then to entice him as near the Tennessee line as possible, before offering battle."[14]

General Hood completed his reversal of the route taken by the Federal army on the way to Atlanta by moving through Snake Creek Gap on his way west where, "the Army passed through the gaps in the mountains, and halted during the 15th and 16th at Cross Roads, in a beautiful valley about nine miles south of Lafayette.[15]

These first two weeks of October were probably the most successful period Hood enjoyed as commander of the Army of Tennessee. He had brought Sherman out of Atlanta, forcing the Federal commander to chase the nimble Confederate army around northern Georgia with little chance of catching up. Hood had captured a few small garrisons of Federal troops and destroyed a large amount of the railroad track that Sherman depended on to keep his army alive. Most important of all, he hoped, Hood was gradually restoring the morale and fighting spirit of his army.

The Confederate authorities were also trying to rally the spirit of the civilian population. Upon assuming command of the Military Division of the West, General Beauregard issued an emotional statement on October 17:

> The army of Sherman still defiantly holds Atlanta. He can and must be driven from it. It is only for the good people of Georgia and surrounding States to speak the word, and the work is done. We have abundant provisions. There are men enough in the country, liable to and able for service, to accomplish the result....
>
> My countrymen, respond to this call as you have done in days that are past, and, with the blessing of a kind and overruling Providence, the enemy shall be driven from your soil. The security of your wives and daughters from the insults and outrages of a brutal foe shall be established soon, and be followed by a permanent and honorable peace. The claims of home and country, wife and children, uniting with the demands of honor and patriotism, summon us to the field. We cannot, dare not, will not fail to respond. Full of hope and confidence, I come to join you in your struggles, sharing your privations, and, with your brave and true men, to strike the blow that shall bring success to our arms, triumph to our cause, and peace to our country.[16]

Unfortunately for the Confederate cause, after all the suffering and destruction that had been visited upon the people of northern Georgia by both sides it was unlikely that mere words could arouse a great deal more enthusiasm for the war. One Union officer, Thomas Osborn, remembered:

> Wherever we have been on this campaign we have, so far as the country afforded supplies, lived off of the country and have pretty effectively cleaned it of all that man or beast could eat. The people who were so unfortunate as to live on the line of march of either of the armies will be sufficiently hungry this winter to regret that Hood ever made this raid. But this is one of the misfortunes of war, and war, at the best, is scientific cruelty.[17]

While Hood was pleased with the results of the raid through northern Georgia, he accomplished more than he knew. The pointless marching around in pursuit of Hood helped to solidify Sherman's conviction that Atlanta was not worth what it cost to hold it. As long as a substantial Confederate army could cut across the lines of communication with Chattanooga and Nashville almost at will, the risk of having a Federal army cut off hundreds of miles from is base was too great.

After following the Confederate army for two weeks Sherman decided that Hood would be

> compelled to go on to Chattanooga and Bridgeport, or to pass around by Decatur and abandon altogether his attempt to make us let go our hold of Atlanta by attacking our communications. It was clear to me that he had no intention to meet us in open battle, and the lightness and celerity of his army convinced me that I could not possibly catch him on a stern-chase.

It was time to consider a new plan of action.[18]

Not long after entering Atlanta, Sherman began formulating a plan for a new and different kind of campaign. He began the battle to get his plan approved on October 1, by cable with his superiors. In a telegram to Grant, Sherman suggested that if Hood marched off to the west or north,

> why would it not do for me to leave Tennessee to the force which Thomas has and the reserves soon to come to Nashville, and for me to destroy Atlanta, and then march across Georgia to Savannah or Charleston, breaking roads and doing irreparable damage? We cannot remain on the defensive.[19]

On October 2, Sherman communicated with Thomas at Nashville:

> Out of the forces now here, and at Atlanta I propose to organize an efficient army of 60, to 65,000 men, with which I propose to destroy Macon, Augusta, and it may be Savannah and Charleston.... By this I propose to demonstrate the vulnerability of the South and make its inhabitants feel that war & individual Ruin are synonymous terms. To pursue Hood is folly, for he can twist & turn like a fox and wear out any army in pursuit. To continue to occupy long lines of Railroad simply exposes our small detachments to be picked up in detail and forces me to make countermarches to protect lines of Communication. I know I am right in this and shall proceed to its maturity.[20]

Throughout the rest of the month Sherman continued to make his case for leaving Atlanta, ignoring whatever Hood did, and marching his army to some location on the coast. In a message to General Grant on the 9th he argued:

> It will be a physical impossibility to protect the roads, now that Hood, Forrest, Wheeler, and the whole batch of devils, are turned loose without home or habitation. ... I propose that we break up the railroad from Chattanooga forward, and that we strike out with our wagons for Milledgeville, Millen, and Savannah. Until we can repopulate Georgia, it is useless for us to occupy it; but the utter destruction of its roads, houses, and people, will cripple their military resources. By attempting to hold the roads, we will lose a thousand men each month, and will gain no result. I can make this march, and make Georgia howl![21]

The more he thought about it the more convinced Sherman became that he needed to change the direction of the war in the South. On the 11th he again telegraphed Grant:

> We cannot now remain on the defensive. With twenty-five thousand infantry and the bold cavalry he has, Hood can constantly break my road. I would infinitely prefer to make a wreck of the road and of the country from Chattanooga to Atlanta, including the latter city; send back all my wounded and unserviceable men, and with my effective army move through Georgia, smashing things to the sea. Instead of being on the defensive, I will be on the offensive. Instead of my guessing at what he means to do, he will have to guess at my plans. The difference in war would be fully twenty-five per cent.[22]

During late October Sherman was busy putting together the force he would take to the coast. General Grant was still nervous about allowing Hood to roam freely around northern Georgia and Tennessee and a flurry of telegrams passed between Grant and Sherman during the first week of November. On November 1, Grant wrote to his friend:

> Do you not think it advisable now that Hood had gone so far north to entirely settle with him before starting on your proposed campaign? With Hood's army destroyed you can go where you please with impunity. I believed, and still believe, that if you had started south whilst Hood was in the neighborhood of you he would have been forced to go after you. Now that he is so far away, he might look upon the chase as useless and go in one direction whilst you are pushing in the other. If you can see the chance for destroying Hood's army, attend to that first and make your other move secondary.[23]

Sherman telegraphed back informing Grant that the Confederate army was now at Tuscumbia waiting to cross into Tennessee and that General Thomas would soon have well over 40,000 men under his command in Tennessee, more than enough troops to deal with Hood. Sherman repeated his reasons for not wanting to chase after Hood again, saying, "If I were to let go Atlanta and North Georgia and make for Hood, he would, as he did here, retreat to the southwest, leaving his militia ... to occupy our conquests, and the work of last summer would be lost."[24]

As always Sherman's first goal was the Confederate railroad system, or rather the destruction of the railroad system. In one sentence he stated all the reasons he thought were necessary to make the campaign through Georgia: "I will destroy all the railroads of Georgia and do as much substantial damage as is possible, reaching the sea-coast near one of the points hitherto indicated...."[25]

Apparently reassured by Sherman's confidence, General Grant wired on the 2nd reversing his earlier position and saying, "With the force, however, you have left with Thomas, he must be able to take care of Hood and destroy him. I do not really see that you can withdraw from where you are to follow Hood, without giving up all we have gained in territory. I say, then, go as you propose."[26]

Sherman quickly replied reinforcing his previous arguments:

> If I could hope to overhaul Hood I would turn against him with my whole force. Then he retreats to the southwest, drawing him as a decoy from Georgia, which is his chief object.... Thomas will have a force strong enough to prevent his reaching any country in which we have an interest, and he has orders if Hood turns to follow me to push for Selma. No single army can catch him, and I am convinced the best results will result from defeating Jeff. Davis' cherished plan of making me leave Georgia by maneuvering. Thus far I have confined my efforts to thwart his plans, and reduced my baggage so that I can pick up and start in any direction, but I would regard a pursuit of Hood as useless.[27]

In another telegram to Grant on the 2nd, Sherman wrote that he had ordered Thomas to fortify and hold Nashville, Chattanooga, and Decatur until all the reinforcements heading to his command arrived, then attack and destroy the invaders.

Sherman also noted what he believed could be an extra benefit from his campaign: "I think Jeff. Davis will change his tune when he finds me advancing into the heart of Georgia instead of retreating, and I think it will have an immediate effect on your operations at Richmond."[28]

On November 6, Sherman sent a long telegram to Grant summarizing his reasons for making the campaign through Georgia and what he hoped to accomplish. He is also unswerving in his opposition to abandoning Atlanta under circumstances that would make it appear that he was forced or maneuvered out of the city. There are abundant supplies in Atlanta and Sherman regarded "Davis' threat to get his army on my rear, or on my communications, as a miserable failure." If Sherman were to go after Hood's army it was probable that the Confederates would have simply moved back into the city, easily taking back what cost so much to gain: "I am more than satisfied that Beauregard has not the men to attack fortifications or meet me in battle, and it would be a great achievement for him to make me abandon Atlanta by mere threats and maneuvers."[29]

In addition to damaging the ability of the Confederacy to make war Sherman is well aware of the political implications. The timing of the campaign is especially interesting. Not wanting to do anything that could jeopardize the reelection of President Lincoln, the campaign will not start until after the election. Sherman's explanation of the reasons for his march exhibits his understanding of the big picture:

> I propose to act in such a manner against the material resources of the South as utterly to negative Davis' boasted threat and promises of protection. If we can march a well-appointed army right through his territory, it is a demonstration to the world, foreign and domestic, that we have a power which Davis cannot resist. This may not be war, but rather statesmanship, nevertheless it is overwhelming to my mind that there are thousands of people abroad and in the South who will reason thus: If the North can march an army right through the South, it is proof positive that the North can prevail in this contest, leaving only open the question of its willingness to use that power.[30]

Confident that President Lincoln would win the election, Sherman believed that the guarantee that the war would be prosecuted to the end coupled with the physical and psychological damage wrought by his campaign "makes a complete, logical whole. Even without a battle, the result operating upon the minds of sensible men would produce fruits more than compensating for the expense, trouble, and risk."[31]

There were three possible routes for Sherman to take: southeast to Savannah, south past Andersonville to the Apalachicola River, or down the Chattahoochee toward Pensacola, Florida. The route eventually taken, to Savannah, was chosen, at least partially, because this destination allowed the quickest way for Sherman to take his army north to aid in ending the war in Virginia. Well aware that his army would be out of touch with the North during the campaign Sherman told General Grant that he would "trust to the Richmond papers to keep you well advised." And in a final note on what kind of campaign he expected to wage Sherman stated that, "I will see that the road is broken completely between the Etowah and the Chattahoochee, including their bridges, and that Atlanta itself is utterly destroyed."[32]

General Sherman issued Special Field Order No. 119 on November 8 informing his army of the coming campaign. Since the route and final destination was still not settled on the men were told little but generalities such as:

> It is sufficient for you to know that it involves a departure from our present base, and a long and difficult march to a new one. All the chances of war have been considered and provided for, as far as human sagacity can. All he asks of you is to maintain that discipline, patience, and courage which have characterized you in the past, and he hopes, through you, to strike a blow at our enemy that will have a material effect in producing what we all so much desire — his complete overthrow. Of all things the most important is that the men, during marches and in camp, keep their places and not scatter about as stragglers or foragers, to be picked up by a hostile people in detail.[33]

On November 9th Special Field Order No. 120 was issued detailing the organization of the army and what was expected along the march:

> 1. The army was divided into two wings with the Right Wing consisting of the Fifteenth and Seventeenth Corps and commanded by Major General Howard. The Left Wing had Major General Slocum commanding the Fourteenth and Twentieth Corps.
>
> 2. When on the move the army would use at least four roads as close to parallel as possible and coming together only on Sherman's order.
>
> 3. There would be no general supply train for the entire army. Each corps would provide transportation with each regiment using one wagon and one ambulance and each brigade responsible for supplies and ammunition.
>
> 4. The men were encouraged to "forage liberally on the country during the march." Each brigade would have its own foraging party led by an officer. They were to keep a 10-day supply of provisions in the wagons. In addition, "Soldiers must not enter the dwellings of the inhabitants, or commit any trespass."
>
> 5. Only corps commanders were to have the authority to destroy property. In areas where there was no opposition there was to be no destruction. But "should guerrillas or bushwhackers molest our march, or should the inhabitants

Union Major General Oliver O. Howard

burn bridges, obstruct roads, or otherwise manifest local hostility, then army commanders should order and enforce a devastation more or less relentless...."

6. The cavalry and artillery were free to impress horses and mules as needed "discriminating, however, between the rich, who are usually hostile, and the poor and industrious, usually neutral or friendly."

7. Former slaves who were able to work could be taken along if they wished but commanders had to be careful that there were enough supplies, the soldiers coming first.

8. A pioneer battalion was to be organized for each army corps to repair roads and bridges. Able-bodied former slaves were to be assigned to this work.[34]

Sherman considered these orders "so clear, emphatic, and well-digested" that there were few if any changes during the campaign. Justifiably proud of his army he later wrote that "though they called for great sacrifice and labor on the part of the officers and men, I insist that these orders were obeyed as well as any similar orders ever were."[35]

The army that marched to the sea was comprised of the best men Sherman could collect.

> The most extraordinary efforts had been made to purge this army of non-combatants and of sick men, for we knew well that there was to be no place of safety save with the army itself; our wagons were loaded with ammunition, provisions, and forage, and we could ill afford to haul even sick men in the ambulances, so that all on this exhibit may be assumed to have been able-bodied, experienced soldiers....[36]

The officers commanding this army of picked soldiers were highly competent veterans that could be relied on under any circumstances. Oliver O. Howard was a native of Maine and a career soldier who graduated from West Point in 1854. He originally was stationed in Virginia and lost his right arm at Fair Oaks in the spring of 1862. After returning to service he fought at Antietam, Fredericksburg, Chancellorsville and Gettysburg before being transferred to the Army of the Cumberland, succeeding to the command after General McPherson was killed.[37]

Henry W. Slocum was born in New York and graduated from West Point in 1852. He was out of the army for several years but volunteered when the war began. He also fought in Virginia and came west with Howard. Unable to get along with General Hooker, Slocum was assigned to the garrison at Vicksburg and joined the army when Hooker left.[38]

General Howard's Right Wing contained the Fifteenth Corps, commanded by Maj. Gen. P.J. Osterhaus and the Seventeenth Corps, under Maj. Gen. Frank P. Blair. General Slocum's Left Wing was made up of the Fourteenth Corps, Maj. Gen. Jefferson C. Davis commanding, and the Twentieth Corps, commanded by Brig. Gen. A.S. Williams. General Sherman retained personal control of the cavalry division commanded by General Kilpatrick.[39]

In addition to all the preparations being carried out in Atlanta there was one additional item that was indispensable for Sherman's campaign to become a success: George Thomas. No matter how much damage Sherman caused in Georgia if Hood were able to invade Tennessee, defeat the Federal forces there, and move into Kentucky or even further, disaster for the Union could be the result.

General Cox wrote: "Sherman had the most implicit confidence in General Thomas' ability to bear the great responsibilities to be imposed upon him, writing to Halleck that he was better suited to the emergency than any man he had." Thomas' temperament was ideally suited to the task assigned to him. He was to conduct a "cautious and purposely dilatory campaign till his reinforcements should be well in hand, and then ... drive Hood southward and follow him wherever he should go."[40]

Sherman returned to Atlanta on the 14th of November to find that all the preparations for the campaign had been made. The army would be taking about 2,500 wagons and 600 ambulances. Each man would carry 40 rounds of ammunition, with another 200 per man carried in the wagons. There would be only 65 pieces of artillery to accompany the army and each of these had about 200 rounds of ammunition. The most pressing issue, as always, was food:

> Colonel Beckwith, chief commissary, reporting one million two hundred thousand rations in possession of the troops, which was about twenty days' supply, and he had on hand a good supply of beef-cattle to be driven along on the hoof. Of forage, the supply was limited, being of oats and corn enough for five days, but I knew that within that time we would reach a country well stocked with corn, which had been gathered and stored in cribs, seemingly for our use, by Governor Brown's militia.[41]

Inside Atlanta the destruction had already begun. The railroad depot, roundhouse, and machine shops of the Georgia Railroad had been demolished and the rubble set on fire. The Confederates had been using one of the machine shops as a storeroom for artillery shells and when the fire hit the building there were massive explosions with shell fragments flying everywhere. Much of the business district near the depot and the center of the city caught fire and burned all night. By the next day there was little of Atlanta left for the Federal army to occupy. All was ready and it was time to go.[42]

In his memoirs Sherman later wrote about the irony of the situation he had worked so hard to bring about:

> It surely was a strange event—two hostile armies marching in opposite directions, each in the full belief that it was achieving a final and conclusive result in a great war, and I was strongly inspired with the feeling that the movement on our part was a direct attack upon the rebel army and the rebel capital at Richmond, though a full thousand miles of hostile country intervened, and that, for better or worse, it would end the war.[43]

Maj. George Nichols described what he saw in Atlanta before the Federal army departed, and before the fires destroyed most of it.

> Atlanta is entirely deserted by human beings, excepting a few soldiers here and there. The houses are vacant; there is no trade or traffic of any kind; the streets are empty. Beautiful roses bloom in the gardens of fine houses, but a terrible stillness and soli-

tude cover all, depressing the hearts even of those who are glad to destroy it. In the peaceful homes at the North there can be no conception how these people have suffered for their crimes.[44]

Now it was time for the army to move on and administer more punishment, hoping that the war would end sooner because of it.

Chapter 14

The Tide Turns

In a letter to a friend, Grant gave his appraisal of the current military situation. To most people in the North this year's campaign looked like another failure, but Grant could see something else. Both of the Confederacy's main armies, Lee in Virginia and Johnston in Georgia, were as good as trapped by stronger Federal armies. They could not come out of their fortifications and fight and they could not run away. Grant was convinced that as long as the people of the North did not give up the war would eventually be won. At that woeful time this type of confidence in the future was rare, but accurate, and soon Grant's positive outlook would be rewarded.[1]

After the horrendous casualties and perceived lack of progress through the spring and most of the summer there was a marked change starting in August that brought with it a string of victories that virtually assured President Lincoln's reelection and the continuation of the war until victory was won.

The first of these victories occurred at Mobile, Alabama. Early on the morning of August 5, the man who captured New Orleans, Adm. David Farragut, led a Union fleet of 18 vessels, four of which were ironclad monitors, into Mobile Bay. The fleet's objective was not to capture the city of Mobile; it was too well-protected and the water was too shallow for the larger vessels of the fleet. Admiral Farragut's goal was to pass the forts protecting the bay and capture or destroy the small Confederate fleet led by the powerful Confederate ironclad *Tennessee*. A Federal fleet safely inside the bay would effectively cut the city of Mobile off from the outside world.[2]

The wooden ships were lashed together in pairs, if one were damaged the other could bring them both through. The monitors started in advance because of their slower speed and it was hoped they would at least partially protect the wooden ships from the fire of the forts. Behind the ironclads the *Brooklyn* and *Octorora* led the wooden ships followed by Farragut's flagship *Hartford* and the *Metacomet*.[3]

The passage into the bay was difficult as the fleet was pounded by fire from Fort Morgan on one side of the channel and Fort Gaines on the other side. The most serious loss was the monitor *Tecumseh*, sunk with 120 officers and men. For some reason the *Brooklyn* stopped in an area that was right between both Confederate forts and despite several orders to move forward she held up the fleet under heavy fire until Farragut ordered the *Hartford* to pass her.[4]

After passing the forts the Federal ships anchored in the harbor and began to make repairs and care for the many wounded. It was now that the *Tennessee* came out into the bay and attacked the fleet, making straight for the *Hartford*. Fortunately for the Union vessel when the *Tennessee* came up to exchange broadsides only one of her guns fired and she soon became the target of the entire Federal fleet. Although most of the shot bounced off the Confederate ship's armor the storm of cannon balls finally took its toll and with her smoke-stack and rudder-chain shot away and her admiral wounded by a shell fragment the *Tennessee* put out a white flag and the battle was over.[5]

Admiral Farragut's hard-won victory closed one of the few ports left to the Confederacy and provided a much-needed break in the constant stream of disappointing news that had been flooding the North throughout the summer.

During the month of September the North began receiving some desperately needed good news. Sherman's capture of Atlanta was the biggest Federal victory since Vicksburg but later in the month there was finally news to celebrate from Virginia.

The Shenandoah Valley had caused nothing but problems for Federal commanders since the beginning of the war. After Jubal Early's daring raid on Washington in July, General Grant decided it was time to consolidate several military districts into one and put them under a competent and aggressive commander. He had to look no farther than the cavalry commander of the Army of the Potomac. Maj. Gen. Philip H. Sheridan was a pugnacious little man that Grant had brought east when he assumed command of all the armies. Sheridan had proven himself to be an excellent battlefield commander in several battles and Grant remembered that it was Sheridan who wanted to continue pursuing the beaten Confederates after leading his division up Missionary Ridge at Chattanooga. Here was a man who was competent to lead a large body of men, and who was aggressive enough to tackle Jubal Early and his tough veterans. Despite some reservations by Lincoln and Stanton that Sheridan was too young, Grant gave the command of the consolidated districts to Sheridan: "I want Sheridan put in command of all the troops in the field, with instructions to put himself south of the enemy and follow him to the death. Wherever the enemy goes let our troops go also."[6]

In addition to defeating the Confederate military forces in the Shenandoah Valley, Grant's orders to Sheridan envisioned the removal of the valley as a source of supplies for the Confederacy: "Do all the damage to railroads and crops you can. Carry off stock of all descriptions, and negroes, so as to prevent further planting. If the war is to last another year, we want the Shenandoah Valley to remain a barren waste."[7]

For about six weeks Sheridan organized his command and moved up and down the Shenandoah Valley with Early, each looking for an advantage to strike the other. Finally Sheridan found what he had been looking for at Winchester. Early had split his forces and Sheridan saw an opportunity to strike and destroy one part before they could be joined. Early on the morning of September 19, Sheridan launched an attack with his entire force of three infantry corps and three divisions of cavalry, more than double his opponent's number. At first it went badly for the Federals; narrow roads were blocked by wagon trains and the delay allowed Early to bring his army together before Sheridan could attack with his full force. The result was a hard-fought battle with heavy casualties for both sides. In the afternoon the combination of a flank attack by Sheridan's reserves and a simultaneous attack by Federal cavalry on the same flank and rear broke the Confederates and as Sheridan reported he "sent them flying through Winchester." Both sides suffered heavy casualties with the Federals losing about 1,000 more men than the Confederates; but Sheridan could afford the loss, and Early could not.[8]

Sheridan closely followed the retreating Confederates and on September 22 used the same tactics of a flank attack to rout them from an excellent defensive position at Fisher's Hill. Early suffered nearly three times the number of casualties as did Sheridan's army, including about 1,000 prisoners. Sheridan's second victory in four days thrilled the people of the North. At last a Federal army was having success in the Shenandoah Valley. After all the disappointment with the bloody offensive against Lee that seemed to produce nothing but casualties the victories in the valley and Sherman's capture of Atlanta earlier in the month provided hope that the war was being won after all. In just a few short days the anguish of three years of defeat and humiliation suffered by the Federal armies in the Shenandoah Valley had been replaced with joy and optimism.[9]

Faced with only minor harassment from guerrilla bands Sheridan now set out to fulfill the second part of his orders: destroy the valley. Like locusts the Federal troops spread out burning barns and mills and killing the livestock they did not take for their own use. Never before had America seen such widespread and organized destruction. One Union soldier wrote: "Before the army was a fertile region filled with the stores of an abundant harvest just gathered; behind was a devastated region."[10]

The final battle in the valley was one of the most amazing of the entire war. On October 19, Early launched a predawn attack on the Federal army while it slept peacefully at Cedar Creek. The surprise was complete and the vast majority of the Federal troops were driven back several miles. Sheridan had been at a meeting in Washington and was just returning to his command when he saw thousands of his men strung out along the road retreating from the battlefield. As he rode toward Cedar Creek he rallied the beaten troops with the force of his personality and the trust they had in him as their leader. Thousands returned to the front to join the men who were still fighting and later that afternoon they attacked and routed the Confederates. It was an expensive victory with Sheridan losing nearly twice as many men as Early but it was worth the price in the long run. The surviving Confederates were devastated, not just from the loss of men and equipment but their morale was shattered beyond repair. No Confederate force in the valley would be more than a minor irritation for the rest of the war.[11]

The victory at Cedar Creek allowed Sheridan to continue his work in making the valley useless to the Confederacy. A Confederate staff officer wrote about what he saw at the end of October: "No one can imagine how utterly destroyed is this fine country, unless he could see it...."[12]

And Wilber Smith, a private in the Sixth Corps, wrote:

> I don't know how the citizens are going to live this winter. They say we have taken away from them everything they have — their wheat, their corn, their cattle, and everything we could find, and now as winter is coming on, they are entirely destitute. Some of these citizens are going North before we leave. The rest I suppose have deliberately embraced the idea, that they are going to starve to death, and become reconciled to it.[13]

Sherman's capture of Atlanta and Sheridan's victories in the Shenandoah Valley helped to compensate for the standoff at Petersburg and gave the people in the North a new confidence that real progress was being made toward winning the war. This confidence also produced a similar turnabout in the political fortunes of President Lincoln and the Republican Party.

Through the late summer and fall the political activities of a presidential election year continued. Abraham Lincoln was a practical politician who knew it was always best to do what it took to keep the voters happy. He frequently considered the wishes of the voters when forming policy, and had appointed some highly incompetent generals because of their political influence. As he had expected, the same people who had been unreasonably hopeful early in May became the most deeply depressed because the speedy victory they expected was nowhere in sight. But instead of trying to soften their disappointment he made it clear that if reelected the war would not end short of victory.[14]

President Lincoln took little active part in the campaign for his reelection. He made a few appearances for charities that cared for sick and wounded soldiers and occasionally gave short speeches to groups of soldiers returning to their homes after their term of service was over. To one regiment he said:

> I happen, temporarily, to occupy this house. I am a living witness that any one of your children may look to come here as my father's child has done. It is in order that each of you may have, through this free government which we have enjoyed, an open field and a fair chance for your industry, enterprise, and intelligence — that you may all have equal privileges in the race of life with all its desirable human aspirations — it is for this that the struggle should be maintained, that we may not lose our birthright.... The nation is worth fighting for to secure such an inestimable jewel.[15]

In a speech to a regiment that had just returned from Virginia and was heading back home to Ohio, the president spoke about the essence of our form of government:

> I wish it might be more generally and universally understood what the country is now engaged in. We have, as all will agree, a free government, where every man has a right to be equal with every other man. In this great struggle this form of government, and every form of human rights, is endangered if our enemies succeed.... There is involved in this struggle the question whether your children and my children shall enjoy the privileges we have enjoyed.... When you return to your homes, rise up to the height of a generation of men worthy of a free government, and we will carry out the great work we have commenced.[16]

As the Union's military situation improved the probability that the opponents of the Lincoln administration could bring about a change of government weakened drastically. John G. Nicolay and John Hay, President Lincoln's private secretaries, wrote how the president's opponents' dreams of obtaining power went up in the same smoke that rose above Atlanta:

> From the moment the Democratic convention named its candidates the stars in their courses seemed to fight against them. During the very hours when the streets of Chicago were blazing with torches, and the air was filled with the perfervid rhetoric of the peace men rejoicing over their work, Hood was preparing for the evacuation of Atlanta; and the same newspapers which laid before their readers the craven utterances of the Vallandigham platform announced the entry of Sherman into the great manufacturing metropolis of Georgia.[17]

On September 17, John C. Fremont, who was supported by the extreme radical faction of the Republican Party, withdrew his name as a presidential candidate. Fremont's statement announcing the end of his campaign illustrates the deep divide that existed within the president's own party. He stated that he withdrew from the campaign

> not to aid in the triumph of Mr. Lincoln, but to do my part toward preventing the election of the democratic candidate. In respect to Mr. Lincoln, I continue to hold exactly the sentiments contained in my letter of acceptance. I consider that his administration has been, politically, militarily, and financially, a failure, and that its necessary continuance is a cause of regret for the country.[18]

The improving military situation was especially troublesome for George B. McClellan and the Democrats. McClellan, who was honestly devoted to preserving the Union, found it impossible to strictly follow many of the proposals that came out of his party's convention. He had deep misgivings about the situation and struggled over his letter of acceptance.[19]

The final document, dated September 8, clearly showed that McClellan would run on his own interpretation of the party's platform. He wrote:

> The reëstablishment of the Union in all its integrity is, and must continue to be, the indispensable condition in any settlement. So soon as it is clear, or even probable, that our present adversaries are ready for peace, upon the basis of the Union, we should exhaust all the resources of statesmanship practiced by civilized nations and taught by the traditions of the American people, consistent with the honor and interests of the country, to secure such peace, reestablish the Union, and guarantee for the future the constitutional rights of every State. The Union is the one condition of peace. We ask no more.[20]

He also promised that individual states that desired to return to the Union would be welcomed back

> with a full guarantee of all its constitutional rights.... But the Union must be preserved at all hazards. I could not look in the face of my gallant comrades of the army

and navy, who have survived so many bloody battles, and tell them that their labors and the sacrifice of so many of our slain and wounded brethren had been in vain, that we had abandoned that Union for which we have so often periled our lives. A vast majority of our people, whether in the army and navy or at home, would, as I would, hail with unbounded joy the permanent restoration of peace, on the basis of the Union under the Constitution without the effusion of another drop of blood. But no peace can be permanent without union.[21]

In other words, if the Confederacy, or any individual state, agreed to reunion, McClellan promised to observe and preserve all of the state's rights that are guaranteed by the Constitution. Implicit in this statement was that a McClellan administration would not interfere with states that continued to permit slavery.[22]

One of the more interesting aspects of the election was that for the first time the soldiers in the field would be able to vote. When General Grant was asked his opinion on allowing the soldiers to vote he replied with irrefutable logic:

> The exercise of the right of suffrage by an army in the field has generally been considered dangerous to constitutional liberty, as well as subversive to military discipline. But our circumstances are novel and exceptional. A very large proportion of the legal voters of the United States are now either under arms in the field, or in hospitals, or otherwise engaged in the military service of the United States ... they are American citizens, having still their homes and social and political ties binding them to the states and districts from which they come and to which they expect to return. They have left their homes temporarily, to sustain the cause of their country in its hour of trial. In performing this sacred duty they should not be deprived of a most precious privilege. They have as much right to demand that their votes shall be counted in the choice of their rulers, as those citizens who remain at home; nay more, for they have sacrificed more for their country.[23]

Theodore Lyman, a colonel in the Army of the Potomac, made this observation:

> The soldiers vote is an unexpected one; they are said to show five to one for the Administration, which tells me that they identify it with the support of the war; for the troops in their private thoughts make the thrashing of the Rebs a matter of pride, as well as of patriotism.
>
> I venture to say that at no time during the war have the Rebel papers talked so desperately; they speak of the next month settling the question, and of arming the negroes. If they do this latter, the slavery candle will burn at both ends. I have no idea that the next month will settle it, though, of course, there is a chance for important movements during the autumn, as at other seasons of good weather. We must keep at them — that is the only way; no let up, no armistice.[24]

There was similar support from Sherman's army. General Alpheus Williams wrote to his daughter on October 18:

> Now I think that to abandon the war now, to submit after all that has been done and suffered, would be disgraceful to us of the North, who now live, and would entail dishonor and disaster upon our posterity for many generations.
>
> I have no particularly strong personal reasons for loving the existing administration, nor do I, in everything, admire its policy or measures. Still its great aim, in the

emergency which absolves small things, is right. It goes for fighting this rebellion until the Rebels cry, "Enough!"[25]

George W. Squier wrote home that he was "so sure as the sun shines at noon day, might the success of the democracy be considered the death nell of our Republic."[26] And, in another letter Squier wrote:

> They would have peace on any terms, howsoever dishonorable to the nation, howsoever degrading to the northern people. Having killed or crippled two thirds of the traitorous scoundrels of the south, the peace-loving democracy would require us to deify what remains. And having also by untold hardships and privations and at the cost of hundreds of thousan[d]s of lives conquered and reclaimed two thirds of the territory once subject to secession, we are now to give it all back without complaint.... Never, never, so long as life remains, as there is a God in Heaven, will we now submit to this base, cowardly concession. The soil of a thousand battlefields is sprinkled with the blood of martyrs to the union. The submissionsist[s] at Chicago are mistaken in the spirit of the army if they suppose they will submit to the vile principals there promulgated. Submission is for the week and erring, for those whose cowardly hearts would accept any terms so that safety was secured, and not for the strong and virtuous.[27]

Another Union soldier, William G. Bentley, wrote home on September 25 that if McClellan should be elected president "I shall almost despair of ever seeing our country restored to peace and happiness. If the Peace party prevails I shall be ashamed to own myself an American citizen."[28]

As the situation brightened in the North there was no hiding the gloom that was slowly enveloping the people of the South. The situation called for drastic measures. One of these measures was General Order No. 77 of October 8, which stated that all men between 18 and 45 years old had to report to camps for military instruction, no matter what civilian job they held. Only experts in certain technical fields and men with backgrounds in ordnance and munitions were exempted. The result being that there was no such thing as a white male civilian of military age, other than those physically unable to serve and those needed to produce food.[29]

Despite such drastic measures there were simply not enough men left in the Confederacy to make much of a difference in the outcome of the war. At the start of the war most Confederates believed that despite the superiority of the North in all things that it took to make war, southern valor would overcome any obstacles and victory would be given to the faithful. By now, however, it had become painfully obvious that, at least on the battlefield, men and guns were more important than good breeding and manners.

The basic problems of the Confederate war effort were linked together in a vicious circle. The southern armies were suffering from the lack of the two basic necessities to make war: men and material. The soldiers complained that there were not enough men in the army because too many were at home, exempt from military service, while they worked their farms, maintained railroads, or manufactured weapons. Part of the reason that there were shortages of food and clothing was that too many men were in the army and not enough men were at home growing the crops or repairing the railroads that transported the crops to the army. The lack of food and clothing caused more soldiers to desert, which decreased further the number of men in the army. No matter what the Confederate authorities did there simply were not enough men to go around.

After the victories in Georgia and the Shenandoah Valley there was only one really important area where the Union forces had not achieved a signal victory: Petersburg. Month after month Grant and Lee faced each other across the torn-up landscape. But, despite appearances, the Federal army was in a much better position than most northerners could see. General Lee's Army of Northern Virginia was as trapped as anything could be. He could not attack Grant's forces without suffering a disastrous slaughter that his army could not afford. The Confederates could not run away to better ground because that would cause the loss of Petersburg and Richmond and soon after, the war. Every day General Lee's army was growing weaker as the Federal lines stretched farther on each flank and Lee had longer lines to defend with the same or fewer men. It looked like a stalemate but it was just a matter of time before the Confederate lines snapped and both Grant and Lee knew it. And, eventually the people back home came to realize it too.

All through the South the people at home were feeling the unpleasant realities of war. Sallie Brock Putnam remembered,

> There was no one so obscure or humble, so far remote in the wilds and mountain fastness of our country, but that he shared in the common distress ... we had only to step out on our streets to meet here a soldier with one leg, there one with one arm, another who had lost an eye ... there was no one in our Southern land who did not "feel the war."[30]

The presidential election of 1864 took place on November 8. John G. Nicolay, one of the president's secretaries, later wrote:

> To Mr. Lincoln this was one of the most solemn days of his life. Assured of his personal success, and devoutly confident that the day of peace and the reestablishment of the Union was not far off, he felt no elation and no sense of triumph over his opponents. His mind seemed filled with mingled feelings of deep and humble gratitude to the vast majority of his fellow-citizens who were this day testifying to him their heartfelt confidence and affection, and of a keen and somewhat surprised regret that he should be an object in so many quarters of so bitter and vindictive an opposition.[31]

The results of the election were a lopsided victory for the president. The Lincoln and Johnson ticket received 212 electoral votes, leaving only 21 for General McClellan. In fact, the Democrats carried only the states of New Jersey, Delaware, and Kentucky.[32]

On November 10, newly reelected President Abraham Lincoln gave an impromptu speech to a group of citizens serenading him outside the White House:

> It has long been a grave question whether any government not too strong for the liberties of its people, can be strong enough to maintain its existence in great emer-

gencies. On this point the present rebellion brought our republic to a severe test, and a presidential election occurring in regular course during the rebellion, added not a little to the strain.

But the election was a necessity. We cannot have free government without elections; and if the rebellion could force us to forego or postpone a national election, it might fairly claim to have already conquered and ruined us. The strife of the election is but human nature practically applied to the facts of the case. What has occurred in this case must ever recur in similar cases. Human nature will not change. In any future great national trial, compared with the men of this, we shall have as weak and as strong, as silly and as wise, as bad and as good. Gold is good in its place, but living, brave, patriotic men are better than gold.[33]

Chapter 15

The March Through Georgia

The march from Atlanta to the sea began on the morning of November 15. In an attempt to confuse the Confederate defenders and obscure his intended objective Sherman sent General Howard, commanding the right wing, southeast down the railroad toward Jonesboro. General Slocum, who rode with the Twentieth Corps from his left wing, set out east by Decatur. As Sherman explained, "These were divergent lines, designed to threaten both Macon and Augusta at the same time, so as to prevent a concentration at our intended destination, or 'objective,' Milledgeville, the capital of Georgia, distant about one hundred miles." Before the march even began Sherman had decided it would take each column seven days to reach Milledgeville.[1]

Among the last acts of the Federal army before leaving Atlanta was to destroy any military property or materials that might be of use to the Confederacy. With the army leaving there were few people left to fight these fires and they soon spread to business and residential areas. Union soldier Rice Bull marched out of Atlanta on the 15th and remembered:

> Looking back, but not like Lot's wife with any desire to return, we could see the smoke and flames of the burning city rise to the sky. It was yet early morning, there was little wind and the smoke hung like a great pall over the doomed town we had just left. Soon we were out of sight of burning Atlanta but the smoke rose in black columns and was visible all day.[2]

Another man, Charles E. Benton, also remembered the burning city as his unit marched away:

> Reaching a little rise of ground at a distance from the city we halted for a rest, and turning to take a last look I beheld a column of black smoke ascending to the sky. Then another column of smoke arose, then another, and another, until it seemed that they all merged together and the whole city was in flames. The jet black smoke of the southern pine, of which the city was mostly built, spread and thickened until it covered the sky and made the day dark.[3]

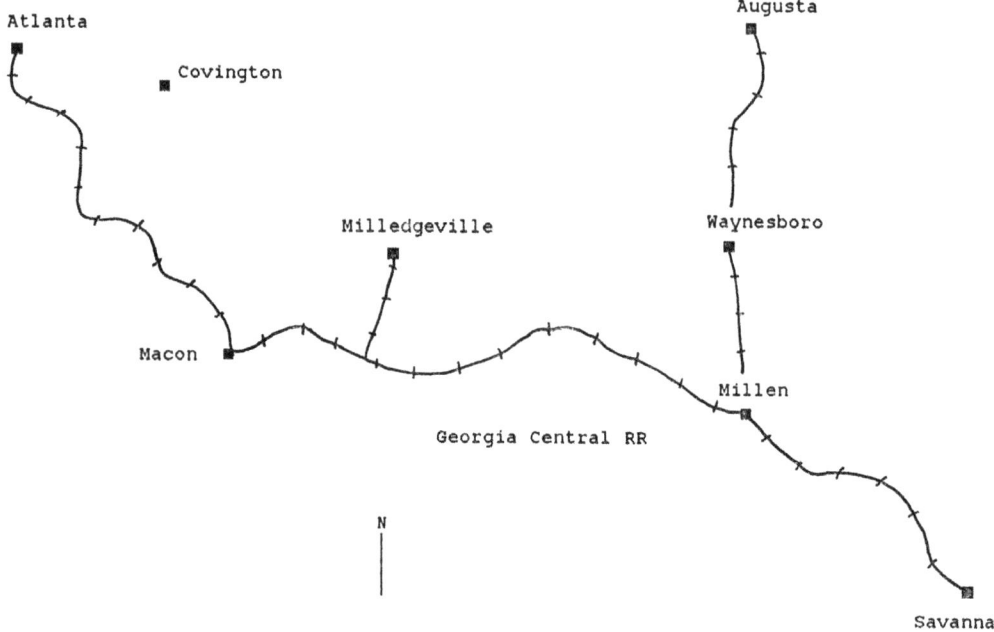

Atlanta to the Sea

As he was riding out of Atlanta, Major Nichols later remembered that he was thinking: "The city, which, next to Richmond, has furnished more material for prosecuting the war than any other in the South, exists no more as a means for injury to be used by the enemies of the Union."⁴

General Sherman also recorded what he remembered of the day he rode from the doomed city into the Georgia countryside:

> About 7 A.M. of November 16th we rode out of Atlanta by the Decatur road, filled by the marching troops and wagons of the Fourteenth Corps; and reaching the hill, just outside of the old rebel works, we naturally paused to look back upon the scenes of our past battles. Behind us lay Atlanta, smouldering and in ruins, the black smoke rising high in air, and hanging like a pall over the ruined city. Away off in the distance, on the McDonough road, was the rear of Howard's column, the gun-barrels glistening in the sun, the white-topped wagons stretching away to the south; and right before us the Fourteenth Corps, marching steadily and rapidly, with a cheery look and swinging pace, that made light of the thousand miles that lay between us and Richmond. Some band, by accident, struck up the anthem of "John Brown's soul goes marching on"; the men caught up the strain, and never before or since have I heard the chorus of "Glory, glory, hallelujah!" done with more spirit, or in better harmony of time and place.
>
> Then we turned our horses' heads to the east; Atlanta was soon lost behind the screen of trees, and became a thing of the past.... The day was extremely beautiful, clear sunlight, with bracing air, and an unusual feeling of exhilaration seemed to pervade all minds—a feeling of something to come, vague and undefined, still full

of venture and intense interest.... Indeed, the general sentiment was that we were marching for Richmond, and that there we should end the war, but how and when they seemed to care not; nor did they measure the distance, or count the cost in life, or bother their brains about the great rivers to be crossed, and the food required for man and beast, that had to be gathered by the way. There was a "devil-may-care" feeling pervading officers and men, that made me feel the full load of responsibility, for success would be accepted as a matter of course, whereas, should we fail, this "march" would be adjudged the wild adventure of a crazy fool.[5]

As his army marched off into the countryside one of the few things that General Sherman was sure of was that he would face little opposition no matter what route he took. While still at Rome he told one of the officers who was being sent to Tennessee to serve with General Thomas that the only hard fighting would be there. The Confederates simply did not have any force large enough to delay, let alone stop, 60,000 veteran soldiers. Confidence abounded in the army and from privates to generals they were ready to get going. In a letter to his wife on the day of departure Sherman wrote: "I never saw a more confident army. The soldiers think I know everything and that they can do anything...."[6]

With Confederate general Hood going in the opposite direction General Sherman had a clear path to accomplish his two main goals. The first was the destruction of railroads and military property. Sherman believed that if he could plant an army in South Carolina the war would soon end. By isolating Virginia and North Carolina from the rest of the South the Confederate army at Petersburg would soon starve. The other goal of marching through Georgia was simply to show that it could be done. What could demoralize the people of the Confederacy more than having a Federal army run rampant through what had been their most secure territory? Marching through Georgia was a perfect example of Sherman's concept of total war. In addition to victory on the battlefield it was necessary to destroy the enemy's will to fight.[7]

Even the soldiers tramping along in the dust could tell that this campaign was going to be different from anything they had previously done in the war. General Sherman certainly did not share his reasons for making the march but his men were veterans and most could figure out that part of the plan was to show southerners that they could march wherever they wanted, proving that the Confederacy was finished. Capturing cities like Macon, Augusta, or Savannah would be important victories, but crossing the heart of the Confederacy unscathed would have an impact far beyond any physical damage they could cause.[8]

The most difficult decision Sherman faced was where to end the march. While the army was moving through Georgia there would be no difficulty in finding enough food, but the army had to keep moving. The country through which the army would pass was hostile, no local government would assist in gathering supplies, and the actions of the foragers themselves meant that all nearby supplies would be quickly used up. Any long-term delay in one location could cause serious problems in feeding men and animals. The march had to be made as rapidly as possible and opening communications with the Federal fleet at a port along the coast was imperative for the campaign to succeed. Sherman left open the possibility that he would "reach the sea-coast first at Savannah or Port Royal, South Carolina, and even kept in mind the alternative of Pensacola."⁹

The first objective of the campaign was the state capital at Milledgeville. The left wing, comprising the Fourteenth and Twentieth Corps, commanded by General Slocum, moved east with the Fourteenth Corps on the left and the Twentieth several miles to the south. Two days out the Fourteenth Corps passed through Covington, "the soldiers closing up their ranks, the color-bearers unfurling their flags, and the bands striking up patriotic airs. The white people came out of their houses to behold the sight, spite of their deep hatred of the invaders, and the negroes were simply frantic with joy."¹⁰

From Covington the Fourteenth Corps turned south in the direction of Milledgeville. General Slocum and the Twentieth Corps had been moving south of Davis, reaching the town of Madison. Both corps had been destroying portions of the Georgia railroad as they marched and General Geary's division was dispatched to burn the bridge over the Oconee River.¹¹

The destruction of railroads was a prime goal of the march and a personal passion with General Sherman. The troops had the process of tearing up track down to a science. Most southern railroads were made of lighter iron than that used in the North and since the start of the war maintenance had been neglected. All the tools necessary to tear up the tracks were carried in wagons. Rice Bull described how the work was done:

The way we did the work was to line our men along the track, then with bars made of wood or iron raise the track, with both rails and ties clinging together, push the rails over on the ties where they could then be separated by iron malls. The ties would be gathered and piled up crosswise to a height of four feet with the rails placed on top. When the ties were fired the rails would become red hot and could be twisted and destroyed. The rapidity with which this could be done was surprising.¹²

Union Major General Henry W. Slocum

In addition to destroying railroads when the Federal troops came upon a farm or plantation they were very adept at quickly grabbing everything in sight that was edible. On

November 19 local resident Dolly Lunt wrote about her experience with Federal foragers:

> There they came filing up.
> I hastened back to my frightened servants and told them that they had better hide, and then went back to the gate to claim protection and a guard. But like demons they rush in! My yards are full. To my smoke-house, my dairy, pantry, kitchen, and cellar, like famished wolves they come, breaking locks and whatever is in their way. The thousand pounds of meat in my smoke-house is gone in a twinkling, my flour, my meat, my lard, butter, eggs, pickles of various kinds—both in vinegar and brine—wine, jars, and jugs are all gone. My eighteen fat turkeys, my hens, chickens, and fowls, my young pigs, are shot down in my yard and hunted as if they were rebels themselves.[13]

Maj. Henry Hitchcock later wrote:

> Evidently it is a material element in this campaign to produce among the people of Georgia a thorough conviction of the personal misery which attends war, and of the utter helplessness and inability of their "rulers," State or Confederate, to protect them. It is a terrible thing to consume and destroy the sustenance of thousands of people, and most sad and distressing in itself to see and hear the terror and grief of these women and children. But personally they are protected and their dwellings are not destroyed; and if that terror and grief and even want shall help to paralyze their husbands and fathers who are fighting us and bringing like terror and grief into more innocent homes in our Border States ... it is mercy in the end.[14]

About 20 miles south of General Slocum's troops General Howard's right wing had turned eastward once they passed Jonesboro moving through McDonough. On the far right of the column Kilpatrick's cavalry drove the few Confederate defenders further south and out of the way. They crossed the Ocmulgee River on November 19 after which General Blair's Seventeenth Corps, accompanied by General Howard, marched through Monticello as they moved southeast toward Millegeville. General Osterhaus' Fifteenth Corps and Kilpatrick's cavalry made a swing to the south to threaten Macon and destroy railroad tracks and equipment in the area.[15]

The daily routine for both wings was pretty much the same; everything had been planned ahead of time and the schedule was closely followed. As Sherman wrote: "Habitually we started from camp at the earliest break of dawn, and usually reached camp soon after noon. The marches varied from ten to fifteen miles a day, though sometimes on extreme flanks it was necessary to make as much as twenty, but the rate of travel was regulated by the wagons; and, considering the nature of the roads, fifteen miles per day was deemed the limit."[16]

On the 22nd the left wing made camp on a plantation about 10 miles from Milledgeville. Sherman discovered that it belonged to Howell Cobb, who was currently serving as a general in the southern army, and who had been United States secretary of the Treasury under President Buchanan. To William T. Sherman, the property of a former high-ranking U.S. official now a leading rebel deserved to receive no mercy.

> Of course, we confiscated his property.... Extensive fields were all round the house; I sent word back to General Davis to explain whose plantation it was, and instructed him to spare nothing. That night huge bonfires consumed the fence-rails, kept our soldiers warm, and the teamsters and men, as well as the slaves, carried off an immense quantity of corn and provisions of all sorts.[17]

While General Davis' troops were destroying Howell Cobb's plantation the Twentieth Corps had reached Milledgeville and the next day, November 23, Sherman and the rest of the left wing entered the capital of Georgia. The Federal army marched through the deserted streets with flags waving and bands playing. Most of the town's white citizens had already fled or were staying at home behind locked doors, but the troops received a joyous welcome from former slaves who came out to see their deliverers.[18]

While Sherman and Slocum were moving in on Milledgeville, General Howard's right wing was fighting the only real battle that occurred during the march until Savannah was in sight. General Woods, of the Fifteenth Corps, sent a brigade commanded by Brig. Gen. Charles C. Walcutt to protect the Union wagon trains. Walcutt took a position on a hill east of the village of Griswoldville. Posted nearby was a mixed Confederate force with Georgia state militia, artillery units and a reserve battalion, about 3,000 men, under the command of the inexperienced Pleasant J. Philips. Believing that he faced only a small advance party Philips boldly decided to attack.[19]

As the Confederate formation advanced across an open field Walcutt's veterans, many armed with new repeating rifles, cut loose with a storm of bullets, decimating the attacking ranks. The courageous southerners charged again, with the same result, before the survivors fled. General Walcutt lost about 60 men against Confederate losses of 500 to 600. After the fight many of the Federal troops were shocked and dismayed to find that their opponents were not regular troops but mostly old men and teenage boys, amateurs who sacrificed themselves for nothing. By November 23 the right wing was concentrated around Gordon, about 20 miles or so south of Milledgeville.[20]

The Confederate response to Sherman's campaign was limited by the fact that there were very few things they could do against the Federal juggernaut. The only organized troops available were Wheeler's cavalry, a division of Georgia militia, and a small force of volunteers. They gathered around Macon where Governor Brown and members of the state government had fled when Slocum approached Milledgeville. General Hardee had been put in command of the operations in Georgia and he supposed that Sherman would be heading either toward Augusta or Savannah. Doing the best he could with what he had General Hardee sent the militia to protect Augusta and ordered General Wheeler to continue to harass the flanks of the advancing Federals. Hardee then went back to his headquarters in Savannah to strengthen its defenses.[21]

On November 18, General Beauregard issued a proclamation intended to inspire resistance to the invaders:

> Arise for the defense of your native soil! Rally around your patriotic governor, and gallant soldiers. Obstruct and destroy all roads in Sherman's front, flank and rear, and his army will soon starve in your midst. Be confident and resolute. Trust in our over-ruling Providence, and success will crown your efforts. I hasten to join you in defense of your homes and firesides.[22]

Also on the 18th the Georgia Legislature passed an act calling into military service all white males between 16 and 55 and issuing a dramatic call to the people to fight:

> The whole people understand how imminent is the danger that threatens the state. Our cities are being burned, our fields laid waste, and our wives and children mercilessly driven from their homes by a powerful enemy. We must strike like men for freedom, or we must submit to subjugation.
> Death is to be preferred to loss of liberty. All must rally to the field for the present emergency, or the state is overrun.

Of course this call to the public to stand up and fight the invaders might have had more meaning if the legislators had not run away as Slocum's column approached Milledgeville.[23]

The state capital held no special meaning for Sherman so the army was soon on its way. Although few major structures and residences had suffered serious physical damage, virtually every fence and outbuilding in the area had vanished. For the residents survival now became the immediate concern since there was little food to be found anywhere and most families had lost their winter stores to the hungry soldiers.[24]

While the army occupied Milledgeville, General Sherman moved Kilpatrick's cavalry over to the left side of the army and issued orders for the next phase of the march. The right wing was to advance along the south side of the Savannah Railroad, the left wing was to move along the same general route on the north side of the railroad toward Louisville, and the cavalry was to swing around to the north and make a quick march to Millen in an attempt to liberate a nearby prisoner of war camp.[25]

General Kilpatrick reported:

> During this march my flanks and rear had been attacked again and again by Wheeler's cavalry, but without serious results, and did not prevent the column from steadily marching on. We passed through Waynesborough and.... Here, to my great regret, I learned that our prisoners had been removed two days previous. After destroying sufficient track to prevent transportation on the road for a few days, I deemed it prudent to retire to our infantry.[26]

The next week was basically a repeat of the previous week, plenty of marching and foraging with little opposition for the infantry. Theodore F. Upson wrote,

> we have regularly detailed foragers under command of officers, and they find plenty of forage of all kinds. The country seems very rich. We have had but little opposition so far—now and then a few Cavalry at some cross roads or at a stream. Meanwhile the main body of troops marches along as though nothing has happened. Such

an Army as we have I doubt if ever was got together before ... all the boys are ready for a meal or a fight and don't seem to care which it is.[27]

Sherman's "March to the Sea" is mostly famous for the devastation that was left behind as the troops moved toward the coast. Unlike many instances in history the facts in this case need no exaggeration. Union soldier Thomas Osborn wrote:

> Since I wrote you from Marietta this army has marched about 300 miles, through the enemy's country, and that without serious difficulty. We have torn up and destroyed about 200 miles of railroad, burned all bridges and cleaned up the country generally of almost every thing upon which the people could live. The Army in this movement covered a strip of country about forty miles wide. We burned all cotton, took all provisions, forage, wagons, mules, horses, cattle, hogs and poultry and the many other things which a country furnishes and which may be made available for the support of an army. In fact, as we have left the country I do not see how the people can live for the next two years.[28]

Eliza Frances Andrews wrote in her journal about some of the scenes she witnessed as she traveled through the countryside:

> About three miles from Sparta we struck the "Burnt Country," as it is well named by the natives, and then I could better understand the wrath and desperation of these poor people. I almost felt as if I should like to hang a Yankee myself. There was hardly a fence left standing all the way from Sparta to Gordon. The fields were trampled down and the road lined with carcasses of horses, hogs, and cattle that the invaders, unable either to consume or to carry away with them, had wantonly shot down to starve out the people and prevent them from making their crops. The dwellings that were standing all showed signs of pillage, and on every plantation we saw the charred remains of the gin-house and packing-screw, while here and there, lone chimney-stacks, "Sherman's Sentinels," told of homes laid in ashes.[29]

General Sherman had laid out a strict policy of what was acceptable and what was not. Foragers were not to enter private homes and were to respect private property, but anything of military value was a fair target. Of course, it was up to the leader of the foraging party to determine what constituted "private property." The same corn and pigs that would feed a family through the winter could also be used to feed Confederate soldiers.[30]

Major Hitchcock expressed the feelings of most of the army when he wrote,

> the only possible way to end this unhappy and dreadful conflict ... is to make it terrible beyond endurance. Not with wanton barbarity nor with useless destruction; but it is neither barbarous nor useless but just and indispensable to utterly destroy everything, no matter whose, or what, that does or can uphold, sustain or encourage this gigantic crime....
>
> Either we must acknowledge the "C.S.A." or we must conquer them: to conquer, we must make war, and it must be war, it must bring destruction and desolation, it must make the innocent suffer as well as the guilty, it must involve plundering, burning, killing.[31]

The frightened residents along the line of march did what they could to protect their valuables, including articles of food, but frequently to no avail. Sometimes they hid their treasures in nearby swamps or woods, but the favorite and most convenient method of concealment was simply to bury the items somewhere on their property. Some people even went so far as to use graveyards to hide their property, hoping that the invaders would not desecrate these places. More often than not, however, the Union foragers, who by now were becoming experts at locating hidden goods, would find the items. Newly turned soil, or wagon tracks, and sometimes betrayal by their slaves, would lead foragers to the family's secret hiding places.[32]

General Cox later wrote about the growing problem of stragglers:

> Little by little the stragglers became numerous enough to cause serious complaint, and they followed the command without joining it for days together, living on the country, and shirking the labors of their comrades. It is perhaps vain to hope that a great war can ever be conducted without abuses of this kind, and we may congratulate ourselves that the wrongs done were almost without exception to property, and that murders, rapes, and other heinous personal offences were nearly unknown.[33]

While the growing number of stragglers caused some serious problems there were also lighter moments. Major Hitchcock tells a story of how General Davis dealt with two thieves who he witnessed just coming out of a house, "each with a *dress* in hand. He arrested both, turned them over to his Provost Marshal, and presently each was tied and walking behind a wagon, wearing his dress with 'stolen' marked on it, amid shouts of laughter from comrades."[34]

The only real problem the Federal army faced along the route was the growing number of former slaves that attached themselves to the columns. Sherman tried to discourage these camp followers since they added thousands of extra mouths to feed. As the army moved from one plantation to another, however, it would not be reasonable to expect the slaves to just sit there and wait for the promised freedom at the end of the war when liberty could be instantly obtained by simply following the men in blue.[35]

General Slocum reported:

> Negro men, women, and children joined the column at every mile of our march; many of them bringing horses and mules, which they cheerfully turned over to the officers of the quartermaster's department. I think at least 14,000 of these people joined the two columns at different points on the march, but many of them were too old and infirm, and others too young, to endure the fatigues of the march, and were therefore left in rear. More than one-half of the above number, however, reached the coast with us. Many of the able-bodied men were transferred to the officers of the quartermaster and subsistence departments, and others were employed in the two corps as teamsters, cooks, and servants.[36]

By December 3, both wings of the army were concentrated in the vicinity of Millen where the Georgia Central met the Augusta & Savannah Railroad. The destruction of track and equipment continued unabated and soon the only direct railroad connection between Augusta and Savannah was gone. When the march continued both wings moved southeast along the Ogeechee River toward the final destination, Savannah. On the north side of the Ogeechee, General Slocum's two corps were joined by the Seventeenth Corps between the Ogeechee and Savannah Rivers, while General Osterhaus led the Fifteenth Corps along the right bank of the Ogeechee accompanied by General Howard.[37]

Not long after leaving Millen, the Confederate cavalry that had been annoying the Federal columns since the march began crossed to the north side of the Savannah River and there was virtually no opposition until the army approached Savannah. Sherman wrote,

> the whole army was in good position and in good condition. We had largely subsisted on the country; our wagons were full of forage and provisions; but as we approached the sea-coast, the country became more sandy and barren, and food became more scarce; still with little or no loss, we had traveled two-thirds of our distance, and I concluded to push on for Savannah.[38]

The next week was more like an excursion than an invasion of enemy territory. Sherman observed

> all the columns then pursued leisurely their march toward Savannah.... The weather was fine, the roads good, and every thing seemed to favor us. Never do I recall a more agreeable sensation than the sight of our camps by night, lit up by the fires of fragrant pine-knots. The trains were all in good order, and the men seemed to march their fifteen miles a day as though it were nothing.[39]

While there was no fighting to speak of as the army got closer to the coast the going got more difficult because of the terrain. As General Williams reported:

> As we approached the coast the surface of the country became flat and swampy. Large ponds or pools were met every mile or so, and the creeks spread out into several miry branches. The roads between the creeks and ponds, though apparently of sandy and substantial character, proved to be upon a thin crust, which was soon cut through by our long trains into the deep quicksand, requiring miles of corduroy.[40]

During the 9th and 10th of December, Sherman's army finally reached its destination as the columns of Federal troops closed in on the defenses of Savannah. The space between the Savannah and Ogeechee rivers was filled with Union blue. General Davis formed his corps with his left resting on the Savannah River with Generals Williams, Blair, and Osterhaus continuing the lines to the right to the Ogeechee. Cavalry detachments cut the Gulf Railroad south of the city, severing Savannah's last link to the South.[41]

The long trek was over and it was time to total up the damage. In addition to destroying the Georgia Railroad from Atlanta to Madison and the majority of the Georgia Central Railroad from Macon, through Millen, to Savannah Sherman's report further details the destruction to Georgia:

> We have also consumed the corn and fodder in the region of country thirty miles on either side of a line from Atlanta to Savannah, as also the sweet potatoes, cattle,

> hogs, sheep and poultry, and have carried away more than 10,000 horses and mules, as well as a countless number of their slaves. I estimate the damage done to the State of Georgia and its military resources at $100,000,000; at least, $20,000,000 of which has inured to our advantage, and the remainder is simple waste and destruction. This may seem a hard species of warfare, but it brings the sad realities of war home to those who have been directly or indirectly instrumental in involving us in its attendant calamities.[42]

The commanding general readily gave credit to the success of the march to the men who made it happen.

> As to the rank and file, they seem so full of confidence in themselves that I doubt if they want a compliment from me; but I must do them the justice to say that whether called on to fight, to march, to wade streams, to make roads, clear out obstructions, build bridges, make corduroy, or tear up railroads, that have done it with alacrity and a degree of cheerfulness unsurpassed. A little loose in foraging, they "did some things they ought not to have done," yet, on the whole, they have supplied the wants of the army with as little violence as could be expected, and as little loss as I calculated.[43]

The value of the march to the sea was not only in the amount of property destroyed but also, as Sherman expected, in the demoralization caused by a Federal army casually moving through an area that had been previously untouched by the war. It could have turned out much worse than it did. General Sherman knew that Bragg had gathered about 10,000 troops in Augusta and that Hardee was also working hard to build up a force to defend Savannah. While there was no Confederate force available that could have stopped the Federal army, even an overwhelming victory over a smaller force could have left the Federal army with more casualties than it could care for. That is why it was so important to avoid a fight, and that is why Sherman went to such great lengths to disguise his route and final objective as long as possible.[44]

Major Nichols wrote,

> [T]his campaign, in execution as well as in conception, was the best example of grand strategy in the war. If the enemy could have anticipated the objective point he might have gathered a sufficient force to arrest the progress of our army; he might have hung upon its flanks and rear, and endangered its existence. In that case, hindered, strangled, starved, and decimated, if it had ever reached the sea, it might have been only to surrender its feeble fragments to a merciless foe. Sherman's combinations, carefully studied, and planned with a wisdom which seems prophetic, completely obscured the great objective point of the march, and divided the confused ranks of the enemy at every point.[45]

Now that the Federal army had reached Savannah, General Sherman had to figure out how to capture it.

Chapter 16

Savannah

The Federal army was drawing close to its final destination during the second week of December. The weather was warm and dry, unseasonably good, in fact. But the terrain the army had to pass through was terrible. The few roads in the area were in dreadful condition and the countryside was full of marshes and swamps. There was so much wet, marshy terrain that most of the roads and railroad track had to be built up on causeways raised above the wetlands.[1]

General Sherman described the conditions the army faced on the outskirts of Savannah:

> As we approached Savannah the country became more marshy and difficult, and more obstructions were met in the way of felled trees, where the roads crossed the creek, swamps, or narrow causeways; but our pioneer companies were well organized, and removed these obstacles in an incredibly short time. No opposition from the enemy worth speaking of was encountered until the heads of columns were within fifteen miles of Savannah, where all the roads leading to the city were obstructed more or less by felled timber, with earth-works and artillery. But these were easily turned and the enemy driven away.[2]

Gradually the Federal skirmishers pushed the Confederates back, and on the 10th of December the defenders had been driven within the lines around Savannah. General Hardee had built and strengthened the city's fortifications from the Savannah River on the north down to near the Little Ogeechee on the south, making good use of the numerous swamps and flooded rice fields. There were only five ways to reach the city, two railroads and three roads, all of which were built up on narrow causeways and completely covered by heavy artillery which Sherman decided were "too strong for us to fight with our light field-guns."[3]

The Confederate fortifications around Savannah were altogether too impressive for Sherman to launch an immediate attack. He felt that

> [t]o assault an enemy of unknown strength at such a disadvantage appeared to me unwise, especially as I had so successfully brought my army, almost unscathed, so great a distance, and could surely attain the same result by the operation of time. I

therefore instructed my army commanders to closely invest the city from the north and west, and to reconnoiter well the ground in their fronts, respectively, whilst I gave my personal attention to opening communications with our fleet, which I knew was waiting for us in Tybee, Wassaw, and Ossabaw Sounds.[4]

No bloody frontal assaults for Sherman; he was content to settle down for a siege.

Major Hitchcock described an incident that occurred on a road about nine miles from the city that illustrates the changing nature of the war and the desperation of the Confederate defenders. Several Federal soldiers had been wounded, one lost a foot, by torpedoes buried in the road and it was assumed that others were still hidden beneath the earth. A nearby group of Confederate prisoners were ordered to precede the column and dig up the remaining torpedoes. Naturally they protested and several pleaded with Sherman to avoid the obviously dangerous duty.

> He told them their people had put these things there to assassinate our men instead of fighting them fair, and they must remove them; and if they got blown up he didn't care. These cowardly villains call us "barbarous Yankees"—and then adopt instruments of murder in cold blood where they dare not stand and fight like men. Torpedoes at the entrance to a fort are perhaps justifiable, for the fort itself is a warning. But here they run away, refuse to defend the road, but leave hidden in an open public road, without warning or chance of defense, these murderous instruments of assassination—contrary to every rule of civilized warfare.[5]

As the Federal army neared the coast Sherman had to change his priorities. The days of easy marching and tearing up railroad track were over. Savannah was a large, heavily fortified city, defended by thousands of determined troops who were led by a very capable commander. Sherman had heard rumors that General Lee had sent James Longstreet from Virginia to reinforce the city. Most importantly Sherman needed to find someplace to meet the naval vessels carrying supplies for his army. In spite of the liberal foraging during the march from Atlanta food supplies were getting low and there was little to eat in the country around Savannah. There may have been some doubt as to what was waiting for the Federals around Savannah but there was none about what lay behind them, and moving forward was the only option.[6]

The commander of the garrison at Savannah was an old foe of Sherman's, Gen. William Hardee. After being relieved of his command under Hood, at his own request, Hardee had been appointed commander of the Department of South Carolina, Georgia, and Florida in September. Hardee had made a survey of Macon and other points along Sherman's march but there was never any doubt that his main responsibility was to protect Savannah. By concentrating all the available Confederate strength he could find Hardee had been able to build up the garrison at Savannah to about 18,000 men.[7]

The defenders of the city included Confederate regulars, state and local militia and more than a few civilians. On November 28 Richard Arnold, the mayor of Savannah, issued a call for volunteers to fight the invaders:

> The time has come when every male who can shoulder a musket can make himself useful in defending our hearths and homes. Our city is well fortified, and the old

men can fight in the trenches as well as the young; and a determined and brave force can, behind entrenchments, successfully repel the assaults of treble their number.... I call upon every man not already enrolled in a local corps to come forward at once.... Let us emulate the noble examples of our sister cities of Macon and Augusta where the whole male population is in arms. By manning the fortifications we will leave free the younger men to act in the field. By prompt action a large force can be organized from our citizens above the military age, and from those who have been exempted from field service. No time is to be lost. The man who will not comprehend and respond to the emergency of the times, is forsworn to his duty and to his country.[8]

Savannah was one of the most elegant cities of the Old South. With a population of about 25,000 the city was located on the Georgia side of the Savannah River. Tree-lined streets of beautiful homes displayed the wealth that had been built up from decades of commerce, including the slave trade. The city was built on a sandy plateau about 40 feet above the water level and 15 miles from where the harbor opens onto the Atlantic Ocean. Once off the plateau the surrounding area is almost at sea level and cut into islands by numerous swamps, creeks and salt marshes. The land on which the city is built appears almost like an island in the midst of all the wetlands. Here and there are other heights on which are built plantation homes in the midst of vast rice fields that had been reclaimed from the marshes.[9]

Hardee had established two lines of fortifications to protect the city. The only remaining railroad connection to the North and Charleston was the Charleston Railroad which crossed the Savannah River about 15 miles above the city. Hardee's outside line, therefore, was set up between the Savannah and Ogeechee Rivers, far enough out to protect the railroad bridge. The defenses started at a point above the bridge and ran southwest behind Monteith Swamp to the Great Ogeechee River. Making good use of the impassable swamps in the area, detached works were strategically built along this line with sufficient artillery to cover the infantry manning the forts.[10]

The outer line was well-placed and strong enough to cause Sherman's army a great deal of trouble, except that it was not quite long enough. Sherman had three corps between the Savannah and Ogeechee rivers but the Fifteenth Corps was on the lower or south side of the Ogeechee. Howard reported:

> As the enemy was reported in some force near the twelve Mile Post, having a line of works in his front, I resolved to turn his position by sending two divisions of the Fifteenth Corps down the west bank of the Ogeechee, which were to force a crossing of the Cannouchee and send sufficient force to break the Gulf railroad and secure, if possible, King's Bridge, over the Ogeechee River, about a mile above the railroad.[11]

General Osterhaus led two divisions along the right bank of the river while General Corse's division, accompanied by Howard, advanced along a ridge road on the left bank. The road was obstructed with felled trees, but these were easily cleared and Corse passed a set of abandoned field works. Moving further they reached the Savannah Canal, quickly rebuilding a burned bridge, and came to a bridge over the Ogeechee that had also been burned. About a mile and a half above the bridge Corse built a pontoon bridge at Dillon's Ferry and crossed the river. Near King's Bridge they ran into a heavily fortified position and halted for the day.[12]

On the 9th General Blair led the Seventeenth Corps in attacks on rifle pits and an entrenched line across a road north of Howard's men. Howard described the advance as Blair moved his troops through a swamp:

> At this place the road led through a dense swamp covered with wood and undergrowth peculiar to this region. The swamp was apparently impassable, yet General Blair moved three lines of battle, preceded by a skirmish line, along on the right and left of the road for some two or three miles, occasionally in water knee-deep. He drove the enemy from every position where he made a stand.[13]

While Blair was moving forward north of the river, Howard's men were closing on King's Bridge from the south. Corse dislodged a small Confederate force and halted in a strong position about 12 miles from Savannah with his advance closing to about eight miles from the city. With Corse's success the Confederates opposing Osterhaus withdrew and the Savannah and Gulf Railroad was destroyed in several places. King's Bridge was burned but repairable and except for Fort McAllister the Confederates had vacated the outer defenses to the south.[14]

On December 10, Howard's troops closed on the inner line of defense. As General Corse advanced he

> found no opposition west of the north fork; but behind that stream, which is rather a wide swamp subject to the influence of the tides, the rebel fortifications and camps were stretched out. The rebel troops gathered on and behind the parapets, and with their banners defiantly unfurled awaited the approach of our column. The open and exposed ground, swamps, and stream in front of the rebel works forbade all sudden attacks, and the men of the advance were kept accordingly under cover, while skirmishers probed all along the lines as closely and carefully as possible.[15]

With his outer line breached on the south Hardee had little choice but to destroy the Charleston Railroad Bridge and pull his troops back within the inner defensive lines. The fortifications around Savannah had only recently been completed, as there had been no need to protect the city against an attack from the interior until the last few months. The works began on the south bank of the Savannah River at Williamson's plantation. As the line moved south much of it was fronted by rice fields, which were frequently under water. Following most of the high ground in the area the fortifications continued south, across the Georgia Central tracks, through several plantations and ended south of the city on the banks of the Little Ogeechee River near the Atlantic and Gulf Railroad bridge.[16]

The fortifications were of the same type as Sherman's men had seen all through northern Georgia: trenches, forts, and the usual felled trees and sharpened wood obstacles. What made the defenses even more formidable were the marshes and virtually impassable swamps that ran across much of the front of the lines. In addition, on Hardee's orders, the river dam at Williamson's plantation was cut so that at high tide the water would flow into the rice fields. This caused much of the land in front of the Confederate lines to be either under several feet of water or knee deep in heavy, sticky mud.[17]

After the Confederates withdrew to their inner defenses Sherman's troops moved forward to completely invest the city by the 12th. The Twentieth Corps, commanded by General Williams, was on the left between the Savannah River and the Georgia Central Railroad. General Davis' Fourteenth Corps continued the line from the railroad south just past the Ogeechee Canal where they joined General Blair's Seventeenth Corps. The Fifteenth Corps, under General Osterhaus, completed the line to the Ogeechee, near King's Bridge. Although the 1,000-foot bridge had been burned by the retreating Confederates, Sherman's engineers had performed another miracle and it was rebuilt and ready to use on the morning of the 13th.[18]

The shortage of supplies was becoming more pressing and about the only thing edible that could be found in the surrounding countryside was rice. It was imperative that a base be established and communications opened with the Federal fleet sailing off the coast. The Ogeechee River was the best way to bring supplies inland but this route was blocked by Fort McAllister, a free-standing fort constructed on the sands south of the river. Outside the fortifications of the city the fort's 200 defenders were on their own and their primary job was to buy time for Hardee to improve the city's inner defenses and delay the landing of Sherman's supplies as long as possible. As soon as King's Bridge was useable Sherman ordered Howard to immediately attack the fort.[19]

Gen. William B. Hazen's division of the Fifteenth Corps was given the assignment to take Fort McAllister and by noon of the 13th they were in position. General

Fort McAllister

Sherman gave Hazen his orders in person: "to march rapidly down the right bank of the Ogeechee, and without hesitation to assault and carry Fort McAllister by storm. I knew it to be strong in heavy artillery, as against an approach from the sea, but believed it open and weak to the rear." As an extra incentive so that there would be no delay Sherman told Hazen "that on his action depended the safety of the whole army, and the success of the campaign."[20]

Late that afternoon Hazen's troops assaulted Fort McAllister, capturing it in a short but deadly fight. Hazen later wrote:

> To make the chance of hits by the enemy as small as possible, the formation was in single rank, resembling a close line of skirmishers, and there were not more than half a dozen casualties before reaching the line of torpedoes, which was continuous around the fort and about one hundred yards in front of the entanglements. Beyond these was a palisade, and then the ditch and parapet. The two flanks of the fort were the weak points, the one on the Ogeechee side presenting a broad gravelly shore left by the receding tide. Our charge, however, carried the whole front. Our losses, which numbered one hundred and thirty, were nearly all from torpedoes, and at close quarters. The garrison did not surrender; they fought within the works, and were overcome man by man.[21]

In an amazing coincidence Sherman and Howard had been impatiently watching Fort McAllister from the top of Cheves's mill, signaling Hazen to make haste. Just then, a small steamer from the Federal fleet came into sight and cautiously moved up the river. Sherman related the interesting story:

> Soon we made out a group of officers on the deck of this vessel, signaling with a flag, "Who are you?" The answer went back promptly, "General Sherman." Then followed the question, "Is Fort McAllister taken?" "Not yet, but it will be in a minute!" Almost at that instant of time, we saw Hazen's troops come out of the dark fringe of woods that encompassed the fort, the lines dressed as on parade, with colors flying, and moving forward with a quick, steady pace. Fort McAllister was then all alive, its big guns belching forth dense clouds of smoke, which soon enveloped our assaulting lines.... On the lines advanced faintly seen in the white, sulphurous smoke; there was a pause, a cessation of fire; the smoke cleared away, and the parapets were blue with our men, who fired their muskets in the air, and shouted so that we actually heard them, or felt that we did.

About 15 minutes later the fort was in Federal hands and the Ogeechee was opened all the way to King's Bridge. The question of supplying the army was over.[22]

In addition to the much-needed supplies the Federal fleet brought some items that were appreciated almost as much — newspapers and mail. Theodore Upson remembered his thoughts at the time:

> We got some Northern papers to day. It seems that the good people up there were teribly worried about us. They called us the *Lost Army*. And some thought we never would show up again. I don't think they know what kind of an Army this is that Uncle Billy has. Why, if Grant can keep Lee and his troops busy we can tramp all over this Confederacy; and by the time we were through with that, there would be nothing left but the ground and that would be in a state primeval as the Poet says.[23]

Upon reaching the main line of fortifications Sherman's men were stopped cold. Frequent artillery duels and sharpshooting continued for days. There were several small, local attacks looking for weak points, but none were found. General Williams reported

> the assailable points in our front were very few; almost every foot was covered deep by artificial ponds from the irrigating canals, behind which and upon the approaches were strong earthworks for artillery, connected throughout by rifle-pits well constructed. The confidence of the troops in carrying these works was, however, perfect and earnest.[24]

Noting his ability to receive supplies and heavy artillery now that the river was open, Sherman sent a formal request for surrender to General Hardee on December 17:

> You have doubtless observed, from your station at Rosedew that sea-going vessels now come through Ossabaw Sound and up the Ogeechee to the rear of my army, giving me abundant supplies of all kinds, and more especially heavy ordnance necessary for the reduction of Savannah. I have already received guns that can cast heavy and destructive shot as far as the heart of your city; also I have for some days held and controlled every avenue by which the people and garrison of Savannah can be supplied, and I am therefore justified in demanding the surrender of the city of Savannah and its dependent forts; and shall wait a reasonable time for your answer, before opening with heavy ordnance. Should you entertain the proposition, I am prepared to grant liberal terms to the inhabitants and garrison; but should I be forced to resort to assault, or the slower and surer process of starvation, I shall then feel justified in resorting to the harshest measures, and shall make little effort to restrain my Army — burning to avenge a great National wrong they attach to Savannah and to large Cities which have been so prominent in dragging our Country into civil war.[25]

Along with this note Sherman enclosed a copy of General Hood's surrender demand at Resaca where he threatened to take no prisoners if an assault was necessary.

Hardee immediately sent a reply that same day repeating much of Sherman's note and stating that his lines were intact:

> Your statement that you have, for some days, held and controlled every avenue by which the people and garrison can be supplied, is incorrect. I am in free and constant communication with my department. Your demand for the surrender of Savannah and its dependent forts is refused.
>
> With respect to the threats conveyed in the closing paragraphs of your letter [of what may be expected in case your demand is not complied with], I have to say that I have hitherto conducted the military operations intrusted to my direction in strict accordance with the rules of civilized warfare, and I should deeply regret the adoption of any course by you that may force me to deviate from them in future.[26]

Hardee was correct in stating that Sherman did not have control of all the routes to the city. On the South Carolina side of the Savannah River was a plank road known as the Union Causeway. Sherman's troops did not try to cut this road because he thought it was impracticable or unwise to push any considerable force across the Savannah River, for the enemy held the river opposite the city with ironclad gun-boats, and could destroy any pontoons laid down by us between Hutchinson's Island and the South Carolina shore, which would isolate any force sent over from that flank.[27]

Despite his negative reply to Sherman's request for surrender Hardee could certainly see that he could not hold out for very long, especially once a serious bombardment began. Col. Charles C. Jones Jr., Hardee's chief of artillery, later wrote:

> The further retention of Savannah was rendered impracticable, and the salvation of its garrison became the problem of the hour. General Hardee's instructions from General Beauregard were to hold Savannah only so long as, in his judgment it might be advisable to do so; and that whatever it became necessary to decide between a sacrifice of the garrison or the city, to preserve the former for operation elsewhere.[28]

As good an officer as he was, Hardee had probably already decided that he would have to evacuate the city before receiving Sherman's request for surrender. The only real question facing the Confederate commander was how much longer he could stay in the city knowing that his only way out might be lost at any time.

Evacuating Savannah by boat was impracticable simply because of the amount of men and equipment that needed to be moved. The only way to accomplish the task was to bridge the waterways to the South Carolina shore. A series of bridges constructed with pontoons and rice flats were built across the Savannah River. One bridge stretched nearly 1,000 feet from the end of West Broad Street to Hutchinson's Island, in the middle of the river. Two other shorter bridges connected Hutchinson's Island to Pennyworth Island and then across another section of river to the South Carolina shore. The rice flats, about 70 or 80 feet long, were strapped together and covered with wood planks taken from wharves along the riverfront. The escape route then extended along the top of a rice dam that was just wide enough to accommodate artillery and wagons. All was ready by the morning of December 20.[29]

During the day of the 20th artillery fire from the Confederate works and gunboats in the river was dramatically increased. Several times during the day Federal soldiers reported movement toward the South Carolina shore but apparently no one was willing to order the troops forward to interfere with the enemy withdrawal. General Sherman had left the army and at that time was on Hilton Head Island meeting with the commander of the Federal fleet, Adm. John A. Dahlgren, and Gen. John G. Foster, commander of the Department of the South. Before leaving for the meeting Sherman had left orders that no action was to be taken until he returned.[30]

Inside Savannah the exodus was on. Military and civilian traffic over the rickety bridges was continuous as hundreds of wagons and carriages crossed the river. To keep the noise down as much as possible straw was put down on the bridges while most of the civilians who were leaving walked next to wagons filled with as many of their possessions as they could pack. Since the guns in the works were going to have to be abandoned the Confederates kept up their fire until the last possible moment before they pulled out. This helped to convince Federal commanders that the lines were still manned and keep any patrols far enough away from the escape route so that the withdrawal would not be discovered until it was too late to do anything about it.[31]

General Williams reported:

> In the night General Geary reported to me that the movements across the river were apparently still going on. Division commanders were instructed to keep in the alert and press their pickets closer to the rebel works.... At 3:30 o'clock on the morning of the 21st Geary reported that Barnum's brigade was in the rebel main line. Orders were sent him and General Ward to advance the picket-lines and follow with their divisions into the city.[32]

With the Confederate army gone, Mayor Arnold and several city officials rode out on the Louisville Road under a flag of truce to surrender the city and ask for protection of the lives and property of the remaining civilians. Troops from Henry Barnum's brigade were the first to enter the city and quickly spread out to keep order. Hardee's rear guard had destroyed the bridges behind them and the large Confederate ironclad *Savannah* remained off Screven's Ferry, sending occasional shells over to discourage any pursuit of the fleeing Confederates. Federal artillery fired on the ship but did no damage and later that night she was destroyed by her crew.[33]

In an ironic twist, the man who had engineered the remarkable march from Atlanta and the capture of Savannah missed the final event. While returning from Hilton Head Island, Sherman's ship ran aground and it was not until the evening of the 21st that he received news of the capture of Savannah from a tugboat sent out to pull his ship free. Returning to camp that night, Sherman did not enter Savannah until the morning of the 23rd.[34]

In a telegram to President Lincoln on the 22nd, Sherman wrote: "I beg to present you as a Christmas-gift the city of Savannah, with one hundred and fifty heavy guns and plenty of ammunition, also about twenty-five thousand bales of cotton."[35]

Also on the 22nd Sherman sent a lengthy telegram to Grant:

> I take great satisfaction in reporting that we are in possession of Savannah and all its forts.... Our troops entered at daylight yesterday, took about 800 prisoners, over 100 guns [some of the heaviest caliber], and a perfect string of forts from Savannah around to McAllister, also 12,000 bales of cotton, 190 cars, 13 locomotives, 3 steamboats, and an immense supply of shells, shot, and all kinds of ammunition. There is a complete arsenal here, and much valuable machinery. The citizens mostly remain, and the city is very quiet....[36]

In addition to reporting on the capture of the city and the military equipment found inside, Sherman continued to advance his plans for continuing the campaign: "The capture of Savannah, with the incidental use of the river, gives us a magnificent position in this quarter; and if you can hold Lee, and if Thomas can continue as he did on the 18th, I could go on and smash South Carolina all to pieces, and also break up roads as far as the Roanoke."[37]

Aside from the normal fear of the unknown the remaining citizens of Savannah suffered very little under the Federal occupation. Because the city had been so far removed from the destruction caused by the armies there were few shortages of basic supplies. Luxuries were in short supply but overall the residents of Savannah were much better off than in most other parts of the Confederacy.[38]

In his official report General Sherman explained why he decided to show the residents of Savannah a degree of mercy that was as unexpected as it was welcome:

> Formal demand having been made for the surrender, and having been refused, I contend that everything within the line of intrenchments belongs to the United States, and I shall not hesitate to use it, if necessary, for public purposes. But inasmuch as the inhabitants generally have manifested a friendly disposition, I shall disturb them as little as possible....[39]

The occupation of Savannah was mild compared to what had happened in other Confederate cities; very little damage occurred while the Federal troops were in residence. Sherman wrote that he considered the behavior of his troops "so manly, so quiet, so perfect, that I take it as the best evidence of discipline and true courage. Never was a hostile city, filled with women and children, occupied by a large army with less disorder, or more system, order, and good government."[40]

On December 26, President Lincoln wrote to Sherman to thank him for the Christmas gift and comment on the campaign:

> Many, many, thanks for your Christmas-gift — the capture of Savannah.
> When you were about leaving Atlanta for the Atlantic coast, I was anxious, if not fearful; but feeling that you were the better judge, and remembering that "nothing risked, nothing gained," I did not interfere. Now, the undertaking being a success, the honor is all yours; for I believe none of us went farther than to acquiesce. And taking the work of Gen. Thomas into the count, as it should be taken, it is indeed a great success. Not only does it afford the obvious and immediate military advantages; but, in showing to the world that your army could be divided, putting the stronger part to an important new service, and yet leaving enough to vanquish the old opposing force of the whole — Hood's army — it brings those who sat in darkness, to see a great light. But what next? I suppose it will be safer if I leave Gen. Grant and yourself to decide.[41]

Chapter 17

Hood Invades Tennessee

John Bell Hood's plan to invade Tennessee was conceived while he paused on October 15th and 16th at Cross Roads, near the Alabama border in northwest Georgia. General Hood had decided to wait for Sherman and offer him battle:

> Upon the eve of action, I considered it important to ascertain by personal inquiry and through the aid of officers of my staff, not alone from corps commanders, but from officers of less rank, whether or not my impressions after the capture of Dalton were correct, and I could rely upon the troops entering into battle at least hopeful of victory.[1]

The answer Hood received was unexpected and disappointing. "[T]he opinion was unanimous that although the Army had much improved in spirit, it was not in condition to risk battle against the numbers reported by General Wheeler." Even Hood was not reckless enough to start a fight when he knew his officers were unanimously opposed. But he also could not dig in and hope Sherman would smash his army against the Confederate works; the Federal commander had learned his lesson at Kennesaw Mountain.[2]

Unable to stand and fight and unwilling to continue marching aimlessly around Georgia and Alabama, Hood devised a plan that was simultaneously a daring scheme that just might win the war and unbridled wishful thinking. Hood proposed to cross the Tennessee River and destroy the armies of Schofield and Thomas before they could be united. Afterward he would occupy Nashville, gather supplies and increase the size of his army with local Confederate sympathizers.[3]

The next phase of General Hood's plan was the truly interesting part. Instead of heading back south, perhaps to Atlanta, Hood would move into Kentucky, threatening Cincinnati and the Ohio River. If General Sherman moved toward the Georgia coast, as Hood expected, he would be too far away to interfere with Hood's movements. If Sherman turned and followed the Confederates, Hood felt his well-fed and well-rested army would be able to defeat the exhausted Federal forces, after which Hood would march East and attack the Army of the Potomac at Petersburg.[4]

There was another possibility that Hood considered:

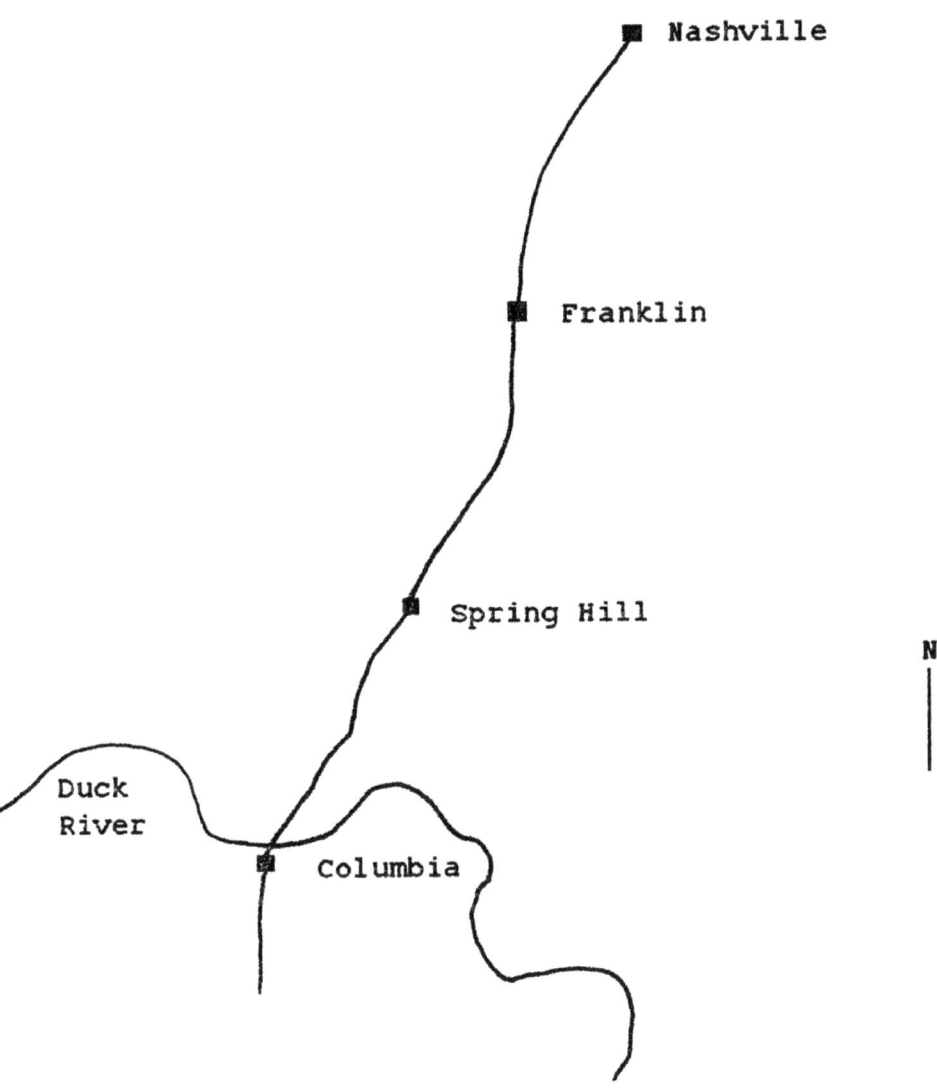

Route to Nashville

If on the other hand he marched to join Grant, I could pass through the Cumberland gaps to Petersburg, and attack Grant in rear, at least two weeks before he, Sherman, could render him assistance. This move, I believed, would defeat Grant, and allow General Lee, in command of our combined Armies, to march upon Washington or turn upon and annihilate Sherman.[5]

Considering the result of General Hood's campaign into Tennessee it is easy to say that this was the plan of a man who has lost his grasp of reality. At the time, however, there were no such conclusions, especially since another such improbable scheme had almost brought disaster to the Union war effort. It was just over three months earlier that Jubal Early marched an army less than half the size of Hood's from Lynchburg, through the Shenandoah Valley, across Maryland, defeated a smaller Federal army, threatened Baltimore, reached the very gates of Washington, D.C., and at one point was literally hours from marching into the nation's capital.

Long after events had played out and the concern, if not panic, that pervaded the Federal high command had faded, General Grant wrote: "Hood, instead of following Sherman, continued his move northward, which seemed to me to be leading to his certain doom. At all events, had I had the power to command both armies, I should not have changed the orders under which he seemed to be acting."[6]

General Hood's army left Cross Roads on October 17, marching southwest into Alabama. They reached Gadsden on the 20th and with enough supplies to last 20 days they left on the 22nd marching northwest in the direction of Guntersville, on the Tennessee River. Hood had learned that Forrest's cavalry, in the western part of Tennessee near Jackson, was unable to cross the rain-swollen river to meet the rest of the army in the center of the state. Having only a small force of cavalry with the army Hood decided to continue further west, join with General Forrest's cavalry and cross the river at Florence. On the 30th Gen. Stephen Lee's corps reached the Tennessee and General Johnson's division crossed the river and occupied Florence. The rest of the army demonstrated against Decatur then moved on to Tuscumbia, on the south side of the river, on the 31st of October.[7]

While at Gadsden, Hood was joined by his immediate superior, the newly appointed commander of the Military Division of the West, Gen. G. T. P. Beauregard, who later reported:

> In an interview with General Hood he informed me that he was then *en route* to Middle Tennessee, via Gunter's Landing, on the Tennessee River. At Gadsden I had conferences during two days with him in relation to the future operations of the army, in the course of which he stated that his general plan had been submitted to and approved by General Bragg, then commanding the Armies of the Confederate States. In view of existing condition of affairs the movement then in progress met my approval also....[8]

It was imperative that Hood move quickly to cross the Tennessee and engage the enemy. The only realistic chance Hood had to make his plan succeed was to beat the Federal armies of Schofield and Thomas one at a time. If General Schofield could fall back to the heavily fortified city of Nashville and add his small army to Thomas' the Confederates would have walked a long way for nothing. Beauregard wrote:

> It was, therefore, our clear policy to strike Thomas with the utmost celerity before he could be re-enforced, rather than to retrace our march and pursue Sherman. But the offensive in Middle Tennessee could only be successful if undertaken at once and executed with energy, without any division or material diminution of our forces.[9]

When General Hood arrived at Tuscumbia he received the worst possible news:

> Notwithstanding my request as early as the 9th of October that the railroad to Decatur be repaired, nothing had been done on the 1st of November towards the accomplishment of this important object.
>
> I had expected upon my arrival at Tuscumbia to find additional supplies, and to cross the river at once. Unfortunately, I was constrained to await repairs upon the railroad before a sufficient amount of supplies could be received to sustain the Army till it was able to reach Middle Tennessee.[10]

Day after frustrating day Hood suffered through one delay after another at Tuscumbia. There was a 10-mile gap in the railroad between Tuscumbia and Cherokee and the frequent heavy rains slowed the repairs to a crawl. The rains also flooded roads and caused the level of the river to rise. A pontoon bridge that had been built across the river was partly submerged and the rest of the army could not cross over to join the troops from Lee's corps in Florence. The only good news for the Confederate commander was that because of the long delay Forrest and his command were able to join the army.[11]

General Beauregard remained with the army at Tuscumbia for two weeks during which time he and Hood carefully went over all aspects of the coming campaign. It was suggested that since Sherman was still in the area of Rome, Georgia, there was still time to turn around and engage him there. But Hood was adamant:

> I adhered to the conviction I had held at Lafayette and Gadsden, and a second time desired General Beauregard to consult the corps commanders, together with other officers, in regard to the effect a return to Georgia would produce upon the Army. I also urged the consideration that Thomas would immediately overrun Alabama, if we marched to confront Sherman. I had fixedly determined, unless withheld by Beauregard or the authorities at Richmond, to proceed, as soon as supplies were received, to the execution of the plan submitted at Gadsden.[12]

General Hood spent three frustrating weeks at Tuscumbia, watching the advantage of surprise slip through his fingers. It was not until November 20 that Hood's entire army was across the river and into Tennessee. Edward McMorries, of the 1st Alabama, remembered it for the rest of his life:

> The day was cold, cloudy and windy, and scattering snowflakes were falling as Hood's army, thinly clad, poorly shod and half-fed, marched through the streets of Florence to the promised land of Tennessee. A few ladies appeared on galleries and at windows, giving the usual salutation by waving handkerchiefs, but their tears revealed that they were without any hope of success.[13]

Whatever the ladies of Florence might have thought, the lack of food or proper clothing never caused the Army of Tennessee to despair. Capt. W. O. Dodd later wrote:

> It was as gallant an army as ever any Captain commanded. The long march from Atlanta had caused the timid and sick to be left behind, and every man remaining was a veteran. Then the long and sad experience of retreating was now reversed, and we were going to redeem Tennessee and Kentucky, and the morale of the army was excellent.[14]

When Hood entered Tennessee he had three corps of infantry: Lee's, Stewart's, and Cheatham's, and Forrest's cavalry, a total of about 35,000 men. The weather was awful; cold temperatures and snow mixed with freezing rain, turning the roads into rivers of mud. On the 21st the entire army was together and Forrest's cavalry led the march north toward the first objective, Columbia, and the Duck River. General Hood hoped that "by a rapid march to get in rear of Schofield's forces, then at Pulaski, before they were able to reach Duck river." The next day the front of the column reached Lawrenceburg, west of Pulaski and on the direct road to Columbia.[15]

Back in Atlanta the threat of Hood's invasion of Tennessee caused little disruption in the preparations for the campaign through Georgia. Since the Federal army occupying Atlanta was leaving soon, a disruption in the supply lines was of little concern. At least Maj. Henry Hitchcock, a member of Sherman's staff, was not too worried about it. In a letter home he wrote:

> Of course this will interrupt our communications, both by mail and telegraph…. Hood's movement is a bold one, but it will be a failure in its real purpose, which is to strike behind Sherman, and frighten him into bringing his whole army northward and so give up Atlanta. When Gen. Sherman gives up Atlanta it will not be worth much to the Johnnies.[16]

The first part of Hood's plan was to cut off and destroy Schofield's army based at Pulaski, about 25 miles south of Columbia. Maj. Gen. John Schofield had only assumed command of the forces at Pulaski on November 14 with instructions to "hold the enemy in check, should he advance, long enough to enable General A. J. Smith's corps, then expected from Missouri, to reach Nashville." The other troops in the Department of the Cumberland were to be brought together at the same time, giving Thomas enough troops to oppose Hood's army. "To effect this concentration was, therefore, of vital importance — a consideration to which all others were secondary." At Pulaski, General Schofield commanded Stanley's Fourth Corps, Cox's division of the Twenty-third Corps, and about a division and a half of cavalry at various locations in the area, a total of about 22,000 men.[17]

The first positive knowledge of Hood's movements reached Schofield on the 22nd when the head of the Confederate column reached Lawrenceburg, obviously heading to Columbia to cut off Schofield's route to Nashville. Justifiably worried, Schofield concentrated his troops and set out for Columbia the next afternoon. Hood's route was slightly longer and on the morning of the 24th Schofield just barely won the race to Columbia. General Cox's division made a forced march and arrived just in time to prevent Forrest's cavalry from capturing the bridge over Duck River, cutting off the Federal line of retreat.[18]

As the Federal troops arrived they threw up a strong line of breastworks just south of Columbia. Hood's army trickled in and both armies were concentrated opposite each other by the night of the 25th. There were some skirmishing and probing attacks but Hood did not launch an assault on the Federal line and both armies held their positions until the night of the 27th. Hood was "determined not to attack them in their breastworks, if I could possibly avoid it, but to permit them to cross undisturbed to the north bank of Duck river that night, as I supposed they would do; to hasten preparations, and endeavor to place the main body of the Confederate Army at Spring Hill, twelve miles directly in the enemy's rear, and about mid-way upon the only pike leading to Franklin...."[19]

Allowing Schofield to get away from Columbia without fighting a battle was certainly not an act of kindness on Hood's part; he was setting a trap. Hood believed, correctly as it turned out, that once Schofield was sure the Confederates were not going to launch an attack he would try to escape north and continue on toward Nashville. Lee and most of the artillery were to remain facing the Federal works while Hood would lead the rest of his army on a secret march around Columbia and cut off the Federal line of retreat. Hood then could "attack as the Federals retreated, and put to rout and capture, if possible, their Army which was the sole obstacle between our forces and Nashville — in truth, the only barrier to the success of the campaign."[20]

The operation began at dawn of the 29th as General Hood personally led Cleburne's division across the river to the right of Columbia. Soon after, General Lee's troops moved toward the Federal line and opened up with artillery. Hood must have been feeling pretty good about his chances. The weather had cleared and it was a cool fall day. The Confederate troops certainly understood what was happening and were enthusiastically looking forward to victory. The Federal army was still in Columbia, occupied with defending against Lee's fake attack. Forrest's cavalry had gone on ahead and the rest of Hood's army was well on its way to Spring Hill and it seemed as if nothing could prevent Hood from achieving a brilliant victory.[21]

Back at Duck River, General Schofield was not as ignorant about what was going on as Hood believed. Almost from the moment Forrest had crossed the river the Federal commander was aware of Hood's movements. What Schofield had to determine was whether Hood was trying to flank Columbia and strike the Federal rear or was he moving farther north to cut the road to Nashville. The artillery and wagons were started on the road to Spring Hill early on the 29th with General Stanley and two infantry divisions right behind them. They moved quickly and by noon the head of the column was nearing the village of Spring Hill.[22]

General Stanley's column arrived in Spring Hill just in time to drive off a detachment of Confederate cavalry that was preparing to attack the lightly defended Federal wagon trains. With the trains secured Stanley entrenched in a good position to meet Hood's infantry as it came up from the south. Stanley's force drove off two Confederate assaults but the third attack forced them back to the outskirts of the village. Here they were able to form another line and with the aid of artillery support were able to hold their position until dark.[23]

General Schofield remained at the Duck River position with General Cox until about 3:00 P.M. when he "became satisfied the enemy would not attack my position on Duck River, but was pushing two corps direct for Spring Hill. I then gave the necessary orders for the withdrawal of the troops after dark." Schofield accompanied General Ruger's troops at the head of the main column. Moving quickly they ran into Confederate cavalry about three miles from Spring Hill but pushed past and arrived in the town about 7:00 P.M.[24]

General Schofield had been fortunate to reach Spring Hill, but he would need even more luck to save his army. Stanley had kept Hood's infantry from cutting the road during the afternoon but now the Federal army had to get past Spring Hill on the road to Franklin. Their danger was apparent to all and Col. Henry Stone, one of General Thomas' staff, later wrote:

> When night came, the danger rather increased than diminished. A single Confederate brigade ... planted square across the pike, either south or north of Spring Hill, would have effectually prevented Schofield's retreat, and daylight would have found his whole force cut off from every avenue of escape by more than twice its numbers, to assault whom would be madness, and to avoid whom would be impossible.[25]

But, instead of Schofield's army being trapped and destroyed, what actually happened that afternoon and evening around Spring Hill was an unbelievable failure at every level of the command structure of the Army of Tennessee. Unfortunately, there is no sure way to know what really happened as the explanations of most of the principals involved in the controversy contradict each other.

During the day General Hood led the main body of his army to within a few miles of Spring Hill. About three o'clock Hood stated that he "requested General Cheatham, commanding the leading corps, and Major General Cleburne to advance to the spot where, sitting upon my horse, I had in sight the enemy's wagons and men passing at double-quick along the Franklin Pike." Pointing out the retreating Federal column Hood ordered both generals to advance and take possession of the road. Soon afterward Hood watched Cheatham's corps march off toward what he was confident would be a glorious victory.[26]

Hood later described how he waited for the sounds of battle:

> Listening attentively to the fire of the skirmishers in that direction, I discovered there was no continued roar of musketry, and being aware of the quick approach of darkness, after four o'clock at that season of the year, I became somewhat uneasy, and again ordered an officer to go to General Cheatham, inform him that his supports were very near at hand, that he must attack at once, if he had not already so done, and take and hold possession of the pike. Shortly afterwards, I entrusted another officer with the same message.[27]

Hood waited and waited, but still no battle. By this time General Stewart had come up with his corps and he was ordered to take control of the pike north of Spring Hill. General Cheatham returned to report that the Federal line was too long for him to successfully assault and requested that Stewart form on his right before making the attempt to cut the road. As Hood remembers it,

> I then asked General Cheatham whether or not Stewart's Corps, if formed on the right, would extend across the pike. He answered in the affirmative. Darkness ... soon closed upon us, and Stewart's Corps, after much annoyance, went into bivouac for the night, near but not across the pike, at about eleven or twelve o'clock.[28]

The individual Confederate soldiers were just as astonished at the failure to take control of the pike as was their commanding general. Captain Dodd wrote:

> I remember distinctly the beautiful day, and as we got in sight of the little village of Spring Hill the old rugged veterans of Cheatham's corps came marching up on our left with their battle-flags waving in the mellow sunlight, and we felt that a long-sought opportunity had at last arrived. Lee's guns at Columbia kept up a lively music, admonishing us that he was meeting his part of the contract. We were satisfied that a few minutes — at most an hour — would be ample time in which to place our command across the pike, and then the surrender of Schofield would follow as night follows day.[29]

John M. Copley, of the 49th Tennessee Infantry, remembered that his unit

> arrived on the scene just after dark.... We were halted in a cornfield, ordered to lie down under arms, be ready for action at a moment's notice, and not to speak above breath. We were informed that ... our columns were within about two hundred yards of the Federal army.... We felt confident that on the following day the whole army would be captured.[30]

Edward McMorries, of the 1st Alabama, later wrote:

> About 9 P.M. we were halted one-quarter of a mile from the Franklin pike north of Spring Hill, and in rear of Schofield, who was then being hard pressed at Spring Hill, by Forrest. Stacking our arms and eating, we spread down our blankets upon the ground and were soon asleep, feeling sure that we had the enemy bagged. We supposed our corps extended across the Franklin pike. The extreme right was in two hundred yards of it, as we saw next morning. Why were we halted just there, leaving a way for the enemy to escape after all our hard marching?[31]

From General Hood's reports it would seem that General Cheatham was totally to blame for the failure to cut the Franklin Pike that afternoon and evening. The problem is that Hood's reports contain glaring inaccuracies. The first is that the Franklin Pike is not visible from where Hood claimed to have seen the Federal column. The other discrepancy is that there were no Federal wagons on the road at 3:00 P.M. By that time the artillery and trains were already in Spring Hill protected by Wagner's division, and the rest of Schofield's army was just leaving or still at the Duck River position. It is possible that Hood made some honest mistakes concerning his location and the time of day. It is also possible that he was trying to place all the blame for the failure at Spring Hill on a subordinate.[32]

Whatever the reason the Federal army was most fortunate. General Stanley reported, "As night closed we could see the enemy rapidly extending his lines, and by 8 o'clock it was evident that at least a corps of Hood's army was formed in line of battle, facing the turnpike, and at a near distance of but little more than a half a mile from it." In addition, Stanley's pickets reported that other Confederate troops were heading past Spring Hill on the east, perhaps to cut the road farther to the north. General Schofield pushed on past Spring Hill with Ruger's division to locate the Confederate positions and was amazed to discover that the road was clear at least as far as Thompson's Station, a few miles north.[33]

By the time General Schofield returned to Spring Hill it was nearly midnight. Cox and Wood had brought their divisions up from Columbia and the entire army was together. Schofield wrote:

> As the road was clear and the Confederates all sound asleep, while the Union forces were all wide awake, there was no apparent reason for not continuing the march that night. A column of artillery and wagons, and another of infantry, moved side by side along the broad turnpike, so that if the redoubtable Forrest should wake up and make his appearance anywhere, he would be quickly brushed away.[34]

As the Federal army marched out of Spring Hill they could hardly believe their luck. They moved quickly and as quietly as possible, within sight of the Confederate campfires. General Stanley reported, "The enemy's skirmishers fired into the column frequently, but instructions were sent to push on and not get into a fight if the enemy kept off the road."[35]

G.W. Lewis, of the 124th Ohio Infantry, remembered years later

> it was about midnight when Adjutant Hammer came riding back directing the company commandants to have the men so adjust their canteens and bayonet scabbards that as little noise be made as possible, that we were in the immediate presence of the enemy. This we could hardly believe. Soon we saw two lines of fires running away to the northeast, and the left end of the line nearest us was so near the pike one could have cast a stone into it without much effort.... And yet our division, the 3d, and a wagon train twelve miles long, passed along that pike, with all the noise incident to the moving of a wagon train and artillery attached to our division, without hindrance or molestation from the enemy.[36]

Even though Schofield's troops were already moving past the inert Confederate army Hood still had one last chance to stop them. Sometime after midnight Hood learned of the enemy movements and sent a message to General Cheatham to at least send out a line of skirmishers to delay the Federals so that they might be attacked in the morning. But, as Hood states, "Nothing was done. The Federals, with immense wagon trains, were permitted to march by us the remainder of the night, within gunshot of our lines. I could not succeed in arousing the troops to action, when one good division would have sufficed to do the work."[37]

General Stanley reported that about 3:00 A.M.

> General Kimbal was directed to push on with the First Division and clear the road. General Wood's division, which had deployed in the night north of Spring Hill and, facing the east, had covered the road, was directed to move on, keeping off the road and on the right flank of the train, and General Wagner's division, although wearied by the fighting of the day before, was detailed to bring up the rear.[38]

On through the darkness the Federal army marched. By 5:00 a.m. the rear of the army was at least a mile north of Spring Hill. Just before dawn a detachment of General Forrest's cavalry made a dash for the wagons train but was repulsed by troops of Wood's division. About two hours later another cavalry attack was easily driven off and the army continued on toward Franklin with no further interruptions.[39]

On the morning of November 30 Hood's anger knew no limits. In fact all the army commanders were upset. Several of the generals had breakfast at the home of Maj. Nat Cheairs and there are rumors of angry confrontations and accusations of neglect and incompetence. There most certainly was enough blame to go around and Hood seemingly blamed everyone except himself. Unfortunately, and unfairly, he also blamed his soldiers.

> The best move in my career as a soldier, I was thus destined to behold come to naught. The discovery that the Army, after a forward march of one hundred and eighty miles, was still, seemingly, unwilling to accept battle unless under the protection of breastworks, caused me to experience grave concern. In my inmost heart I questioned whether or not I would ever succeed in eradicating this evil. It seemed to me I had exhausted every means in the power of one man to remove this stumbling block to the Army of Tennessee.[40]

Hood had every right to be angry that morning. His design to trap Schofield should have resulted in a brilliant victory. All the pieces were there, but somehow they couldn't be put together properly. All the senior commanders involved were too experienced to have made the mistakes they apparently made, and too committed to the Confederacy to simply disobey an order that all could see would result in a victory. Perhaps General Cheatham misunderstood his orders or perhaps Hood did not explain himself clearly, or perhaps in the darkness everyone believed they had followed orders and were just too exhausted to take the extra effort to make sure. In the end, however, the responsibility for the failure rests squarely on the head of John Bell Hood. He was the commanding officer, he was on the field and could have checked in person to see that his orders were carried out, as he desired.

General Hood was not alone in his dismay that cold November morning. Most of his soldiers could not understand how the Union army had been able to escape any more than their commander. John M. Copley later wrote that at dawn on the morning of the 30th:

> [N]ot a Federal soldier could be seen, except their rear guard, and that far beyond the range of our guns. When we discovered their successful escape on the morning of the 30th, our chagrin and disappointment can be better imagined than described. General Forrest was so enraged that his face turned almost to a chalky whiteness, and his lips quivered. He cursed out some of the commanding officers, and censured them for allowing the Federal army to escape. I looked at him, as he sat in his saddle pouring forth his volumes of wrath, and was almost thunderstruck to listen to him, and to see no one dare resent it.[41]

Captain Dodd remembered:

> Even after dark there would have been no material trouble in crossing the pike. It was a clear day and a starlight night.... But we slept, and the Federals marched by without molestation ... there was not a soldier who did not realize that a golden opportunity was at hand, and every one felt mortified at the inglorious result. We lost confidence in general Hood, not that we doubted his courage, but we clearly saw that his capacities better suited him to command a division.[42]

The opportunity to trap and destroy General Schofield's army was gone. Once he reached Franklin, Schofield was only 18 miles from Nashville, less than a good day's march. The still-furious Hood was in no mood to rationally assess the situation. He felt that somehow he had to recover the initiative and destroy Schofield's army:

> I hereupon decided, before the enemy would be able to reach his stronghold at Nashville, to make that same afternoon another and final effort to overtake and rout him, and drive him in the Big Harpeth river at Franklin, since I could no longer hope to get between him and Nashville, by reason of the short distance from Franklin to that city, and the advantage which the Federals enjoyed in the possession of the direct road.[43]

So the Army of Tennessee would follow the fleeing Federal army to Franklin, and disaster.

Chapter 18

Slaughter at Franklin

Just as the sun was rising on November 30 the advance troops of the Federal column wearily walked into the town of Franklin. The tense night march had taken its toll on his soldiers but General Schofield had no intention of stopping and allowing the Confederates to catch up and cut him off from Nashville. As Schofield wrote later: "The troops were very much fatigued by their long night march, rendering considerable rest indispensable. Hence there could not be much time in which to prepare defensive works with such obstructions as to insure successful defense against a very heavy assault." But, more important at the moment than rest for the troops, was the possibility that Hood might cross the river above Franklin with a large force before Schofield could move enough men to the north side to provide a suitable defense.[1]

When they entered Franklin the Federals found the wagon bridge across the Harpeth River had been burned; all that remained were the supports at the waterline. Schofield ordered that the existing railroad bridge be prepared to handle wagon traffic and put his men to work rebuilding the wagon bridge as quickly as possible. "I hoped, in spite of the difficulties, to get all my material, including the public property, and a large wagon train at Franklin, across the river, and move the army over before the enemy could get up force enough to attack me."[2]

Even while Schofield's troops were still in the process of filing into Franklin the Army of Tennessee was in hot pursuit and closing fast. General Hood later wrote:

> At early dawn the troops were put in motion in the direction of Franklin, marching as rapidly as possible to overtake the enemy before he crossed the Big Harpeth, eighteen miles from Spring Hill. Lieutenant General Lee had crossed Duck river after dark the night previous, and in order to reach Franklin, was obliged to march a distance of thirty miles. The head of his column arrived at Spring Hill at 9 A.M. on the 30th, and, after a short rest, followed in the wake of the main body.[3]

It is very probable that no army ever rushed toward battle in the frame of mind that infected the Army of Tennessee that morning. From generals to the lowest private the men were disappointed and angry, mostly with themselves. Some angry words had been exchanged between several of the top commanders and the responsibility for allowing the Federal army to escape the trap at Spring Hill was freely spread around. The generals were not alone in their frustration. The rest of the Army of Tennessee was anxious to catch up with the fleeing Federals and General Hood saw that, "A general feeling of mortification and disappointment pervaded its ranks. The troops appeared to recognize that a rare opportunity had been totally disregarded, and manifested, seemingly, a determination to retrieve, if possible, the fearful blunder of the previous afternoon and night."[4]

The village of Franklin is situated on the south side of the Harpeth River, which bends around the town in a deep curve to the northeast. Before the war Franklin was a pleasant little village of well-kept homes surrounded by prosperous farms. There was a direct connection to Nashville, some 18 miles away, by railroad and turnpike. On the northeast side of town, across the river, the ground was higher and an earthwork called Fort Granger occupied a hill commanding both the railroad and wagon bridges with its artillery. There were also several batteries of artillery situated along the riverbank. From the south, three roads and the Nashville & Decatur Railroad entered the village. Near the town the railroad ran close to the river and parallel to one of the roads, the Columbia Pike.[5]

The Federal fortifications consisted of two lines of breastworks about 800 yards from the center of town and between 300 and 400 yards apart. The lines formed a semicircle from the extreme left, or northeast, at a railroad cut near the river, southwest across the Columbia Pike, then bending west and then north across the Carter's Creek Pike around the west side of town and back to the river. Artillery was strategically placed at various locations on the lines that could not only fire forward but was able to sweep the interval between the lines. The works had been built when the Federal army first occupied the town about two years earlier. Schofield wasted no time in putting his men to work strengthening them and by noon the work was completed.[6]

The troops of the Twenty-third Corps manned the left side of the Federal works. Since General Schofield was in overall command of the army Maj. Gen. Jacob Cox was given the responsibility of commanding the men in the fortifications. Cox's division, commanded by Brigadier General James W. Reilly, was stationed on the left. Closest to the river was Col. I.N. Stiles commanding the Third Brigade, then came Col. J.S. Casement with the Second Brigade and finally, with its right resting on the Columbia Pike, was Reilly's First Brigade. Defending the area between the Columbia and Carter's Creek turnpikes was Brigadier General Thomas H. Ruger's Second Division of the Twenty-third Corps. Along the right of the Columbia Pike was the Third Brigade, commanded by Col. Silas Strickland, with Col. Jesse Moore's Second Brigade was to the right. General Wagner's division was split with Colonel Opdyke's brigade inside the lines along the Columbia Pike as a reserve. The other two of Wagner's brigades were manning a rear-guard position outside of town. When these troops returned they occupied a short barricade about 800 yards in front of the main line across the Columbia Pike. Along the whole front the ground sloped very gently from the line, and was obstructed only by a small grove of locust trees a short distance in front of Ruger, and by farm buildings, with orchards here and there in the distance.[7]

Major General Stanley's Fourth Corps formed on the right of the Federal fortifications. Gen. Nathan Kimball's division was on the right of Ruger's division and filled in the line to the north back to the river. General Wood's division was stationed on the north side of the Harpeth River as a reserve and to protect the wagon trains as they crossed the river.⁸

As General Hood's army marched toward Franklin on the Columbia Pike, Stewart's corps was in the lead, followed by Cheatham's corps and then, a few miles back, Lee's corps. About three miles outside town General Wagner had formed two brigades as a rear guard along a ridge that crossed the Columbia Pike. As the Confederates approached, General Stewart sent a formation of skirmishers forward and the Federals quickly fell back to their position in front of the rest of the Federal line.⁹

Union Major General John M. Schofield

About 3:00 P.M. General Stewart moved his troops off the pike and established his line of battle. General French's division was to the right of the pike with the divisions of Walthall and Loring continuing the line east. General Cheatham formed his corps with Cleburne's division on the east side of the Columbia Pike and Generals Brown and Bate placing their divisions in that order toward the west. Detachments of Forrest's cavalry were sent to both flanks to block the escape of any fleeing Federal troops.¹⁰

With few obstructions to block their view it was obvious to Hood and his subordinate commanders that the Federal lines were strong and well-manned. Generals Cheatham and Forrest both advised against making a frontal assault, suggesting instead that they cross the river and attack Schofield's flank. Hood, however, would have nothing to do with that; he wanted no more delays in bringing the enemy to battle. The men who had escaped his perfect trap the night before were right in front of him and he was consumed with the need to attack and destroy them. General Hood later wrote:

> I knew that it was all important to attack Schofield before he could make himself strong, and if he should escape at Franklin he would gain the works about Nashville. The nature of the position was such as to render it inexpedient to attempt any further flank movement, and I therefore determined to attack him in front, and without delay.[11]

It was getting late in the afternoon and Hood was in such a hurry that he decided there was no time to wait for Lee's troops to strengthen the thin Confederate line, so thousands of veteran troops were left behind when his men moved forward. He later wrote that he didn't want to use artillery for fear of hitting the village. However, the first Federal line was far enough away from the town that it was unlikely any stray shells would have done much harm to civilians or their property, and even a brief artillery barrage might have softened up the Federal line; Hood was simply not interested in waiting to launch his attack.[12]

Within the Federal works the men had worked all morning to make their fortifications as strong as possible and were now just waiting to see if there was going to be a fight. By the time General Hood's army was making their dispositions most of the Federal trains had crossed the Harpeth River and were moving north. Earlier that day Schofield had issued orders that if they had not been attacked by sunset the rest of the army was to follow and continue the march to Nashville.[13] General Stanley reported that all afternoon "the enemy's entire force was in sight and forming for attack, yet in view of the strong position we held, and reasoning from the former course of the

Union Major General Jacob D. Cox

rebels during this campaign, nothing appeared so improbable as that they would assault."[14]

As soon as Stewart and Cheatham informed Hood that their lines had been formed he ordered the assault to proceed. It was just about four o'clock when the Confederate line surged forward with their bayonets flashing in the afternoon sun and tattered flags waving in the breeze. Six divisions of infantry, with their cavalry support, set off in a straight line across the open field. Few Civil War battlefields had such an open view as at Franklin and the Federal defenders were treated to the terrifying yet beautiful sight of the Confederate line, stretching nearly a mile and a half, approaching like an irresistible wave of gray.[15]

General Stewart reported that his men "moved forward in fine order, the men in high spirits."[16] Out in front of the main Federal line the two brigades of Wagner's division waited for the Confederates behind their crude barricades. According to General Wood, "Their orders were to maintain their position as long as it could be done without becoming too severely engaged, and then retire to the main line."[17] For some unknown reason, however, they chose to stay and fight as the enemy came closer and closer. With the Confederate line moving swiftly over the open ground the two Federal brigades barely had enough time to let loose a single volley of musket fire before the Confederates were on them. One of Hood's soldiers, John Copley, remembered that as they moved forward,

> [t]hey received us with a volley of musketry, but all opposition was inadequate to check our columns in the slightest degree, and with one prolonged and loud cheer we carried the first line of works at the very point of the Federal bayonets. They stood their ground until we mounted the top of their works, but as we went over, part of their line of battle broke and fled....[18]

Now occurred the only real chance for victory that the Confederates would have that day. As the advance works were overwhelmed by the Confederate line the surviving soldiers turned and went streaming to the rear in a disorganized mass of blue. The triumphant Confederates were close on their heels and hundreds of Federal soldiers were captured before reaching their main lines. The center of the line, where it crossed the Columbia Pike, was manned by the brigades of Reilly and Strickland. As the survivors from the two forward brigades came running back the men in the works had to hold their fire so they didn't hit their retreating comrades. The Confederates were following so closely behind the fleeing troops that there was no real gap between the two groups and they arrived at the Federal line almost simultaneously.[19]

The tremendous noise and confusion of battle coupled with the sudden onrush of their terrified comrades fleeing toward them, and the sight of the Confederates pouring in right behind, overwhelmed the men at the breast works. Capt. Edward P. Bates, of the 125th Ohio, was in the reserve force behind the lines and he saw that "the next moment the line at the works was broken, a mass of frightened recruits and panic-stricken men came surging back, and the clash of arms, the whizzing of bullets, and the demoniac yell of an elated foe was all that could be heard."[20]

A portion of General Reilly's brigade, along with most of Strickland's brigade joined the growing stream of men pouring down the pike past the Carter house. The guns were abandoned and the works for over 100 yards on either side of the pike were left unmanned, only to be occupied by Cleburne and Brown's men, who swarmed into the empty works. Disaster for the Union army was just moments away. From his vantage point behind the second line of works General Schofield saw with dismay

> [t]he charging ranks of the enemy, the flying remnants of our broken troops, and the double ranks of our first line of defense, coming back from the trenches together, produced the momentary impression of an overwhelming mass of the enemy passing over our parapets. It is hardly necessary to say that for a moment my "heart sank within me."[21]

This was the critical point of the battle and it was now that Col. Emerson Opdycke led his brigade forward. Fortunately this reserve force had been stationed along the pike right behind the area where the line was broken. Opdycke's brigade, joined by Reilly's second line under the command of Colonel White, sprang forward and charged toward the breach in the line. Opdycke reported that he witnessed the

> most horrible stampede of our front troops come surging and rushing back past Carter's house, extending to the right and left of the pike. When I gave the order "First Brigade, forward to the works," bayonets came down to a charge, the yell was raised, and the regiments rushed most grandly forward, carrying many stragglers back with them. We deployed as we charged....[22]

The fighting behind the breach in the line was as desperate a hand-to-hand fight as the men from either army had ever been engaged in. Gradually the Confederates were forced back and after about 20 minutes the Federal troops once again occupied their line. General Stanley, who left his sickbed to join the fight, was wounded trying to rally his troops near the breach.[23]

General Schofield could see little of the fighting because everything had become hidden by "a dense mass of smoke, and not a man was visible except the fragments of the broken brigades and others, afterward known to be prisoners, flocking to the rear. A few seconds of suspense and intense anxiety followed, then the space in the rear of our line became clear of fugitives" and Schofield could tell from the sound of the firing that the fighting had moved back to the line of works and the breach had been restored. General Cox later wrote that there was a "fierce melee, but the guns were retaken and all of the men in gray who were inside the parapet were dead or prisoners."[24]

During the fight to regain the front line Colonel Opdycke reported that the enemy was "put to rout with a loss of 394 prisoners." And later, at the works, Opdycke stated that he "never saw the dead lay near so thick"[25]

Despite being pushed back out of the Federal works the Confederates continued the pressure with no respite. On the right side of the breach where part of Strickland's brigade was stationed, the Confederates from Brown's division were able to hold on to the outside of the fortifications, firing over the works at the Federal troops inside the line. Brutally close firing and hand-to-hand fighting took place across the top of the works. Despite horrible losses the Confederates stubbornly hung on to this foothold, but could not gain control of the fortifications.[26]

On the east side of the pike Gen. Patrick Cleburne was in his customary position, at the head of his division, as it chased after Wagner's retreating brigades and it was here that the brave Irishman was killed just outside the works. In addition to Cleburne, one of his brigade commanders, Hiram Granberry, was killed. General Brown was wounded and all four of his brigade commanders were lost. Generals Otho Stahl and Statesright Gist were also killed on that bloody field and General Carter mortally wounded. The worst of the crisis in the center was over but much more desperate fighting and slaughter was to take place there as well as all along the lines.[27]

On the left of the Federal lines, near the river and railroad, the men of Stewart's corps displayed unsurpassed courage as they tried to break the lines and reach the bridges on that flank. General Loring's division was on the right end of the Confederate battle line with Walthall's division on his left. They quickly advanced across the open field, meeting no obstructions except for the railroad cut and some hedges near the Federal works.[28]

As soon as the Confederates were in range a tremendous storm of artillery fire struck them from all sides. In addition to six guns stationed in the line directly in front of the attackers, there were several batteries on the banks of the river that, along with the guns in Fort Granger, swept the field in front of the fortifications from that side, and another battery of a dozen guns in the line that fired into the advancing men from their left. The grape and canister came at the advancing Confederates like a hailstorm of lead.[29]

When the advancing Confederates came within range of the Federal muskets the slaughter began in earnest. In front of Colonel Stiles' brigade the fire swept the field, mowing down Confederates in rows. Some of General Loring's men tried to pass around the end of the line by moving through the railroad cut but the artillery along the river pounded them with shrapnel and canister and they were driven back.[30]

When the Confederates reached the hedges on Stiles' left they at first tried to tear them down, then tried to move around them, all the while under a withering musket and artillery fire. Finally they gave up and, using the partial cover of the hedges, began firing into the Federal lines, with little effect.[31]

A little to the right of the end of the Federal line, in front of Casement and to the right of Stiles, there were few obstructions and the Confederates advanced rapidly and in good order. Time after time they threw themselves at the works only to be repulsed with horrible loss. Union colonel Henry Stone later wrote,

> It is impossible to exaggerate the fierce energy with which the Confederate soldiers, that short November afternoon, threw themselves against the works, fighting with what seemed the very madness of despair. There was not a breath of wind, and the dense smoke settled down upon the field, so that, after the first assault, it was impossible to see at any distance. Through this blinding medium, assault after assault was made, several of the Union officers declaring in their reports as many as thirteen distinct attacks.[32]

The Confederate officers also exhibited amazing courage that afternoon, riding right up to the works and encouraging their men by example. Gen. John Adams, at the head of his brigade, rode straight at the works and when his horse was killed as he tried to jump over the parapet, the general fell among Casement's troops, mortally wounded. Another of Loring's brigade commanders, General Thomas Scott, was also killed leading his men forward. In Walthall's division General Quarles fell at the head of his brigade and the loss of officers in that brigade was so great that at the end of the day the highest-ranking survivor was a captain. Despite the almost insane courage and determination of the Confederate soldiers, General Cox was able to later report, "In all this part of the line our men stood steadily without flinching, and repulsed the enemy, inflicting terrible loss upon him and suffering but little in return."[33]

Confederate soldier John M. Copley later wrote about the terrible scenes he witnessed that November afternoon:

> The slaughtering of human life could be seen down the line as far as the Columbia and Franklin pike and where the works crossed the pike the destruction was indescribable. Along that portion of the works in front of the batteries on the right, our troops were killed by whole platoons; our front line of battle seemed to have been cut down by the first discharge, for in many places they were lying on their faces in almost as good order as if they had lain down on purpose; but no such order prevailed amongst the dead who fell in making the attempt to surmount the *cheval-de-frise*, for hanging on the long spikes of this obstruction could be seen the mangled and torn remains of many of our soldiers who had been pierced by hundreds of mini balls and grape shot....[34]

Union soldier William G. Bently wrote home that there were

> [v]ery few wounded outside of the works, but you can't imagine the appearance of the field. The ditch was literally piled with dead and wounded and for rods you could scarcely walk without stepping on a body. They laid in every position imaginable. Some were in the act of loading, some drawing the trigger. Our fire had been very effective, nearly all were struck below the breast.[35]

The fighting along the line from around the Columbia Pike to the far left continued unabated until after dark. In many places only the top of the parapet separated the troops and all they had to do was hold their rifles over the top and fire down into the enemy. The ditch outside the works was filled with Confederate troops, some dead, some wounded, and some still fighting as long as they were able. John Copley wrote:

> [S]treams of blood ran here and there over the entire battle ground, in little branches, and one could have walked upon the dead and wounded men from one end of the column to the other; the ditch was full of dead men and we had to stand and sit upon them, the bottom of it, from side to side, was covered with blood to the depth of the shoe soles.

Some of the Confederates ended up falling or being pulled over into the Federal side to become prisoners but most that were able to move eventually crawled away in the darkness.[36]

While the vast majority of the heaviest fighting and casualties occurred east of the Columbia Pike, the far right of the Federal line also came under attack. General Bate reported that he received orders from Cheatham "to move my command by the left flank, pass a gap in the ridge to the left, circle around a mound which rose in the plan below, and move toward the Carter Creek turnpike." Bate's division had the most distance to cover and his men reached the federal lines well after the fighting began to his right. The fighting on this side was nowhere as deadly as the rest of the field and Bate gives few details in his report. "My line, now a single one without support, charged the works of the enemy. My right got to the works and remained there until morning; the left was driven back."[37]

Exhaustion finally overcame the men on both sides and the fighting gradually died down although General Cox reported: "Even as late as 9 o'clock attacks were made, which were, however, easily repulsed.... Alarms occurred frequently until 11 o'clock, and frequently caused a general musketry fire on both sides from our center toward the right."[38]

Having been ordered by General Thomas to join him in Nashville as soon as possible Schofield decided, "To remain longer at Franklin was to seriously hazard the loss of my army, by giving the enemy another chance to cut me off from reenforcements."[39] The withdrawal was carried out quickly and quietly. The artillery was pulled out of the line and moved over the river first, then, as General Wood reported, "At midnight the troops on the south side of the river began to withdraw from the lines and pass to the north side of the stream; this work was rapidly and successfully accomplished. The enemy probably suspected what was going on, but did not attempt to interfere with the movement."[40]

General Wood's division, which had been stationed on the north side of the river during the battle, remained as the rear guard until about 4 o'clock in the morning. Wood's troops set fire to the bridges making sure they would be destroyed before following the rest of the army toward Nashville. When the Confederates discovered their enemy had fled they began shelling the empty fortifications.[41]

The next morning a ghastly scene greeted the surviving Confederates. Edward McMorries later wrote:

> It seldom happens in any battle that the ratio of killed to wounded is so great as was in this. Viewed next morning by daylight, the space between the outer and inner lines to the right of the pike was heartrending. Gen. Hood is said to have wept when he beheld it. The bodies of our dead [for there were no wounded on the field the next morning] lay thicker and thicker as you go from the outer to the inner line, and in the ditches they were literally banked up three or four men deep. The immense ditch in front of the redoubt was nearly full of our dead. There were also many lying along the top of the breastworks, and some even within the enemy's lines.[42]

General Hood's army paid a staggering cost in human life at Franklin. Confederate dead were nearly 10 times that of the Federals. Schofield reported that his losses were 189 killed, 1,033 wounded, and 1,104 missing, making a total of 2,326. The casualties of the Army of Tennessee were not fully learned until Federal troops returned to the area in mid-December. In addition to 700 prisoners taken to Nashville by

Schofield's army Hood lost, "buried upon the field, 1,750; disabled and placed in hospital at Franklin, 3,800, which with the 702 prisoners already reported, makes an aggregate loss to Hood's army of 6,252, among whom were 6 general officers killed, 6 wounded, and 1 captured."[43]

All armies are made up of individual soldiers. After a battle, when the human cost of victory and defeat are determined, individual deaths sometimes leave a greater impression than the deaths of hundreds. Tod Carter, a 20-year-old captain on General Smith's staff, had traveled hundreds of miles the last two years to meet his destiny. The Carter house, around which much of the deadliest fighting took place, was his home. As the rest of the Carter family sought shelter in their cellar, young Tod was trying to rally some troops when he was killed within sight of his home. After the battle his family found Tod's body and he was laid to rest on his family's land.[44]

The slaughter at Franklin had a lasting effect on the Confederates that fought there. Weeks later many of the wounded were being treated back in Georgia. Volunteer nurse Fannie Beers saw frightening testimony to the horrors these men had faced:

> These men were unlike any I have ever nursed. Their shattered forms sufficiently attested courage and devotion to duty, but the enthusiasm and pride which had hitherto seemed to me so grand and noble when lighting up the tortured faces of wounded soldiers, appearing like a reflection of great glory, I now missed. It seemed as if they were yet revengeful and unsatisfied; their countenances not yet relaxed from the tension of the fierce struggle, their eyes yet gleaming with the fires of battle.... It turns me sick even now when I remember the terrible things I then heard, the awful wounds I then saw.[45]

Apparently John Bell Hood had no such qualms as he surveyed the mangled bodies that were spread all over the battlefield. Not long after the sun illuminated that terrible landscape he was ready to continue the campaign with his battered army.

Chapter 19

Debacle at Nashville

Before dawn on December 1 Confederate search parties had gone out with torches to recover any of the wounded that could be helped. Soon the field hospitals were full and farmhouses and homes in the village were crowded with the wounded. Even Hood's hard, veteran soldiers were stunned when the sun came up and the full horror of that ghastly field was revealed. But there was no time to waste on sorrow or giving thanks for survival. The dead of both armies were buried in shallow trenches, Confederates and Federals in separate graves.[1]

There was only decision General Hood had to make that morning, whether to turn back or continue to Nashville. Common sense would seem to dictate that he should turn his battered army around and head home, living to fight another day. His army had suffered terrible losses and the officer corps had been decimated. Schofield was safely on his way to join General Thomas at Nashville, giving the Federals a vastly superior force. But John Bell Hood's reputation as a fighter who never gave up was well earned. As long as he could field any sort of a fighting force retreat was simply out of the question. So Hood gave the only command he could—forward to Nashville.[2]

Many of the Confederates that trudged toward Nashville that morning were despondent and bitter over the slaughter of their comrades and confidence in General Hood's ability to command was lower than ever. One of the most critical was Capt. Samuel T. Foster of Granbury's Brigade. The entry in his diary for the 1st reads:

> All the army follow the Yanks this morning on to Nashville. Our Brigd and the Ark. Brigd are so badly cut up that we can't move. Some officers have no men, and some companies have [no?] officers. So we have to reorganize and consolidate, a Captain has to command the Brigade.
>
> Gen. Hood has betrayed us [The Army of Tenn]. This is not the kind of fighting he promised us at Tuscumbia and Florence Ala. When we started into Tenn.
>
> And the wails and cries of widows and orphans made at Franklin Tenn Nov 30th 1864 will heat up the fires of the bottomless pit to burn the soul of Gen JB Hood for Murdering their husbands and fathers at that place that day. It can't be called anything else but cold blooded Murder.
>
> He sacrificed those men to make the name of Hood famous; when if the History of it is ever written it will make him *infamous*.

> ... he brings this Army here into middle Tenn. And by making them false promises and false statements get these men killed.[3]

Although it was seemingly a foolish and dangerous gesture, Hood did have his reasons for continuing on to Nashville.

> After the failure of my cherished plan to crush Schofield's Army before it reached its strongly fortified position around Nashville, I remained with an effective force of only twenty-three thousand and fifty-three. I was therefore well aware of our inability to attack the Federals in their new stronghold with any hope of success.... The President was still urgent in his instructions relative to the transferrence of troops to the Army of Tennessee from Texas, and I daily hoped to receive the glad tidings of their safe passage across the Mississippi river.
>
> I therefore determined to move upon Nashville, to entrench, to accept the chances of reinforcements from Texas, and, even at the risk of an attack in the meantime by overwhelming numbers to adopt the only feasible means of defeating the enemy with my reduced numbers, viz., to await his attack, and, if favored by success, to follow him into his works.[4]

General Hood's plan, or rather dream, had little chance of succeeding. The army that General Thomas was gathering in Nashville was vastly superior to the Confederates in numbers and equipment. Hood must have known enough about his opponent to realize that the careful Thomas would not come out from behind his fortifications until he was sure he could crush Hood's depleted army. About all that Hood really accomplished was to bring his army close enough to Thomas so that what was left of the Army of Tennessee could be smashed whenever it was convenient for the Federal army to do so.[5]

As the Army of Tennessee arrived in front of Nashville during the day of December 2, Hood put Lee's corps, which was now the strongest, in the center of his lines across the Franklin Pike. General Cheatham's corps filed off to the right and Stewart took the left. General Forrest's cavalry occupied the area between Stewart and the Cumberland River below Nashville.[6]

The countryside around Nashville is mostly undulating terrain with several high hills and occasional forests. The city is located in a bend of the Cumberland River open from the southwest to the east. To the south rise the Brentwood Hills, about four miles from the city. Both Brown's Creek on the east and Richland Creek flowing northwest begin in these hills. The creeks run close together coming down the hillsides then branch off, nearly encircling the city as they flow into the Cumberland. The creeks also provide natural defensive positions. Several turnpikes radiate in all directions from the city. Along a ridge line between the creeks is the Granny White Turnpike. About a mile eastward is the Franklin Pike and further to the east are the Nolensville and Murfreesboro turnpikes. About a mile to the west of the Granny White Pike is the Hillsboro Pike, then continuing northwest is the Hardin and the Charlotte turnpikes.[7]

The city that General Hood's troops were investing was one of the most heavily fortified in the country. Close to town was a seven-mile-long inner line supported by 20 batteries of artillery. This line went from the Granny White Pike to the river on the west and was defended by garrison troops and men from the quartermaster's corps, but few of them expected to ever face the enemy. General Thomas' army occupied the outer line that stretched from the Cumberland River on the west of the city along a range of hills to where the river bent around the city on the east, covering all the roads into Nashville.[8]

The Confederates immediately began digging earthworks, building their line along a string of hills between the Nolensville Pike on the right westward to the hills near Richland Creek, then along the creek to the Hillsborough Pike. This line covered only about half of the Federal lines, from the center going east, but even this was too much to be properly manned. To protect the open western end of his line Hood ordered the building of five redoubts stretching south along the Hillsborough Pike. These small forts contained artillery supported by infantry from Walthall's division.[9]

A few days after arriving in front of Nashville, Hood decided to split his meager force. General Bate's division, from Lee's corps, and 2,500 men of Forrest's cavalry were sent to the southeast to attack the Federal garrison at Murfreesboro, which consisted of about 8,000 troops under the command of General Rousseau. The Confederates built works a short distance from the town but did not attack. On the 8th Gen. Robert Milroy led seven regiments of infantry in a successful attack on the Confederate position, capturing over 200 prisoners. On the same day Confederate

Federal lines outside Nashville

cavalry under Gen. Abraham Buford entered Murfreesboro but were quickly driven out by Federal infantry. The Confederate force then returned to the main army at Nashville with nothing to show for their long march.[10]

During the first week of December the weather was unseasonably fair and the Confederates were able to complete much of the work on their fortifications. On the night of the 8th, however, the weather changed suddenly and a winter storm covered the area with snow and ice. For most of the next week the weather was terrible; the whole area around Nashville was covered with ice. It was difficult enough to move on level ground and virtually impossible to accomplish much of anything on the hillsides.[11]

The Confederates suffered greatly in this weather. Edward McMorries of the 1st Alabama remembered, "Our men were daily occupied in strengthening our works, the weather was intensely cold, snow several inches deep covered the frozen ground, and one-third of our men without shoes, were going about with their feet wrapped with rags."[12]

As difficult as the weather was on the Confederates it helped to bring about near panic in the Federal high command. As soon as Hood had arrived in front of Nashville President Lincoln and Secretary of War Stanton wanted Thomas to attack immediately. General Grant telegraphed Thomas on the 2nd advising him to leave the defense of Nashville to the garrison and attack Hood at once. When the weather changed the ground turned to ice and any kind of movement was impossible. On the 6th Grant once again sent orders for Thomas to attack. The telegraph was also busy between Washington and Grant's headquarters at City Point. On the 7th Stanton sent a dispatch to Grant saying, "Thomas seems unwilling to attack, because it is hazardous—as if all war was anything but hazardous." Grant replied that, "There

Union Major General George H. Thomas

is no better man to repel an attack than Thomas, but I fear he is too cautious to take the initiative."[13]

On December 8 General Grant once again sent orders to attack saying in part: "Now is one of the finest opportunities ever presented of destroying one of the three armies of the enemy. If destroyed, he can never replace it. Use the means at your command, and you can do this, and cause a rejoicing that will resound from one end of the land to another."[14]

It is easy to say that Grant was being unreasonable considering the conditions that Thomas had to deal with. In fact, however, Grant had his reasons. Since coming east to command all the armies time and time again he had seen plans frustrated and opportunities for victory lost because of delays in moving troops or launching attacks. Now, at Nashville, an entire Confederate army was just sitting there, waiting to be destroyed, and now, once again, delays were postponing a Federal attack. Even from Virginia, Grant saw that Thomas had an opportunity to win a great victory if he would only act, and the possibility that it could slip from his grasp was driving Grant crazy. While there are no sure things on a battlefield it would have taken something like divine intervention to save Hood's army if Thomas delivered the smashing attack that Grant wanted.

General Thomas replied that same day saying that he had not yet been able to satisfactorily concentrate his troops. General Grant's limited patience was now exhausted and he instructed General Halleck to have Thomas relieved of command and put Schofield in his place. Before implementing this order Halleck wired Thomas to advise him of the government's dissatisfaction. Thomas then called a meeting of his corps commanders explaining that he had been ordered to attack at once or be removed from command. Since General Schofield was the next senior officer it was apparent that he would take over, however, he was the first to state that no attack should be made until the weather was better, and all the others agreed.[15]

On the 9th Thomas sent another telegram to Grant explaining,

> I had nearly completed my preparations to attack the enemy to-morrow morning, but a terrible storm of freezing rain has come on to-day, which will make it impossible for our men to fight to any advantage. I am therefore compelled to wait for the storm to break, and make the attack immediately after. Major-general Halleck informs me that you are very much dissatisfied with my delay in attacking. I can only say I have done all in my power to prepare, and if you should deem it necessary to relieve me I shall submit without a murmur.[16]

That evening General Grant wired Thomas saying, "I have as much confidence in your conducting a battle rightly as I have in any other officer; but it has seemed to me that you have been slow, and I have had no explanation of affairs to convince me otherwise." He then told Thomas that the order removing him had been suspended until further information became available. Grant closed with, "I hope most sincerely that there will be no necessity of repeating the order, and that the facts will show that you have been right all the time." General Thomas would remain in command, at least for the time being.[17]

While the telegrams were flying between Nashville and Washington the Confederate high command was having problems of its own. With General Sherman tearing up Georgia the wisdom of allowing Hood to take his army in the opposite direction was being questioned. General Beauregard wrote to President Davis on December 6 restating the reasons why it was "inexpedient to countermand the campaign of General Hood into Tennessee to attempt the pursuit of Sherman." There were several reasons for continuing the current campaign, all of them quite reasonable sounding: the roads were too poor to allow swift movement, Sherman was too far away to be able to catch up with him, a retreat now could cause many desertions, without Hood's army in place the way would be open for Thomas to invade Alabama, and the state officials of Georgia had promised thousands of militia to throw across Sherman's path.[18]

But perhaps the most important reason that Beauregard did not interfere with Hood's plans was that "he possessed in a high degree the confidence of the Government as like wise of General Bragg."[19]

In his report of April 1865, General Beauregard was to write, "It is clear, also, to my mind that after the great loss and waste of life at Franklin, the army was in no condition to make a successful attack on Nashville—a strongly fortified city, defended by an army nearly as strong as our own, which was being re-enforced constantly...." Perhaps if he had expressed those feelings in December 1864 there might have been a brighter future for many of the brave men in the Army of Tennessee.[20]

Thomas was not as slow or unprepared as was feared back in Washington. By December 6 he had formed a detailed plan of attack and it was understood by both officers and men that the attack would be launched as soon as the weather allowed. General Schofield later wrote about the anxiety and pressure coming from outside Nashville:

> Considering the feeling of nervous anxiety which prevailed in Washington and throughout the country at the time, possibly he ought to have assumed the offensive on the 2d or 3d of December. But that state of anxiety was at first unknown at Nashville, even to General Thomas, and was never fully appreciated or understood. No one at Nashville, so far as I am aware, shared that feeling. We knew, or thought we knew, that Hood could do nothing, unless it were to retreat, before we would be prepared to meet him, and that every day's delay strengthened us far more than it possibly could him ... hence all at Nashville awaited with confidence the period of complete preparation which was to give us decisive victory.[21]

Despite the confidence in Nashville and Grant's protestations about his confidence in General Thomas, the pressure to attack continued. On the 11th Grant telegraphed the following:

> If you delay attack longer, the mortifying spectacle will be witnessed of a rebel army moving for the Ohio River, and you will be forced to act, accepting such weather as you find. Let there be no further delay. Hood cannot stand even a drawn battle, so far from his supplies of ordnance stores. I am in hopes of receiving a dispatch from you to-day announcing that you have moved. Delay no longer for weather or reinforcements.

General Grant need not have worried about being mortified because the same weather that kept Thomas from attacking would have prevented Hood from going anywhere.[22]

Thomas sent two telegrams to Grant on the 12th saying that he would obey the order as soon as possible but the country was covered with ice and making an attack under the current conditions would put him under a disadvantage and probably cause higher losses. The next day another telegram containing the same information arrived at Grant's headquarters.[23]

General Grant's patience had finally run out. Maj. Gen. John A Logan, one of Sherman's most vigorous fighters, who happened to be visiting between assignments, was dispatched to Nashville to relieve Thomas if the attack had not been launched by the time Logan arrived. On the 14th Grant, who was getting more worried by the hour, decided to go to Nashville and take command in person. This would solve two problems: with Grant on the scene there would be no delay for any reason, and by taking command in person Grant could avoid the embarrassing necessity of relieving Thomas. Grant had just arrived in Washington on the evening of the 15th when he received notice that Thomas had sent Halleck a telegram the night before stating that the weather had changed and that the attack would be launched on the morning of the 15th.[24]

General Thomas originally arranged his forces in the Nashville works with A.J. Smith's Sixteenth Corps on the right, the Fourth Corps in the center commanded by General Wood, and Schofield with the Twenty-third Corps on the left. Wilson's cavalry was behind Smith's line, and Gen. James B. Steedman was stationed a short distance in front of the Federal left, with Brown's Creek before him. For the coming battle Steedman was to demonstrate against the right of the Confederate line. The main attack would come from the Federal right with Wood advancing almost straight ahead and Smith bringing his corps down and to the southeast in a swinging motion to crush the Confederate left. General Wilson, with three divisions of cavalry was to move even farther west and clear the Hardin and Charlotte turnpikes while supporting Smith's right flank. Schofield's corps was moved from the left and placed behind Wood's corps as a reserve to strengthen the right during the attack.[25]

A little before six o'clock on the morning of the 15th General Steedman's division, on the far left of the Federal line, moved forward along the Murfreesboro Pike. There was a heavy fog that morning and the Federals were able to advance undiscovered until about eight o'clock when they attacked the Confederate right between the road and the Nashville and Chattanooga Railroad. The attack on this end of the line was supposed to be merely a demonstration to attract the enemy's attention from the main assault. Steedman, however, made a fairly vigorous assault and soon heavy fire from small arms and artillery filled the air.[26]

On the other end of the Federal works General Smith's corps had farther to go than was originally thought and it was not until about 10 o'clock that the infantry on the far right was clear of the Hardin Pike so that Wilson's cavalry could move around them. The cavalry spread out to the right of the infantry with Brig. Gen. Richard W. Johnson's division moving forward on the Charlotte Pike Brig. Gen. John T. Croxton's brigade filling the space east to the Hardin Pike and Brig. Gen. Edward Hatch's division connected to and covering the right flank of Smith's infantry.[27]

As the Sixteenth Corps swept forward Brig. Gen. John McArthur's division was on the right with Brig. Gen. Kenner Garrard's division on the left, connecting to the Fourth Corps, and Col. Jonathan B. Moore's Third Division in reserve. The Confederates of Walthall's division on the far left were driven back by the wave of blue that came down upon them. About half a mile past the Hardin Pike the Federals encountered the first of the Confederate redoubts. The advance was momentarily stalled while artillery was brought up and the redoubt was blasted from all sides. Infantry from McArthur's division assaulted the fort after their guns were silenced. General Smith reported "the cavalry on our right, at the same time charging directly under the guns of the rear fort on the hill, entered the first fort simultaneously with our skirmishers. The guns in the fort were all captured and about 150 prisoners."[28]

General Stewart tried to reinforce Walthall's position, along a low stone wall on the east side of the Hillsboro Turnpike. This left the remaining redoubts without infantry support and, in little more than an hour, they were reduced and captured one by one. The right end of Smith's corps now reached the Hillsboro Pike and struck the extreme left flank of Walthall's division, driving Reynold's brigade back from the stone wall. While the Sixteenth Corps was advancing against the Confederate left, Schofield had brought his Twenty-third Corps forward and pushed Gen. Darius Couch's division past the right of Smith's flank. Here was open country and Schofield's troops, now accompanied by part of Smith's corps, advanced past the Confederate flank to a group of hills near the Granny White Turnpike.[29]

When the Federal attack was fully developed and it was obvious that they were trying to turn the Confederate left General Hood sent reinforcements from Lee's Corps to Stewart. Two brigades of Major General Johnson's division were sent to strengthen the line near the redoubts but they, and two other brigades that arrived soon after, were unable to stem the flood of Federal soldiers that were streaming over the Hillsborough Pike and as General Stewart reported "completely turning our flank and gaining the rear of both Walthall and Loring, whose situation was becoming perilous in the extreme." It was obvious that the Confederates needed to fall back to avoid being overwhelmed. Orders to fall back and regroup were dispatched but Walthall had already taken it upon himself to order his men back, and not a moment too soon.[30]

While the main thrust of the Federal attack was on their right, in the center General Wood's Fourth Corps was the anchor of the pivoting movement that was to sweep the Confederates from the field. Along the center and right of the Federal line General Wood had deployed his corps with Brig. Gen. Washington L. Elliott's division on his right, connected with Smith's corps, and Brig. Gen. Nathan Kimball's division in the center with Brig. Gen. Samuel Beatty's division on the left. Wood had to wait for the right of the army to deploy before moving out and it was not until about one o'clock in the afternoon that Wood gave the order to advance.[31]

The first target was the steep and heavily wooded Montgomery Hill, a high point about one half-mile in front of Beatty's division, that was the Confederate advance position in this part of their line. The hill was heavily fortified with a strong line of trenches just below the crest. A heavy artillery barrage preceded the attack and after a tough fight "driving every object before it, so swept the brigade up the wooded slope, over the enemy's intrenchments; and the hill was won."[32]

As the pressure from Smith's troops on Walthall's line on the left grew stronger Kimball's division attacked the fortified hill near the center of the Confederate line. "With the most exalted enthusiasm and with loud cheers it rushed forward up the steep ascent and over the intrenchments."[33] The rest of General Wood's corps had advanced along with Kimball's men and soon the Confederate line was reeling. With Federals coming at them from two sides Walthall's line gave way with Johnson's and then Shelley's brigades falling back. As Walthall was pushed back the Federal troops from Elliott's division of Wood's corps closed with Garrard's division from Smith's corps and the angle where the two Confederate lines met was carried away.[34]

General Wood reported, "The onset was so fierce, the movement of the troops so rapid, that a very brief interval elapsed between the first shout of the advancing line and the planting of our colors on the enemy's works."[35]

Although Hood's army had been forced from its works it was not yet beaten. With the coming of darkness the Confederates were able to fall back to a new line along the base of the Harpeth Hills. They were positioned across the Granny White and Franklin pikes, facing north with the left flank bent back.[36]

George Thomas had to have been pleased; perhaps he even allowed a slight smile to disturb his normally grim countenance. His army had crushed the left of the enemy's lines sending them streaming back. All Hood could do now was to reorganize his army the best he could and retreat back to Georgia, or so Thomas believed. General Schofield was ordered to pursue the fleeing Confederates in the morning but he and Hood had been classmates at West Point and Schofield knew Hood too well to believe that the Confederate commander would give up yet.[37]

General Schofield was right; Hood apparently refused to face reality and formed his army in a new and shorter line along the Overton hills, about two miles behind the original positions. The Confederate forces were realigned with Lee's corps, which had done little fighting, placed on the right with Stewart's corps, which had borne the brunt of the fighting, in the center and Cheatham's corps was pulled from the right and put on the left flank. Why Hood decided to just sit there, basically asking to be destroyed, is difficult to fathom. He must have had some doubts as to his ability to withstand another Federal attack since he ordered the wagon trains to move back to the Harpeth River and assigned Lee's corps the task of protecting the Franklin Pike, over which his and Stewart's corps should withdraw, while Cheatham was to fall back on the Granny White Pike.[38]

The Federal lines were also adjusted during the night with Schofield, covered by the cavalry, in position on the right, Smith's corps in the center, and Wood on the left, Steedman stayed in his position farther east. The right of the Federal line ran parallel to and about halfway between the Hillsboro and Granny White pikes, then, as it went back toward Nashville, turned east crossing both the Granny White and Franklin pikes.[39]

The statistics from the first day of battle were decidedly in Thomas' favor, as he reported:

> The total result of the day's operations was the capture of sixteen pieces of artillery and 1,200 prisoners…. The enemy had been forced back at all points, with heavy

loss; our casualties were unusually light. The behavior of the troops was unsurpassed for steadiness and alacrity in every movement.[40]

Nowhere was the news of the first day's victory at Nashville welcomed more than in Washington. General Grant received the news as he arrived in the capital on his way to Nashville. He immediately telegraphed to Thomas:

> I was just on my way to Nashville, but receiving a dispatch from Van Duzer detailing your splendid success of to-day, I shall go no farther. Push the enemy now, and give him no rest until he is entirely destroyed. Your army will cheerfully suffer many privations to break up Hood's army and render it useless for future operations. Do not stop for trains or supplies, but take them from the country, as the enemy has done. Much is now expected.[41]

When Grant arrived at his hotel he received a cable from Thomas announcing that "I attacked the enemy's left this morning and drove it from the river, below the city, very nearly to the Franklin Pike, distance about eight miles." Before retiring Grant sent his congratulations to Thomas and his army adding "that tomorrow will add more fruits to your victory." President Lincoln also cabled Thomas: "You have made a magnificent beginning. A grand consummation is within your easy reach. Do not let it slip." At this point in the war a mere victory was not sufficient. The enemy must be destroyed.[42]

Gen. John Logan had gotten as far as Louisville when he his chance of having an independent command evaporated. He telegraphed to Grant saying: "People here jubilant over Thomas's success. Confidence seems to be restored…. All things going right. It would seem best that I return to join my command with Sherman." Grant replied, "The news from Thomas so far is in the highest degree gratifying. You need not go farther."[43]

For the attack on the 16th General Thomas decided to stick with a winning strategy: attack the Confederate right while using overwhelming numbers to turn the left flank and get behind the enemy lines to cut off their retreat. General Wood opened the battle about 6:00 A.M. by moving toward the Franklin Pike, supported by Steedman's troops on the left. The Confederate skirmishers were pushed across the road to the east and then south. Wood deployed Elliott's division across the pike with Beatty's division on his left and Kimball behind Elliott. As the troops advanced they ran into a strong skirmish line and, about half a mile behind that, the even-stronger main line manned by Lee's corps.[44]

About 3:00 P.M. the preparations for the main assault were finished and Wood gave the order to advance. The Confederate position on Overton Hill was a strong one and a heavy artillery barrage tried to soften up the Confederate works before the assault. G.W. Lewis, of the 124th Ohio, wrote later that "the firing was so intense and ceaseless that not an individual gun could be distinguished, but there was one dreadful roar of shot and shell, and all along the rebel lines and beyond, the bursting misses filled the air with clouds of smoke."[45]

General Wood sent two brigades forward to assault the hill. General Steedman sent the Fourteenth U.S. Colored Troops to support the attack from the east. The ground was open and the defenders, seeing what the Federals were up to, had time to reinforce the threatened position. General Wood reported:

> The assaulting force was instructed to move steadily forward to within a short distance of the enemy's works, and then, by a "bold burst," ascend the steep parapet, and secure the coveted goal. The troops were full of enthusiasm, and the splendid array in which the advance was made gave hopeful promise of success.[46]

This portion of the Confederate line was defended by the relatively fresh troops of Lee's corps and they put up a valiant fight, throwing back the waves of Federal troops. Wood reported that when his men reached the position:

> Near the foot of the ascent the assaulting force dashed forward for the last great effort. It was welcomed with a most terrific fire of grape and canister and musketry; but its course was onward. When near the enemy's works his reserves on the slope of the hill rose and poured in a fire before which no troops could live.... After the repulse our soldiers, white and colored, lay indiscriminately near the enemy's works at the outer edge of the abatis.[47]

While the Federal troops were throwing themselves in vain against the Confederate line on Overton Hill, the action shifted to the west. Like the day before, the left of the Confederate line was the weak point. And, also as on the day before, the far left of the Confederate line bent back to the south. The angle where the left flank joined the main line to the east was based on a hill, later known as Shy's Hill, for the colonel of the Twentieth Tennessee who died defending the position. The divisions of Gen. Mark Lowry and James A. Smith, now commanding Cleburne's division, defended the left flank, extending the line to the Brentwood Hills. Bate's division filled in the line from Shy's Hill to the right connecting to Stewart's corps.[48]

Early in the morning Smith and Schofield brought up several batteries of artillery and, placing them on high ground that commanded the enemy's left, rained shells down on the angle at Shy's Hill throughout the day. A little after noon General McArthur was able to place a battery in some woods along the front of the line, firing point-blank into the works on Shy's Hill. By late afternoon much of the Confederate fortifications had been battered to pieces. General Bate reported, "These rifled guns of the enemy being so close razed the works on the left of the angle for fifty or sixty yards."[49]

While the Federal artillery pounded the Confederate position General Wilson's cavalry had been advancing on foot from the south. They outflanked Govan's brigade, which Hood had sent to protect the end of the line. Coming close to Schofield's troops the cavalrymen were joined by Stiles' brigade and closed in on the rear of Bate and Lowry's position.[50]

About 3:00 P.M. General McArthur sent word to General Smith that it was time to make the assault. McArthur did not receive any reply and, concerned that it would be dark soon, he ordered the attack. His First Brigade, commanded by Col. W.L. McMillen, was to storm the hill from the left while the Second and Third Brigades would attack in the front. As his men moved forward General Smith saw that "the enemy opened with a fierce storm of shell, canister, and musketry, sadly decimating the ranks of many regiments, but nothing save annihilation could stop the onward progress of that line."[51]

Just after Smith's troops began their attack, General Schofield sent Cox's division forward and "the whole Confederate left was crushed in like an egg-shell."[52] General Bate saw that "the brigade on the extreme left of our infantry line of battle was driven back, down the hill into the field in my rear, and the balls of the enemy were fired into the backs of my men."[53] Colonel McMillan's troops swept over the ruined works on Shy's Hill and, with no reserves left, the Confederates were forced to run. At almost the same time that Cox's men were pouring over the Confederate works the cavalry divisions of Hatch and Knipe rushed in from the right and "the Confederates west of the Granny White road crowded eastward, running for their lives." In fact, Smith's men, heading east, and Schofield's troops, rushing north, were converging so quickly that they had to be halted to prevent them from crashing into each other.[54]

As on the day before, when the Confederate left failed the center also gave way. But today there was no orderly retreat to a new position. In the center of the Federal line General Wood and his men could hear the firing and the shouts of the victorious Union troops from his right. "I at once ordered the whole corps to advance and assault the enemy's works, but the order was scarcely necessary." Inspired by their comrades and sensing that victory was within their grasp, Wood's men "rushed forward like a mighty wave, driving everything before it. The sharp fire of musketry and artillery did not cause an instants pause." Overton Hill was captured by the same troops that had been beaten back earlier in the day. With Federals pouring over their works the rest of Stewart's line collapsed under the relentless pressure and fled in confusion. Whole batteries of artillery were captured as well as hundreds of prisoners.[55]

Only the far right of the Confederate line held its positions. With Wilson's Federal cavalry commanding the Granny White Pike the only route south for the Confederates was the Franklin Pike. General Lee's troops gallantly protected this last avenue of escape for Hood's army. They were forced back a short distance but Lee rallied his men and they held a new line until the remainder of the Confederates were able to make their way through the Brentwood Hills to the Franklin Pike.[56]

Many of Cheatham and Stewart's men were near panic that dismal and rainy December evening as they fled through the muddy hills. They hardly had time to recover from the nightmare at Franklin and now they had taken a beating two days in a row. These tough Confederate veterans were, after all, just men. They were beaten and they knew it, and now it was time to save themselves. General Bate reported that men

> climbed over the rugged hills in our rear and passed down a short valley which debouched into the Franklin turnpike. The whole army on this thoroughfare seemed to be one heterogeneous mass, and moving back without organization or government. Strenuous efforts were made by officers of all grades to rally and form line of battle, but in vain.[57]

19. Debacle at Nashville

The two-day battle of Nashville was the culmination of a campaign that virtually destroyed the Army of Tennessee as a force to be reckoned with. George Thomas had completely beaten Hood in every facet of warfare. It would be easy to simply say that it was the difference in numbers that gave victory to Thomas. But the real question is what was Hood doing outside Nashville in the first place. He knew his smaller army could never capture the well-fortified city. He knew he was outnumbered. He should have known enough about George Thomas to know that the Federal commander would do nothing rash enough that could give Hood an opening to steal a victory. His army had just suffered devastating losses at Franklin and the troops were exhausted. Their morale had hit bottom and any confidence they might have had in Hood's leadership must surely have dissipated by then. It looks as if Hood put his army in harm's way in the hope of some sort of miracle.

There was no miracle for the Army of Tennessee at Nashville, just a stunning defeat. During the two-day battle the Federal army captured 4,462 prisoners, including 287 officers, and 53 pieces of artillery.[58] General Thomas reported that for the entire Tennessee campaign his army captured 13,189 prisoners of war, 72 pieces of artillery and received over 2,000 deserters. There are no accurate records of Confederate killed and wounded but based on what is known about the casualties at Franklin and taking into account that many of the men listed as prisoners were probably wounded, a reasonable estimate for those killed and those wounded men that were able to travel with the army would probably add another 5,000–6,000 men lost. These Confederate losses do not take into consideration the many men who, realizing that the war was as good as lost, simply slipped away from the army during the retreat and went home. The total loss for the Federal armies was less than 10,000.[59]

The immediate pursuit of Hood's broken army was not pressed with much enthusiasm. Near the Granny White Pike, Chalmers' Confederate cavalry had been able to halt Wilson's advance toward the Franklin Pike, keeping the Federals from cutting the one remaining Confederate escape route. The infantry followed for a short distance but with the darkness and rain everyone was too exhausted to force the pursuit.[60]

During the night General Wood received orders to move his corps down the Franklin Pike as soon as possible on the morning of the 17th. The day was cold and wet and dark but Wood's men made good time, reaching Franklin about 1:30 in the afternoon. Wood reported: "The whole line of march of the day bore unmistakable evidence of the signalness of the victory our arms had achieved and the completeness of the rout. The road was strewn with small-arms, accounterments, and blankets." The bridges over the Harpeth River had been destroyed, halting the pursuit until repairs were made.[61]

For the rest of the pursuit the weather was bitterly cold. The Confederates abandoned their wounded in the hospitals at Franklin and for the next week suffered through one of the most terrible retreats of the war. Federal pursuers nipped at the rear of the broken army but, protected by Forrest's troopers, they made their way through Pulaski toward the Tennessee River where they began crossing at Bainbridge on Christmas Day. Hood's army finished crossing the Tennessee on the 27th and, destroying the bridge behind them, finally reached safety. What was left of the Army of Tennessee moved through Tuscumbia and Corinth, Mississippi, finally going into camp at Tupelo on January 10.[62]

The Federal victory at Nashville sealed the fate of the Confederacy west of Virginia. The Army of Tennessee had virtually fallen apart and what was left was later transferred east to oppose Sherman once again. After all General Grant's worried, and sometimes threatening, telegrams, he later wrote about George Thomas that "his final defeat of Hood was so complete that it will be accepted as a vindication of that distinguished officer's judgment."[63]

John Bell Hood, on the other hand, apparently was living in a different reality from the brave soldiers who suffered under his command. He later wrote: "It is my firm conviction that, notwithstanding that disaster, I left the army in better spirits and with more confidence in itself than it had at the opening of the campaign."[64]

Chapter 20

The End in Sight

Another year of this terrible war was over and after 12 months of the most horrible slaughter and destruction there was no longer any doubt about the outcome. As Union soldier Rice Bull wrote:

> The prevailing feeling among the men was a desire to finish the job; they wanted to get back home. The mass of those in this Army were veterans, nearly all had served three years, many much longer, and all were tired of army life ... they were intelligent and could see that the Rebellion was nearing its end, so were willing and anxious to meet quickly any privation or danger that would bring a speedy end to the war.[1]

With Abraham Lincoln in the White House and hard-driving Generals Grant and Sherman commanding the two principal armies, the Union was prepared to continue the fight to the bitter end. There was no good reason to expect anything less than total victory because, as Lincoln said:

> The important fact remains demonstrated that we have more men now than we had when the war began; that we are not exhausted, nor in process of exhaustion; that we are gaining strength, and may, if need be, maintain the contest indefinitely. This as to men. Material resources are now more complete and abundant than ever.
> On careful consideration of all the evidence accessible, it seems to me that no attempt at negotiation with the insurgent leader could result in any good. He would accept nothing short of severance of the Union – precisely what we will not and cannot give. His declarations to this effect are explicit and oft repeated.[2]

The situation was well known among the people of the South, and her soldiers, brave as any who ever walked the earth, certainly saw the futility of their cause. David E. Johnson, of the 7th Virginia Infantry, wrote:

> The situation was grave in the extreme.... The dark clouds that had been for some time overhanging us were settling down. The patriotism, enthusiasm and untold sacrifices of the past four years seemed all for naught, and our men could not be required to shoulder a heavier cross than was now the lot of the Confederate sol-

diers. But a patriotic people and a valiant soldiery might yet accomplish success, looking we were, but in vain, for foreign intervention, or something else to turn up. If to satisfy the Northern people and gain our separate existence meant to give up slavery, the army was ready to see it abolished. In fact, the great bulk of the army was ready to make almost any sacrifice required for independent and separate government. Dark and discouraging as were these days, the spirit of the army was yet unbroken, and the men were willing to fight it out, although it appeared but a question of time when we should all go down.

Thus closed the year of 1864, and to us it seemed final overthrow must come, for our foe was growing stronger, we weaker. Our star was surely on the wane.[3]

The cost for the last four years in treasure and property for both sides had been enormous, but the human cost had been beyond anything anyone had thought possible when the war began. Hundreds of thousands had lost family members and loved ones, millions had lost friends and neighbors, but some had lost more than could be imagined.

On November 21, President Lincoln wrote to a Mrs. Bixby of Boston:

> I feel how weak and fruitless must be any words of mine which should attempt to beguile you from the grief of a loss so overwhelming. But I cannot refrain from tendering to you the consolation that may be found in the thanks of the Republic they died to save. I pray that our heavenly Father may assuage the anguish of your bereavement, and leave you only the cherished memory of the loved and lost, and the solemn pride that must be yours to have laid so costly a sacrifice upon the alter of freedom.

Mrs. Bixby lost five sons, killed fighting for their country.[4]

In addition to the sadness that was everywhere there was also anger. George Templeton Strong wrote in his diary on November 20:

> It is sad to think of the misery rebellion has brought upon Rebeldom, of the many thousand households it has ruined and is starving. They have brought it on themselves in the great majority of cases.... They deserve no sympathy. But think of the poor little children who do not know good from evil! Think of the thousands of little people ... who have pined and wasted and perished under privation and exposure inflicted on them by this war.... Treason so groundless and gratuitous cannot be found in the history of man. But the nation should execute justice on the guilty all the more sternly because their crime has inflicted so much suffering on the innocent.[5]

On the last day of 1864 Emma Florence LeConte, of Columbia, South Carolina, wrote in her diary:

> Yes, the year that is dying has brought us more trouble than any of the other three long dreary years of this fearful struggle. They are preparing to hurl destruction upon the State they hate most of all, and Sherman the brute avows his intention of converting South Carolina into a wilderness. But is this a time to talk of submission? Now when the Yankees have deepened and widened the breach by a thousand new atrocities? A sea rolls between them and us—a sea of blood. Smoking houses, outraged women, murdered fathers, brothers and husbands forbid such a union.

Reunion! Great Heavens! How we hate them with the whole strength and depth of our souls!

Hope has fled, and in its place remains only a spirit of dogged sullen resistance.[6]

Sitting in Savannah, William T. Sherman was more than ready to do his part to end the war. In letters to Grant and Halleck, Sherman outlined a plan for what he believed would be the last campaign. His army, soon to be reinforced with General Schofield's men from Nashville, would move north to join the Army of the Potomac to finish off the Army of Northern Virginia at Petersburg. On the way to this rendezvous he would move through South Carolina, occupying, and as it turned out pretty well destroying, the capital of Columbia. Then the army would turn on Charleston, South Carolina, or the port of Wilmington, North Carolina, "according to the importance of either."[7]

After taking care of business in South Carolina, Sherman proposed to make a movement "direct on Raleigh. The game is then up with Lee, unless he comes out of Richmond, avoids you and fights me; in which case I should reckon on your being on his heels. Now that Hood is used up by Thomas, I feel disposed to bring the matter to an issue as quick as possible." Sherman was confident that after destroying the railroads in the Carolinas he could arrive in the vicinity of Raleigh, North Carolina, by early spring. Sherman informed Grant "if you feel confident that you can whip Lee outside of his intrenchments, I feel equally confident that I can handle him in the open country. I do not like to boast, but believe this army has a confidence in itself that makes it almost invincible."[8]

In an earlier letter General Halleck had suggested to Sherman that, "Should you capture Charleston, I hope that by some accident the place may be destroyed, and, if a little salt should be sown upon its site, it may prevent the growth of future crops of nullification and secession." Such was the mindset of many Union men toward the state that had taken the lead in plunging the nation into bloody civil war.[9]

Sherman wrote back to Halleck, giving a hint of what was to come:

> I think the time has come now when we should attempt the boldest moves, and my experience is, that they are easier of execution than more timid ones, because the enemy is disconcerted by them....
>
> I think our campaign of the last month, as well as every step I take from this point northward, is as much a direct attack upon Lee's army as though we were operating within the sound of his artillery.
>
> I attach more importance to these deep incisions into the enemy's country, because this war differs from European wars in this particular; we are not only fighting hostile armies, but a hostile people, and must make old and young, rich and poor, feel the hard hand of war, as well as their organized armies....
>
> I will bear in mind your hint as to Charleston, and do not think "salt" will be necessary. When I move, the Fifteenth Corps will be on the right of the right wing, and their position will naturally bring them into Charleston first; and, if you have watched the history of that corps, you will have remarked that they generally do their work pretty well. The truth is, the whole army is burning with an insatiable desire to wreak vengeance upon South Carolina. I almost tremble at her fate, but feel that she deserves all that seems in store for her.[10]

General Sherman planned to begin the march north on January 15, 1865. Heavy rains delayed the army but by the end of the month the Federal army was moving through South Carolina, and revenge was on the minds of many. Major Nichols wrote: "Houses are burning, and South Carolina has commenced to pay an installment, long overdue, on her debt to justice and humanity. With the help of God, we will have principal and interest before we leave her borders."[11]

During the march through South Carolina, General Sherman used the same tactics that served him so well in Georgia. The army was split into several columns, making it difficult for Confederate defenders to determine if the target was Columbia or Augusta, until it was too late. Sherman bypassed Charleston and entered the state capital of Columbia on February 17. Sherman had issued orders that the troops "were to destroy absolutely all arsenals and public property not needed for our own use, as well as all railroads, depots, and machinery useful in war to an enemy," but they were to spare all dwellings, schools, and harmless private property. By the next day much of the city was nothing but smoldering ruins. Of course, Sherman's men were blamed for using the incendiary skills they had perfected in Georgia. The truth is that most likely the fires were started by flying embers from hundreds of bales of cotton the Confederate rear guard set on fire to prevent them from falling into the hands of the Federal army. Several thousand Union soldiers were brought into the city to fight the fires but they generally burned out of control until the wind died down early the next morning. As for who started the fires General Sherman says, "I disclaim on the part of my army any agency in this fire, but, on the contrary, claim that we saved what of Columbia remains unconsumed."[12]

General Sherman never had the opportunity to complete his plan to join General Grant to confront the Army of Northern Virginia. By the time he had reached Raleigh, North Carolina, Lee had surrendered to Grant at Appomattox Court House. Sherman would face his opponent from Georgia one more time when Joseph Johnston was once again called to command what was left of the Army of Tennessee. Unable to do much more than get in Sherman's way Johnston surrendered near Raleigh on April 18, 1865. Sherman offered terms that went well beyond his authority and the surrender was rejected by the new government of President Andrew Johnson. Sherman had to meet with Johnston again on the 26th and draw up new terms of surrender that matched those signed by General Lee. Except for a few scattered Confederate commands that eventually gave up it was finally over.[13]

With the end of the war the muskets were stacked and artillery pieces that once roared like thunder were parked in fields, to be used later at memorials all over the country. The men who did the fighting went their separate ways, some to fame and fortune, some back to their homes and farms where they tried to resume a normal life again, and some had misery and despair in their futures.

After the fighting ended George Thomas was appointed administrator of the Military Division of Tennessee. For four years he worked to smooth the process of bringing the state back into the Union and had to contend with a myriad of problems connected with reconstruction, among them the rise of the Ku Klux Klan. In 1869, Thomas was assigned to command the Military District of the Pacific with headquarters in San Francisco.

On March 28, 1870, Thomas collapsed from a stroke and died that same day. He was only 54 years old but, always heavy, he had ballooned up to over 300 pounds. His funeral procession in New York was over a mile long and attended by a host of dignitaries including President Ulysses Grant and eight Union generals serving as pallbearers. Thomas was always considered an outstanding general and a decent and honorable man and both his friends and former foes mourned his passing. Almost everyone, that is, except his family in Virginia who never forgave him for choosing the Union over his home state.[14]

After surrendering what was left of his beloved Army of Tennessee to Sherman, Joseph Johnston continued a life of public service for many years. He was elected to the United States House of Representatives from Virginia and later was appointed U.S. commissioner of railroads. Like many of the Civil War leaders he eventually wrote his memoirs; unlike most he became involved in an acrimonious war of words with several of his former comrades.

Johnston criticized Hood for what he considered the pointless sacrifice of the Army of Tennessee in the attacks around Atlanta and the campaign in Tennessee. Hood responded that Johnston had ruined the army through his constant retreats. The two men, and their supporters, exchanged charges in books and articles for several years, settling little.

In February 1891, on a cold and rainy winter day, Johnston was in New York to pay his respects at the funeral of his old friend, William Sherman. He stood in the rain with his hat in hand, as any gentleman of the Old South would have done, when a friend told him he should put his hat on so he didn't become ill from the weather. Johnston replied that he could not, that his friend Sherman would have shown the same respect to him. A few weeks later Johnston contracted pneumonia and one of the South's most loved and respected leaders passed away at the age of 84.[15]

John Bell Hood's luck did not improve after the disaster at Nashville. He resigned command of the Army of Tennessee on January 13, 1865. Still a favorite of Jefferson Davis, Hood was later assigned to the Trans-Mississippi Department and was on his way west when the war ended.[16]

After the war Hood settled down in New Orleans where he became successful as a cotton merchant and head of an insurance company. In 1868 he married the daughter of a prominent Louisiana family and his future seemed full of promise. Unfortunately the debate between Hood and Johnston about who was to blame for ruining the Army of Tennessee was a constant distraction during these years.

In 1874, Hood published his memoirs giving his version of events. That summer tragedy again struck John Bell Hood when his wife and oldest child contracted yellow fever and died in the same week. Hood had little time to mourn because he too was stricken with the deadly disease and died a few days later at the age of 48. While many could argue that Hood was out of his depth as an army commander no one, on either side, ever doubted his courage and commitment to the Confederacy.[17]

William Tecumseh Sherman would have to be considered the most remembered and respected of the Civil War commanders after Grant and Lee. For years after the war he was reviled in the South because of the devastation that followed his army in Georgia and the Carolinas. But the simple fact is that he was ahead of his time in the use of total war to bring a population to its knees, thus probably saving many lives in the long run.

He remained in the army after the war serving as commander of the Mississippi District. When Grant was elected president in 1869, Sherman succeeded him as general in chief and served as the nation's highest-ranking military officer until his retirement in 1883.

After returning to civilian life, Sherman spent much of his time at speaking engagements and writing his memoirs. During this time he was frequently urged to run for president but he had a deep-seated distrust of politics and repeatedly declined.

William Tecumseh Sherman died in New York City on February 14, 1891. In a nation that was filled with Civil War heroes he was among the most revered.[18]

After the war the city that was at the center of the campaign of 1864, Atlanta, made a remarkable recovery from her near-total destruction. Once again the railroads played a large part in the history of the "Gate City." It was primarily because of her position as a rail center that Atlanta became a target for destruction and it was the same reason that she was able to recover and prosper in the years after the war. In a strange twist many northerners flocked to Atlanta; in fact, within a few years they outnumbered the native-born residents. The new residents brought new businesses to the city as well as a new way of life, and soon Atlanta became a northern city that happened to be located in the Deep South.[19]

One event illustrates the recovery of Atlanta as well as anything could. In 1881 the city hosted the International Cotton Exposition. A slim, gray-haired gentleman was persuaded by the organizers to make a few remarks from the speaker's platform. William Tecumseh Sherman, once the most hated man in the South, and the destroyer of Atlanta, received more applause than a former Confederate general and governor of Georgia.[20]

Shortly after he won reelection, President Lincoln told a visiting delegation from Maryland, "Those who differ from and oppose us will yet see that defeat was better for their own good than if they had been successful."[21]

Notes

Chapter 1

1. Dolly Sumner Lunt, *A Woman's Wartime Journal* (New York: Century, 1918), 1.
2. J. B. Jones, *A Rebel War Clerk's Diary at the Confederate States Capital* (New York: Time-Life Books, 1982), 331.
3. Robert G. Evans, ed., *The 16th Mississippi Infantry: Civil War Letters and Reminiscences* (Jackson, Miss.: University Press of Mississippi, 2002), 232–33.
4. Clifford Dowdey, ed., *The Wartime Papers of R. E. Lee* (Boston: Little, Brown, 1961), 659–60.
5. Michael J. Forsyth, *The Red River Campaign of 1864 and the Loss by the Confederacy of the Civil War* (Jefferson, N.C.: McFarland, 2002), 40–42.
6. Elizabeth Lyle Saxon, *A Southern Woman's War Time Reminiscences* (Memphis, Tenn.: Press of the Pilcher Printing Co., 1905), 36.
7. Eliza Stinson, *War Days in Fayetteville, North Carolina: Reminiscences of 1861 to 1865* (Fayetteville, N.C.: United Daughters of the Confederacy, J.E.B. Stuart Chapter, 1910), 21.
8. George Cary Eggleston, *A Rebel's Recollections* (New York: Hurd and Houghton, 1875), 197–98.
9. Albert Castel, *Decision in the West: The Atlanta Campaign of 1864* (Lawrence, Kans.: University Press of Kansas, 1992), 24–25.
10. George Cary Eggleston, "A Rebel's Recollections," *Atlantic Monthly*, December 1874: 663.
11. Richard M. McMurry, *Atlanta 1864: Last Chance for the Confederacy* (Lincoln, Neb.: University of Nebraska Press, 2000), 5–6; Castel, 26–28.
12. William Alan Blair, *Virginia's Private War: Feeding Body and Soul in the Confederacy, 1861–1865* (New York: Oxford University Press, 1998), 82. Castel, 27.
13. Mary C. Moffett, ed., *Letters of General James Conner, C.S.A.* (Columbia, S.C: R. L. Bryan, 1950), 116.
14. J. B. Jones, *A Rebel War Clerk's Diary at the Confederate States Capital Vol.2* (Philadelphia: J. B. Lippincott & Co., 1866), 157.
15. Eggleston, 193.
16. *Ibid.*, 193–94.
17. G. S. Bradley, *The Star Corps: or, Notes of an Army Chaplain During Sherman's Famous March to the Sea* (Milwaukee, Wisc.: Jermain & Brightman, 1865), 88.
18. John G. Nicolay and John Hay, "Abraham Lincoln: A History," *Century*, July 1889: 414–15.
19. *Ibid.*, *Abraham Lincoln: Complete Works, Volume 2* (New York: Century, 1894), 508.
20. *Ibid.*
21. *Ibid.*, "Abraham Lincoln: A History," July 1889: 414–15.
22. Benjamin P. Thomas and Harold M. Hyman, *Stanton: The Life and Times of Lincoln's Secretary of War* (New York: Knopf, 1962), 307–08.
23. Castel, 4.
24. *Ibid.*
25. *Ibid.*
26. *Ibid.*
27. Gary Gallagher, ed., *The Wilderness Campaign* (Chapel Hill, N.C.: University of North Carolina Press, 1997), 1–2.
28. Bruce Catton, *Bruce Catton's Civil War* (New York: The Fairfax, 1984), 474.
29. *Ibid.*, 475.
30. *Ibid.*, 475.

Chapter 2

1. S. M. Bowman and R. B. Irwin, *Sherman and His Campaigns* (New York: Richardson, 1865), 167–68; Castel, 68.
2. Bowman, 167–68. Castel, 68.
3. United States War Department, *The War of the Rebellion: A Compilation of the Official Records of the*

Union and Confederate Armies (Washington, D.C.: Government Printing Office, 1880–1901), Volume 38, Part 1, 3.
　4. Bowman, 167–68. Castel, 68.
　5. *Official Records*, Volume 38, Part 1, 1.
　6. Ulysses S. Grant, *Personal Memoirs of U. S. Grant* (New York: Webster, 1886), 130.
　7. *Official Records*, Volume 38, Part 1, 1–2.
　8. *Official Records*, Volume 38, Part 1, 2.
　9. Adam Badeau, *Military History of Ulysses S. Grant, from April, 1861 to April, 1865, Volume 2* (New York: Appleton 1885), 10.
　10. Bruce Catton, *Grant Takes Command* Boston: Little, Brown, 1968), 112.
　11. Catton, *Grant Takes Command*, 112.
　12. *Official Records*, Volume 32, Part 1, 176.
　13. McMurry, 5–6.
　14. John Bell Hood, *Advance and Retreat* (Edison, N.J.: Blue and Gray Press, 1985), 89.
　15. Hood, 90.
　16. Joseph E. Johnston, "Opposing Sherman's Advance to Atlanta," *Century*, August 1887: 585.
　17. *Ibid.*
　18. *Ibid.*
　19. *Ibid.*
　20. *Official Records*, Volume 38, Part 3, 613.
　21. Hood, 91–92.
　22. Jefferson Davis, *The Rise and Fall of the Confederate Government, Volume 3* (New York: Yoseloff, 1958), 549.
　23. Joseph E. Johnston, *Narrative of Military Operations Directed, During the Late War Between the States* (Bloomington, Ind.: Indiana University Press, 1959), 274–75.
　24. Davis, 549.
　25. Hood, 92.
　26. *Ibid.*, 94–95.
　27. Andrew Haughton, *Training, Tactics and Leadership in the Confederate Army of Tennessee: Seeds of Failure* (London: Cass, 2000), 148–49; Douglas Hale, *The Third Texas Cavalry in the Civil War* (Norman, Okla.: University of Oklahoma Press, 1993), 217.
　28. Haughton, 148–49; Hale, 217.
　29. William T. Sherman, *Memoirs of Gen. W. T. Sherman, Written by Himself, Volume 2* (New York: Webster, 1891), 8–9.
　30. *Ibid.*, 10.
　31. Castel, 91–93.
　32. Sherman, 10–11.
　33. *Ibid.*
　34. Mark Coburn, *Terrible Innocence: General Sherman at War* (New York: Hippocrene Books, 1993), 78–80.
　35. Castel, 69; Hale, 216–17.
　36. F. N. Boney, *Rebel Georgia* (Macon, Ga.: Mercer University Press, 1997), 43.
　37. Bradley T. Johnson, *A Memoir of the Life and Public Service of Joseph E. Johnston* (Baltimore: Woodward, 1891), 113–14.
　38. Sherman, 29.
　39. Gideon Welles, "The Opposition to Lincoln in 1864," *Atlantic Monthly*, March 1878: 376.

Chapter 3

　1. Sherman, 5.
　2. Stanley F. Horn, *The Army of Tennessee* (Norman, Okla.: University of Oklahoma Press, 1952), 316; Samuel Carter III, *The Siege of Atlanta, 1864* (New York: St. Martin's Press, 1973), 102–03; Bowman and Irwin, 169–70.
　3. Bowman, 170.
　4. Carter, 102; Bowman, 170; W. F. G. Shanks, "Recollections of Thomas," *Harper's New Monthly Magazine*, May 1865: 756–57.
　5. Bowman, 170.
　6. Carter, 103.
　7. Bowman, 169–70.
　8. Carter, 104.
　9. *Ibid.*, 100–01.
　10. John C. Ropes, "General Sherman," *Atlantic Monthly*, August 1891: 191; Brooks D. Simpson and Jean V. Berlin, eds., *Sherman's Civil War: Selected Correspondence of William T. Sherman, 1860–1865* (Chapel Hill, N.C.: University of North Carolina Press, 1999), 651–52.
　11. Ropes, 191–92.
　12. *Ibid.*, 192–94.
　13. W. F. G. Shanks, "Recollections of Sherman," *Harper's New Monthly Magazine*, April 1865: 646.
　14. Badeau, 19; Shanks, "Recollections of Sherman": 641–42.
　15. McMurry, 51; William Tecumseh Sherman, "The Grand Strategy of the War of the Rebellion," *The Century*, February 1888: 593.
　16. M. A. DeWolfe Howe, ed., *Home Letters of General Sherman* (New York: Charles Scribner's Sons, 1909), 287.
　17. Simpson, 599.
　18. *Ibid.*, 599–600.
　19. *Ibid.*, 601.
　20. *Ibid.*, 599–601.
　21. *Ibid.*, 596.
　22. *Ibid.*, 587.
　23. Jennifer Cain Bohrnstedt, ed., *Soldiering with Sherman: Civil War Letters of George F. Cram* (DeKalb, Ill.: Northern Illinois University Press, 2000), 73.
　24. C. Flavel Barber and H. Robert Ferrel, eds., *Holding the Line: The Third Tennessee Infantry 1861–1864* (Kent, Oh.: Kent State University Press, 1994), 157.
　25. Steven E. Woodworth, *No Band of Brothers: Problems in the Rebel High Command* (Columbia, Mo.: University of Missouri Press, 1999), 82; Castel, 28.
　26. McMurry, 8; Woodworth, 83.
　27. Woodworth, 84.
　28. Boney, 62; Richard M. McMurry, *The Road Past Kennesaw: The Atlanta Campaign of 1864* (Washington, D.C.: National Park Service, 1972), 4.
　29. Jacob D. Cox, *Sherman's Battle for Atlanta* (New York: Da Capo Press, 1994), 26.
　30. McMurry, *Atlanta 1864*, 10–11.

31. Johnston, *Narrative of Military Operations*, 279; *Official Records*, Volume 38, Part 3, 613.
32. Castel, 31; Johnston, *Narrative of Military Operations*, 273–74.
33. Johnston, *Narrative of Military Operations*, 272.
34. McMurry, *Atlanta 1864*, 37–38; Horn, 312.
35. McMurry, *Atlanta 1864*, 37–39; Horn, 318; Carter, 94–95.
36. Horn, 316–17; Thomas Robson Hay, *Hood's Tennessee Campaign* (New York: Neale, 1929), 35–37.
37. Hay, 35–37. Horn, 316–17; Woodworth, 124.
38. Hood, 92–93.
39. Carter, 88–89.
40. *Ibid.*

Chapter 4

1. Johnston, "Opposing Sherman's Advance to Atlanta": 586.
2. George W. Pepper, *Personal Recollections of Sherman's Campaigns in Georgia and the Carolinas* (Zanesville, Oh.: Dunne, 1866), 57.
3. Horn, 311; Cox, 30.
4. William C.P. Breckinridge, "The Opening of the Atlanta Campaign," *Battles and Leaders of the Civil War, Volume 4*, ed. Robert Underwood Johnson and Clarence Clough Buel (New York: Yoseloff, 1956), 958.
5. Davis, 551.
6. Johnston, *Narrative of Military Operations*, 317.
7. *Ibid.*, 317–18.
8. *Official Records*, Volume 38, Part 1, 62–63.
9. *Ibid.*, Volume 38, Part 1, 59.
10. *Ibid.*, Volume 38, Part 1, 63. Oliver Otis Howard, *Autobiography of Oliver Otis Howard* (New York: The Baker & Taylor Company, 1908), 504.
11. *Official Records*, Volume 38, Part 1, 63.
12. *Ibid.*, Volume 38, Part 3, 816.
13. *Ibid.*, Volume 38, Part 2, 510.
14. *Ibid.*, Volume 38, Part 3, 375–76; Oliver O. Howard, "The Struggle for Atlanta," *Century*, July 1887: 445.
15. Philip L. Secrist, *The Battle of Resaca: Atlanta Campaign 1864* (Macon, Ga.: Mercer University Press, 1998), 14.
16. *Official Records*, Volume 38, Part 3, 375.
17. Secrist, 15.
18. *Official Records*, Volume 38, Part 3, 16–17.
19. Sherman, 33.
20. *Ibid.*, 34.
21. *Official Records*, Volume 38, Part 3, 721.
22. *Official Records*, Volume 38, Part 1, 64; Howard, "The Struggle for Atlanta": 445.
23. Cox, 31–32, 41.
24. Secrist, 18.
25. *Official Records*, Volume 38, Part 3, 721.
26. Johnston, "Opposing Sherman's Advance to Atlanta": 589.
27. *Official Records*, Volume 38, Part 3, 91.
28. *Ibid.*, Volume 38, Part 3, 91.
29. *Ibid.*, Volume 38, Part 2, 510–11, 676–77; Norman D. Brown, ed., *One of Cleburne's Command: The Civil War Reminiscences and Diary of Capt. Samuel T. Foster, Granbury's Texas Brigade, CSA* (Austin, Tex.: University of Texas Press, 1980), 76.
30. *Official Records*, Volume 38, Part 2, 582.
31. *Ibid.*, Volume 38, Part 1, 521.
32. *Ibid.*, Volume 38, Part 2, 677–78.
33. Secrist, 33; *Official Records*, Volume 38, Part 1, 190.
34. Secrist, 33.
35. *Ibid.*, 33–34.
36. *Official Records*, Volume 38, Part 1, 190; Secrist, 34–35.
37. *Official Records*, Volume 38, Part 1, 488–89.
38. Secrist, 35–36.
39. *Official Records*, Volume 38, Part 3, 92–93.
40. *Official Records*, Volume 38, Part 3, 93.
41. Howard, "The Struggle for Atlanta": 447.
42. *Official Records*, Volume 38, Part 1, 190–91; Johnston, "Opposing Sherman's Advance to Atlanta": 589.
43. *Official Records*, Volume 38, Part 1, 191; Cox, 47.
44. *Official Records*, Volume 38, Part 3, 812.
45. *Ibid.*, Volume 38, Part 3, 817.
46. *Ibid.*, Volume 38, Part 3, 817.
47. *Ibid.*, Volume 38, Part 3, 813.
48. *Ibid.*, Volume 38, Part 3, 377–78.
49. Johnston, "Opposing Sherman's Advance to Atlanta": 590.
50. *Official Records*, Volume 38, Part 3, 615.
51. Cox, 47–48.
52. *Ibid.*, 49.
53. *Official Records*, Volume 38, Part 3, 615.
54. Johnston, "Opposing Sherman's Advance to Atlanta": 591. McMurry, *The Road Past Kennesaw*, 16.
55. David Coe, ed., *Mine Eyes Have Seen the Glory: Combat Diaries of Union Sergeant Hamlin Alexander Coe* (Rutherford, N.J.: Fairleigh Dickinson University Press, 1975), 133–34.
56. Bell Irvin Wiley, ed., *Confederate Letters of John W. Hagen* (Athens, Ga.: University of Georgia Press, 1954), 36–37.
57. *Official Records*, Volume 38, Part 3, 616.
58. McMurry, *The Road Past Kennesaw*, 14–15.
59. *Official Records*, Volume 38, Part 3, 616.
60. Cox, 55.
61. Daniel E. Sutherland, ed., *Reminiscences of a Private: William E. Bevens of the First Arkansas Infantry, C.S.A.* (Fayetteville, Ark.: The University of Arkansas Press, 1992), 161.
62. Frank A. Montgomery, *Reminiscences of a Mississippian in Peace and War* (Cincinnati, Oh.: Clarke, 1901), 166.
63. Johnston, *Narrative of Military Operations*, 323.
64. *Ibid.*, 323–24.
65. McMurry, *The Road Past Kennesaw*, 16.
66. Johnston, *Narrative of Military Operations*, 324.

67. *Ibid.*; *Official Records*, Volume 38, Part 3, 616; Joseph E. Johnston, "Opposing Sherman's Advance to Atlanta": 590.
68. Jack K. Bauer, ed., *Soldiering: The Civil War Diary of Rice C. Bull, 123rd New York Volunteer Infantry* (San Rafael, Calif.: Presidio Press, 1977), 111–12.
69. Howard, "The Struggle for Atlanta": 449.
70. Lucille Griffith, ed., *Yours Till Death: Civil War Letters of John W. Cotton* (Tuscaloosa, Ala.: University of Alabama Press, 1951), 106.
71. G. W. Lewis, *The Campaigns of the 124th Regiment Ohio Volunteer Infantry* (Akron, Oh.: Werner, 1894), 144.

Chapter 5

1. *Official Records*, Volume 38, Part 1, 60.
2. *Ibid.*, Volume 38, Part 1, 65; Webb Garrison, *Atlanta and the War* (Nashville, Tenn.: Rutledge Hill Press, 1995), 85.
3. Coburn, 84; Garrison, 84.
4. Howard, "The Struggle for Atlanta": 451; Coburn, 84.
5. Howard, *Autobiography*, 543, 548.
6. McMurry, *Atlanta 1864*, 88–89; *Official Records*, Volume 38, Part 1, 66.
7. *Official Records*, Volume 38, Part 1, 66; McMurry, *Atlanta 1864*, 89.
8. McMurry, *Atlanta 1864*, 88.
9. Bauer, 117.
10. McMurry, *Atlanta 1864*, 88; *Official Records*, Volume 38, Part 3, 855.
11. Howard, "The Struggle for Atlanta": 452.
12. *Official Records*, Volume 38, Part 2, 382.
13. Howard, "The Struggle for Atlanta": 452; *Official Records*, Volume 38, Part 2, 124.
14. McMurry, *Atlanta 1864*, 88–89. *Official Records*, Volume 38, Part 3, 828.
15. J. H. Segars, ed., *Life in Dixie During the War: Mary A. H. Gay* (Macon, Ga.: Mercer University Press, 2001), 91.
16. Coburn 84–85; *Official Records*, Volume 38, Part 1, 194.
17. *Official Records*, Volume 38, Part 1, 194; William B. Hazen, *A Narrative of Military Service* (Boston: Ticknor, 1885), 257.
18. *Official Records*, Volume 38, Part 1, 195, 724.
19. Hazen, 257.
20. *Official Records*, Volume 38, Part 1, 194.
21. *Ibid.*, Volume 38, Part 3, 725.
22. Hazen, 257.
23. Howard, "The Struggle for Atlanta": 452; *Official Records*, Volume 38, Part 1, 195.
24. *Official Records*, Volume 38, Part 3, 95.
25. *Ibid.*, Volume 38, Part 3, 129.
26. *Ibid.*, Volume 38, Part 3, 316.
27. *Ibid.*, Volume 38, Part 3, 129.
28. *Ibid.*, Volume 38, Part 3, 95.
29. *Ibid.*, Volume 38, Part 3, 96.
30. *Ibid.*, Volume 38, Part 3, 96.
31. *Ibid.*, Volume 38, Part 3, 131.
32. Lot D. Young, *Reminiscences of A Soldier of the Orphan Brigade* (Paris, Ky.: self-published, 1918), 86–87.
33. *Official Records*, Volume 38, Part 3, 96; Howard, "The Struggle for Atlanta": 452.
34. C. Knight Aldrich, ed., *Quest for a Star: The Civil War Letters and Diaries of Colonel Francis T. Sherman of the 88th Illinois* (Knoxville, Tenn.: University of Tennessee Press, 1999), 116.
35. *Official Records*, Volume 38, Part 1, 60.
36. *Ibid.*
37. Bauer, 121–22.
38. *Official Records*, Volume 38, Part 1, 60–61.
39. Howard, *Autobiography*, 550–51.
40. McMurry, *Atlanta 1864*, 92–93.
41. *Ibid.*
42. Bauer, 118–19.
43. McMurry, *Atlanta 1864*, 93.
44. *Ibid.*, *Atlanta 1864*, 94.
45. *Ibid.*, *Atlanta 1864*, 95.
46. Johnston, *Narrative of Military Operations*, 175.
47. Coburn, 85–86.

Chapter 6

1. Bauer, 137.
2. Coe, 146.
3. Edward Young McMorries, *History of the First Regiment Alabama Volunteer Infantry C.S.A.* (Freeport, N.Y.: Books for Libraries Press, 1970), 73–74.
4. Sherman, *Memoirs*, 51; *Official Records*, Volume 38, Part 1, 67.
5. William Alan Blair, ed., *A Politician Goes to War: The Civil War Letters of John White Geary* (University Park, Pa.: Pennsylvania State University Press, 1995), 179.
6. Mark K. Christ, *Getting Used to Being Shot At: The Spence Family Civil War Letters* (Fayetteville, Ark.: The University of Arkansas Press, 2002), 94.
7. Carter, 139. Howard, "The Struggle for Atlanta": 453; McMurry, *Atlanta 1864*, 100–01.
8. Henry H. Wright, *A History of the Sixth Iowa Infantry* (Iowa City, Ia.: State Historical Society of Iowa, 1923), 283.
9. *Official Records*, Volume 38, Part 1, 67.
10. *Ibid.*
11. Bohrnstedt, 104.
12. Janet Correll Ellison, ed., *On to Atlanta: The Civil War Diaries of John Hill Ferguson, Illinois Tenth Regiment of Volunteers* (Lincoln, Neb.: University of Nebraska Press, 2001), 47.
13. Coe, 150.
14. Milo M. Quaife, ed., *From the Cannon's Mouth: The Civil War Letters of General Alpheus S. Williams* (Detroit, Mich.: Wayne State University Press and the Detroit Historical Society, 1959), 316.

15. L. W. Day, *Story of the One Hundred and First Ohio Infantry* (Cleveland, Oh.: Bayne, 1894), 216–18).
16. *Official Records*, Volume 38, Part 1, 67.
17. Coburn, 87; Carter, 147.
18. *Official Records*, Volume 38, Part 1, 67.
19. Bauer, 127–28.
20. *Official Records*, Volume 38, Part 1, 197.
21. S. G. French, "Paper Read Before Louisville Branch of the Southern Historical Society," *Southern Historical Society Papers*, Volume 9, November-December 1881: 506; McMurry, *Atlanta 1864*, 104.
22. Wright, 286–87; *Official Records*, Volume 38, Part 1, 68.
23. Mrs. Irby Morgan, *How It Was: Four Years Among the Rebels* (Nashville, Tenn.: Publishing House Methodist Episcopal Church, South, 1892), 98–99.
24. Howard, "The Struggle for Atlanta": 454; Coburn, 88.
25. *Official Records*, Volume 38, Part 3, 815.
26. Ibid., Volume 38, Part 2, 513; Ibid., Volume 38, Part 3, 815; McMurry, *Atlanta 1864*, 105–06. Coburn, 88.
27. Howard, "The Struggle for Atlanta": 454; Coburn, 88.
28. Sherman, *Memoirs*, 59–60.
29. McMurry, *Atlanta 1864*, 107.
30. Sherman, *Memoirs*, 60.
31. *Official Records*, Volume 38, Part 1, 68.
32. Howard, "The Struggle for Atlanta": 454.
33. Ibid., *Official Records*, Volume 38, Part 3, 85.
34. Wright, 291.
35. Ibid., 292. *Official Records*, Volume 38, Part 3, 85.
36. Howard, "The Struggle for Atlanta": 454.
37. *Official Records*, Volume 38, Part 1, 632.
38. Howard, "The Struggle for Atlanta": 454; *Official Records*, Volume 38, Part 1, 335–36.
39. Howard, "The Struggle for Atlanta": 454–55.
40. *Official Records*, Volume 38, Part 1, 336.
41. Ibid., Oscar Osburn Winther, ed., *With Sherman to the Sea: The Civil War Letters, Diaries & Reminiscences of Theodore F. Upson* (Bloomington: Indiana University Press, 1958), 116.
42. Sutherland, 175.
43. *Official Records*, Volume 38, Part 1, 632.
44. Ibid., Volume 38, Part 1, 680.
45. Ibid., Volume 38, Part 1, 632–33.
46. Howard, "The Struggle for Atlanta": 455; Sherman, *Memoirs*, 61.
47. Coburn, 90.
48. McMurry, *Atlanta 1864*, 109–10; Coburn, 91; *Official Records*, Volume 38, Part 1, 69.
49. McMurry, *Atlanta 1864*, 114; *Official Records*, Volume 38, Part 1, 69.
50. Howard, "The Struggle for Atlanta": 456; Coburn, 91.
51. Wright, 299.
52. Coburn, 91; *Official Records*, Volume 38, Part 2, 515–16.
53. Howard, "The Struggle for Atlanta": 456; *Official Records*, Volume 38, Part 1, 70.
54. Carter, 185.
55. McMurry, *Atlanta 1864*, 118–20.
56. Howard, "The Struggle for Atlanta": 456.
57. Howe, *Home Letters*, 298.

Chapter 7

1. George T. Stevens, *Three Years in the Sixth Corps* (New York: Time-Life Books, 1984), 303.
2. Badeau, 311.
3. Horace Porter, *Campaigning with Grant* (New York: Mallard, 1991), 72–73.
4. Badeau, 131.
5. Porter, 110.
6. Hunt Rhodes, ed. *All for the Union: The Civil War Diary and Letters of Elisha Hunt Rhodes* (New York: Orion Books, 1991), 158.
7. Catton, *Bruce Catton's Civil War*, 569.
8. Ibid., 572–75.
9. Badeau, 324–25.
10. Catton, *Grant Takes Command*, 246.
11. Orton S. Clark, *The One Hundred and Sixteenth Regiment of New York State Volunteers* (Buffalo, N.Y.: Printing House of Matthews & Warren, 1868), 206.
12. Catton, *Grant Takes Command*, 248; John D. Imboden, "The Battle of New Market, Va., May 15th, 1864," *Battles and Leaders of the Civil War*, Robert Underwood Johnston and Clarence Clough Buel, eds. (New York: Yoseloff, 1956), 485.
13. Richard Duncan, *Lee's Endangered Left* (Baton Rouge: Louisiana State University Press, 1998), 247.
14. Jubal A. Early, *A Memoir of the Last Year of the War for Independence in the Confederate States of America* (New Orleans: Blelock & Co., 1867), 35; Duncan, 256; A. L. Long, *Memoirs of Robert E. Lee: His Military and Personal History* (Edison, N.J.: The Blue and Gray Press, 1993), 256.
15. Henry Kyd Douglas, *I Rode with Stonewall* (Chapel Hill, N.C.: University of North Carolina Press, 1940), 293–94.
16. Catton, *Bruce Catton's Civil War*, 610–12.
17. Long, 359–60.
18. Horace Greeley, *The American Conflict: A History of the Great Rebellion in the United States of America, 1860–65* (New York: Negro Universities Press, 1969), 660–61.
19. Allan Nevins, ed., *Diary of the Civil War 1860–1865: George Templeton Strong* (New York: Macmillan, 1962), 467.
20. Badeau, 11.
21. Nicolay and Hay, "Abraham Lincoln: A History" August 1889: 551.
22. Ibid., 552.
23. Ibid., 555.
24. Jedediah Mannis and Galen R. Wilson, eds., *Bound to Be A Soldier: The Letters of Private James T. Miller, 11th Pennsylvania Infantry, 1861–1864* (Knoxville, Tenn.: University of Tennessee Press, 2001), 129–30.

25. McMurry, *Atlanta 1864*, 125.
26. Greeley, 657–58; McMurry, *Atlanta 1864*, 123.
27. Thomas, *Stanton*, 312.
28. Nicolay and Hay, "Abraham Lincoln: A History," July 1889: 411.
29. *Ibid.*, *Abraham Lincoln: Complete Works*, 534.
30. McMurry, *Atlanta 1864*, 125.
31. *Ibid.*
32. *Ibid.*, 124–25.
33. Greeley, 668; Gideon Welles, "Lincoln's Triumph in 1864," *Atlantic Monthly*, April 1878: 457.
34. McMurry, *Atlanta 1864*, 125–26.
35. Davis, 611.
36. Welles, "Lincoln's Triumph": 455.
37. Nicolay and Hay, *Abraham Lincoln: Complete Works*, 550.
38. Bruce Catton, *Never Call Retreat* (Garden City, N.J.: Doubleday, 1965), 288–89.
39. *Ibid.*, 289–90; Nicolay and Hay, "Abraham Lincoln: A History," July 1889: 418.
40. Catton, *Never Call Retreat*, 289–90; Nicolay and Hay, "Abraham Lincoln: A History," July 1889: 418.
41. Carl Sandburg, *Abraham Lincoln: The War Years, Volume 3* (New York: Harcourt, Brace, World, 1939) 128.
42. Nicolay and Hay, "Abraham Lincoln: A History," July 1889: 418; Sandburg, 128.
43. Nicolay and Hay, "Abraham Lincoln: A History," July 1889: 419.
44. *Ibid.*, "Abraham Lincoln: A History," August 1889: 548.
45. *Ibid.*, *Abraham Lincoln: Complete Works*, 568.
46. Isabella D. Martin and Myrta Lockett Avary, eds., *A Diary from Dixie, as Written by Mary Boykin Chesnut* (New York: D. Appleton, 1905), 316.
47. Welles, "The Opposition to Lincoln in 1864": 372.

Chapter 8

1. Sarah Woolfolk Wiggins, ed., *The Journals of Josiah Gorgas, 1857–1878* (Tuscaloosa, Ala.: University of Alabama Press, 1995), 111.
2. Davis, 556.
3. Thomas Cooper DeLeon, *Four Years in Rebel Capitals* (New York: Time-Life Books, 1983), 341.
4. *Official Records*, Volume 38, Part 5, 878–79; Robert M. Hughes, *General Johnston* (New York: Appleton, 1897), 246; Garrison, 138–39.
5. *Official Records*, Volume 38, Part 5, 878.
6. Hughes, 246–47; *Official Records*, Volume 38, Part 5, 880.
7. *Official Records*, Volume 38, Part 5, 882–83.
8. Davis, 557.
9. *Official Records*, Volume 38, Part 5, 885.
10. Hood, 126.
11. *Official Records*, Volume 38, Part 5, 888.
12. *Ibid.*
13. Davis, 556–57.
14. *Official Records*, Volume 38, Part 5, 887.
15. McMorries, 75–76.
16. Wiley, 51.
17. W. J. McMurray, *History of the Twentieth Tennessee Regiment Volunteer Infantry, C.S.A.* (Nashville, Tenn.: Elder's Bookstore, 1976), 319.
18. Brown, 106–07.
19. Montgomery, 182.
20. Fannie A. Beers, *Memories: A Record of Personal Experience and Adventure During Four Years of War* (New York: Time-Life Books, 1985), 138.
21. McMurry, *Atlanta 1864*, 141–42.
22. Sherman, *Memoirs*, 71–72.
23. John M. Schofield, *Forty-six Years in the Army* (New York: Century, 1897), 231–32.
24. Sherman, *Memoirs*, 72.
25. Coburn, 99; McMurry, *Atlanta 1864*, 146–47; Hood, 165–66.
26. *Official Records*, Volume 38, Part 3, 871.
27. Coburn, 99; *Official Records*, Volume 38, Part 3, 871.
28. McMurry, *Atlanta 1864*, 150; Oliver O. Howard, "The Battles About Atlanta I," *Atlantic Monthly*, October 1876: 389.
29. McMurry, *Atlanta 1864*, 150; *Official Records*, Volume 38, Part 3, 698.
30. *Official Records*, Volume 38, Part 1, 290. Howard, "Battles About Atlanta I": 390.
31. Howard, "Battles About Atlanta I": 389.
32. *Official Records*, Volume 38, Part 1, 290.
33. *Ibid.*, Volume 38, Part 3, 306.
34. *Ibid.*, Volume 38, Part 3, 298.
35. Howard, "Battles About Atlanta I": 390.
36. *Official Records*, Volume 38, Part 2, 328.
37. Howard, "Battles About Atlanta I": 390–91; *Official Records*, Volume 38, Part 2, 328.
38. *Official Records*, Volume 38, Part 2, 138; Howard, "Battles About Atlanta I": 391.
39. *Official Records*, Volume 38, Part 2, 138; Howard, "Battles About Atlanta I": 391.
40. Howard, "Battles About Atlanta I": 391; *Official Records*, Volume 38, Part 2, 34.
41. *Official Records*, Volume 38, Part 2, 34; Bauer, 149.
42. Bauer, 149; Howard, "Battles About Atlanta I": 391.
43. Hood, 168; *Official Records*, Volume 38, Part 3, 698.
44. *Official Records*, Volume 38, Part 3, 871.
45. *Ibid.*, Volume 38, Part 3, 877.
46. Coburn, 100; Howard, "Battles About Atlanta I": 392.
47. Wallace P. Reed, *History of Atlanta, Georgia* (Syracuse, N.Y.: Mason, 1889), 175.

Chapter 9

1. Hood, 173.
2. McMurry, *Atlanta 1864*, 152–53; *Official Records*, Volume 38, Part 1, 73.

3. McMurry, *Atlanta 1864*, 152.
4. *Official Records*, Volume 38, Part 3, 544.
5. *Ibid.*
6. *Ibid.*
7. Hood, 176–77.
8. *Ibid.*, 177.
9. *Official Records*, Volume 38, Part 3, 699; McMurry, *Atlanta 1864*, 153.
10. T. B. Roy, "General Hardee and the Military Operations Around Atlanta," *Southern Historical Society Papers*, Volume 8, August-September 1880: 360.
11. *Official Records*, Volume 38, Part 3, 699; W. H. Chamberlin, "Hood's Second Sortie at Atlanta," *Battles and Leaders of the Civil War, Volume 4*, Robert Underwood Johnson and Clarence Clough Buel, eds. (New York: Thomas Yoseloff, 1956), 326.
12. Chamberlin, 326.
13. Grenville M. Dodge, *The Battle of Atlanta and Other Campaigns, Addresses, Etc.* (Council Bluffs, Ia.: Monarch, 1911), 42.
14. *Official Records*, Volume 38, Part 3, 370.
15. Roy, 369–70.
16. *Official Records*, Volume 38, Part 3, 369–70.
17. Chamberlin, 327.
18. *Official Records*, Volume 38, Part 3, 475.
19. *Ibid.*, Volume 38, Part 3, 476.
20. Chamberlin, 326.
21. *Official Records*, Volume 38, Part 3, 466.
22. *Ibid.*, Volume 38, Part 3, 23.
23. *Ibid.*, Volume 38, Part 3, 370.
24. *Ibid.*
25. Roy, 360; Howard, "Battles About Atlanta I": 393–94; *Official Records*, Volume 38, Part 3, 582.
26. Howard, "Battles About Atlanta I": 393–94; *Official Records*, Volume 38, Part 3, 582.
27. *Official Records*, Volume 38, Part 3, 582.
28. *Ibid.*, Volume 38, Part 3, 582–83.
29. Howard, "The Struggle for Atlanta": 460; Sherman, *Memoirs*, 77.
30. *Official Records*, Volume 38, Part 3, 24.
31. *Ibid.*, Volume 38, Part 3, 23.
32. *Ibid.*
33. Pepper, 139–40.
34. Sherman, *Memoirs*, 80.
35. *Official Records*, Volume 38, Part 3, 24–25.
36. *Ibid.*, Volume 38, Part 3, 25.
37. *Ibid.*
38. *Ibid.*, Volume 38, Part 3, 25–26.
39. Sherman, Memoirs, 81.
40. *Official Records*, Volume 38, Part 3, 26.
41. *Ibid.*, Volume 38, Part 3, 583.
42. *Ibid.*, Volume 38, Part 3, 27.
43. Pepper, 144–45.
44. *Official Records*, Volume 38, Part 3, 547.
45. Dodge, 45.
46. *Official Records*, Volume 38, Part 3, 506.
47. *Ibid.*, Volume 38, Part 3, 506–07.
48. Sherman, *Memoirs*, 82–84.
49. Hood, 182–83.
50. *Ibid.*, 183.

Chapter 10

1. Reed, 170; Segars, 119–20.
2. Carter, 177.
3. Beers, 150.
4. Carter, 178–79.
5. Segars, 127–28.
6. Garrison, 166.
7. McMurry, *Atlanta 1864*, 155–56; Coburn, 97.
8. McMurry, *Atlanta 1864*, 155–56. Coburn, 97.
9. McMurry, *Atlanta 1864*, 155–56; Howard, "The Struggle for Atlanta": 461.
10. Coburn, 104; McMurry, *Atlanta 1864*, 155; Hood, 194.
11. Coburn, 104; Howard, "The Struggle for Atlanta": 461–62.
12. *Official Records*, Volume 38, Part 3, 762–63; McMurry, *Atlanta 1864*, 155–56.
13. *Official Records*, Volume 38, Part 3, 104.
14. *Ibid.*
15. *Ibid.*, Volume 38, Part 1, 78.
16. *Ibid.*, Volume 38, Part 3, 767.
17. *Ibid.*, Volume 38, Part 3, 763.
18. Pepper, 155.
19. Dawson, 72; *Official Records*, Volume 38, Part 3, 41.
20. *Official Records*, Volume 38, Part 3, 927.
21. *Ibid.*, Volume 38, Part 3, 931.
22. *Ibid.*, Volume 38, Part 3, 927.
23. Howard, "Battles About Atlanta I": 397.
24. *Official Records*, Volume 38, Part 3, 281.
25. *Ibid.*, Volume 38, Part 3, 140.
26. Coburn, 105. McMurry, *Atlanta 1864*, 157; *Official Records*, Volume 38, Part 1, 78.
27. *Official Records*, Volume 38, Part 3, 699.
28. Simpson, 676.
29. McMurry, *Atlanta 1864*, 157; Sherman, *Memoirs*, 87–88.
30. McMurry, *Atlanta 1864*, 157–58; Sherman, *Memoirs*, 88, 98.
31. *Official Records*, Volume 38, Part 2, 762–63; Sherman, *Memoirs*, 98; McMurry, *Atlanta 1864*, 157–58.
32. Sherman, *Memoirs*, 98; McMurry, *Atlanta 1864*, 157–58.
33. Sherman, *Memoirs*, 98.
34. *Official Records*, Volume 38, Part 1, 78; James P. Boyd, *The Life of General William T. Sherman* (Philadelphia: Publishers Union, 1891), 301.
35. Simpson, 676; *Official Records*, Volume 38, Part 1, 78–79.
36. *Official Records*, Volume 38, Part 5, 407.
37. *Ibid.*, Volume 38, Part 5, 408.
38. *Ibid.*, Volume 38, Part 5, 408–09.
39. *Ibid.*, Volume 38, Part 3, 386.
40. *Ibid.*, Volume 38, Part 1, 161.
41. Bauer, 160.
42. McMurry, *Atlanta 1864*, 163.
43. *Ibid.*
44. Coburn, 107–08.
45. *Ibid.*, 107.

46. *Official Records*, Volume 38, Part 5, 412, 434, 448, 573.
47. Reed, 179. Coburn, 107.
48. Reed, 182–83.
49. John R. Hornaday, *Atlanta: Yesterday, Today and Tomorrow* (n.p.: American Cities Book Co., 1922), 46.
50. Beers, 166.
51. Hood, 202–03.

Chapter 11

1. Sherman, *Memoirs*, 102.
2. W. S. Morris, L. D. Hartwell and J. B. Kuykendall, ed., *History 31st Regiment Illinois Volunteers* (Carbondale, Ill.: Southern Illinois University Press, 1998), 118; Boyd, 303–04.
3. McMurry, *Atlanta 1864*, 163; Boyd, 304.
4. McMurry, *Atlanta 1864*, 165.
5. *Official Records*, Volume 38, Part 1, 79.
6. Boyd, 304; McMurry, *Atlanta 1864*, 166–67.
7. Sherman, *Memoirs*, 104.
8. Thomas W. Osborn, ed. Richard Harwell and Philip N. Racine, *The Fiery Trail: A Union Officer's Account of Sherman's Last Campaigns* (Knoxville, Tenn.: University of Tennessee Press, 1986), 18; William M. Anderson, ed., *We Are Sherman's Men: The Civil War Letters of Henry Orendorff* (Macomb, Ill.: Western Illinois University Press, 1986), 109.
9. Boyd, 304; *Official Records*, Volume 38, Part 1, 80.
10. Day, 252.
11. Howard, "Battles About Atlanta II": 560.
12. *Ibid*.: 561; Sherman, *Memoirs*, 105.
13. Coburn, 109; *Official Records*, Volume 38, Part 3, 700.
14. Sherman, *Memoirs*, 105; *Official Records*, Volume 38, Part 1, 165.
15. Winther, 123–24.
16. Sherman, *Memoirs*, 105; *Official Records*, Volume 38, Part 1, 165.
17. McMurry, *Atlanta 1864*, 170; *Official Records*, Volume 38, Part 1, 80–81.
18. McMurry, *Atlanta 1864*, 171; *Official Records*, Volume 38, Part 3, 44.
19. McMurry, *Atlanta 1864*, 171; *Official Records*, Volume 38, Part 3, 44.
20. *Official Records*, Volume 38, Part 1, 81.
21. McMurry, *Atlanta 1864*, 172; *Official Records*, Volume 38, Part 3, 700.
22. *Official Records*, Volume 38, Part 3, 700.
23. Hood, 205–06; Roy, 342.
24. McMurry, *Atlanta 1864*, 172; Howard, "Battles About Atlanta IL": 563.
25. Roy, 342.
26. *Official Records*, Volume 38, Part 3, 109.
27. Osborn, 13–14.
28. *Official Records*, Volume 38, Part 3, 109–10.
29. *Ibid*., McMurry, *Atlanta 1864*, 173.
30. Roy, 342; McMurry, *Atlanta 1864*, 173.
31. *Ibid*., Volume 38, Part 2, 518–19.
32. *Ibid*., Volume 38, Part 3, 701.
33. *Ibid*., Volume 38, Part 1, 514–15.
34. *Official Records*, Volume 38, Part 1, 166.
35. Boyd, 305.
36. McMurry, *Atlanta 1864*, 174.
37. *Ibid*., 175; Hornaday, 50; *Official Records*, Volume 38, Part 2, 20.
38. Sherman, *Memoirs*, 108.
39. McMurry, *Atlanta 1864*, 176; *Official Records*, Volume 38, Part 1, 82.
40. Catton, *Never Call Retreat*, 386; *Official Records*, Volume 38, Part 5, 763.
41. *Official Records*, Volume 38, Part 2, 20.
42. Sherman, *Memoirs*, 108–09.
43. McMurry, *Atlanta 1864*, 176; *Official Records*, Volume 38, Part 1, 83.
44. Christ, 102.
45. *Official Records*, Volume 38, Part 5, 777. Carter, 318.

Chapter 12

1. Reed, 195.
2. *Ibid*.
3. Garrison, 203.
4. Hornaday, 54–55.
5. Blair, *A Politician Goes to War*, 199.
6. George Washington Baker, Letter, September 3, 1864, George Washington Baker Papers, University of North Carolina at Chapel Hill.
7. Hornaday, 47.
8. Nicolay and Hay, *Abraham Lincoln: Complete Works*, 572.
9. Sherman, *Memoirs*, 113.
10. *Official Records*, Volume 38, Part 1, 88.
11. DeLeon, 345.
12. Carter, 346–47.
13. Hood, 249.
14. Coburn, 144–45.
15. Sherman, *Memoirs*, 111.
16. *Official Records*, Volume 38, Part 5, 794.
17. Sherman, *Memoirs*, 111–12.
18. A. H. Guernsey, "Sherman's Great March," *Harper's New Monthly Magazine*, October 1865: 574.
19. Sherman, *Memoirs*, 118–19.
20. Hood, 230.
21. Sherman, *Memoirs*, 120–21.
22. Hood, 232.
23. *Ibid*., 235.
24. Sherman, *Memoirs*, 128.
25. *Ibid*., 124.
26. *Ibid*., 125–27.
27. *Ibid*., 128–29.
28. Segars, 168.
29. Garrison, 209; Bauer, 170.
30. Wright, 335; Garrison, 209.
31. Segars, 181.

32. George Ward Nichols, *The Story of the Great March from the Diary of a Staff Officer* (Williamstown, MA: Corner House, 1972), 21–22.
33. Wright, 333.
34. Bohnstedt, 148.
35. George Washington Baker letter.
36. Sherman, *Memoirs*, 129.
37. Hood, 245–46.
38. *Ibid.*, 247.

Chapter 13

1. Hood, 252.
2. *Ibid.*, 253.
3. Davis, 567.
4. *Ibid.*
5. Hood, 255.
6. Howard, "The Struggle for Atlanta": 463; Sherman, *Memoirs*, 146.
7. Hood, 256–57; Coburn, 146–47.
8. Sherman, *Memoirs*, 146; Coburn, 147–48.
9. Coburn, 148; Sherman, *Memoirs*, 148–49.
10. Coburn, 149–50; *Official Records*, Volume 45, Part 1, 660.
11. Sherman, *Memoirs*, 153; Coburn, 152.
12. Sherman, *Memoirs*, 155.
13. Hood, 262; Coburn, 152.
14. Hood, 258–59.
15. *Ibid.*, 262.
16. Sherman, *Memoirs*, 160.
17. Osborn, 34–35.
18. Sherman, *Memoirs*, 157.
19. *Official Records*, Volume 39, Part 3, 3.
20. Simpson, 729–30.
21. Sherman, *Memoirs*, 152.
22. *Ibid.*, 153–54.
23. *Official Records*, Volume 39, Part 3, 576.
24. *Ibid.*
25. *Ibid.*
26. *Ibid.*, Volume 39, Part 3, 594.
27. *Ibid.*, Volume 39, Part 3, 594–95.
28. *Ibid.*, Volume 39, Part 3, 595.
29. *Ibid.*, Volume 39, Part 3, 659.
30. *Ibid.*, Volume 39, Part 3, 660.
31. *Ibid.*
32. *Ibid.*, Volume 39, Part 3, 660–61.
33. Sherman, *Memoirs*, 174.
34. *Official Records*, Volume 39, Part 3, 713–14; Sherman, *Memoirs*, 175–76.
35. Sherman, *Memoirs*, 174.
36. *Ibid.*, 172.
37. Anne J. Bailey, *War and Ruin: William T. Sherman and the Savannah Campaign* (Wilmington, Del.: Scholarly Resources, 2003), 29–30.
38. Bailey, 30.
39. Sherman, *Memoirs*, 171.
40. Cox, March, 6–7.
41. Sherman, *Memoirs*, 176–77.
42. *Ibid.*, 177.
43. *Ibid.*, 170.
44. Nichols, 38.

Chapter 14

1. Catton, *Grant Takes Command*, 305.
2. J. C. Kinney, "An August Morning with Farragut," *Scribner's Monthly*, June 1880: 201–02.
3. Kinney, 202.
4. Catton, *Never Call Retreat*, 390; Kinney, 203–04.
5. Kinney, 206–08.
6. Grant, 317–18. Philip H. Sheridan, *Personal Memoirs of P. H. Sheridan, Volume 1* (New York: Webster, 1888), 462.
7. *Official Records*, Volume 43, Part 1, 917.
8. Catton, *Bruce Catton's Civil War*, 626, 633; *Official Records*, Volume 43, Part 1, 555.
9. Catton, *Bruce Catton's Civil War*, 637; Richard O'Connor, *Sheridan the Inevitable* (New York: Kinecky & Konecky, 1993), 211.
10. John W. Elwood, *Elwood's Stories of the Old Ringgold Cavalry 1847–1865* (Coal Center, Pa.: Elwood, 1914), 246.
11. *Official Records*, Volume 43, Part 1, 137; Douglas, 319.
12. William C. Davis and Meredith L. Swentor, eds., *Bluegrass Confederate: The Headquarters Diary of Edward O. Guerrant* (Baton Rouge: Louisiana State University Press, 1999), 564.
13. Emil and Ruth Rosenblatt, eds., *The Civil War Letters of Private Wilber Fisk 1861–1865* (Lawrence, Kans.: University Press of Kansas, 1992), 275.
14. Catton, *Grant Takes Command*, 295.
15. Nicolay and Hay, "Abraham Lincoln: A History," September 1889: 693.
16. *Ibid.*
17. *Ibid.*: 692.
18. Welles, "Lincoln's Triumph": 464.
19. McMurry, *Atlanta 1864*, 178–79.
20. Nicolay and Hay, "Abraham Lincoln: A History," August 1889: 551.
21. *Ibid.*
22. McMurry, *Atlanta 1864*, 178–79.
23. Badeau, 167–68.
24. George R. Agassiz, ed., *Meade's Headquarters 1863–1865: Letters of Colonel Theodore Lyman From the Wilderness to Appomattox* (Freeport, N.Y.: Books for Libraries Press, 1970), 245.
25. Quaife, 347–48.
26. Julie A. Doyle, John David Smith and Richard M. McMurry, eds., *This Wilderness of War: The Civil War Letters of George W. Squier, Hoosier Volunteer* (Knoxville, Tenn.: University of Tennessee Press, 1998), 77.
27. Doyle, 82.
28. Barbara Bently Smith and Nina Bently Baker, eds., *"Burning Rails as We Pleased": The Civil War Letters of William Garrigues Bently, 104th Ohio Vol-

unteer Infantry (Jefferson, N.C.: McFarland, 2004), 116.
29. Blair, *Virginia's Private War*, 126.
30. Sallie Brock Putnam, *Richmond During the War: Four Years of Personal Observation* (Lincoln, Neb.: University of Nebraska Press, 1996), 273.
31. Nicolay and Hay, "Abraham Lincoln: A History," September 1889: 699.
32. *Ibid.*
33. Nicolay and Hay, *Abraham Lincoln: Complete Works*, 595–96.

Chapter 15

1. Sherman, *Memoirs*, 177.
2. Bauer, 174.
3. Charles E. Benton, *As Seen from the Ranks* (New York: G. P. Putnam's Sons, 1902), 211.
4. Guernsey, 575.
5. Sherman, *Memoirs*, 178–79.
6. Jacob D. Cox, *Sherman's March to the Sea* (New York: Da Capo Press, 1994), 21; Simpson, 767–68.
7. Cox, *Sherman's March*, 21; Simpson, 751.
8. Bailey, 58–59.
9. Cox, *Sherman's March*, 22–23; Sherman, *Memoirs*, 179.
10. Sherman, *Memoirs*, 180.
11. *Official Records*, Volume 44, 157.
12. Bauer, 184.
13. Lunt, 22–23.
14. M. A. DeWolfe Howe, ed., *Marching with Sherman: Passages from the Letters and Campaign Diaries of Henry Hitchcock* (New Haven, Conn.: Yale University Press, 1927), 125.
15. Cox, *Sherman's March*, 26; Sherman, *Memoirs*, 187. *Official Records*, Volume 44, 362.
16. Sherman, *Memoirs*, 184.
17. *Ibid.*, 185–86.
18. *Official Records*, Volume 44, 157; Bailey, 67–68.
19. Bailey, 73.
20. Bailey, 73–74; Coburn, 168; *Official Records*, Volume 44, 66–67.
21. Cox, *Sherman's March*, 28.
22. Charles C. Jones Jr., *The Siege of Savannah in December 1864* (Albany, N.Y.: Munsell, 1874), 12.
23. *Ibid.*, 15; Cox, *Sherman's March*, 29.
24. Bailey, 69.
25. Sherman, *Memoirs*, 190; *Official Records*, Volume 44, 363.
26. *Official Records*, Volume 44, 363.
27. Winther, 134.
28. Osborn, 47.
29. Eliza Frances Andrews, *The War-Time Journal of a Georgia Girl, 1864–1865* (New York: Appleton, 1908), 32.
30. Cox, *Sherman's March*, 40.
31. Howe, *Marching with Sherman*, 35–36, 77.
32. Guernsey, 578.
33. Cox, *Sherman's March*, 41.
34. Howe, *Marching with Sherman*, 76–77.
35. Cox, *Sherman's March*, 37.
36. *Official Records*, Volume 44, 159.
37. Cox, *Sherman's March*, 34; Sherman, *Memoirs*, 192–93.
38. Cox, *Sherman's March*, 34; Sherman, *Memoirs*, 193.
39. Sherman, *Memoirs*, 193.
40. *Official Records*, Volume 44, 207–08.
41. Cox, *Sherman's March*, 34–35; *Official Records*, Volume 44, 158.
42. *Official Records*, Volume 44, 13.
43. *Ibid.*, Volume 44, 14.
44. Coburn, 168–69.
45. George W. Nichols, "How Fort McAllister Was Taken," *Harper's New Monthly Magazine*, August 1868: 368.

Chapter 16

1. Coburn, 180–81.
2. *Official Records*, Volume 44, 9.
3. *Ibid.*, Volume 44, 10.
4. *Ibid.*
5. Howe, *Marching with Sherman*, 161.
6. Bailey, 96; Cox, *Sherman's March*, 52.
7. Bailey, 97; Cox, *Sherman's March*, 51; Sherman, *Memoirs*, 195.
8. Jones, 74.
9. Cox, *Sherman's March*, 43.
10. *Ibid.*, 46–47.
11. *Official Records*, Volume 44, 70.
12. *Ibid.*, Volume 44, 70–71.
13. *Ibid.*, Volume 44, 71.
14. *Ibid.*
15. *Ibid.*, Volume 44, 87.
16. Charles C. Jones Jr., "The Siege and Evacuation of Savannah": 68–69; Bailey, 100.
17. Jones, "The Siege and Evacuation of Savannah": 69.
18. Sherman, *Memoirs*, 194; Cox, *Sherman's March*, 52.
19. Jones, "The Siege and Evacuation of Savannah": 78; Bailey, 100.
20. Cox, *Sherman's March*, 52; Sherman, *Memoirs*, 196.
21. Hazen, 333.
22. Sherman, *Memoirs*, 196–98.
23. Winther, 142.
24. *Official Records*, Volume 44, 209.
25. Sherman, *Memoirs*, 210–11.
26. *Ibid.*, 211–12.
27. *Official Records*, Volume 44, 11.
28. Jones, "The Siege and Evacuation of Savannah": 78.
29. Jones, *The Siege of Savannah*, 133–34; Bailey, 111.
30. *Official Records*, Volume 44, 209; Bailey, 112.
31. *Official Records*, Volume 44, 209; Bailey, 111.
32. *Official Records*, Volume 44, 209.
33. *Ibid.*; Charles Elihu Slocum, *The Life and Ser-*

vices of Major-General Henry Warner Slocum (Toledo, Oh.: Slocum, 1913), 243; Bailey, 114.
34. Sherman, *Memoirs*, 217.
35. *Ibid.*, 231.
36. Simpson, 771–72; *Official Records*, Volume 44, 6–7.
37. Simpson, 772.
38. Bailey, 4–5.
39. *Official Records*, Volume 44, 12.
40. *Ibid.*, Volume 44, 14.
41. Harold Holzer, ed., *Dear Mr. Lincoln: Letters to the President* (Reading, Mass.: Addison-Wesley, 1995), 225.

Chapter 17

1. Hood, 262–63.
2. *Ibid.*, 263–64.
3. *Ibid.*, 266–67.
4. *Ibid.*, 267.
5. *Ibid.*, 267–68.
6. *Official Records*, Volume 38, Part 1, 29.
7. *Ibid.*, Volume 45, Part 1, 659–60; Hood, 270–71.
8. *Official Records*, Volume 45, Part 1, 647.
9. *Ibid.*, Volume 45, Part 1, 649.
10. Hood, 271–72.
11. Horn, 382–83.
12. Hood, 272.
13. McMorries, 82.
14. W. O. Dodd, "Reminiscences of Hood's Tennessee Campaign," *Southern Historical Society Papers*, Volume 9, November-December, 1881: 519.
15. Henry Stone, "Hood's Invasion of Tennessee," *Century*, August 1887: 598; Hood, 281.
16. Howe, *Marching with Sherman*, 21.
17. *Official Records*, Volume 45, Part 1, 340–41.
18. Horn, 384; *Official Records*, Volume 45, Part 1, 341.
19. Horn, 384; Hood, 282.
20. Horn, 384; Hood, 282.
21. Horn, 385–86; Hood, 284.
22. *Official Records*, Volume 45, Part 1, 113, 341.
23. *Ibid.*, Volume 45, Part 1, 113–14, 342; Schofield, 172.
24. *Official Records*, Volume 45, Part 1, 342; Horn, 389.
25. Stone, 601.
26. Hood, 284–85.
27. *Ibid.*, 285.
28. *Official Records*, Volume 45, Part 1, 652; Hood, 286.
29. Dodd, 520.
30. John M. Copley, *A Sketch of the Battle of Franklin Tenn.: With Reminiscences of Camp Douglas* (Austin, Tex.: Eugene von Boeckmann, Printer, 1893), 33–34.
31. McMorries, 83–84.
32. Horn, 387.
33. *Ibid.*, 393; *Official Records*, Volume 45, Part 1, 114.
34. Schofield, 174.
35. *Official Records*, Volume 45, Part 1, 114.
36. G. W. Lewis, 190–91.
37. Hood, 287.
38. *Official Records*, Volume 45, Part 1, 115.
39. *Ibid.*, Volume 45, Part 1, 123–24.
40. Hood, 290.
41. Copley, 34–35.
42. Dodd, 521–22.
43. Hood, 291.

Chapter 18

1. Schofield, 176.
2. *Official Records*, Volume 45, Part 1, 342.
3. Hood, 292.
4. Horn, 395l Hood, 292.
5. Cox, *Sherman's March*, 82; Horn, 395–96; Copley, 36–37.
6. Horn, 397; Cox, *Sherman's March*, 82; Copley, 39.
7. Cox, *Sherman's March*, 82–84; *Official Records*, Volume 45, Part 1, 351.
8. *Official Records*, Volume 45, Part 1, 124, 342.
9. Hood, 292–93.
10. *Ibid.*; Cox, *Sherman's March*, 88.
11. Horn, 397–98; *Official Records*, Volume 45, Part 1, 653.
12. Horn, 398.
13. Cox, *Sherman's March*, 87.
14. *Official Records*, Volume 45, Part 1, 115.
15. Horn, 399; Cox, *Sherman's March*, 88.
16. *Official Records*, Volume 45, Part 1, 708.
17. *Ibid.*, Volume 45, Part 1, 124.
18. Copley, 48–50.
19. Cox, *Sherman's March*, 88–89.
20. *Official Records*, Volume 45, Part 1, 251.
21. *Ibid.*, Volume 45, Part 1, 353, 116. Schofield, 178.
22. Cox, *Sherman's March*, 89; Schofield, 178; *Official Records*, Volume 45, Part 1, 240.
23. *Official Records*, Volume 45, Part 1, 353.
24. Schofield, 178; Cox, *Sherman's March*, 90.
25. *Official Records*, Volume 45, Part 1, 240–41.
26. Cox, *Sherman's March*, 90–92; *Official Records*, Volume 45, Part 1, 125; Horn, 401.
27. Cox, *Sherman's March*, 90–92; *Official Records*, Volume 45, Part 1, 125; Horn, 401.
28. *Official Records*, Volume 45, Part 1, 708.
29. *Ibid.*, Volume 45, Part 1, 352; Copley, 50.
30. Cox, *Sherman's March*, 91.
31. *Ibid.*; *Official Records*, Volume 45, Part 1, 353.
32. Stone, 607.
33. Cox, *Sherman's March*, 91; *Official Records*, Volume 45, Part 1, 708.
34. Copley, 52.
35. Barbara Bently Smith, 126–27.
36. Copley, 55.
37. *Official Records*, Volume 45, Part 1, 742–43.
38. *Ibid.*, Volume 45, Part 1, 354–55.
39. *Ibid.*, Volume 45, Part 1, 344.

40. *Ibid.*, Volume 45, Part 1, 126.
41. *Ibid.*, Volume 45, Part 1, 117.
42. McMorries, 87.
43. *Official Records*, Volume 45, Part 1, 35.
44. Winston Groom, *Shrouds of Glory, from Atlanta to Nashville: The Last Great Campaign of the Civil War* (New York: Atlantic Monthly Press, 1995), 204.
45. Beers, 176–77.

Chapter 19

1. Horn, 404–05.
2. *Ibid.*
3. Brown, 150–51.
4. Hood, 299–300.
5. Horn, 405–06.
6. Cox, *Sherman's March*, 101; Hood, 300.
7. Cox, *Sherman's March*, 108–10.
8. Horn, 407.
9. *Official Records*, Volume 45, Part 1, 35; Cox, *Sherman's March*, 107; Horn, 410.
10. *Official Records*, Volume 45, Part 1, 36.
11. Horn, 410.
12. McMorries, 88.
13. Cox, *Sherman's March*, 104–06; Horn, 410–11; Porter, 343.
14. Porter, 343.
15. Cox, *Sherman's March*, 104–06; Horn, 410–11.
16. Porter, 344.
17. *Ibid.*, 345.
18. *Official Records*, Volume 45, Part 1, 649–50.
19. *Ibid.*, Volume 45, Part 1, 650.
20. *Ibid.*, Volume 45, Part 1, 651.
21. Schofield, 236–37.
22. Porter, 346.
23. *Ibid.*, 347; Horn, 411.
24. Porter, 348; Horn, 411.
25. Horn, 411–12; Cox, *Sherman's March*, 102.
26. Cox, *Sherman's March*, 110; *Official Records*, Volume 45, Part 1, 38.
27. Cox, *Sherman's March*, 110; *Official Records*, Volume 45, Part 1, 38.
28. *Official Records*, Volume 45, Part 1, 38, 434; Cox, *Sherman's March*, 111; Horn, 412–13.
29. Cox, *Sherman's March*, 111–12; Horn, 413–14.
30. *Official Records*, Volume 45, Part 1, 709–10.
31. Horn, 413; Cox, *Sherman's March*, 112; *Official Records*, Volume 45, Part 1, 128–29.
32. Horn, 413; Cox, *Sherman's March*, 112; *Official Records*, Volume 45, Part 1, 128–29.
33. *Official Records*, Volume 45, Part 1, 129.
34. Cox, *Sherman's March*, 113; *Official Records*, Volume 45, Part 1, 39.
35. *Official Records*, Volume 45, Part 1, 130.
36. Cox, *Sherman's March*, 113; *Official Records*, Volume 45, Part 1, 130.
37. Horn, 414–15.
38. Horn, 415; *Official Records*, Volume 45, Part 1, 710.
39. *Official Records*, Volume 45, Part 1, 39.
40. *Ibid.*
41. Porter, 349.
42. *Ibid.*
43. *Ibid.*
44. *Official Records*, Volume 45, Part 1, 130–31.
45. Lewis, 207–08.
46. *Official Records*, Volume 45, Part 1, 133; Cox, *Sherman's March*, 121.
47. *Official Records*, Volume 45, Part 1, 133–34.
48. Cox, *Sherman's March*, 115, 122–23.
49. Horn, 417; *Official Records*, Volume 45, Part 1, 749.
50. Cox, *Sherman's March*, 122.
51. *Official Records*, Volume 45, Part 1, 435.
52. Cox, *Sherman's March*, 123.
53. *Official Records*, Volume 45, Part 1, 749.
54. Cox, *Sherman's March*, 123.
55. *Official Records*, Volume 45, Part 1, 134.
56. Horn, 416–17; Cox, *Sherman's March*, 124.
57. *Official Records*, Volume 45, Part 1, 750.
58. *Ibid.*, Volume 45, Part 1, 40.
59. *Ibid.*, Volume 45, Part 1, 46. Haughton, 175.
60. Horn, 419.
61. *Official Records*, Volume 45, Part 1, 135.
62. Horn, 420–21; *Official Records*, Volume 45, Part 1, 135–37; Cox, *Sherman's March*, 125.
63. *Official Records*, Volume 45, Part 1, 31.
64. *Ibid.*, Volume 45, Part 1, 656.

Chapter 20

1. Bauer, 196.
2. Nicolay and Hay, *Abraham Lincoln: Complete Works*, 614.
3. David E. Johnston, *The Story of a Confederate Boy in the Civil War* (Portland, Ore.: Glass & Prudhomme, 1914), 282–83.
4. Nicolay and Hay, *Abraham Lincoln: Complete Works*, 600.
5. Nevins, 518.
6. Emma Florence LeConte, *A Journal* (Chapel Hill, N.C.: University of North Carolina).
7. Sherman, *Memoirs*, 226.
8. *Ibid.*, 225–26.
9. *Ibid.*, 223.
10. *Ibid.*, 227–28.
11. Guernsey, 579.
12. *Official Records*, Volume 47, Part 1, 21–22.
13. Catton, *Never Call Retreat*, 464–65.
14. Groom, 279–80.
15. *Ibid.*, 283.
16. Hood, 307, 311.
17. *Ibid.*; Groom, 290.
18. Groom, 282.
19. Garrison, 245–46.
20. *Ibid.*, 248–49.
21. Nicolay and Hay, "Abraham Lincoln: A History," September 1889: 701.

Bibliography

Books

Abernethy, Byron R., ed. *Private Elisha Stockwell, Jr. Sees the Civil War*. Norman, OK: University of Oklahoma Press, 1958.

Agassiz, George R., ed. *Meade's Headquarters 1863–1865: Letters of Colonel Theodore Lyman from the Wilderness to Appomattox*. Reprint, Freeport, NY: Books for Libraries Press, 1970.

Aldrich, C. Knight, ed. *Quest for A Star: The Civil War Letters and Diaries of Colonel Francis T. Sherman of the 88th Illinois*. Knoxville, TN: University of Tennessee Press, 1999.

Anderson, William M., ed. *We Are Sherman's Men: The Civil War Letters of Henry Orendorff*. Macomb, IL: Western Illinois University, 1986.

Andrews, Eliza Frances. *The War-Time Journal of A Georgia Girl, 1864–1865*. New York: Appleton, 1908.

Aten, Henry J. *History of the Eighty-fifth Regiment Illinois Volunteer Infantry*. Hiawatha, KS: Regimental Association, 1901.

Badeau, Adam. *Military History of Ulysses S. Grant: From April, 1861, to April, 1865, 3 Volumes*. New York: Appleton, 1885.

Bailey, Anne J. *The Chessboard of War: Sherman and Hood in the Autumn Campaigns of 1864*. Lincoln, NE: University of Nebraska Press, 2000.

_____. *War and Ruin: William T. Sherman and the Savannah Campaign*. Wilmington, DE: Scholarly Resources, 2003.

Bailey, Ronald H. *Battles for Atlanta: Sherman Moves East*. Alexandria, VA: Time-Life Books, 1985.

Barber, C. Flavel. *Holding the Line: The Third Tennessee Infantry 1861–1864*. Edited by H. Robert Ferrel. Kent, OH: Kent State University Press, 1994.

Barber, Lucius W. *Army Memoirs of Lucius W. Barber, Company "D," 15th Illinois Volunteer Infantry*. Chicago: J. M. Jones Stationary and Printing, 1894.

Basler, Roy P., ed. *The Collected Works of Abraham Lincoln, Volume VII*. New Brunswick, NJ: Rutgers University Press, 1953.

Bauer, K. Jack, ed. *Soldiering: The Civil War Diary of Rice C. Bull, 123rd New York Volunteer Infantry*. San Rafael, CA: Presidio Press, 1977.

Beach, John N. *History of the Fortieth Ohio Volunteer Infantry*. London, OH: Shepherd & Craig, Printers, 1884.

Beers, Fannie A. *Memories: A Record of Personal Experience and Adventure During Four Years of War*. New York: Time-Life Books, 1985.

Benton, Charles E. *As Seen from the Ranks*. New York: G. P. Putnam's Sons, 1902.

Blair, William Alan, ed. *A Politician Goes to War: The Civil War Letters of John White Geary*. University Park, PA: Pennsylvania State University Press, 1995.

_____. *Virginia's Private War: Feeding Body and Soul in the Confederacy, 1861–1865*. New York: Oxford University Press, 1998.

Bohrnstedt, Jennifer Cain, ed. *Soldiering with Sherman: Civil War Letters of George F. Cram*. DeKalb, IL: Northern Illinois University Press, 2000.

Boney, F. N. *Rebel Georgia*. Macon, GA: Mercer University Press, 1997.

Bowman, S. M. and R. B. Irwin. *Sherman and*

His Campaigns. New York: Charles B. Richardson, 1865.
Boyd, James P. *The Life of General William T. Sherman.* Philadelphia: Publishers Union, 1891.
Bradley, G. S. *The Star Corps, or, Notes of an Army Chaplain During Sherman's Famous March to the Sea.* Milwaukee, WI: Jermain & Brightman, Book & Job Printers, 1865.
Brown, Campbell H., ed. *The Reminiscences of Sergeant Newton Cannon.* Franklin, TN: Carter House Association, 1963.
Brown, Norman D., ed. *One of Cleburne's Command: The Civil War Reminiscences and Diary of Capt. Samuel T. Foster, Granbury's Texas Brigade, CSA.* Austin, TX: University of Texas Press, 1980.
Carter, Samuel III. *The Siege of Atlanta, 1864.* New York, St. Martin's Press, 1973.
Castel, Albert. *Decision in the West: The Atlanta Campaign of 1864.* Lawrence, KS: University Press of Kansas, 1992.
_____. *Tom Taylor's Civil War.* Lawrence, KS, University Press of Kansas, 2000.
Catton, Bruce. *Bruce Catton's Civil War.* New York: Fairfax Press, 1984.
_____. *Grant Takes Command.* Boston: Little, Brown, 1968.
_____. *Never Call Retreat.* Garden City, NJ: Doubleday, 1965.
Christ, Mark K., ed. *Getting Used to Being Shot At: The Spence Family Civil War Letters.* Fayetteville, AR.: University of Arkansas Press, 2002.
Clark, Orton S. *The One Hundred and Sixteenth Regiment of New York State Volunteers.* Buffalo, NY: Printing House of Matthews & Warren, 1868.
Coburn, Mark. *Terrible Innocence: General Sherman at War.* New York: Hippocrene Books, 1993.
Coe, David, ed. *Mine Eyes Have Seen the Glory: Combat Diaries of Union Sergeant Hamlin Alexander Coe.* Rutherford, NJ: Fairleigh Dickinson University Press, 1975.
Connelly, Thomas Lawrence. *Autumn of Glory: The Army of Tennessee, 1862–1865.* Baton Rouge: Louisiana State University Press, 1971.
Copley, John M. *A Sketch of the Battle of Franklin Tenn.: with Reminiscences of Camp Douglas.* Austin, Texas: Eugene Von Boeckmann, Printer, 1893.
Cox, Jacob D. *Sherman's Battle for Atlanta.* New York: Da Capo Press, 1994.
_____. *Sherman's March to the Sea.* New York: Da Capo Press, 1994.

Crist, Lynda Lasswell, ed. *The Papers of Jefferson Davis.* Baton Rouge: Louisiana State University Press, 1999.
Dana, Charles A. *Recollections of the Civil War.* New York: Appleton, 1899.
Davis, Burke. *Sherman's March.* New York: Random House, 1980.
Davis, Jefferson. *The Rise and Fall of the Confederate Government, Vol. III.* Reprint, New York: Thomas Yoseloff, 1958.
Davis, Stephen. *Atlanta Will Fall: Sherman, Joe Johnston, and the Yankee Heavy Battalions.* Wilmington, DE: Scholarly Resources, 2001.
Davis, William C., and Meredith L. Swentor, eds. *Bluegrass Confederate: The Headquarters Diary of Edward O. Guerrant.* Baton Rouge: Louisiana State University Press, 1999.
Dawson, George Francis. *Life and Services of Gen. John A. Logan as Soldier and Statesman.* Chicago: Belford, Clarke, 1887.
Day, L. W. *Story of the One Hundred and First Ohio Infantry.* Cleveland, OH: W. M. Bayne, 1894.
DeLeon, Thomas Cooper. *Four Years in Rebel Capitals.* New York: Time-Life Books, 1983. Reprint of 1890 edition.
Derry, Joseph T. *Story of the Confederate States.* New York: Arno Press, 1979. Reprint of 1895 edition.
Dodge, Grenville M. *The Battle of Atlanta and Other Campaigns, Addresses, Etc.* Council Bluffs, IA: Monarch, 1911.
Douglas, Henry Kyd. *I Rode with Stonewall.* Chapel Hill, NC: University of North Carolina Press, 1940.
Dowdey, Clifford, ed. *The Wartime Papers of R. E. Lee.* Boston: Little, Brown, 1961.
Doyle, Julie A., John David Smith, and Richard M. McMurry, eds. *This Wilderness of War: The Civil War Letters of George W. Squier, Hoosier Volunteer.* Knoxville: University of Tennessee Press, 1998.
Duncan, Richard R. *Lee's Endangered Left.* Baton Rouge, LA: Louisiana State University Press, 1998.
Dupré, Louis J. *Fagots from the Camp Fire.* Washington: Charles, 1881.
Dyer, Frederick H. *A Compendium of the War of the Rebellion.* New York: Thomas Yoseloff, 1959.
Early, Jubal A. *A Memoir of the Last Year of the War for Independence in the Confederate States of America.* New Orleans: Blelock, 1867.
Eggleston, George Cary. *A Rebel's Recollections.* New York: Hurd and Houghton, 1875.
Eicher, David J. *The Longest Night: A Military*

History of the Civil War. New York: Simon & Schuster, 2001.

Ellison, Janet Correll, ed. *On to Atlanta: The Civil War Diaries of John Hill Ferguson, Illinois Tenth Regiment of Volunteers.* Lincoln, NE: University of Nebraska Press, 2001.

Elwood, John W. *Elwood's Stories of the Old Ringgold Cavalry 1847–1865*. Coal Center, PA: Elwood, 1914.

Evans, Clement A., ed. *Confederate Military History, Vol. III*. Atlanta: Confederate, 1899.

Evans, Robert G., ed. *The 16th Mississippi Infantry: Civil War Letters and Reminiscences*. Jackson, MS: University Press of Mississippi, 2002.

Fellman, Michael. *Citizen Sherman: A Life of William Tecumseh Sherman*. New York: Random House, 1995.

Foote, Corydon Edward, and Olive Deane Hormel. *With Sherman to the Sea: A Drummer's Story of the Civil War*. New York: Day, 1960.

Foote, Shelby. *The Civil War, A Narrative: Red River to Appomattox*. New York: Random House, 1974.

Forsyth, Michael J. *The Red River Campaign of 1864 and the Loss by the Confederacy of the Civil War*. Jefferson, NC: McFarland, 2002.

Fox, William F. *Regimental Losses in the American Civil War 1861–1865*. Albany, NY: Albany, 1889.

Freeman, Douglas Southall. *Lee's Lieutenants: A Study in Command*. New York: Scribner's, 1944.

Gallagher, Gary, ed. *The Wilderness Campaign*. Chapel Hill, NC: University of North Carolina Press, 1997.

Garrison, Webb. *Atlanta and the War*. Nashville, TN: Rutledge Hill Press, 1995.

Gibbon, John. *Personal Recollections of the Civil War*. New York: Putnam's, 1928.

Gibson, John M. *Those 163 Days: A Southern Account of Sherman's March from Atlanta to Raleigh*. New York: Bramhall House, 1961.

Glazier, Willard. *Battles for the Union*. Hartford, CT: Dustin, Gilman, 1875.

Grant, Ulysses S. *Personal Memoirs of U. S. Grant*. New York: Webster, 1886.

Greeley, Horace. *The American Conflict: A History of the Great Rebellion in the United States of America, 1860–65*. Reprint, New York: Negro Universities Press, 1969.

Griffith, Lucille, ed. *Yours Till Death: Civil War Letters of John W. Cotton*. University, AL: University of Alabama Press, 1951.

Grimsley, Mark, and Todd D. Miller, eds. *The Union Must Stand: The Civil War Diary of John Quincy Adams Campbell, Fifth Iowa Volunteer Infantry*. Knoxville, TN: University of Tennessee Press, 2000.

Groom, Winston. *Shrouds of Glory, from Atlanta to Nashville: The Last Great Campaign of the Civil War*. New York: Atlantic Monthly Press, 1995.

Hale, Douglas. *The Third Texas Cavalry in the Civil War*. Norman, OK: University of Oklahoma Press, 1993.

Haughton, Andrew. *Training, Tactics and Leadership in the Confederate Army of Tennessee: Seeds of Failure*. London: Cass, 2000.

Hay, Thomas Robson. *Hood's Tennessee Campaign*. New York, Neale, 1929.

Hazen, William B. *A Narrative of Military Service*. Boston: Ticknor, 1885.

Hoehling, A. A. *Last Train from Atlanta*. New York: Yoseloff, 1958.

Holzer, Harold. *Dear Mr. Lincoln: Letters to the President*. Reading, MA: Addison-Wesley, 1995.

Hood, J. B. *Advance and Retreat*. Reprint, Edison, NJ: Blue and Grey Press, 1985.

Horn, Stanley F. *The Army of Tennessee*. Norman, OK: University of Oklahoma Press, 1952.

Hornady, John R. *Atlanta: Yesterday, Today and Tomorrow*. n.p.: American Cities Book, 1922.

Howard, Oliver Otis. *Autobiography of Oliver Otis Howard*. New York: Baker & Taylor, 1908.

Howe, M. A. DeWolfe, ed. *Home Letters of General Sherman*. New York: Scribner's, 1909.

_____, ed. *Marching with Sherman: Passages from the Letters and Campaign Diaries of Henry Hitchcock*. New Haven, CT: Yale University Press, 1927.

Hughes, Robert M. *General Johnston*. New York: Appleton, 1897.

Imboden, John D. "The Battle of New Market, VA., May 15th, 1864." *Battles and Leaders of the Civil War*. Edited by Robert Underwood Johnson and Clarence Clough Buel. New York: Thomas Yoseloff, 1956.

Johnson, Bradley T. *A Memoir of the Life and Public Service of Joseph E. Johnston*. Baltimore: Woodward, 1891.

Johnson, Ludwell H. *Red River Campaign: Politics and Cotton in the Civil War*. Baltimore: Johns Hopkins Press, 1958.

Johnston, David E. *The Story of a Confederate Boy in the Civil War*. Portland, OR: Glass & Prudhomme, 1914.

Johnston, Joseph E. *Narrative of Military Operations Directed, During the Late War Between the States*. Bloomington: Indiana University Press, 1959.

Joiner, Gary Dillard. *One Damn Blunder from Beginning to End: The Red River Campaign of 1864*. Wilmington, DE: Scholarly Resources, 2003.

Jones, Charles C., Jr. *The Siege of Savannah in December 1864*. Albany, NY: Munsell, 1874.

Jones, Charles Edgeworth. *Georgia in the War 1861–1865*. Jonesboro, GA: Freedom Hill Press, 1988.

Jones, J. B. *A Rebel War Clerk's Diary at the Confederate States Capital, 2 Volumes*. New York: Time-Life Books, 1982. Reprint of 1866 edition.

Lane, Mills, ed. *Marching Through Georgia: William T. Sherman's Personal Narrative of His March Through Georgia*. New York: Arno Press, 1978.

Lewis, G. W. *The Campaigns of the 124th Regiment Ohio Volunteer Infantry*. Akron, OH: Werner, 1894.

Lewis, Lloyd. *Sherman: Fighting Prophet*. New York: Harcourt, Brace, 1932.

Long, A. L. *Memoirs of Robert E. Lee: His Military and Personal History*. Edison, NJ: Blue and Grey Press, 1993.

Losson, Christopher. *Tennessee's Forgotten Warriors: Frank Cheatham and His Confederate Division*. Knoxville: University of Tennessee Press, 1989.

Lunt, Dolly Sumner. *A Woman's Wartime Journal*. New York: Century, 1918.

Key, William. *The Battle of Atlanta and the Georgia Campaign*. New York: Twayne, 1958.

Mannis, Jedediah and Galen R. Wilson, eds. *Bound to Be A Soldier: The Letters of Private James T. Miller, 11th Pennsylvania Infantry, 1861–1864*. Knoxville, TN: University of Tennessee Press, 2001.

Marszalek, John F. *Sherman: A Soldier's Passion for Order*. New York: The Free Press, 1993.

Martin, Isabella D., and Myrta Lockett Avary, eds. *A Diary from Dixie, as Written by Mary Boykin Chesnut*. New York: Appleton, 1905.

Matloff, Maurice, ed. *The Civil War: A Concise Military History of the War Between the States 1861–1865*. New York: Promontory Press, 1982.

McCaffrey, James M. *This Band of Heroes: Granbury's Texas Brigade, C.S.A*. College Station, TX: Texas A&M University Press, 1996.

McCormick, Edgar L., Edward G. McGehee, and Mary Strahl, eds. *Sherman in Georgia*. Boston: Heath, 1961.

McMorries, Edward Young. *History of the First Regiment Alabama Volunteer Infantry C. S. A.* Freeport, NY: Books for Libraries Press, 1970. Reprint of 1904 edition.

McMurray, W. J. *History of the Twentieth Tennessee Regiment Volunteer Infantry, C. S. A.* Reprint, Nashville, TN: Elder's Bookstore, 1976.

McMurry, Richard M. *Atlanta 1864: Last Chance for the Confederacy*. Lincoln, NE: University of Nebraska Press, 2000.

_____. *The Road Past Kennesaw: The Atlanta Campaign of 1864*. Washington: National Park Service, 1972.

McPherson, James M. *Battle Cry of Freedom: The Civil War Era*. New York: Oxford University Press, 1988.

_____. *Ordeal by Fire: The Civil War and Reconstruction*. New York: Knopf, 1982.

Moffett, Mary C. ed. *Letters of General James Conner, C.S.A.* Columbia, SC: Bryan, 1950.

Montgomery, Frank A. *Reminiscences of A Mississippian in Peace and War*. Cincinnati, OH: Clarke, 1901.

Morgan, Mrs. Irby. *How It Was: Four Years Among the Rebels*. Nashville, TN: Publishing House Methodist Episcopal Church, South, 1892.

Morris, W. S., L. D. Hartwell, and J. B. Kuykendall, eds. *History 31st Regiment Illinois Volunteers*. Carbondale, IL: Southern Illinois University Press, 1998.

Nanzig, Thomas P., ed. *The Badax Tigers: From Shiloh to the Surrender with the 18th Wisconsin Volunteers*. Lanham, MD: Rowman & Littlefield, 2002.

Nichols, George Ward. *The Story of the Great March from the Diary of a Staff Officer*. Reprint, Williamstown, MA: Corner House, 1972.

Nevins, Allan, ed. *Diary of the Civil War 1860–1865: George Templeton Strong*. New York: Macmilian, 1962.

Nicolay, John G., and John Hay. *Abraham Lincoln: Complete Works, Volume 2*. New York: Century, 1894.

O'Connor, Richard. *Sheridan the Inevitable*. Reprint, New York: Konecky & Konecky, 1993.

Osborn, Hartwell. *Trials and Triumphs: The Record of the Fifty-fifth Ohio Volunteer Infantry*. Chicago: A. C. McClurg, 1904.

Osborn, Thomas W. *The Fiery Trail: A Union Officer's Account of Sherman's Last Campaigns*. Edited by Richard Harwell and Philip N. Racine. Knoxville, TN: University of Tennessee Press, 1986.

Pepper, George W. *Personal Recollections of Sherman's Campaigns in Georgia and the Carolinas.* Zanesville, OH: Dunne, 1866.

Porter, Horace. *Campaigning with Grant.* Reprint, New York: Mallard Press, 1991.

Putnam, Sallie Brock. *Richmond During the War: Four Years of Personal Observation.* Lincoln, NE: University of Nebraska Press, 1996.

Quaife, Milo M., ed. *From the Cannon's Mouth: The Civil War Letters of General Alpheus S. Williams.* Detroit, MI: Wayne State University Press and Detroit Historical Society, 1959.

Reed, Wallace P. *History of Atlanta, Georgia.* Syracuse, NY: Mason, 1889.

Reyburn, Philip J., and Terry L. Wilson, eds. *"Jottings from Dixie": The Civil War Dispatches of Sergeant Major Stephen F. Fleharty, U. S. A.* Baton Rouge: Louisiana State University Press, 1999.

Rhodes, Robert Hunt, ed. *All for the Union: The Civil War Diary and Letters of Elisha Hunt Rhodes.* New York: Orion Books, 1991.

Ridley, Bromfield L. *Battles and Sketches of the Army of Tennessee.* Dayton, OH: Press of Morningside Bookshop, 1978.

Rosenblatt, Emil, and Ruth Rosenblatt, eds. *The Civil War Letters of Private Wilbur Fisk 1861–1865.* Lawrence, KS: University Press of Kansas, 1992.

Rowell, John W. *Yankee Cavalrymen: Through the Civil War with the Ninth Pennsylvania Cavalry.* Knoxville, TN: University of Tennessee Press, 1971.

Sandburg, Carl. *Abraham Lincoln: The War Years, Volume 3.* New York: Harcourt, Brace, World, 1939.

Saxon, Elizabeth Lyle. *A Southern Woman's War Time Reminiscences.* Memphis, TN: Pilcher, 1905.

Schofield, John M. *Forty-six Years in the Army.* New York: Century, 1897.

Secrist, Philip L. *The Battle of Resaca: Atlanta Campaign 1864.* Macon, GA: Mercer University Press, 1998.

Segars, J. H., ed. *Life in Dixie During the War: Mary A. H. Gay.* Macon, GA: Mercer University Press, 2001. Reprint of 1892 edition.

Senour, F. *Major General William T. Sherman and His Campaigns.* Chicago: Sherwood, 1865.

Shapiro, Larry, ed. *Abraham Lincoln: Mystic Chords of Memory.* New York: Book-of-the-Month Club, 1984.

Sheridan, Philip H. *Personal Memoirs of P. H. Sheridan.* New York: Webster, 1888.

Sherman, William T. *Memoirs of Gen. W. T. Sherman, Written by Himself.* New York: Webster, 1891.

Simon, John Y., ed. *The Papers of Ulysses S. Grant.* Carbondale, IL: Southern Illinois University Press, 1982.

Simpson, Brooks D., and Jean V. Berlin, eds. *Sherman's Civil War: Selected Correspondence of William T. Sherman, 1860–1865.* Chapel Hill, NC: University of North Carolina Press, 1999.

Slocum, Charles Elihu. *The Life and Services of Major-General Henry Warner Slocum.* Toledo, OH: Slocum, 1913.

Smith, Barbara Bently, and Nina Bently Baker, eds. *"Burning Rails as We Pleased": The Civil War Letters of William Garrigues Bently, 104th Ohio Volunteer Infantry.* Jefferson, NC: McFarland, 2004.

Stanley, David S. *Personal Memoirs of Major-General D. S. Stanley, U. S. A.* Cambridge, MA: Harvard University Press, 1917.

Stevens, George T. *Three Years in the Sixth Corps.* New York: Time-Life Books, 1984. Reprint of 1866 edition.

Stinson, Eliza. *War Days in Fayetteville North Carolina: Reminiscences of 1861 to 1865.* Fayetteville, NC: United Daughters of the Confederacy, J. E. B. Stuart Chapter, 1910.

Sutherland, Daniel E., ed. *Reminiscences of a Private: William E. Bevens of the First Arkansas Infantry, C. S. A.* Fayetteville, AR: University of Arkansas Press, 1992.

Taylor, F. Jay, ed. *Reluctant Rebel: The Secret Diary of Robert Patrick 1861–1865.* Baton Rouge: Louisiana State University Press, 1987.

Taylor, Richard. *Destruction and Reconstruction: Personal Experiences of the Late War.* New York: Appleton, 1879.

Tenney, W. J. *The Military and Naval History of the Rebellion in the United States.* New York: Appleton, 1866.

Thomas, Benjamin P., and Harold M. Hyman. *Stanton: The Life and Times of Lincoln's Secretary of War.* New York: Knopf, 1962.

United States War Department. *The War of the Rebellion: A Compilation of the Official Records of the Union and Confederate Armies.* Washington: Government Printing Office, 1880–1901. Series I unless noted.

Walton, Clyde C., ed. *Private Smith's Journal: Recollections of the Late War.* Chicago: Donnelley, 1963.

Warner, Ezra J. *Generals in Blue.* Baton Rouge: Louisiana State University Press, 1964.

_____. *Generals in Gray*. Baton Rouge: Louisiana State University Press, 1959.

Wheeler, Richard. *Sherman's March*. New York: HarperPerennial, 1991.

Wiggins, Sarah Woolfolk, ed., *The Journals of Josiah Gorgas, 1857–1878*. Tuscaloosa, AL: University of Alabama Press, 1995.

Wiley, Bell Irvin, ed. *Confederate Letters of John W. Hagan*. Athens, GA: University of Georgia Press, 1954.

Williams, T. Harry. *Lincoln and His Generals*. New York: Knopf, 1952.

_____. *McClellan, Sherman and Grant*. New Brunswick, NJ: Rutgers University Press, 1962.

Williamson, David. *The Third Battalion Mississippi Infantry and the 45th Mississippi Regiment*. Jefferson, NC: McFarland, 2004.

Winther, Oscar Osburn, ed. *With Sherman to the Sea: The Civil War Letters, Diaries & Reminiscences of Theodore F. Upson*. Bloomington, IN: Indiana University Press, 1958.

Woodworth, Steven E. *No Band of Brothers: Problems in the Rebel High Command*. Columbia, MO: University of Missouri Press, 1999.

Wright, Henry H. *A History of the Sixth Iowa Infantry*. Iowa City, IA: State Historical Society of Iowa, 1923.

Wynne, Lewis N., and Robert A. Taylor, eds. *This War So Horrible: The Civil War Diary of Hiram Smith Williams*. Tuscaloosa, AL: University of Alabama Press, 1993.

Articles, Letters, Diaries

Baker, George Washington. Letter to Mother, September 3, 1864. George Washington Baker Papers, University of North Carolina at Chapel Hill.

Breckinridge, William C.P. "The Opening of the Atlanta Campaign." *Battles and Leaders of the Civil War, Volume 4*. Edited by Robert Underwood Johnson and Clarence Clough Buel. New York: Yoseloff, 1956.

Byers, S. H. M., "The March to the Sea." *North American Review* (September 1887).

Chamberlin, W. H. "Hood's Second Sortie at Atlanta." *Battles and Leaders of the Civil War, Volume 4*. Edited by Robert Underwood Johnson and Clarence Clough Buel. New York: Yoseloff, 1956.

Dodd, W. O. "Reminiscences of Hood's Tennessee Campaign." *Southern Historical Society Papers*, Volume 9 (November-December 1881).

Dwight, Henry O. "How We Fight at Atlanta." *Harper's New Monthly Magazine* (October 1864).

Eggleston, George Cary. "A Rebel's Recollections." *Atlantic Monthly* (December 1874).

Fisher, Julia Johnson. *Diary by Julia Johnson Fisher*. University of North Carolina at Chapel Hill.

French, S. G. "Paper read before Louisville Branch of the Southern Historical Society." *Southern Historical Society Papers*, Volume 9, November-December 1881.

Guernsey, A. H. "Sherman's Great March." *Harper's New Monthly Magazine* (October 1865).

Howard, Oliver O. "The Battles About Atlanta I." *Atlantic Monthly* (October 1876).

_____. "The Battles About Atlanta II." *The Atlantic Monthly* (November 1876).

_____. "The Struggle for Atlanta." *Century* (July 1887).

_____. "Sherman's Advance from Atlanta." In *Battles and Leaders of the Civil War, Volume 4*. Edited by Robert Underwood Johnson and Clarence Clough Buel. New York: Thomas Yoseloff, 1956.

Irwin, Richard B. "The Red River Campaign." *Battles and Leaders of the Civil War, Volume 4*. Edited by Robert Underwood Johnson and Clarence Clough Buel. New York: Yoseloff, 1956.

Johnston, Joseph E. "Opposing Sherman's Advance to Atlanta." *Century* (August 1887).

Jones, Charles. C. Jr. "General Sherman's March from Atlanta to the Coast." Address Before the Survivors Association of Augusta, Georgia, April 20, 1884." *Southern Historical Society Papers*. Volume 12.

_____. "The Siege and Evacuation of Savannah, Georgia, in December 1864." Address Before the Survivors' Association of Augusta, Georgia, April 26, 1890. *Southern Historical Society Papers*. Volume 17.

King, William. *Diary of William King, Cobb County, Georgia 1864*. University of North Carolina, Chapel Hill.

Kinney, J. C. "An August Morning with Farragut." *Scribner's Monthly* (June 1880).

LeConte, Emma Florence. *A Journal*. University of North Carolina, Chapel Hill.

Lee, Stephen D. "Sherman's Expedition from Vicksburg to Meridian, Feb. 3, to March 6, 1864." *Southern Historical Society Papers*, Volume 32.

Nicolay, John G., and John Hay. "Abraham Lincoln: A History." *Century* (June-September 1889).

Nichols, George W. "How Fort McAllister Was Taken." *Harper's New Monthly Magazine* (August 1868).

Oakey, Daniel. "Marching Through Georgia and the Carolinas." *Century* (October 1887).

Ridley, B. L. "The Battle of New Hope Church." *Confederate Veteran* (September 1897).

Ropes, John C. "General Sherman." *Atlantic Monthly* (August 1891).

Roy, T. B. "General Hardee and the Military Operations Around Atlanta." *Southern Historical Society Papers*. Volume 8 (August and September 1880).

Sea, Andrew M. "An Incident of Rocky Face Ridge." *Confederate Veteran* (July 1898).

Shanks, W.F.G. "Recollections of Sherman." *Harper's New Monthly Magazine* (April 1865).

_____. "Recollections of Thomas." *Harper's New Monthly Magazine* (May 1865).

Sherman, William Tecumseh. "The Grand Strategy of the War of the Rebellion." *Century* (February 1888).

_____. "Letters of Two Brothers: Passages from the Correspondence of General and Senator Sherman." *Century* (March 1893).

Smith, Gustavus W. "The Georgia Militia About Atlanta." In *Battles and Leaders of the Civil War, Volume 4*. Edited by Robert Underwood Johnson and Clarence Clough Buel. New York: Yoseloff, 1956.

Stone, Henry. "Hood's Invasion of Tennessee." *Century* (August 1887).

Vandiver, Frank E. "Forward." *Southern Historical Society Papers*. Volume 50. 1958.

_____. "Forward." *Southern Historical Society Papers*. Volume 51. 1958.

Welles, Gideon. "The Opposition to Lincoln in 1864." *Atlantic Monthly* (March 1878).

_____. "Lincoln's Triumph in 1864." *Atlantic Monthly* (April 1878).

Wilson, James Harrison. "Reminiscences of General Grant." *Century* (October 1885).

Young, Lot D. *Reminiscences of a Soldier of the Orphan Brigade*. Paris, Kentucky: Self published, 1918.

Index

Ackworth, Georgia 55
Adairsville, Georgia 41
Adams, Confederate Gen. John: killed 190
Allatoona, Georgia 41, 44; battle 132–33; casualties 133; secured 52, 55; warehouses 132
Andersonville, Georgia 104, 116
Andrews, Eliza Frances: destruction 158
Army of Northern Virginia 3, 13, 27, 68; trapped 149, 209
Army of Tennessee 3, 12; defeat 204; improved 17; Jonesboro 123, 129, 131, 175, 178; Nashville, works 194–95; new commander 15; organization 22, 28, 34, 53, 56, 83, 93; retreat 205–6; Spring Hill anger 183; surrender 210
Army of the Cumberland: occupy Atlanta 120; organization 21, 34, 65
Army of the Ohio: at Atlanta 87; Decatur 120; organization 21, 34; Resaca 37
Army of the Potomac 3; Wilderness 66, 72, 209
Army of the Tennessee 3; East Point 120; organization 22, 34, 52, 81, 93, 97, 100, 105
Arnold, Richard (Savannah mayor): surrender Savannah 170; volunteers 163–64
Atlanta and West Point Railroad 100, 112
Atlanta, Georgia: casualties 97, 100; condition 120; destroyed 140; Hood battle plan 88; railroads and manufacturing 19, 65, 86; recovery, Sherman speech 212; shelling 108, 113, 119

Augusta and Savannah Railroad: destroy 159

Badeau, Adam: disappointment 68, 70; failed strategy 14; fight Lee 67
Baird, Union Gen. Absalom 21
Baker, George Washington: Atlanta condition 129; letter to mother 121
Bald Hill, Georgia 35, 36, 37
Barber, Union Maj. Flavel: diary 26
Bate, Confederate Gen. William B.: Atlanta 90, 185; Franklin 191, 195; line broken, retreat 204; Resaca 38, 82; Shy's Hill 203
Bates, Union Capt. Edward P.: 125th Ohio, broken line 187
Beatty, Union Gen. Samuel: Nashville 200, 202
Beauregard, Confederate Gen. P. G. T. 27, 132; approve invasion 174; chase Sherman 198; after Franklin 198; Military Division of the West 134; proclamation 156–57
Beers, Fannie: Confederate wounded 192; patients 99; replace Johnston 80; shelling Atlanta 108
Bentley, William G.: on election 148; Franklin casualties 190
Benton, Charles E.: Atlanta fire 151
Bevens, William E.: Cassville 42
Big Kennesaw Mountain, Georgia 57
Big Shanty, Georgia 56, 132
Blair, Union Gen. Frank P., Jr. 22; Atlanta 96; bald hill 88; cut off Hardee 116; foraging 56, 87; Ogeechee attack 165, 166; reinforcements 55, 101; 17th Corps on march 139, 155
Bounties: Union soldiers 10
Bradley, G. S.: about revenge 7
Bragg, Confederate Gen. Braxton: collect troops 161; letter to Johnston 15; military advisor to Davis 29, 32; new strategy 16, 27; report on Johnston 76–77
Brentwood Hills, Tennessee 194; Confederate retreat 203–4
Brown, Confederate Gen. John C.: Ezra Church 102, 185; fortifications 188; wounded 189
Brown's Creek 194, 199
Brush Mountain, Georgia 57
Buford, Confederate Gen. Abraham: Murfreesboro 196
Bull, Rice C.: Cassville 42; destroy tracks 154; end of war 207; evacuation 128; leave Atlanta 151; maneuvering 58–59; New Hope 46–47; Peachtree Creek 85; picket duty 106; weather 52, 55
Burnet House: Grant and Sherman meeting 12
Butler, Union Gen. Benjamin 13; Bermuda Hundred 68
Butterfield, Union Gen. Daniel 21
Buzzard's Roost, Georgia: location 32, 34–35

Calhoun, James M.: Atlanta mayor, protest evacuation 126
Camp Creek 36, 37–38; attack 39
Cantey, Confederate Gen. James 35

Carter, Confederate Gen. John C.: killed 189
Carter, Confederate Capt. Tod: killed near home 192
Carter's Creek Turnpike 184
Casement, Union Col. J. S. 184, 189
Cassville, Georgia 41
Cedar Creek, Virginia 144
Chamberlin, Union Maj. W. H.: Atlanta 90–91
Charleston Railroad 164
Charleston, South Carolina 209
Charlotte Turnpike 194, 199
Chattahoochee River 64, 65, 110
Cheairs, Confederate Maj. Nat: confrontations 180–81
Cheatham, Confederate Gen. Frank: Atlanta 94, 95, 176; blame for escape 179, 181; cut Franklin Pike 178; Franklin 185, 187, 191, 194; Granny White Pike 201, 204; Kennesaw 62, 81, 82, 87, 88, 89; Resaca 38
Chesnut, Mary: sacrifice 75
Cleburne, Confederate Gen. Patrick: Franklin Pike 178, 185; Jonesboro 114, 115, 177; lead attack, killed 188–89; on McPherson 36; Pickett's Mill 48–49, 87, 89, 92; Resaca 37–38
Cobb, Confederate Gen. Howell: commander Georgia and Florida 99; destroy plantation 155–56
Coburn, Union Col. John: 33rd Indiana, New Hope 47
Coe, Hamlin: enemy contacts 58; march 41; weather 55
Cold Harbor, Virginia 67
Columbia, South Carolina: destruction 210
Columbia, Tennessee: fortify 176
Columbia Pike 184, 190
Confederate General Order No. 77: general conscription 148
Connasauga River: location 32, 37, 38, 40
Conner, Confederate Gen. James: new laws 6
Cooper, Confederate Gen. Samuel 27, 78
Copley, John M.: Confederate dead 190; disappointment 181; 49th Tennessee, Franklin Pike 179; Union advance line 187
Corse, Union Gen. John M. 22; Allatoona 132–33; Ogeechee River 164–65
Cotton, John W.: Cassville 43

Couch, Union Gen. Darius: Nashville 200
Covington, Georgia 154
Cox, Union Brig. Gen. Jacob D. 21; broken line 188; Franklin works 184; about Johnston 28; late attacks 191; Nashville 204; recover line 190; Resaca 37–38; stragglers 159, 176, 177; about Thomas 140;
Cram, George F.: Atlanta condition 129; letter home 57; 105th Illinois, new campaign 26
Crawford, J. B.: letter to wife 4
Cross Roads, Georgia: 133, 172
Croxton, Union Gen. John T.: Nashville 199
Cumberland River 194, 195

Dallas, Georgia: battle, losses 51
Dalton, Georgia 18, 24, 28; Army of Tennessee base 32, 34, 36; Hood captures 133
Davis, Congressman Henry Winter: peace terms 74
Davis, Jefferson, Confederate president: on Atlanta 76; background 5; influence north 73; new laws 6; office as military headquarters 15, 16, 26, 28; reason for change 79; rebuild army 32–33, 53; relieve Johnston 78; reply to Hood 79; visit army, new plan 131, 198; wire to Johnston 77–78
Davis, Union Gen. Jefferson C. 21; command 14th Corps 105; 14th Corps on march 139, 156; Jonesboro 116; Kennesaw 62–63; Savannah River 160, 166
Day, L. W.: Atlanta south 111; 101st Ohio, skirmish line 58
Decatur, Georgia 65, 120
DeLeon, Thomas: on Atlanta 76; loss of Atlanta 123
Democratic Party: convention 72; platform 72
Dilworth, Union Col. Caleb: Kennesaw 63
Dodd, Confederate Capt. W.O.: army morale 175; disappointment 181; Franklin Pike 178–79
Dodge, Union Gen. Grenville M. 22; Atlanta 90–91, 97, 101; Atlanta fighting 106; Resaca 35, 50, 87
Douglas, Confederate Maj. Henry Kyd: Early's campaign 69

Duck River 176

Early, Confederate Gen. Jubal: Lynchburg, threaten Washington 69, 143
East Point, Georgia 100, 105, 110, 111, 114, 120
Eggleston, George C.: duty 5; government 6–7
Eighty-first Ohio Regiment 91
Elliott, Union Gen. Washington L.: Nashville 200, 202
Etowah River 40–41
Ezra Church, Georgia: battle 101–4; casualties 103

Farragut, Union Adm. David: Mobile Bay 142–43
Ferguson, John Hill: 10th Illinois, rain 57–58
Fifteenth U.S. Army Corps: at Atlanta 87, 89, 93, 94, 155, 164; organization 22, 35, 50
First Arkansas: Lt. Col. Martin, Kennesaw 63
Fisher's Hill, Virginia 144
Flint River 113
Florence, Alabama 175
Forrest, Confederate Gen. Nathan Bedford 14, 174, 177; Spring Hill 180, 185, 194, 195, 205
Fort Granger 184; fire on Confederates 189
Fort McAllister 165–66
42nd Georgia Infantry 47
Foster, Confederate Capt. Samuel: criticize Hood 193–94; Texas Brigade, replace Johnston 80
14th Kentucky Regiment 60
Fourteenth U.S. Army Corps: organization 21, 36, 37, 40, 154
14th U.S. Colored Regiment: Overton Hill 202–3
Fourth U.S. Army Corps: Franklin 185; Nashville 199; organization 21, 35, 36, 40
Franklin Pike: to Nashville 178, 179, 194, 201, 204
Franklin, Tennessee 181, 182; about 184; battle losses 191–92; Schofield enters 183
Fremont, John C.: presidential candidate 71; withdraw from race 146
French, Confederate Gen. S. G.: attack Allatoona 132; Franklin 185
Fuller, John W. 89; Atlanta 90–91

Gadsden, Alabama 174

Index

Garrard, Union Gen. Kenner 23, 52; Nashville 200
Gay, Mary: evacuation 127–28; inside Atlanta 99, 100
Geary, Union Gen. John W. 21; letter to wife 121, 154; New Hope 46–47; Peachtree Creek 84
General Order No. 44: Southern conscription 148
Georgia Central Railroad: cut 81; destroy 159, 166
Georgia Legislature: call to people 157
Gibson, Confederate Gen. Randall L.: New Hope 47
Gist, Confederate Gen. States Rights: killed 189
Gorgas, Confederate Gen. Josiah: criticize Johnston 76
Govan, Confederate Gen. Daniel: Pickett's Mill 48, 203
Granbury, Confederate Gen. Hiram: killed 189; Pickett's Mill 48–49
Granny White Turnpike 194, 200, 201, 204
Grant, Union Gen. Ulysses S.: attack Hood 196, 197; campaign instructions 19–20; about Georgia march 136; on Hood's plan 174; to Nashville 199; orders to Sheridan 143; replace Thomas 197, 198; on Sherman's progress 105; on soldier vote 147; strategy 12–14; summer situation 142; to Thomas praise and attack 202; Thomas right 206; Vicksburg, Chattanooga 3; Wilderness 66; wire Sherman 121
Greeley, Horace: Confederate agents 73; Northern sentiment 69–70
Griswoldville, Georgia 156
Guntersville, Alabama 174

Hagan, John: letter to wife 41; replace Johnston 80
Hall, Union Col. William: Atlanta 92
Halleck, Union Gen. Henry W. 23; Atlanta plan 124; destroy Charleston 209; evacuation 127, 197, 199; note to Lincoln 119; from Sherman 60, 111
Hardee, Confederate Gen. William 28; abandon outer line, flood fields 165; blame for defeat 97; Cassville 42; Dallas 45–46, 50, 53, 81, 88; defend Savannah 161, 162; about Ezra Church 104, 113; garrison 163; about him 30; Jonesboro 114–15; night march 89; position 116, 118; reassigned 132, 156; refuse surrender 168; Resaca 37–38
Hardin Turnpike 194, 199
Harker, Union Gen. Charles C.: Kennesaw 62
Harpeth Hills, Tennessee 201
Harpeth River: bridge burned 183
Harrow, Union Gen. William 22; Ezra Church 103; Resaca 37, 50
Hascal, Union Gen. Miles S. 21, 60
Hatch, Union Gen. Edward: Nashville 199, 204
Hay, John: opposition groups 70; president secretary 146
Hazen, Union Gen. William B.: Fort McAllister 166–67; Pickett's Mill 48–49; 115
Hillsboro Turnpike 194, 195, 200
Hitchcock, Union Maj. Henry: destruction 155, 158, 159; on Hood move 176; torpedoes 163
Hodges, A. G.: Lincoln letter 8
Hood, Confederate Lieut. Gen. John Bell: to Alabama 174; angry 180; army determined 184; army morale 172; army size 176; Atlanta battle plan 88; about Atlanta civilians 108, 110; Atlanta defeat 97; attack columns 40, 41; attack Franklin 186, 191; begin offensive 15; blame for loss 123; blame others 97–98; blame troops 181; Cassville 42; cavalry raid 112; decide to move 130; evacuate Atlanta 116–17, 118; force Union attack 131–32; gap in Union lines 87; Hardee south 113; about him 29; invade Tennessee, move east 172; Johnston feud, family, death 211; Lee 101; letter to Bragg 17; letter to Davis 16–17, 77; letters to Sherman 125–26; to Nashville 193–94; New Hope 46, 53, 59, 60; ordered attack 178; overtake Schofield 182–83; postpone change 78, 81, 85; prepare retreat 201; realign army 201; reality 206; replace Johnston 78; request reserves 123; Resaca 37–39; resume operations 129; Spring Hill trap 176–77; into Tennessee 175; to Tennessee River 133; Tuscumbia 174; urge advance 30; why Nashville 204
Hooker, Union Gen. Joseph 21; New Hope 46, 58, 60; Resaca 39–40, 41; resign 105; Snake Creek Gap 36
Howard, Union Gen. Oliver O. 21; Army of the Tennessee 100; below Savannah 164, 165; Cassville 43; Ezra Church 103, 105; Flint River bridge 113; to Jonesboro 114, 115; Jonesboro feint 151, 155, 156; Kennesaw 62–63, 64; landscape 45; leave Atlanta works 112; Lost Mountain 59; New Hope 46–48, 50, 53, 58; Peachtree Creek 82, 84; Resaca 37–38; Rocky Face Ridge 36
Hunter, Union Gen. David: Lynchburg retreat 69; Piedmont victory 68
Hurlbut, Union Gen. Stephen A. 22

Imboden, Confederate Gen. John 68

Johnson, Andrew: president 210; vice-presidential candidate 71
Johnson, David E.: 7th Virginia, futility 207–8
Johnson, Union Gen. Richard W. 21; Nashville 199–200; Pickett's Mill 48–49; Resaca 38
Johnston, Confederate Gen. Joseph Eggleston 13; abandon Kennesaw 64; abandon Resaca 40; Allatoona 44; army condition 15, 28–29, 31, 32; Army of Tennessee 15; arrive Dalton 28; Cassville 41–42; criticized by Hood 97–98; at Dalton 33–34; enemy strength 16; farewell to army 79; Hood feud, death 211; new strategy 16–17; Pine Mountain 58; relation with Davis 27–28; relieved of command 78; Resaca 37–38; strategy 53; surrender 210; wire to Davis 77
Jones, Confederate Col. Charles C.: Nashville 200; save troops 169
Jones, John B.: diary 3; new confidence 6
Jonesboro, Georgia 111, 113, 131
Judah, Union Gen. Henry M.: Resaca 37–38

Kennesaw Mountain, Georgia 56; battle losses 63; Confederate lines 59; plan of attack 61
Kilpatrick, Union Gen. Judson 23, 35; cavalry on march 139, 155; Louisville raid 157; Macon & Western raid 111
Kimball Union Gen. Nathan 62; Franklin 185; Nashville 200–1, 202; Peachtree Creek 83
King's Bridge 154–65; captured 165, 166
Kingston, Georgia 41
Knights of the Golden Circle 70
Kolb's Farm, Georgia: battle 59–60

Lawrenceburg, Tennessee 176
Lay's Ferry, Georgia 39–40
LeConte, Emma Florence: Southern hate 208–9
Lee, Confederate Gen. Robert E.: Army of Northern Virginia 3; letter to Seddon 4, 23, 142, 210
Lee, Confederate Gen. Stephen D.: attack Howard 101; Ezra Church 101–2; Franklin 185, 194, 200; Franklin Pike 201, 204; Tennessee River 174, 176, 177
Leggett, Union Gen. Miles D. 22; Atlanta 93; Bald Hill 87–88
Lewis, G. W.: Cassville 43; to Franklin 180; heavy fire 202
Lightburn, Union Gen. A. J.: Atlanta 95; Resaca 39
Lincoln, Abraham: cabinet letter 75, 119; on Emancipation Proclamation 8; on final victory 207; letter to Grant 20, 71; letter to Mrs. Bixby 208; peace plan 7; peace terms 73; politics 145; Sanitary Commission speech 72; Sherman on march 171, 196; slavery letter 8; Southern defeat 207; speeches 145; to Thomas 202; Wade-Davis bill 74; win election 149–50; wire Sherman 121, 142
Little Kennesaw Mountain, Georgia 57
Logan, Union Gen. John A. 22, 35; Army of the Tennessee 93; Atlanta 91; on Blair attack 94, 95, 96, 101; Camp Creek 39; Dallas 50–51; Ezra Church 102; Flint River bridge 113; Jonesboro 115; Kennesaw 61, 87; toward Nashville 199; Resaca 37–38; return 202

Long, Confederate Gen. A. L.: Early's campaign 69
Loring, Confederate Gen. William W. 59; Ackworth 132, 185; Franklin 189, 200; Peachtree Creek 85
Lost Mountain, Georgia 57
Lovejoy's Station, Georgia 104, 116; Hood arrives 118, 129
Lowry, Confederate Gen. Mark 203
Lunt, Dolly Sumner: diary 3; Union foragers 155
Lyman, Union Col. Theodore: on soldier vote 147

Macon and Western Railroad 81, 104, 111, 113; destroy 116
Macon, Georgia: rail center 19, 99, 104, 156
Maney, Confederate Gen. George E. 82, 92
Marietta, Georgia 44, 56, 57
McArthur, Union Gen. John: Nashville 200; Shy's Hill 203
McClellan, George B.: change platform 146–47, 149; democratic presidential candidate 72
McCook, Union Col. Daniel: Kennesaw 63
McCook, Union Gen. Edward 23; cavalry raid 104–5
McLean, Union Gen. Nathaniel C.: Resaca 38, 49
McMillen, Union Col. W. L.: Shy's Hill 203–4
McMorries, Edward: cold weather 196; 1st Alabama, marching 55; Florence 175; Franklin battlefield 191; Franklin Pike 179; replace Johnston 79–80
McMurray, W. J.: 20th Tennessee, replace Johnston 80
McPherson, Union Gen. James Birdseye: about 22; killed 93; occupy Bald Hill 37, 39, 41, 50, 52, 61, 64, 81; Resaca 34, 38; right of Atlanta 82, 87; Snake Creek Gap 35, 36
Meridian, Mississippi 14
Military Division of the Mississippi 14; departments 21
Mill Creek Gap, Georgia: location 32, 34
Milledgeville, Georgia: capital 19, 99, 151, 156; capture 157; first objective 154
Millen, Georgia 159
Miller, James T.: letter to father 71
Milroy, Union Gen. Robert: Murfreesboro 195

Mitchell, Union Col. John G.: Kennesaw 63
Mobile Bay, Alabama 142
Montgomery, Confederate Lt. Col. Frank A.: Cassville 42; replace Johnston 80
Montgomery Hill 200
Moore, Union Col. Jesse: Franklin 184
Moore, Union Col. Jonathan: Nashville 200
Morgan, Mrs. Irby: Marietta 59
Murfreesboro, Tennessee 195
Murfreesboro Turnpike 194, 199

Nashville and Chattanooga Railroad 199
Nashville, Tennessee 12; bad weather 196; battle losses 205; concentrate troops 176, 181, 184, 193; Confederate works 195; fortifications 194–95; supplies 18; terrain 194
New Hope Church, Georgia: battle 46; losses 47, 52
Newton, Union Gen. John 21; Kennesaw 62; Peachtree Creek 82–83; Rocky Face Ridge 35
Nichols, Union Maj. George: Atlanta deserted 140; Atlanta fire 152; hate of residents 128; on march 161; on South Carolina 210
Nickajack Creek 64
Nicolay, John G.: Lincoln on winning 149; opposition groups 70; president secretary 146
Ninth U.S. Army Corps 21
Nolensville Turnpike 194, 195
Noyes' Creek, Georgia 59

Ocmulgee River 104, 155
Oconee River 104; burn bridge 154
Ogeechee River: move on both sides 160, 164
123rd New York: Cassville 42
124th Ohio Infantry: Cassville 43
Oostanaula River 37, 39, 40, 53
Opdycke, Union Col. Emerson: charge broken line, casualties 188; Franklin reserve 184
Orendorff, Henry: close lines 111
Osborn, Thomas: civilians 134; destruction 158; Logan at Jonesboro 115
Osterhaus, Union Gen. Peter J. 22; Dallas 50–51; 5th Corps on march 139, 155, 160; Jones-

boro 114; Ogeechee River 164, 166; Resaca 37
Overton Hill, Tennessee 201, 202, 203; captured 204

Palmer, Union Gen. John M. 21; replaced 105; Resaca 36–37, 85
Palmetto, Georgia 131
Peachtree Creek: battle 81–85; casualties 85; gap in Union line 81; terrain 82
Pepper, George: Atlanta 94, 96; Buzzard's Roost description 32; Ezra Church 102
Petersburg, Virginia: missed opportunity 67–68; rail center 67; siege 149
Philips, Pleasant J.: Griswoldville 156
Pickett's Mill, Georgia: battle, losses 49–50
Pine Mountain, Georgia 57, 58
Polk, Confederate Gen. Leonidas 15, 32; Cassville 42; killed 58; New Hope 46; Resaca 37, 39, 41
Porter, Horace: Wilderness 66
Potts, Union Col. Benjamin F.: Atlanta 92
Pulaski, Tennessee 176
Pumpkin Vine Creek 46; casualties 58
Putnam, Sallie Brock: Southern reality 149

Quarles, Confederate Gen. William A.: Ezra Church 103; killed 190

Radical Republicans: convention 71
Raleigh, North Carolina 209, 210
Ranson, Union Gen. Thomas E.G. 22
Reed, Wallace: shelling Atlanta 108
Reilly, Union Gen. James W. 184; line broken 187
Renfroe's Plantation, Georgia 113
Republican Party: convention, platform 71–72
Resaca, Georgia: Hood threaten 133; location 34, 37
Rhodes, Elisha Hunt: Cold Harbor 67
Richland Creek 194, 195
Ringgold, Georgia 35
Robinson, Union Col. J. S.: Resaca 39
Rocky Face Ridge, Georgia 32
Rome, Georgia 132, 133

Rome Railroad 32
Rough and Ready, Georgia 113; evacuation 128; Union force approach 115, 116
Rousseau, Union Gen. Lovell H.: cavalry raid 65; Murfreesboro 195
Ruger, Union Gen. Thomas H. 184

Savannah and Gulf Railroad: destroyed 165
Savannah Canal 164
Savannah, Georgia 137, 164; bridges, evacuate 169–70; fortifications 162, 164; inner line 165; occupation 171
Savannah River 160, 168
Saxon, Elizabeth Lyle: home life 4
Schofield, Union Gen. John M. 21; advance 34–35; arrive Franklin 183, 184; leave Franklin 191, 193, 197; on Hood 81, 94, 100, 105, 111; Hood not done 201; Kennesaw 64; line broken 188; night march 179–80; in open country 200; pressure to attack 198, 199; at Pulaski, army size 176; Resaca 37, 41, 49, 55, 60, 61; Rough and Ready 115–16, 132, 174; cross Soap Creek 64; to Spring Hill 177
Scott, Confederate Gen. Thomas: killed 190
Seddon, Confederate Secretary of War James A.: letter from Lee 4, 28
Seventeenth U.S. Army Corps: at Atlanta 87, 89, 94, 155; organization 22, 55
Seward, U.S. Secretary of State William H. 74
Shenandoah Valley, Virginia 68; 143; destruction 144
Sheridan, Union Gen. Philip H.: destruction, Cedar Creek 144; Fisher's Hill 144; Shenandoah Valley, Winchester 143–44
Sherman, Union Col. Francis T.: 88th Illinois, Dallas 51
Sherman, U.S. Senator John 25
Sherman, William T. 23–26; Allatoona 44, 50; army condition 160; ask for surrender 168–69; after Atlanta 129, 132; Atlanta captured 119, 121; Atlanta explosions 118; Atlanta fire, begin march 152; attack other positions 94; to Calhoun 126–27; casualties 97; to Chattahoochee River 64;

Cobb plantation 155–56, 158; command changes 105; confidence 153; daily routine 155; damage to Georgia 160–61; destroy rails 113; direction 140, 151; enlistments 107; Ezra Church 102; final campaign 209–10; flank Dallas 52; general in chief, death 212; to Grant 110, 170; to Grant on Georgia march 135–37; to Halleck 124; follow Hood 133–34; on Hood 81; to Hood 124–25; Johnston surrender 210; Kennesaw 61; landscape 57; letter to Grant 105–6; letter to Halleck 60, 106; to Lovejoy's Station 118; to McPherson 34, 36, 40; meet ship, Fort McAllister 167; mercy on Savannah 171; Meridian raid 14; Military Division of the Mississippi 12, 13; move South 100, 111, 112; move to Jonesboro 113–14; no attack 162–63; outside Atlanta 65; outside Savannah 162; Pine Mountain 58; remove civilians 123–24; routes to sea 137; Savannah Christmas gift 170; shelling Atlanta 107–8; supplies 18, 140; take over railroad 18–19; to Thomas on Georgia march 135; troop condition 139; where to end 153–54
Shoupe, Confederate Gen. Francis: Cassville 42
Shy's Hill, Tennessee 203
Sigel, Union Gen. Franz 13; defeat at New Market 68
Simonson, Union Capt. Peter: 5th Indiana Battery at Resaca 39
Sixteenth U.S. Army Corps: at Atlanta 87, 89, 94; Nashville 199–200; organization 22, 35, 39, 50
6th Iowa Regiment 50
Slocum, Union Gen. Henry W.: 22; enter Atlanta, wire Stanton 118; in Atlanta 132; command 20th Corps 105; toward Decatur 151, 154; former slaves 159, 160; left wing 139
Smith, Union Gen. A. J. 22, 176; Nashville plan 199; redoubt 200, 201; Shy's Hill 203–4
Smith, Confederate Gen. G. W.: Georgia state troops 88
Smith, Union Gen. Giles A.: Atlanta 92–93, 95, 97; Resaca 39, 89
Smith, Confederate Gen. James A. 203

Smith, Union Gen. John E. 22
Smith, Union Gen. Morgan L. 22, 50; Kennesaw 61, 95
Smith, Wilber: Shenandoah destruction 144–45
Smyrna Camp Ground, Georgia 64
Snake Creek Gap, Georgia: Hood 133; location 32, 34, 36
Soap Creek 64
Special Field Order No. 68: Sherman praise troops 121–22
Special Field Order No 119: inform troops on march to sea 138
Special Field Order No. 120: organization on march 138–39
Spence Alex: Atlanta lost 119; 1st Arkansas, retreating 57
Spotsylvania, Virginia 67
Sprague, Union Gen. John W.: at Decatur 96–97
Spring Hill, Tennessee 177, 179
Squier, George W.: on election 148
Stahl, Confederate Gen. Otto: killed 189
Stanley, Union Gen. David S. 21, 35; command 4th Corps 105; Confederates in view 186–87; to Franklin 180, 185; Resaca 38, 82; Rough and Ready 115–16, 176; Spring Hill 177–78, 179; Utoy Creek 111; wounded 188
Stanton, U.S. Secretary of War Edward 196; complain Thomas 197
Steedman, Union Gen. James B.: Nashville 199, 201; Overton Hill 202
Stevenson, Confederate Gen. Carter: Kolb's Farm 60; Resaca 38, 40
Stewart, Confederate Gen. A.P.: attack Howard 101, 103; Big Shanty 132, 176, 178, 185; flank turned 200, 201, 204; Franklin 187, 194; Peachtree Creek 85, 88; report 35; Resaca 38, 40, 46, 81, 84
Stiles, Union Col. I.N. 184; Franklin 189
Stinson, Eliza: home life 5
Stokes, Thomas: New Hope letter 48
Stone, Union Col. Henry: Franklin 189; Schofield danger 178
Stone Mountain, Georgia 65
Stoneman, Union Gen. George 23, 52, 64, 65; cavalry raid 104–5

Strickland, Union Col. Silas 184; fight at works 188; line broken 187
Strong, George Templeton: anger toward South 208; discouragement at home 70
Strong, Union Lt. Col. W.E.: Atlanta 90
Sugar Valley, Georgia 34
Sweeney, Union Gen. Thomas W. 22; Resaca 39–40, 89, 90, 91

Third Missouri Infantry 39
Thirty-ninth Ohio Regiment 91
Thirty-Seventh Mississippi 35
Thomas, Union Gen. George H. 21–22, 34; administer Tennessee, death 210–11; Atlanta fighting 106, 111, 113, 115, 116, 118; 1st day victory 201; to Nashville 132, 136, 139, 191, 193, 194; order to attack 198–99; realign army 201; Resaca 36–37, 41, 62, 81, 94, 100; 2nd day victory 202–4, 205; victory notice 201–2; weather delay 197
Thomas, Confederate Capt. Lovick P.: New Hope 47–48
Tourtellotte, Union Lt. Col. John: command Allatoona 132
Tunnel Hill, Georgia: Hood 133; location 32, 34–35
Tuscumbia, Alabama: railroad damage 174–75
Twelfth Illinois Regiment 91
Twentieth U.S. Army Corps: Chattahoochee River 110, 154; New Hope 46; organization 21, 36, 40
Twenty-seventh Ohio Regiment 91
Twenty-third U.S. Army Corps: Franklin 184; Nashville 199; organization 21, 40

Union Causeway, Georgia 168
Upson, Theodore F.: destroy rails 112; Kennesaw 63; march routine 157–58; supplies from ships 167
Utoy Creek 111
Vallandingham, Clement L.: peace party 72

Wade, Senator Benjamin: peace terms 74
Wade-Davis Bill 74
Wagner, Union Gen. George D.: Franklin advance line 187; Kennesaw 62, 179, 184

Walcutt, Union Gen. Charles C.: Atlanta 93, 94; Dallas 50; Griswoldville 156
Walker, Confederate Gen. Leroy P.: Resaca 40, 82, 90
Walthall, Confederate Gen. Edward G.: Ezra Church 103; Franklin 185, 189; Nashville 200–1
Wangelin, Union Col. Hugo: Atlanta 93
Ward, Union Gen. William T.: Peachtree Creek 83–84
Weaver, Union Col. Clark R.: defend Resaca 133
Weed, Thurlow: letter to Seward 74–75
Welles, Secretary of the Navy Gideon: wounded soldiers 75
West Point Railroad 131
Western and Atlantic Railroad 29, 32, 110; damage 133
Wheeler, Confederate Gen. Joseph 31, 88, 96: cavalry raid 107; Western & Atlantic 110–11, 156
The Wilderness, Virginia 66–67
Williams, Union Gen. Alpheus S. 21; on election 147–48; enemy contacts 58, 60; evacuate Savannah 170; near coast 160, 166; Peachtree Creek 84, 111; Savannah works 168; 20th Corps on march 139
Wilson, Union Gen. James: cavalry move south 203–4; Nashville 199
Winchester, Virginia 143
Woods, Union Gen. Charles R. 22, 35; Ezra Church 103, 156; Pickett's Mill 48–49, 95; Resaca 39
Wood, Union Gen. Thomas J. 21, 48, 82; advance line 187; break Confederate line 204; capture hill 201; evacuate Franklin 191; Nashville plan 199, 200; Overton Hill 203; pursuit 204; reserve 185; 2nd day attack 202
Wright, Henry: Chattahoochee swamps 64; Kennesaw 61; 6th Iowa 57
Wright, Union Col. William: railroad construction 19, 53

Young, Confederate Lt. Lot: Orphan Brigade, Dallas 51

www.ingramcontent.com/pod-product-compliance
Ingram Content Group UK Ltd.
Pitfield, Milton Keynes, MK11 3LW, UK
UKHW050533150426
5217IPUK00026B/1913